Advances in
THE STUDY OF BEHAVIOR
VOLUME 7

Contributors to This Volume

RONALD J. BARFIELD
PATRICIA S. GOLDMAN
MONICA IMPEKOVEN
ERIC B. KEVERNE
BENJAMIN D. SACHS
YUKIMARU SUGIYAMA
H. PHILIP ZEIGLER

Advances in
THE STUDY OF
BEHAVIOR

Edited by

JAY S. ROSENBLATT
Institute of Animal Behavior
Rutgers University
Newark, New Jersey

ROBERT A. HINDE
Medical Research Council
Unit on the Development and Integration of Behavior
University Sub-Department of Animal Behavior
Madingley, Cambridge, England

EVELYN SHAW
Department of Biological Sciences
Stanford University
Stanford, California

COLIN BEER
Institute of Animal Behavior
Rutgers University
Newark, New Jersey

——————— VOLUME 7 ———————

ACADEMIC PRESS   New York San Francisco London 1976
A Subsidiary of Harcourt Brace Jovanovich, Publishers

ACADEMIC PRESS, INC.
111 Fifth Avenue, New York, New York 10003

United Kingdom Edition published by
ACADEMIC PRESS, INC. (LONDON) LTD.
24/28 Oval Road, London NW1

LIBRARY OF CONGRESS CATALOG CARD NUMBER: 64-8031

ISBN 0-12-004507-9

PRINTED IN THE UNITED STATES OF AMERICA

Contents

Maturation of the Mammalian Nervous System and the Ontogeny of Behavior
PATRICIA S. GOLDMAN

Functional Analysis of Masculine Copulatory Behavior in the Rat
BENJAMIN D. SACHS AND RONALD J. BARFIELD

Sexual Receptivity and Attractiveness in the Female Rhesus Monkey
ERIC B. KEVERNE

Prenatal Parent–Young Interactions in Birds and Their Long-Term Effects
MONICA IMPEKOVEN

Life History of Male Japanese Monkeys
YUKIMARU SUGIYAMA

Feeding Behavior of the Pigeon

H. PHILIP ZEIGLER

List of Contributors

Numbers in parentheses indicate the pages on which the authors' contributions begin.

RONALD J. BARFIELD, *Department of Biology, Livingston College, Rutgers University, New Brunswick, New Jersey (91)*

PATRICIA S. GOLDMAN, *National Institute of Mental Health, Bethesda, Maryland (1)*

MONICA IMPEKOVEN, *Institute of Animal Behavior, Rutgers University, Newark, New Jersey (201)*

ERIC B. KEVERNE, *Department of Anatomy, University of Cambridge, Cambridge, England (155)*

BENJAMIN D. SACHS, *Department of Psychology, The University of Connecticut, Storrs, Connecticut (91)*

YUKIMARU SUGIYAMA, *Primate Research Institute, Kyoto University, Inuyama, Japan (255)*

H. PHILIP ZEIGLER, *Department of Psychology, Hunter College, City University of New York, and Department of Animal Behavior, American Museum of Natural History, New York, New York (285)*

Preface

The study of animal behavior is attracting the attention of ever-increasing numbers of zoologists and comparative psychologists in all parts of the world, and is becoming increasingly important to students of human behavior in the psychiatric, psychological, and allied professions. Widening circles of workers, from a variety of backgrounds, carry out descriptive and experimental studies of behavior under natural conditions, laboratory studies of the organization of behavior, analyses of neural and hormonal mechanisms of behavior, and studies of the development, genetics, and evolution of behavior, using both animal and human subjects. The aim of *Advances in the Study of Behavior* is to provide workers on all aspects of behavior an opportunity to present an account of recent progress in their particular fields for the benefit of other students of behavior. It is our intention to encourage a variety of critical reviews, including intensive factual reviews of recent work, reformulations of persistent problems, and historical and theoretical essays, all oriented toward the facilitation of current and future progress. *Advances in the Study of Behavior* is offered as a contribution to the development of cooperation and communication among scientists in our field.

Contents of Previous Volumes

Maturation of the Mammalian Nervous System and the Ontogeny of Behavior[1]

PATRICIA S. GOLDMAN

NATIONAL INSTITUTE OF MENTAL HEALTH
BETHESDA, MARYLAND

[1] This work was sponsored by the Intramural Research Program of the National Institute of Mental Health and is therefore not subject to copyright.

I. INTRODUCTION

The aim of developmental research, broadly considered, is to discover fundamental principles and mechanisms governing the ontogenesis of structure and
function in the nervous system. Of the numerous issues that arise in the study of
ontogeny, none is more basic than the question of the degree of latitude that is
permissible in the relationship between structure and function. Clarification of
this basic issue will ultimately require answers to the persisting question of the
degree to which behavioral capacities are determined by inexorable biological
forces and the extent to which they may be molded by the pervasive and
cumulative imprint of experience.

This century has witnessed radical shifts in opinion concerning these matters
and, in particular, the matter of how experience enters into the structure–function equation. The prevailing assumption among psychologists in the 1930s and
1940s was that for all practical purposes, the behavioral repertoire of the
organism was the product of accumulated training or conditioning. Watson's
(1924) oft-cited claim that he could select any child at random and teach it to
become any type of specialist is an extreme example of the environmentalism of
the period. If there were any biological limits to educability, the forgers of
behaviorism in this country and elsewhere were only vaguely mindful of them.
To a large extent, this view persists to the present day in many quarters of
academic and clinical psychology with its emphasis on operant conditioning and
behavior modification approaches to such human disorders as childhood autism
and mental retardation. Learning models of behavioral development have also
exerted some influence on the thinking of ethologists. In his recent Nobel
Lecture, Tinbergen (1974) took the view that autism is a consequence of early
traumatic experience rather than an organic disorder and advocated the continued improvement of behavioral therapies aimed at reducing anxiety.

The physiologically oriented psychology of the 1930s and 1940s conspired
unwittingly to advance the behaviorist's position (e.g., see Sperry, 1971). Lashley's (1941) unsuccessful search for the locus of memory tended more to turn
psychologists away from considering the limits set by neural mechanisms than to
reinforce a coalescence of biological and behavioral sciences, as he had hoped.
Similarly, the neurology of Kurt Goldstein (1939) probably diverted the attention of students of behavior away from physiological experiments, even though
his holistic approach to the structure-function problem was in reality a challenge
for such research. Working in the laboratory of John Fulton at Yale, Kennard
(1936, 1942) claimed that the motor cortex of infant monkeys could be ablated
without seriously compromising the development of their motor behavior.
Studies of brain injury in the laboratory and in the clinic thus seemed to indicate
that neurons in different parts of the brain could substitute for one another to

an almost unlimited extent. Of the extreme claims for plasticity made in this early period by leading figures in psychology and neurology, Sperry (1971) has said, "If you hadn't been there, you wouldn't believe it!"

The 1940s, however, also saw the beginning of a growing appreciation of structural factors in behavior and development. In psychology, Gesell (1942) founded the "developmental" school, which laid stress on genetic endowment and maturational processes. At midcentury, the search for local functions was carried on by scientists like H. Kluver, K.H. Pribram, and D.O. Hebb, the latter proposing a pattern theory of neural activity that attempted to accommodate evidence of both plasticity and specificity by not requiring "any single nerve cell or pathway (to be) essential to any habit or perception" (Hebb, 1949). To Schneirla (1957), biological properties of organisms were inseparable from functional properties, as both were guided by genetic constitution and milieu at different levels of phylogeny and at different stages of development. It was during this period also that the discovery was made of the potent inductive role of hormones during the perinatal period on the organization of mature behavior patterns (Phoenix *et al.,* 1959). During this era, still partly dominated by an overemphasis on plasticity, Sperry (1945) upheld the view that there is a precise and rigidly specified correspondence between structure and function in the nervous system. His classical studies on retinotectal connections in amphibians and fishes stood as a model demonstration that brain pathways and synaptic connections can be elaborated by inherent growth mechanisms. His later work, involving the assessment of deficits in patients given callosal transections for intractable epilepsy (e.g., Sperry *et al.,* 1969), showed clearly that interruption of the major interhemispheric commissure is not without effect on mental processes and behavior, as many had believed. Thus, traditional arguments for independence of structure and function, based, for example, on the absence of behavioral impairments in the special case of persons with callosal agenesis, were largely dispelled.

In the last two decades, there has been a fresh challenge to concepts of strict structure-function specificity and a reemergence of ideas about plasticity in what might superficially appear to be a return to the formulations of earlier times. However, contemporary views are based on new findings concerning the preservation of behavioral capacity following lesions in infants (Harlow *et al.,* 1968; Kling and Tucker, 1968; Goldman, 1971, 1972) or after serial lesions in adults (Stein *et al.,* 1969; Finger *et al.,* 1973), as well as on unprecedented electrophysiological and neuroanatomical evidence for central nervous system (CNS) reorganization in response to injury (e.g., Raisman, 1969; Schneider, 1970, 1973; Moore *et al.,* 1971; Steward *et al.,* 1973) or to modified sensory experience (Hirsch and Spinelli, 1970; Blakemore and Cooper, 1970; Wiesel and Hubel, 1974b). These new findings reawakened interest in the type of study begun by

Kennard and by others (Ades and Raab, 1946; Glees and Cole, 1950) and brought into focus once again the old dialogue on the modifiability of the developing and adult central nervous system.

Recent experimental work in numerous laboratories has opened a new page in the history of ideas about structure-function relationships, ideas that may break the cycle of scientific opinion witnessed throughout the century. The question of the degree to which hereditary and environmental factors govern behavior and its development is no longer formulated in the "either-or" terms of earlier decades; dichotomous thinking has given way to the more sophisticated concepts of integration and interaction (e.g., Lehrman, 1970; Birch, 1971; Eisenberg, 1971), and rhetoric has been more and more replaced by experimentation. There have been major advances, one may even say revolutions, in basic ideas about the central nervous system and about the mechanisms through which organismic and experiential factors inseparably orchestrate its development. Evidence has been brought forth for both a high degree of constraint in the relationship between structure and function and for a remarkable and unexpectedly large measure of neural and behavioral plasticity. Nature, it would appear, has provided for both.

In the pages that follow, an attempt is made to bring together diverse sources of evidence that pertain to the neural basis of behavioral development both in its normal and abnormal manifestations. The scope of this subject is too vast to be covered with any degree of completeness, and the present treatment is therefore necessarily highly selective. Emphasis has been placed on studies in various mammalian species, and the chapter has been organized largely along morpho-genetic lines. The selection of topics has been based, first, on the existence of a substantial body of work concerning the development of specific structures and their functions and, second, on the degree to which a particular line of work highlights a general principle in the development of brain and behavior. Thus, studies on the cerebellum were selected to illustrate the behavioral significance of intrinsic or local connections and the role that neurogenetic mechanisms might play in their formation. Studies on several areas of the cerebral cortex were chosen in an attempt to elucidate the behavioral significance of pathways connecting distant structures, the organization of structures into systems, and the modulation of development by experience. Finally, a section on limbic system structures was included because these structures exemplify particularly well mechanisms of neural and behavioral plasticity in development. In an attempt to place these various specific aspects of development into a broader perspective, the chapter begins with a brief overview of the major events in the chronology of brain development.

II. ORIGINS OF THE CENTRAL NERVOUS SYSTEM

One of the basic premises of the developmental approach is that complex processes and mechanisms can be deciphered through reconstruction of the preceding, less complicated stages from which they emerge. It is desirable, therefore, to begin analysis at the earliest possible stages of life. For this reason, recent studies in the field of neuroembryology are of direct interest to students of neural and behavioral development.

A. CELL DIVISIONS AND MIGRATIONS

The subject of neurogenesis and migration has been reviewed on a number of occasions (Altman, 1969a; Angevine, 1970a; Boulder Committee, 1970; Sidman, 1970, 1974; Sidman and Rakic, 1973) and only certain highlights will be mentioned here. The intricate assembly of the countless neurons and neuronal processes that compose the adult brain begins as a single layer of columnar epithelial cells which form a wall around the neural tube. Initially, each cell stretches from the lumen of the neural tube to the outside surface and thus occupies the entire width of the neural wall. Later, as demonstrated in Fig. 1, the neural wall will expand and develop distinctive layers from which the cortex, the white matter, and the internal structures of the brain will develop, while the lumen of the neural tube is the anlage of the future lateral, third, and fourth ventricles.

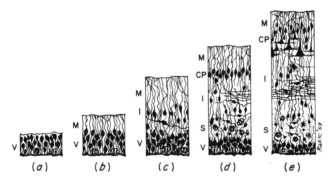

Fig. 1. Schematic drawing of five stages (*a–e*) in the development of the vertebrate central nervous system. The embryonic CNS consists of four fundamental zones from which the adult organization is derived, though none of the four correspond to any adult component: V, ventricular zone; S, subventricular zone; I, intermediate zone; M, marginal zone. A cortical plate (CP) is formed only in the cerebrum and cerebellum at stages *d* and *e*. (Reproduced with permission from Rakic, 1975.)

All of the cells of the ventricular zone[2] (see Fig. 1) are mitotic, though they are in different phases of cell division at any given time (Sauer and Walker, 1959; Sidman *et al.*, 1959). Each cell gives rise to two "daughter" cells, which in turn give rise to new generations of cells. When a ventricular cell has completed its divisions, it begins a migration from its site of origin at the ventricular surface to its final and often remote location as a prospective cortical or subcortical neuron. Both the time and the site of origin of cells may affect their ultimate fate. For example, cells that will eventually form the cerebral cortex, the striatum, and certain intrinsic nuclei of the thalamus arise from the ventricular region lining the embryonic lateral ventricles (Angevine and Sidman, 1961; Angevine, 1970b; Sidman and Rakic, 1973; Rakic, 1974a, b, 1975); cells destined to become the deep nuclei of the cerebellum and the Purkinje cells of the cerebellar cortex originate in the roof of the embryonic fourth ventricle (Miale and Sidman, 1961; Rakic and Sidman, 1970), while brain stem nuclei derive from the floor of the same embryonic zone (Taber Pierce, 1966). However, much as trains leaving from the same station at different hours tend to be destined for different terminals, the same ventricular zone may give rise to different populations of cells at different times. For example, the cells forming the deeper layers of the cerebral cortex are generated earlier from a particular ventricular zone than those of the more superficial layers arising from the same zone (Angevine and Sidman, 1961; Berry and Rogers, 1965; Hicks and D'Amato, 1968; Shimada and Langman, 1970; Rakic, 1974a, 1975); likewise, progenitors of cells that will form the inferior olive, for example, are generated before those forming the pontine grey matter (Taber Pierce, 1966), though both have the same "birthplace." One of the more striking examples of the interplay of spatial and temporal factors in neurogenesis occurs in the formation of the cerebellum. Here, the major efferent neuron of the cerebellar cortex, the Purkinje cell, originates in one germinal zone, the embryonic fourth ventricle, at early prenatal stages, whereas the granule cells that will establish synaptic connections on Purkinje cell dendrites proliferate at later pre- and early postnatal stages in another entirely different germinal zone, the external granular layer, which encapsulates the cerebellum during its development (Ramón y Cajal, 1911, 1960; Miale and Sidman, 1961; Altman, 1969b; Rakic, 1971a; Rakic and Sidman, 1970; del Cerro and Snider, 1972). A sequence of precisely timed and spatially coded events thus characterizes the organization of the brain and establishes its ordered development.

B. MODE OF CELL MIGRATION

One of the basic questions in neuroembryology concerns the mechanisms by which cells generated at the ventricular surface find their way to specific

---

[2] Nomenclature recommended by the Boulder Committee (1970).

locations at some distance from their sites of origin. When the neural plate is narrow in width, as it is at early embryonic stages, it is easy to imagine how a postmitotic cell might migrate from the ventricular zone to the pial surface by transposing the position of its nucleus along the cytoplasmic attachments which it maintains with the outer surface of the neural wall, as has been suggested by Berry and Rogers (1965) and Morest (1970). However, as the neural wall expands and develops layers of greater and greater complexity by migration of previously generated cells and proliferation of their processes, it becomes more difficult to explain how later-arising cells find their way across the considerably longer and now densely populated terrain eventually to reach their appropriate destinations. Although a discussion of this problem is beyond the scope of the present review, it is of some interest to note that recent electron-microscopic investigations in the developing monkey have revealed the presence of numerous radially oriented glial fibers that traverse the entire width of the cerebral wall in fetal brains at late stages of corticogenesis (Rakic, 1971a, b, 1972). These studies show further that young neurons remain in close apposition to the radial glial struts along their entire course of migration, even when the glial fibers deviate from a strictly radial path. The radial glial fibers thus may provide a contact guidance mechanism by which young neurons, and succeeding generations of neurons, perform their orderly migrations. Interestingly, this trellis of elongated radial glial cells eventually disappears or becomes transformed into astrocytes (Schmechel and Rakic, 1973) and is no longer detectable in the mature primate brain.

C. SPECIES DIFFERENCES

The same basic plan of brain development seems to hold in all mammalian species studied thus far, including man (Sidman and Rakic, 1973). Neurogenesis begins in the embryonic neural plate stages and may continue, for some classes of neurons in many mammalian species, until after birth. Except for the aforementioned special and transient class of radial glial cells in different regions of the brain (including also Bergmann glial cells in the cerebellum), neurogenesis generally precedes extensive gliogenesis. It should be emphasized, however, that although a considerable proportion of the brain's glial constituents are generated postnatally, the timetables for neural and glial multiplication overlap considerably (e.g., Dobbing and Sands, 1970).

Notwithstanding the embellishments on the basic plan that have been found in nonhuman primates and man (Rakic and Sidman, 1969, 1970), the main variations in brain maturation among various mammalian species derive principally from differences in the size of the brain and the number of cells, and in the duration and timing of the major developmental events, rather than from divergent principles of organization. For example, in the monkey the proliferation of neocortical neurons is completed over a 50-day period about 2 months prior to birth (Rakic, 1974a, 1975). In other altricial mammals like the rat and the mouse, however, corticogenesis requires less than a week and is completed just before parturition (Angevine and Sidman, 1961; Berry and Rogers, 1965; Hicks and D'Amato, 1968), whereas in the hamster some cortical neurons continue to be generated for a number of days after birth (Shimada and Langman, 1970). On the other hand, the genesis of cerebellar granule cells occurs postnatally to various degrees in all species studied so far (Miale and Sidman, 1961; Rakic and Sidman, 1970; Rakic, 1971a, 1973; Altman, 1972c).

D. CORRELATION BETWEEN THE TIME OF NEURON GENESIS AND EMERGENCE OF FUNCTION

The order in which neurons of various regions of the brain are laid down appears to bear less relationship either to the onset or nature of the functions of these regions than is usually assumed. Although the early development of spinal and brain stem reflexes correlates well with the early genesis of neurons in these regions (e.g., Bodian, 1970), similar correlations do not seem to hold for cell proliferation and migration schedules of the neocortex. Thus, areas of the primate cortex as cytoarchitectonically, spatially, and functionally distinct as the prefrontal granular cortex and the primary visual cortex appear to be formed at roughly the same period of gestation (Rakic, 1974a, b; Rakic and Wikmark, personal communication) even though they ultimately will mediate vastly different functions and, as far as we know, will develop these functions over widely different intervals of time [e.g., compare Goldman (1975) with Hubel and Wiesel (1963)]. Similarly, in primates the deposition of neural elements in the cerebral cortex is completed long before the cerebellar cortex is fully constituted, yet the emergence of mature cerebellar motor functions most likely precedes that of higher cortical functions. The neuroembryological findings thus seem to indicate that the general outlines of brain development may be basically governed by temporospatial factors and inherent growth mechanisms without strict regard to functional destiny.

E. NEURONAL DIFFERENTIATION

The fact that there is little correspondence between the time of neuron origin and the time of emergence of neural function does not, however, negate the strong interdependence of structure and function. At early stages of embryonic development, neurons are "undifferentiated," i.e., they do not possess the cellular characteristics of mature neurons and cannot yet be classified into neuronal types by the usual morphological criteria. While it is a fairly simple matter to recognize an undifferentiated neuron as defined above, it may be considerably more difficult to determine meaningful criteria for levels of differentiation or maturity, since this depends in large measure on the particular parameter of cellular development chosen for study. Thus, a cell may be judged as fully mature in terms of the distribution and complexity of its dendritic field (e.g., Ramón y Cajal, 1911, 1960; Morest, 1969; Scheibel and Scheibel, 1972), the degree of elaboration of its synaptic relationships (e.g., Voeller *et al.*, 1963; Aghajanian and Bloom, 1967; Larramendi, 1969; Mugnaini, 1969; Adinolfi, 1972a, b; Cragg, 1972b), or the maturation of its biosynthetic capacity (e.g., Coyle and Axelrod, 1972; Himwich, 1972; Coyle and Henry, 1973), but the time course for each of these features of neuronal differentiation is rarely the same. Furthermore, the synchrony of cellular maturational events need not be uniform for neurons of different types nor for similar types in different regions of the brain. It should be emphasized, however, that many of these parameters of neuronal maturation that appear after neural multiplication and migration have ended can be linked to functional development, as described in the following sections.

III. CEREBELLUM: INTRINSIC CONNECTIONS AND INHERENT GROWTH MECHANISMS UNDERLYING LOCOMOTOR BEHAVIOR

The fact that motor skills undergo a conspicuous transformation with age may be among the reasons that locomotor behavior was one of the first subjects to be studied in relation to structural differentiation (Soltmann, 1876; Langworthy, 1927; Coghill, 1929; Kennard, 1936; Tower, 1940; Hines, 1942). A useful illustration of structural–functional relations in development is given by recent studies concerned with various aspects of cerebellar morphology in relation to motor behavior. Some additional studies on the development of motor function will be mentioned in a subsequent section (IV, A) concerned with the motor cortex.

A. STRUCTURE AND FUNCTION OF THE ADULT CEREBELLAR CORTEX

Although it is well established that the cerebellum contributes to motor function, there is a divergence of opinion concerning the precise nature of this contribution. While the classical view was that the cerebellum functions solely to refine and smooth out ongoing movements commanded by the motor cortex, contemporary physiologists regard this structure as much more than a regulatory instrument. For example, Brindley (1964) has proposed that the cerebellum has associative functions and is necessary for motor learning and Kornhuber (1974) has emphasized that the cerebellum both initiates and programs rapid movements such as those that are involved in saccadic eye movements and in the rapid and coordinated movements of muscles involved in speech and writing.

In order fully to appreciate the studies of development that follow, it is helpful to have a general picture of the anatomical organization of the cerebellar cortex and its relation to other parts of the brain. Compared with other structures of the brain, the cytoarchitecture and circuit design of the cerebellar cortex have been worked out with an amazing degree of precision and clarity (see Fox, 1962; Eccles *et al.*, 1967; Llinás, 1969; Palay and Chan-Palay, 1973). The cerebellar cortex is composed of only five types of neurons (Purkinje; Golgi type II; stellate; granule; and basket) interconnected with their processes, and with three types of input fibers (climbing fibers, mossy fibers, and axons from the locus ceruleus) and with only one output fiber (the Purkinje axon). The different cell types come to be organized in a rigid geometric fashion to form the characteristic layering pattern of the cerebellar cortex. Figure 2 diagrammatically illustrates a cross section of cerebellar cortex, showing the distribution of major cell types among four major strata: a molecular layer; a Purkinje cell layer; a granule cell layer; and a medullary layer. The Purkinje cell bodies, the largest cells of the cerebellar cortex, form a layer, one cell deep, between the molecular layer above and the granule cell layer below. The dendrites of Purkinje cells are distributed in the molecular layer. Their axons, the only efferent fibers of the cerebellar cortex, project to the cerebellar roof nuclei situated deep within the cerebellum; it is from these nuclei that messages originating at the cerebellar cortical level are conveyed to other portions of the brain. While the main part of the Purkinje cell axon is oriented inward toward the white matter and deep nuclei of the cerebellum, the rather elaborate dendritic portion of the Purkinje cell spreads in a leaf-shaped formation outward from the cell body toward the surface of the cerebellar cortex. Beneath the Purkinje cell layer is the granule cell layer composed of small rounded granule cells. These cells have a small number of simple dendrites that remain in close proximity to the cell body. Their axons ascend into the molecular layer where they bifurcate into two horizontal fibers that form a "T" shape. The horizontal axons run parallel to each other and to the pial surface of the cerebellar cortex. These numerous granule cell axons or parallel fibers synapse upon the spines of the Purkinje cell dendrites that occupy a considerable portion of the molecular layer.

B. DEVELOPMENT OF THE CEREBELLUM

Perhaps more attention has been given to the cerebellum and its development than to any other structure in the central nervous system. Since the original investigations of Ramón y Cajal (1911, 1960), the genesis of the cerebellar cortex has been studied in a number of different species, including the chick (Mugnaini and Forstrønen, 1967; Mugnaini, 1969), rat (Addison, 1911; Dadoune, 1966), mouse (Miale and Sidman, 1961; Fujita, 1967; Larramendi, 1969), and monkey (Rakic, 1971a).

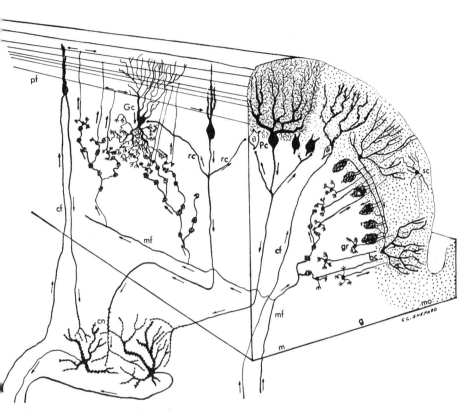

Fig. 2. Schematic view of a folium showing the interneuronal connections of the cerebellar cortex. Abbreviations: bc, basket cells; cf, climbing fiber; cn, deep cerebellar nuclei; g, granular layer; Gc, Golgi cell; gr, granule cell; m, medullary layer; mf, mossy fibers; mo, molecular layer; Pc, Purkinje cell; pf, parallel fiber; rc, recurrent collateral; sc, stellate cell. Recently demonstrated input fibers from the locus ceruleus are not shown in this figure. (Reproduced with permission from Fox, 1962.)

Altman (1975) has recently reviewed his own work and that of others on the postnatal development of the cerebellum in the rat. Figure 3 illustrates the enormous expansion in size of the cerebellum in rats from birth through weaning at 21 days of age, an expansion which is due primarily to the growth of the cerebellar cortex. As has been mentioned, neurons of the deep cerebellar nuclei and the Purkinje cells of the cerebellar cortex are formed prenatally, but basket and stellate cells of the molecular layer and granule cells of the granular layer arise postnatally (Miale and Sidman, 1961; Fujita et al., 1966; Fujita, 1967; Altman, 1969b, 1972c). These latter cells arise from the subpial external germinal layer, a proliferative zone unique to the cerebellum that forms a rind

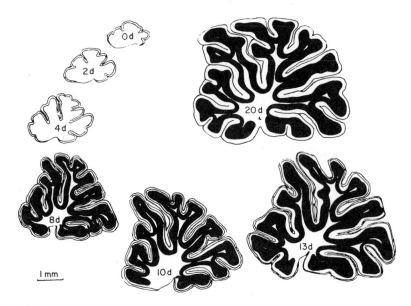

Fig. 3. Tracings of sagittal matched sections of the cerebellum from rats of different ages, as indicated (d equals days). Key: *outer band,* external germinal layer; *black,* granular layer; *white above black,* molecular layer; *white below black,* subcortical. (Reproduced with permission from Altman, 1975.)

over the developing cerebellar cortex (Ramón y Cajal, 1911, 1960). In the rat, this germinal layer will eventually disappear when cell genesis has been completed at around 21 days of postnatal age, and its position will be occupied by the expanding molecular layer beneath it, but during the first 3 weeks of postnatal life the external layer gives rise to the precursors of basket cells (end of the first week), stellate cells (second week), and finally granule cells (second and third weeks); see Altman (1966, 1969b, 1972a, c).

Ramón y Cajal (1911, 1960) first described the interesting process of differentiation and migration exhibited by a developing granule cell. Recent studies in primates have confirmed and amplified this process (Rakic, 1971a). As illustrated in Fig. 4, at early stages of morphogenesis the spindle-shaped granule cell, still located in the lower part of the external germinal layer, develops two processes that are oriented horizontally in each direction. At a subsequent stage, presumably when the horizontal processes have reached a certain length, the cell develops a third vertically oriented process that descends from the base of the cell soma, thus taking on a T-shaped configuration. Finally, the cell nucleus (and the surrounding cytoplasm that constitutes the soma) migrates down the vertical process until it comes to occupy its final position in the granule cell layer. The growth of the vertical process and the translocation of the cell body seem to

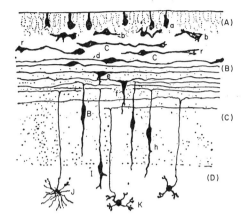

Fig. 4. Schematic figure to show all the forms and locations adopted by the granule cells during their development. Key: (A) indifferent cell layer; (B) layer of granule cells in the horizontal bipolar stage; (C) plexiform layer; (D) granular layer; (a) indifferent granule cell; (b, c, d, e) stages of horizontal bipolarity; (g, h) stage of vertical bipolarity; (i, j) embryonic granule cells; (k) almost fully developed granule cell. (Reproduced with permission from Ramón y Cajal, 1960.)

follow the radially oriented processes of Bergmann glia (see Section II,B). The T-shaped process now trailing above the granule cell becomes its bifurcated axon, and similar processes of successive generations of granule cells become the parallel fibers that are so characteristic of cerebellar architecture. As parallel fibers get "stacked up" one upon the other in the molecular layer, this layer expands and the germinal layer contracts. As the molecular and granule cell layers develop, the prenatally formed Purkinje cell, already in place, begins to develop characteristic morphological features. These include the development of an apical dendrite that ascends into the molecular layer and the formation of secondary and tertiary dendritic branches (Ramón y Cajal, 1911, 1960; Addison, 1911; Altman, 1972b; Rakic and Sidman, 1973b). In the rat, a few synapses between the axons of granule cells (parallel fibers) and the dendrites of Purkinje cells can be detected in the forming molecular layer as early as the first postnatal week (del Cerro and Snider, 1972), but the greater majority of them appear to be formed during the second and third postnatal weeks (Altman, 1972b).

C. EXPERIMENTALLY INDUCED CEREBELLAR PATHOLOGY

Knowledge of the timetables of development of particular cell classes in the cerebellar cortex, and of the fact that dividing cells are selectively vulnerable to low-level X irradiation, has been used to advantage. Thus, many authors, including Hicks *et al.* (1969); Altman *et al.* (1967, 1971) and Altman and Anderson (1971) studied the effects on motor development of destroying the precursors of the postnatally forming interneurons (granule, basket, and stellate cells) by irradiating the cerebellum of infant mice and rats at times when such cells are generated and can be decimated by X irradiation.

Altman *et al.* (1971) studied the emergence of motor skills in intact infant rats and in groups of rats whose cerebellums were focally exposed to different doses of radiation from 2 to 10 days of age. On the basis of earlier parametric work (Altman and Anderson, 1971), the doses of radiation used in this study could be presumed to have affected the population of interneurons (in proportion to dose) without reducing the number of prenatally formed Purkinje cells, which they outnumber by a hundredfold. At 11–30 days of age, after all radiation treatments had ceased, qualitative and quantitative observations were made on the rat pups' spontaneous ambulation in an open-field situation, on their performance in clinging to and descending a vertically positioned tight rope, and on their ability to escape from a cold water bath by climbing a verticle wooden rod to a landing platform above. In general, there was either a delay in or, on some measures, a failure to acquire the progressive motor capacities that un-folded in the normal pups, the degree of retardation being related to the amount of radiation. For example, the ability to rear or stand on the hind limbs with support of the forelimbs was well developed by the third week of life in the controls, but this behavior was almost never seen in the most severely irradiated groups; similarly, the ability to climb a rod and reach an escape platform appeared at 16–18 days in normal pups, but the rats given the highest doses of radiation never succeeded either in climbing the rod or reaching the platform. Most of the deficits were attributed by the authors to a selective impairment of hindlimb coordination. On the basis of cerebellar pathology and behavioral findings, it was suggested that the cerebellum plays a most important role in ambulation but less or little role in controlling the more "manipulatory" forelimbs.

Further dissection of the role of cerebellar interneurons in locomotor behavior comes from a more recent experiment by Altman's group. In this study, intact and irradiated rat pups were first observed as adults on a series of progressively more demanding motor tasks (Brunner and Altman, 1973). The two doses of radiation that were employed in this investigation led to a 49% and 72% reduction in the mean number of granule cells, respectively, and consequently to a progressive diminution in the width of the molecular, granule, and medullary layers, and in the over-all weight and volume of the cerebellum. These cerebellar cell deficits were correlated with deficits in running speeds on horizontal and inclined planes, in jumping across gaps of increasing distance, in climbing narrow metal rods, and in crossing stationary and rotating rods of different widths and textures for food reward. Again, the degree of impairment on these various measures was related to the dose of radiation and hence to the degree of cerebellar pathology. However, the irradiated animals were not impaired in swimming, in endurance in running a treadmill, or in crossing a wide, stable rough rod. Brunner and Altman interpreted the selective pattern of deficits to mean that the cerebellum is especially important for locomotion that involves the concurrent coordination of exteroceptive and proprioceptive information such as may be required in navigating rotating and narrow rods, or in climbing and jumping, but is presumably less necessary in simple terrestrial locomotion or in swimming.

The results of these studies on focal cerebellar irradiation accord well with findings of others using both similar and different techniques of interfering with cerebellar morphogenesis. Hicks and his colleagues (1969), for example, compared the effects on motor behavior of cerebellar irradiation and ablation in infant rats. Their studies showed deficits in the development of motor performance, increasing in proportion to the dose of radiation or to the extent of cerebellum removed. One of their findings is of particular interest for understanding the physiology of cerebellar disorders. They reported that partial ablations of the cerebellar cortex did not appreciably alter motor development unless, in addition, the infant rats sustained damage to certain deep cerebellar nuclei, particularly the fastigial nucleus. In cases with subcortical involvement, the animals were severely and permanently incapacitated: they had difficulty standing up or walking more than a few steps without falling. In view of these findings it might be supposed that at least some of the deficits resulting from irradiation could be due to a primary disruption of the granule cell input to the Purkinje cells and, secondarily, to an abnormal output from the Purkinje cells to the deep nuclei.

As Altman has recently pointed out, X irradiation is only an experimental tool for the study of selective interference with brain and behavior development but is not an environmental hazard to which man is normally exposed. It is important to realize, however, that similar selective cell losses and arrested or abnormal brain development can stem from more commonly occurring human conditions such as undernutrition (e.g., Fish and Winick, 1969; Dobbing et al., 1971; Cragg, 1972a; Barnes and Altman, 1973); hypoxia (e.g., Cheek et al., 1969); hyper- and hypothyroidism (e.g., Balazs et al., 1971; Legrand, 1971; Nicholson and Altman, 1972; Hajos et al., 1973); and exposure to viruses (e.g., Herndon et al., 1971; Llinás et al., 1973); or toxins (e.g., Nathanson et al., 1969; Hirano et al., 1972).

D. GENETICALLY INDUCED CEREBELLAR PATHOLOGY

A number of genetic mutants have been found in inbred strains of mice. Certain of these involve single-gene mutations with recessive modes of inheritance that affect specific features of central nervous system structure and function (Sidman *et al.,* 1965; Sidman, 1968). These so-called neurological mutants have provided useful models for unraveling the normal sequence of steps underlying the development of brain and behavior in general, and of cerebellar structure and function in particular. Only three of the most thoroughly analyzed mutants will be briefly reviewed below.

1. The Weaver Mouse

The weaver mutation is carried on the C57BL/6J strain of mice. The behavior displayed by homozygotes consists of an instability of gait, hypotonia, and fine tremor; such animals rarely survive beyond 3 weeks of age (Lane, 1964). The cerebellum in weaver mice is reduced in size and shows a selective deficit in the number of granule cell neurons (Sidman *et al.,* 1965; Sidman, 1968). The extent of both the behavioral abnormality and the cerebellar pathology are less severe in heterozygotes than in homozygotes, as might be expected from the fact that the latter has a double dose of the mutant gene (Rezai and Yoon, 1972; Rakic and Sidman, 1973b). In the heterozygote, which displays no obvious behavioral impairment, the cerebellar defect is correspondingly mild, with many granule cells attaining their normal morphological characteristics and reaching their ultimate destination in the deeper layers of the cerebellar cortex, though their migration across the molecular layer to the granular layer is slower than normal. The cerebellum of homozygotes is more drastically reduced in size, and the cerebellar cortex of these animals is virtually devoid of granule cells and of the parallel fibers that are so intrinsic a part of normal cerebellar circuitry.

Recent electron-microscopic and rapid Golgi studies (Rakic and Sidman, 1973a, b, c) of the brains of homozygous, heterozygous, and wild-type representatives of the strain, at those postnatal ages when the cerebellum is rapidly forming and granule cell proliferation is at a peak, have considerably clarified the nature of the genetic defect. These studies have established that granule cells are actually generated normally in the external granular layer, but they fail to migrate out of this proliferative zone and subsequently die there during the first 2 weeks after birth. These studies also provide strong evidence that the failure of the granule cells to migrate may be a secondary consequence of a more primary defect involving the radial glial cells (Bergmann glia) that normally guide neuronal migration. Such cells were somewhat abnormal in heterozygotes and much more severely altered in homozygotes.

2. The Staggerer Mouse

The staggerer mouse is another neurological mutant that shares certain behavioral and anatomical similarities with the weaver mutant (Sidman *et al.,* 1962). This mouse displays motor deficits around the second postnatal week—also chiefly recognizable as ataxia and hypotonia—and its cerebellum is also reduced in size. As with the weaver mouse, the granule cell population is qualitatively relatively normal initially and then becomes diminished, virtually disappearing at subsequent stages (Sidman, 1968, 1972). However, in spite of this similarity, the mechanism of cell death in these cases appears to differ from that operating in the weaver mouse. Unlike weaver mutants, in staggerer mice the radial Bergmann glial cells are normal and the migration of granule cells along them proceeds normally. However, the Purkinje cells of the cerebellum, on which the granule cells' parallel axons would ordinarily terminate, fail to develop dendritic spines of the type normally contacted by parallel fibers (Landis and Sidman, 1975). The possibility therefore exists that the developing granule cell depends for its survival on the establishment of appropriate synaptic contacts with Purkinje cells (Sidman, 1972). In the case of weaver mice, then, the failure of granule cells to contact Purkinje cell dendrites appears to be caused by a disorder in granule cell migration, whereas in staggerer mice synaptogenesis may be compromised by defective Purkinje cell dendrites. The common result in both mutants is that normal synapses between granule cells and Purkinje cells fail to develop and the granule cells degenerate.

3. The Reeler Mouse

Another interesting mutant, also of the autosomal recessive variety, is the reeler mouse. The behavior of this mutant was first described by Falconer (1951, p. 198):

> The most striking abnormality is the mouse's inability to keep its hindquarters upright. When the mouse stands still its hindquarters sway slowly from side to side; when it walks the swaying is accentuated and the mouse falls over on to its side. It rights itself immediately, but as soon as progression recommences it falls over again to the same or the opposite side. The whole performance is remarkably suggestive of inebriation, and strongly resembles the behavior of normal mice when recovering from ether anesthesia . . . . Close observation usually discloses a slight tremor of the foot while it is off the ground. A more generalized tremor may sometimes be observed in a reeler that is excited and active . . . . Reelers are less active than normal mice, and it is often difficult to induce them to run about so as to display their abnormality. When the cage is opened they are usually found crouching in a corner, often lying partially on their sides, which a normal mouse does not do, and they pay little attention to the disturbance caused by opening the cage. When induced to run about on a table they often fall off if they come to the edge, a thing that a normal mouse seldom does. The fur of adults assumes an unkempt appearance which is probably due to lack of grooming, though reelers are well able to scratch with their hind legs. Neither males nor females show any sign of normal aggressive behavior toward strange mice. All these features suggest strongly that reelers are mentally deficient.

According to Falconer, some of these symptoms may be detected as early as 15 days of age, but the full-blown syndrome is definitely present by 18 days of age.

Many reelers will die at 3 weeks of age if they are not hand reared. Five males that Falconer kept for a year proved to be sterile, and one female that was successfully bred failed to rear her young.

Although Falconer's use of the term "mentally deficient" was probably colloquial, it is of interest that subsequently anatomical abnormalities were found to be present in the reeler cerebral neocortex (Sidman, 1968, 1972) and hippocampus (Caviness and Sidman, 1973), as well as in the cerebellum (Sidman and Rakic, 1972a, b). The major feature of abnormality in these brain regions is that while all cell types appear to be present and even to establish appropriate synapses with one another, these cells are improperly oriented and drastically misaligned. In some areas of the cerebellum, for example, the cell bodies of granule cells take up positions above the Purkinje cell layer rather than in their normal locations beneath (Sidman, 1968). However, though the granule cells are misaligned, they appear to develop the same major classes of synapses with other neurons that are found in the normal cerebellum (Sidman and Rakic, 1972a, b). Similar reversals of position (and hence disruption of layers) were also described in other areas of the brain, and major fiber bundles such as the anterior commissure were found to be grossly displaced (Caviness and Sidman, 1972, 1973). The striking abnormalities in the positions of cells could be due to a wide-ranging defect in cell migration (Sidman, 1972), to an abnormal distribution of fibers with which they will ultimately establish synaptic contacts, or to an inability of migrating cells to recognize their targets (Caviness and Sidman, 1973).

These studies are important because they indicate that a single gene can control specific aspects of neural development and that different genes can alter development in a number of different ways, even when the phenotypic expression—the behavior, for example—may be remarkably similar, as it is among the mutants here described.

Findings such as these cannot but stimulate curiosity as to whether some individual differences in normal human beings and the numerous mental and behavioral disorders known to be heritable in some degree are not also manifestations of disordered development of the nervous system. Information on dendritic and synaptic development in human neuropathological disorders is practically nonexistent. However, the first detailed morphological studies (Marin-Padilla, 1974) utilizing specialized neurohistological techniques have recently been carried out in the case of a newborn infant with a chromosomal abnormality [D_1(13–15) trisomy or Patau's syndrome] known to be associated with mental retardation. The cerebral motor cortex of this infant was markedly hypocellular, the cortical neurons were structurally less developed than that of normal neonates, and the dendritic spines of the giant pyramidal cells were structurally abnormal, their number being reduced and their distribution altered. As noted by the author (Marin-Padilla, 1974), all of the distinctive features in this human brain, and in particular the abnormal synaptic apparatus, could contribute to the poor motor coordination and mental retardation that becomes apparent in all cases of this type that survive to ages when such symptoms can be judged. Furthermore, mental retardation has been described in other types of genetic anomalies such as mongolism (trisomy 21) and also in association with chromosomal disorders other than trisomy. What morphological abnormalities may be found in the brains of such cases when appropriate anatomical methods are applied can only be imagined. It is already clear that abnormalities in the fine structure of the cerebral cortex exist in mentally retarded individuals with normal karyotypes (Huttenlocker, 1975; Purpura, 1975).

E. FUTURE DIRECTIONS

A number of different approaches to the analysis of structural and functional development of the cerebellum have recently been exploited. The use of low-level X irradiation to alter experimentally the number and type of neuronal components of the cerebellar cortex and the study of genetically altered strains of mice have been highlighted in the present review. The two approaches are complementary, and both have yielded evidence which can be interpreted as indicating that the integrity of a particular class of neurons, the granule cells, and their synapses, particularly those with the Purkinje cell dendrites, are essential for the normal development of motor skills. However, this point is far from well established, and many questions remain to be answered.

Studies of focally X irradiated rats have shown that these rats, in whom the granule cells did not develop in normal numbers, were severely impaired on a variety of motor tasks. However, it is not yet clear from these studies whether other cellular elements in the cerebellum itself or in other regions of the brain were completely spared the destructive effects of radiation, nor is there suffi-cient evidence pertaining to other aspects of the irradiated animals' behavior, such as whether their learning or other nonsensorimotor abilities are intact. Both types of evidence would provide further information on the specificity of the cerebellar defect produced by X irradiation.

Studies of weaver and staggerer mutants, in whom drastic deficits in both the granule cell population and in motor behavior are correlated, provide further evidence for the functional importance of this class of neurons in development. However, the fact that the altered brains of these neurological mutants consti-tute valuable natural experiments does not minimize the difficulty of establish-ing that a particular cellular defect is responsible for a particular behavioral symptom. In the case of weaver and staggerer mice, for example, it is necessary to study all features and parts of their nervous systems in order to be sure that the granule cell defect is critical. In addition, studies of a greater variety of genetic mutants are needed to reveal the extent to which a defect in the granule cell and its synaptic relationships with other cells is a common pathological finding in the brains of animals exhibiting motor symptoms. Such symptoms are present, for example, in the reeler mouse, which does not exhibit a conspicuous loss either of granule cell neurons or of synapses involving this cell. However, the spatial dislocation of the granule cell with respect to other neurons may be a sufficient basis for altering the functional integrity of these synapses; or, alternatively, the motor symptoms in these animals may arise from a different feature of their cerebellar pathology or from the derangement of cellular relationships in other regions of their brains. It is possible also that more sensitive measures of their behavior will reveal them to be less similar in their motor disabilities to other mutants than it would now appear.

Much finer behavioral techniques and electrophysiological studies would greatly clarify the nature of the functional deficits in these cases of experimentally and genetically induced cerebellar pathology. That the field is now ready for such multidisciplinary cooperation is testimony to the many promising directions which have been opened up by the pioneering studies reviewed here. These studies provide a model for the analysis of structure–function relationships in development that can be pursued in the study of other areas of the central nervous system as well as in the cerebellum.

IV. CEREBRAL CORTEX: EXTRINSIC CONNECTIONS AND CNS ORGANIZATION

A. MOTOR CORTEX

While studies of cerebellar development have elucidated the behavioral importance of synapses between neurons in different layers of the same structure, studies on the frontal cortex described below focus on the development of connections between neurons in distant structures.

1. Corticospinal Connections in the Adult

The motor cortex of adult mammals is the site of origin of long fiber tracts that terminate at many levels of the spinal cord and exert control over the initiation and execution of various aspects of voluntary movement. In the adult monkey, some of the fibers originating in the motor cortex descend in the pyramidal tract to interneurons in the intermediate zone of the spinal cord (e.g., Liu and Chambers, 1964; Kuypers, 1960; Kuypers and Brinkman, 1970). As shown in Fig. 5, these projections may be direct or indirect, the latter being routed via nuclei in the brain stem. These pathways from the precentral cortex and brain stem to the intermediate zone of the spinal cord play a role in the animal's ability to maintain posture, to perform integrated body–limb move-

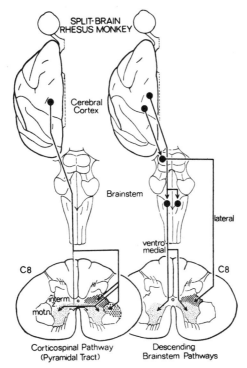

Fig. 5. Diagrams of descending connections from the cerebral cortex and brainstem to the spinal cord in the rhesus monkey. Note that one-half of the brain is connected directly and indirectly to the dorsolateral (hatched) and the ventromedial (stippled) parts of the intermediate zone and to motoneurons (small open circles) of distal extremity muscles *contralaterally*, but mainly to the ventromedial parts of the intermediate zone *ipsilaterally*. (Reproduced with permission from Brinkman and Kuypers, 1973.)

ments, to execute the independent movements of the extremities, and to direct the course of progression (Lawrence and Kuypers, 1968b; Brinkman and Kuypers, 1973; Kuypers, 1974). Precise control over individual finger movements, however, appears to depend upon another group of corticospinal fibers, also originating in the motor cortex but terminating directly upon the motoneurons of the ventral horn rather than on interneurons in the intermediate zone (Bernhard and Bohm, 1954; Kuypers, 1960; Liu and Chambers, 1964; Phillips and Porter, 1964; Beck and Chambers, 1970; Brinkman and Kuypers, 1973).

The role of cortico-motoneuronal fibers in the discrete control of the digits is based on several lines of evidence. First, comparative anatomical studies indicate that direct innervation of the ventral horn motoneurons is present only in species that make extensive manipulative use of the digits. Direct corticospinal projections to motoneurons in the ventral horn have been found in the monkey (Kuypers, 1960, 1962; Liu and Chambers, 1964; Petras, 1969) but not in the cat (Chambers and Liu, 1957; Petras, 1969) or the dog (Buxton and Goodman, 1967), neither of which demonstrate complex digital manipulative skills. Furthermore, within taxonomic orders there is an increasing number of direct cortico-motoneuronal connections with increased complexity of digital usage. In carnivores there are differences between cats and dogs, on the one hand, which show little digital dexterity and an absence of direct cortical connections to ventral horn motoneurons, and kinkajous and raccoons, on the other hand, representatives of the order that show both distal manipulative capacities and direct cortico-motoneuronal innervation (Buxton and Goodman, 1967; Petras, 1969; Wirth *et al.,* 1974). Similarly, in primates cortical innervation of the ventral horn motoneurons appears to be less in the rhesus monkey than in the chimpanzee or man (Kuypers, 1956; Petras, 1969). These anatomical findings are in accord with evidence of varied degrees of functional deficit following interruption of the corticospinal pathways in different species (Magoun and Ranson, 1938; Walker and Fulton, 1938; Tower, 1940; Buxton and Goodman, 1967; Lawrence and Kuypers, 1968a).

A second line of evidence for the dependence of digital dexterity upon direct cortico-motoneuronal fibers comes from behavioral studies of split-brain monkeys (Brinkman and Kuypers, 1972, 1973). As may be seen from Fig. 5, projections from the motor cortex to the spinal cord terminate bilaterally in the intermediate zone of the cord but only contralaterally in the motoneuronal cells of the ventral horn. On the basis of the anatomy, Kuypers and Brinkman (1970) proposed that each half of the brain has full control over arm, hand, *and* finger movements contralaterally but only over arm movements ipsilaterally. Using the split-brain preparation in which visual input was restricted to one half of the brain, Kuypers and Brinkman demonstrated that split-brain monkeys could reach out and pick up pieces of food from recessed foodwells with their contralateral hand and fingers, whereas their ipsilateral hand and fingers could be brought to the proper place but could not execute the relatively independent hand and finger movements necessary to retrieve the food morsels. Thus, individual finger movements could be performed only by the hand innervated by ventral horn neurons that receive a direct projection from the motor cortex, i.e., the contralateral hand.

2. Development of Corticospinal Pathways

Lesions of the motor cortex or of the pyramidal tract in adult monkeys result in abnormalities of tone and paralysis of the affected limbs, the severity of which depends upon a number of factors including the extent of the lesion, the time of recovery, and the age of the animal (Kennard, 1936, 1938, 1940, 1942; Tower, 1940; Travis and Woolsey, 1956; Lawrence and Kuypers, 1968a). In primates the loss of dexterity and control in the use of the digits, such as those involved in apposing the thumb and index finger to remove a morsel of food from a recessed foodwell or in the act of grooming, are permanent and ir-recoverable symptoms following interruption of the corticospinal pathways (Tower, 1940; Lawrence and Kuypers, 1968a; Beck and Chambers, 1970). The lack of manipulatory capacity following such damage in adult animals has been likened to the level of manipulative abilities exhibited by young infants (Hines, 1942). Classical observations on the development of motor skills in infant monkeys indicate that the independent use of the index finger and thumb does not attain adult levels of proficiency until about a year of age, nor are the fine movements of grooming spontaneously displayed until that time (Hines, 1942). Correspondingly, ablations of the motor cortex in the infant monkey do not seem to result in nearly as severe deficits in motor performance as they do in adult monkeys (Kennard, 1936, 1938, 1940, 1942).

Kuypers (1962) suggested that the discrepant motor deficits in the infant and the adult monkey could be due to ontogenetic differences in the pattern of corticospinal projections similar to the phylogenetic differences that exist be-tween, for example, the cat and the monkey. Using silver degeneration tech-niques to study the status of corticospinal fibers in monkeys given motor cortex lesions at different ages, Kuypers found evidence that the adult pattern of fiber degeneration in the spinal cord did not become apparent until at least 8 months after birth. It is of interest that only the 8-month-old infant in this series exhibited the hemiparesis and extremity weakness which "approximated" the adult picture of deficits. A similar ontogenetic study has been carried out in the dog (Buxton and Goodman, 1967) but on a time scale corresponding to canine development. Both the spinal distribution of degenerating cortical fibers and the behavioral consequences of unilateral lesions of the motor cortex were studied in 4-week-old puppies, 3-month-old puppies, and 12-month-old (adult) dogs. In agreement with the findings based on monkeys, early lesions of the motor cortex resulted both in less severe motor deficits than did lesions in the adult and also in correspondingly less evidence of corticospinal terminations in the infants than in the adults. Furthermore, there was a progressive increase with age in the degree of functional loss and the extent of corticospinal terminations over the range of ages employed, with the major developmental changes occurring be-tween 4 and 12 weeks of age.

The anatomical findings in the dog are especially interesting in light of a study which is largely unknown to scientists outside of Eastern Europe. Gorska and Czarkowska (1973) applied electrical stimulation to the surface of the motor cortex in adult dogs and in puppies of various ages and observed the skeletal movements elicited by such stimulation. The methods used were similar to those that had been employed by Woolsey and his colleagues (Woolsey et al. 1952; Welker et al., 1957; Woolsey, 1958) in classical studies on the somatotopic

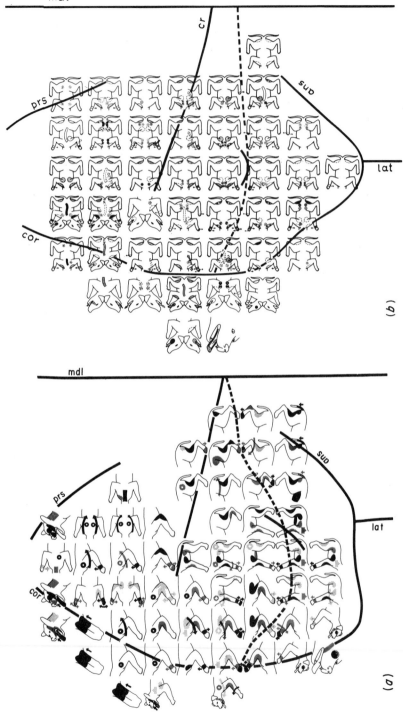

organization of the motor cortex in adult animals. Stimulation of the motor cortex in puppies evoked movements of the skeletal musculature as early as the first day of life, but these movements are very different from those which are elicited in fully mature dogs. The main differences are illustrated in Fig. 6 and summarized here: (1) *Somatotopic organization*—Whereas in the adult dog, stimulation of the medial regions of the sigmoid gyrus yields hindlimb movements and stimulation of the more lateral zones triggers forelimb movements, in puppies both fore- and hindlimb movements were produced by stimulation of either medial or lateral regions of this cortex. Thus, in contrast to adults, in puppies there appears to be a lack of somatotopic organization. (2) *Bilaterality*— In adult dogs, stimulation of the sigmoid gyrus results in movements of the contralateral body parts only; stimulation of this same area in puppies produces movements of both ipsilateral as well as contralateral extremities. (3) *Repertoire*—Whereas in adult dogs, electrical stimulation of the motor cortex yields a variety of movements of the proximal and distal musculature, in puppies a majority of the movements elicited by such stimulation were confined to the

---

Fig. 6. Figurine maps used to illustrate the results for (*a*) an adult dog and (*b*) a 13-day-old dog. The heavy solid lines indicate sulci. The heavy dashed lines indicate the boundary between the somatic sensory (SI) and the motor area. The abbreviations refer to sulci. On each figurine the muscle group or body part engaged in the movement is marked. The symbols of various kinds of movements are similar to those used by Welker *et al.* (1957). Each figurine corresponds to one cortical point stimulated. Unilateral figurines represent the contralateral side of the animal. In order to maintain the appropriate direction of individual figurines within the pattern of somatotopic organization of sensory (SI) and motor areas, right-sided figurines were used for area SI and left-sided figurines for the motor cortex. In bilateral figurines the contralateral side of the body is marked on the corresponding part of the figurine according to the convention used for unilateral figurines, and the mirror-image half of the figurines represents the ipsilateral side of the animal. Abbreviations: prs, presylvian sulcus; cr, cruciate sulcus; ans, ansate sulcus; lat, lateral sulcus; cor, coronal sulcus; mdl, midline.

A variety of symbols has been used to denote various features of movements obtained in puppies and adult dogs. In adultlike forms of responses, solid black represents the earliest, strongest, or lowest-threshold movement; hatched, intermediate grades; and small dots, the weakest or highest-threshold movement elicited. These symbols also indicate that movements were tonic and repetitive, that is, successive stimulations of the same cortical point yielded similar motor responses.

For other movements specific for puppies, the following symbols are used: An interrupted line denotes a variable response which could not be repeated on successive stimulation of the same cortical point. A solid line indicates a repetitive movement. Repetitive responses elicited at threshold value of stimulation are marked by large dots, and dashed hatching means a repetitive response recruited with suprathreshold stimulation. A solid line without any pattern inside denotes a movement which we could not classify, for some reason, as repetitive or variable. (Reproduced with permission from Gorska and Czarkowska, 1973.)

proximal joints. Hindlimb movements, for example, were essentially limited to a retraction of the thigh, a movement which is unusual in adults; similarly, forelimb movements were mainly limited to a protraction of the shoulder. Movements characteristic of the adult dog, such as thigh protraction, shoulder retraction, knee and elbow flexion, and flexion of the wrist were extremely rare responses to electrical stimulation at very early stages of development. (4) *Character of movements*—In adult dogs, movements elicited by cortical stimulation are virtually always tonic, whereas in puppies they were generally jerklike, phasic, or clonic. The movements elicited in puppies were also quite variable. In contrast to studies in the adult dog, successive stimulation of the same cortical point produced different responses at different times. (5) *Threshold*—The currents required to elicit motor responses were higher in puppies than in adult dogs and decreased with age.

On the basis of their results, Gorska and Czarkowska (1973) identified two major periods in postnatal maturation of the organization of the motor cortex and its functions: one period from birth through about 4 weeks of age, and a subsequent period from the fourth week through about 12 weeks of age. The earlier period was characterized by lack of somatotopic representation of the body parts, lack of dominant representation of the contralateral side of the body, meager repertoire of response, variability or lack of tonic character of response, and high thresholds of stimulation. In the subsequent period, somatotopic organization and contralateral representation first made their appearance, the repertoire of movements became enriched, movements became tonic, and responses stable. By 12 weeks of age, electrical stimulation produced effects qualitatively similar to those observed in the adult, although there was some indication in threshold data, for example, that the maturation of motor cortex was not fully complete even at this stage of development. These results correlate remarkably well with the anatomical findings of Buxton and Goodman (1967), who showed that major changes occur in the maturational status of the dog's corticospinal connections between weeks 4–12, and with the electrophysiological findings of Kirk and Breazile (1972), who demonstrated that conduction velocities of corticospinal fibers are still increasing within this period.

The anatomical findings reviewed in this section are subject to the limitation that the absence of degeneration products in the immature animal could be due to various factors such as the smaller diameter of fibers, their degree of myelinization, or to possible metabolic properties that affect the silver impregnation of the tissue, rather than due to the absence of connections per se. However, differences in fiber diameter or argyrophilic reactions themselves can be useful indices of functional immaturity (Leonard, 1973, 1974), as shown, for example, by the correlation in dogs between anatomical indices of neural maturation (Buxton and Goodman, 1967) and the impressive results obtained by mapping the electrically excitable cortex at different stages of development

(Gorska and Czarkowska, 1973). Furthermore, electrophysiological studies in developing dogs (Kirk and Breazile, 1972) and monkeys (Felix and Wiesendanger, 1971) support a picture of protracted corticospinal development. Thus, taken together, the evidence indicates that the maturation of corticospinal connections postnatally, perhaps at the level of ultrastructure, underlies in part the emergence of motor capacity with age. Similarly, in the case of higher primates, the exquisitely precise use of the digits, a hallmark of the evolutionary status of primates, may depend upon the gradual elaboration of synapses between the long axons of the motor cortex and the motoneurons of the ventral horn during the first postnatal year.

3. Corticocortical Connections

The motor cortex not only gives rise to pathways descending to the spinal cord but also establishes many connections with cortical and other subcortical regions. Studies of nervous system development often await advances in understanding of the organization of the adult system. Only recently has there been a revival of interest in the description of corticocortical pathways in the adult (Pandya and Kuypers, 1969; Jones and Powell, 1970), and so it is not surprising that very few studies exist on the status of such connections in the infant. One recent study compared in great detail the extent of corticocortical pathways in the newborn and 24-month-old monkey (Kemper et al., 1973). Using the method of silver impregnation, these authors demonstrated a dramatic difference in the corticocortical connections of the immature and mature brain. In Fig. 7(a–d) it can be observed that a small needle track lesion in the motor cortex of a 24-month-old monkey results in axonal anterograde degeneration over a wide area, extending to the adjacent cortex of the frontal and parietal lobes, thus indicating the existence of an extensive network of corticocortical connections. Following a lesion of the same dimensions in the newborn monkey, however, the resultant degeneration was confined to within only a 600-μm radius of the lesion. A number of other parameters of motor cortex development, including cyto- and myeloarchitectonics and quantitative measures of the dendritic apparatus, were also studied. Altogether the findings supported the view that the corticocortical connections of the motor cortex of newborn primates are not well developed at birth and that significant maturation of these connections occurs postnatally, although the precise time at which the adult pattern of connectivity is established was not determined in this study.

The maturation of corticocortical connections may be presumed to be an important factor in the emergence of motor skills during normal development, and cortical maturity may also have a bearing on certain features of disordered development. Caveness et al. (1973) compared the electroencephalographic (EEG) and clinical expression of penicillin-induced focal seizures in newborn and juvenile monkeys under two experimental conditions. In one condition, the

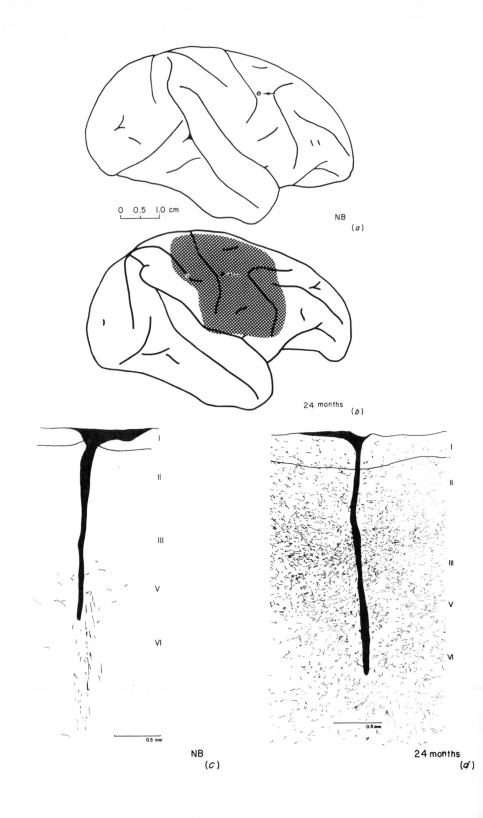

0   0.5   1.0 cm

NB
(a)

24 months
(b)

I

II

III

V

VI

0.5 mm

NB
(c)

I

II

III

V

VI

0.5 mm

24 months
(d)

cortical site of penicillin activation was separated from subcortical structures by undercutting the cortex, a procedure that severs the afferent and efferent connections but leaves the intracortical connections intact. Conversely, the corticocortical connections of the same cortical site were disrupted by circumsecting it without compromising the cortical-subcortical pathways. The undercutting procedure blocked the propagation of paroxysmal activity in the newborn but not in the 24-month-old monkey; in contrast, circumsecting the cortex blocked the spread of seizures in the juvenile but not in the newborn. These dramatic results indicate that the circuitry for both the propagation of focal paroxysmal activity such as may occur in abnormal conditions like epilepsy, as well as for the elaboration of behavior patterns under normal conditions, differs considerably in the young and in the mature brain.

B. PREFRONTAL CORTEX

1. Anatomical Connections of the Dorsolateral Prefrontal Cortex in the Adult

The foundation for an analysis of structure and function in the prefrontal cortex of the primate was begun over 40 years ago by Carlyle Jacobsen (1936). Since his pioneering efforts, it has become clear that this prominent region of neocortex, once regarded as a unitary functional entity, is heterogeneous both in terms of its contribution to psychological processes and in terms of its corticocortical and subcortical connections (Mishkin, 1964; Goldman and Rosvold, 1970; Akert, 1964; Nauta, 1964; Pandya et al., 1971). We shall here be concerned with only one of the major subdivisions of the prefrontal area, the cortex situated on the dorsolateral convexity of the frontal lobe anterior to the arcuate sulcus (Fig. 8).

The dorsolateral cortex is interconnected with many other areas of cortex and with numerous subcortical structures. Of particular interest in the present review are those pathways linking this region of prefrontal cortex with the caudate nucleus and the thalamus (Fig. 8). The dorsolateral prefrontal cortex both projects directly upon and receives a direct afferent innervation from the parvocellular subdivision of the dorsomedial nucleus of the thalamus (Akert, 1964, Nauta, 1964; Johnson et al., 1968). This region of prefrontal cortex also

---

Fig. 7. Diagram to show the extent of the axonal degeneration within the cortex following a needle track lesion in the face-hand area of the motor cortex, as seen in Nauta-Gygax preparations in (a) a newborn and (b) a 24-month-old Macaca mulatta. Camera lucida drawing of anterograde axonal degeneration in the motor cortex of Macaca mulatta as seen in Nauta-Gygax preparations 14 days after a needle track lesion made (c) at birth and (d) at 24 months of age. (Reproduced with permission from Kemper et al., 1973.)

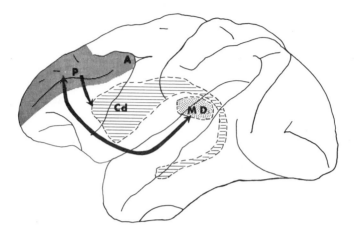

Fig. 8. Schematic figure to show interconnections of the dorsolateral prefrontal cortex (cross-hatching) with the caudate nucleus and the dorsomedial nucleus of the thalamus. Abbreviations: P, principal sulcus; A, arcuate sulcus; Cd, caudate nucleus; MD, dorsomedial nucleus.

projects upon the anterodorsal sector of the head of the caudate nucleus (Nauta, 1964, Kemp and Powell, 1970; Johnson et al., 1968). In addition, there exists a multisynaptic pathway from the caudate nucleus back to the thalamus (Johnson and Rosvold, 1971; Szabo, 1962, 1970).

2. Behavioral and Electrophysiological Properties of Dorsolateral Prefrontal Cortex in the Adult

In the adult monkey, lesions of the dorsolateral prefrontal cortex result in severe impairments on spatial delayed-response and spatial delayed-alternation tasks which require the monkey to remember the *location* of a stimulus (usually a morsel of food) over very brief intervals of time. One of the notable features of the deficit in the adult is its severity. Adult monkeys given bilateral dorsolateral lesions usually cannot reliably regain the ability to perform delayed-response tasks above chance levels of performance. The failure of such monkeys to learn these tasks postoperatively is not attributable to interference with performance by sensory or motor difficulties, nor to insufficient recovery time allowed after surgery, nor to lack of opportunity to relearn. Monkeys with bilateral lesions are not agnostic for the mechanical requirements of the task but simply make incorrect choices and exhibit impairments years after surgery in spite of prolonged efforts to retrain them (Goldman, 1971). The magnitude of impairment exhibited by adult monkeys with dorsolateral lesions on delayed-response tasks stands in marked contrast to the normal abilities which they exhibit on a whole host of problems of equal or greater difficulty (as assessed by the performance records of unoperated monkeys on these tasks). For example, monkeys with such lesions perform as well as unoperated monkeys on relatively easy visual-pattern and object-discrimination problems, but they also perform within the range of normal animals on more complex tasks such as learning set (Mishkin, 1964), object reversal (Goldman, 1971), and delayed nonspatial (go–no go) alternation (Goldman *et al.,* 1971), while at the same time failing to master delayed-response problems. The same pattern of impairments results when only that portion of the dorsolateral cortex lying within the banks and depths of the principal sulcus is excised (Fig. 8). Except in the special circumstance of removing the cortex in the principal sulcus in sequential operations, a circumstance which introduces a degree of behavioral compensation (Butters *et al.,* 1973), monkeys with lesions confined to this sulcal cortex are as severely impaired on the delayed-response tasks as those with more extensive dorsolateral removals. As in the case of these larger removals, monkeys with the more limited lesions exhibit normal performance on tasks which tax mnemonic abilities to an apparently similar degree as the delayed-response tasks but which are nonspatial in character, such as delayed object alternation (Manning and Mishkin, 1975) and delayed matching-to-sample (Passingham, 1975) tasks.

The specificity of the dorsolateral cortex for spatial delayed-response tasks is now supported by convergent evidence from electrophysiological analysis of the properties of prefrontal neurons. Neurons have been found in the dorsolateral prefrontal cortex of unanesthetized monkeys performing delayed-response tasks that respond preferentially during the delay phase of the task (Fuster and Alexander, 1971; Kubota and Niki, 1971). This electrophysiological evidence together with the results of ablation studies have established that, whatever other functions it may have, the dorsolateral prefrontal cortex in the adult monkey is highly specialized for the processing and retention of temporospatial information.

3. Behavioral and Electrophysiological Properties of Related Subcortical Structures in the Adult

The dorsolateral cortex undoubtedly mediates these functions in collaboration with other neural structures with which it is interconnected. Thus, lesions of the dorsomedial nucleus and of the head of the caudate nucleus in the adult monkey also result in impairments on delayed-response tasks. The degree of impairment following lesions in these subcortical structures is related to the extent of the lesion, but monkeys with lesions of sufficient size in the caudate (Goldman and Rosvold, 1972) or the dorsal thalamus (Goldman, 1974; Goldman and Rosvold, unpublished observations; Schulman, 1964), like those with lesions in the cortex, may either be severely impaired or totally incapable of learning these tasks. Moreover, single neurons in the parvocellular portion of the normal monkey's dorsomedial nucleus (which, as mentioned, is reciprocally connected to the dorsolateral prefrontal cortex) exhibit sustained elevations of electrical discharge during the delay phase of the delayed-response task while the monkey is performing this task (Fuster and Alexander, 1973). Thus, the electrophysiological characteristics of dorsomedial thalamic neurons resemble those of dorsolateral cortical neurons, and the similarity between the two populations of cells adds further support for the idea that this cortex and the subcortical structures to which it projects are components of a circuit whose integrity is essential for spatial-mnemonic behavior (Rosvold, 1968).

4. Cortical-Subcortical Interaction in the Adult: The Reversible Lesion Approach

It has now become possible to further elucidate the nature of the functional interrelationships between these cortical and subcortical structures by making use of the recently developed technique of cryogenic depression. By this technique various structures in the brain can be inactivated by local cooling or hypothermia. Further, the effects of cooling are entirely reversible. It is therefore possible to examine the role of a neural structure in behavioral performance without the necessity of ablation, thus avoiding the disadvantages for analysis that neuropathological processes may introduce. Using this technique, Fuster and Alexander (1970) showed that cooling the dorsolateral prefrontal cortex in adult rhesus monkeys produced deficits in their delayed-response performance. Similarly, Krauthamer et al. (1967) showed that delayed-alternation performance in monkeys was impaired by local cooling of the head of the caudate nucleus. In both studies, the effects were reversible. When the cooling was discontinued and the structures allowed to regain their normal temperatures, the performance of the monkeys returned to precooling levels. These studies on nonlesioned animals thus confirm the results of the studies based on the ablation method. Further, the cryogenic depression technique can also be used to examine the influence of the cortex on the ongoing activity in subcortical nuclei. Alexander and Fuster (1973) studied the effects of cooling the dorsolateral prefrontal cortex on the unit activity of neurons in the dorsomedial nucleus of the thalamus, upon which the cortex projects. Their studies showed that cortical cooling concomitantly induced a severe (though reversible) deficit on delayed-response performance and an alteration in the firing characteristics of neurons in the parvocellular portion of the dorsomedial nucleus. The normal firing patterns of 63% of the units related to delayed-response performance were modified. As mentioned earlier, some units exhibit a sustained firing rate preferentially during the delay of a delayed-response trial. Prefrontal cooling either attenuated or abbreviated the delay-related sustained discharge or converted it into a paradoxical inhibition. These studies show that in the adult monkey the cortex has an influence over subcortical activity and that this influence may be critical in the performance of delayed-response tasks.

5. Summary: The Adult Prefrontal Cortex

To summarize, the removal of the influence of the dorsolateral cortex in the adult by ablation or by inactivation through cooling results in profound impairments on delayed-response tasks. In the case of bilateral lesions, the deficits are not only profound, they are irrecoverable. Similar deficits result when lesions are made in anatomically associated subcortical structures—the caudate nucleus and the dorsal thalamus. The deficits are selective to spatial tasks involving mnemonic processes and do not extend to other classes of perceptual or memory tasks. Single neurons in the frontal cortex and in the dorsomedial nucleus of the thalamus in normal animals exhibit similar patterns of electrical activity associated with performance on delayed-response tasks. Cooling the prefrontal cortex has been shown to suppress the activity of those thalamic units which exhibit a pattern of elevated discharge preferentially during the delay. These various findings with respect to the structural and functional characteristics of the dorsolateral cortex and of the subcortical structures with which it is anatomically related are useful descriptors of the mature system and can now be used as a basis for studying its development.

6. Status of Afferent and Efferent Projections of the Dorsolateral Prefrontal Cortex in Developing Monkeys

In contrast to the information about connections of the dorsolateral prefrontal cortex in adults, virtually nothing is known about their status in neonates or developing monkeys. However, a recent study has examined whether the efferent projections from the dorsolateral cortex to the caudate nucleus and the dorsomedial nucleus of the thalamus are fully mature at early stages of development. Johnson et al. (1976) analyzed the terminal distribution of silver-impregnated degenerating axons in these subcortical structures following unilateral removal of the dorsolateral prefrontal cortex in monkeys at 2, 6, and 24 months of age. Following the dorsolateral lesions, which were identical to those used in previous behavioral investigations, considerable numbers of degenerating fibers were found in the parvocellular division of the dorsomedial nucleus in all age groups. Likewise, in accord with previous observations (Goldman, 1971), there was evidence of retrograde degeneration of cell bodies in the thalamus at all ages. Both observations suggest that the thalamocortical and corticothalamic pathways are present by two months of age. In contrast, the degree of fiber degeneration present in the anterodorsal sector of the head of the caudate nucleus was age dependent: degenerating fibers were found in increasing numbers from 2 months of age, when virtually none could be detected to 6 months of age, when they were clearly present, to 24 months of age, when they appeared in relatively dense concentration. These findings with respect to the anatomical status of corticocaudate connections during development are comparable to those found by Kuypers (1962), whose study of the postnatal maturation of the motor cortex indicated that degenerating cortico-moto-neuronal fibers to the spinal cord following ablation of the motor cortex were relatively sparse in baby monkeys but increased in number until 8 months of age. These "negative" results from silver degeneration studies on immature monkeys should not be taken to signify an actual absence of the corticofugal pathways in question at early ages, since autoradiographic studies currently in progress on the postnatal development of prefrontal and motor cortex projections (Goldman and Nauta, unpublished observations) clearly show that cortical efferents to the caudate nucleus and spinal cord are as plentiful in 1-week-old monkeys as they are in mature monkeys. However, as mentioned previously, the silver degeneration evidence could indicate an immaturity in these pathways related perhaps to their degree of myelination or to some other histochemical property of young neurons that alters their argyrophilic response to injury. Taken together with other evidence (e.g., see Leonard, 1974) the results of the study of Johnson et al. (1976) indicates that at least a part of the circuit necessary for normal delayed-response behavior in the adult may not be fully structurally differentiated in the infant and may gradually mature in the course of postnatal development.

7. Functional Development of the Dorsolateral Prefrontal Cortex: Normative Studies

Several lines of investigation have contributed to an understanding of prefrontal cortical development. One category of study has described the normative development of behaviors like delayed response performance known to be dependent on the integrity of the prefrontal cortex. These studies, in which normal subjects of different ages are compared, have been carried out in dogs (Fox and Spencer, 1967), cats (Wikmark, 1974), monkeys (Harlow, 1959), and man (Hunter, 1913; Lynn and Compton, 1966) and have served to delimit the age span over which abilities dependent on prefrontal cortical mechanisms are normally attained. Not surprisingly, in most species studied the capacity to perform delayed-response tasks with adult proficiency is not present in the neonate and develops only gradually over an extended postnatal period. In the monkey, it is doubtful whether fully adult-level delayed-response abilities are attained within the first year or two of life (Harlow, 1959; Goldman, 1971).

8. Functional Development of the Dorsolateral Prefrontal Cortex: Lesion Studies

The timetables of emergence of mature forms of behavior in normal animals are helpful reflections of the status of the central nervous system at different stages of development but yield only inferential statements concerning the maturation of the brain regions underlying that behavior. An extension of this approach is to compare the development of behavior in normal subjects with subjects in whom specific regions of the brain have been extirpated early in ontogeny.

Several laboratories have now investigated the effects on delayed-response performance of removing the dorsolateral prefrontal cortex in monkeys of different ages, and the results have been remarkably consistent (Akert *et al.,* 1960; Tucker and Kling, 1967; Goldman, 1971). Monkeys that have undergone extensive dorsolateral removals within the first 2 months of life do not exhibit the characteristic adult impairments on delayed-response tasks and, in fact, perform as well as unoperated controls as long as such groups are subsequently tested within the first year of life. As after motor cortex lesions at different ages, the degree of impairment following prefrontal cortical lesions increases with increasing age of the animal at the time of injury, although there is still some question as to the exact age when adult-typical deficits can be obtained (see Harlow *et al.,* 1970).

The fact that earlier lesions result in less impairment than later lesions can be interpreted in a variety of ways (Goldman, 1974). One explanation is that the immature brain has a greater capacity for restitution of function than the mature brain. According to this view, the removal of the dorsolateral prefrontal cortex in infancy does not result in impairments because other regions of the brain may take over the functions of the missing area. The implication of such an analysis is that the dorsolateral prefrontal cortex is as committed to its functions in young animals as in older ones but that other undamaged brain structures possess a capacity for compensation, presumably because their own functions are not yet fully specified. An alternative explanation for the lack of effect of dorsolateral removal in infancy is that the dorsolateral cortex (and/or its interconnections with subcortical structures) is itself not functionally mature and hence is not used by the young monkey to solve delayed-response problems. If the "immaturity hypothesis" is correct, then animals raised from infancy without this region of cortex should ultimately show arrested development of delayed-response capacity with age, as delayed-response performance normatively becomes more dependent on cortical mechanisms.

Few observations are available on the long-term consequences of dorsolateral prefrontal injury in infancy. However, when monkeys that were operated upon in infancy are followed into the second year of life, they exhibit increasing evidence of difficulty on delayed-response tasks (Tucker and Kling, 1967; Goldman, 1971, 1974, 1975). This delay in the appearance of deficits with age supports the idea that the dorsolateral cortex can be removed with impunity at early ages simply because it does not contribute to delayed-response performance at these ages. From the limited longitudinal evidence, Goldman (1971, 1972) has proposed that the dorsolateral prefrontal cortex in the monkey does not attain functional maturity until 2 years of age and perhaps even later.

9. Functional Development of Subcortical Structures: Lesion Studies

The findings obtained when the behavioral effects of early and late lesions of subcortical structures are compared stand in sharp contrast to those obtained in studies of cortical lesions. Thus, Kling and Tucker (1967) found no evidence of preserved delayed-response capacity in monkeys in whom caudate lesions had been added to dorsolateral cortical lesions in infancy, and Goldman and Rosvold (1972) showed that lesions limited to the head of the caudate nucleus produced severe and selective impairments at 1 year of age in monkeys operated upon as infants. The pattern and degree of impairment exhibited by these early-operated monkeys was undistinguishable from that produced by comparable lesions in monkeys operated upon as juveniles. Similarly, selective lesions of the dorso-medial nucleus were found to result in the same pattern and degree of deficits in early- and late-operated monkeys (Goldman and Rosvold, unpublished observations; Goldman, 1974). The absence of evidence for a difference in the effect of subcortical lesions in young and old subjects is compatible with the idea that these subcortical structures are already well developed and selectively "tuned" to mediate functions at a time when dorsolateral cortical mechanisms have not yet matured.

The differential effectiveness of cortical and subcortical lesions at different stages of development is illustrated in Fig. 9. If monkeys are operated upon as infants, bilateral caudate lesions produce more severe deficits on three different spatial tasks than do dorsolateral cortical lesions. In animals operated upon as juveniles, however, cortical lesions are more disruptive on these same tasks than are subcortical lesions. (Figure 9 also demonstrates that nonspatial tasks are unaffected by frontal cortical or subcortical damage at any age.) The reversal in the effectiveness of these cortical and subcortical lesions with age indicates that there is a shift in cortical-subcortical relationships with age—a shift which may be characterized as a change from "subcortical dominance" of delayed-response performance to "cortical dominance." Thus, it would appear that subcortical structures participate in the mediation of delayed-response learning well before the cortex does; with the development of cortical influence, however, the relative (though not the absolute) importance of subcortical mechanisms seems to diminish.

10. Functional Inactivation of Developing Cortex by Cooling

The behavioral evidence obtained from normal animals and from those de-prived as infants of the dorsolateral prefrontal cortex, the caudate nucleus, or the dorsomedial nucleus of the thalamus suggests that the cortex only slowly develops its functions over a protracted period of about 2 years and, further-more, that in immature animals subcortical structures are capable of mediating certain functions in the absence of the cerebral cortex. The implication of this

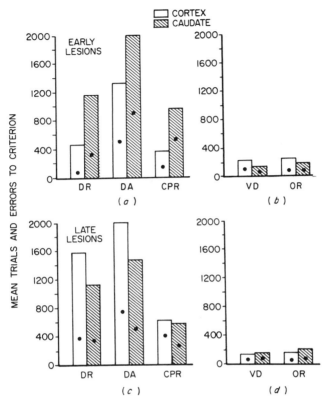

Fig. 9. Contrasting effects of dorsolateral cortical and anterodorsal caudate lesions at different stages of development: (a, b) Performance on tests given after the age of 1 year but before 2 years, after lesions performed in infancy. (c, d) Performance on the same tests given at the same time intervals after surgery performed in young adults. Abbreviations: DR, delayed response; DA, delayed alternation; and CPR, conditioned position response—all spatial tests affected by dorsolateral lesions in adults; VD, visual pattern discrimination; OR, object discrimination reversal; control tests not dependent on the integrity of the dorsolateral cortex. (Goldman, 1974. Reproduced with permission from *Neurosci. Res. Progr. Bull.* **12**, p. 219.)

analysis is that subcortical mechanisms possess a degree of functional autonomy from cortical influence, an autonomy which is lost with age. Recent studies in the author's laboratory have provided further evidence for these conjectures.

The cryogenic depression technique, developed by Fuster and Alexander (1970) for the study of reversible lesions in adult monkeys, has now been applied to the study of developing monkeys. As indicated previously, bilateral prefrontal cooling in adults is associated with systematic and consistent decreases in the number of correct responses on the delayed-response task, without however affecting the animals' general level of activity or motor coordination.

Moreover, the prefrontal cooling concomitantly alters the electrophysiological activity of neurons in the dorsomedial nucleus of the thalamus whose activity is related to task parameters. Applying this method to developing monkeys should reveal the degree of functional maturity of their cortex and may be a way of assessing the interdependence or autonomy of cortical and subcortical mechanisms at different stages of development. Alexander and Goldman (unpublished observations) have investigated the effects of cooling the prefrontal cortex in immature monkeys trained on delayed response. Four monkeys, ranging in age from 11 to 18 months, have been extensively studied under conditions entirely comparable to those used in the investigations on adult monkeys. In sharp contrast to the results obtained in adult monkeys (Fuster and Alexander, 1970), however, cooling the dorsolateral prefrontal cortex in monkeys at 11–18 months of age appears to have no disruptive effect on their level of performance, since they continue to perform at criterion levels, both during cooling and control (noncooling) trials. In the same animals, electrophysiological recordings from subcortical structures can be made while the animals are performing the delayed-response task. Studies are now in progress on the concomitant effects of prefrontal cortical cooling on subcortical activity and delayed-response behavior in immature animals to determine whether neurons in the dorsomedial nucleus of the thalamus respond preferentially in relation to task paramenters as they do in the adult, and if so, whether such neurons are influenced by cortical cooling in the same way or to the same degree as in adult monkeys. The finding to date that prefrontal cooling is ineffective in altering delayed-response performance in juvenile monkeys 18 months of age or younger provides strong support for the view, based on evidence from lesion studies, that the dorsolateral cortex does not become committed to its adult functions until well into the second year of life.

11. Comments on Studies of Motor and Prefrontal Cortical Development

Together the prefrontal and precentral (motor) cortex constitute a considerable portion of the neocortical mantle of the primate frontal lobe. It is of interest that there are certain parallels in their development. Both regions of cortex can be removed in infancy with less severe behavioral consequences than comparable lesions in adults. However, neither area can be removed without eventually producing symptoms at an age when the symptomatic functions can be judged as mature in normal monkeys. In the case of the motor cortex, loss of fine control of the digits is a permanent defect associated with motor neuron damage, though the symptom does not appear in full bloom until about 2 years of age (Lawrence and Hopkins, 1972). In the case of the prefrontal cortex, monkeys who could perform delayed-response tasks as well as unoperated controls at 1 year of age, fail at later stages of development to exhibit that improvement in performance found in unoperated monkeys of the same age. There is parallel anatomical evidence for both systems that corticofugal pathways are not fully mature in the first year of life, a parallelism attributable perhaps to their state of myelination. And each area of the frontal cortex exhibits an immaturity with respect to its interactions with other cortical or subcortical areas.

It should be emphasized that behavioral analysis has been an important tool in our understanding of development in each of these systems. Behavioral observations have not merely been used as markers for critical events in ontogeny; one may say that behavior is a definitive measure for differentiation of neural structure.

C. VISUAL CORTEX

Although almost all readers will be familiar with the important studies on development of orientation specificity and binocularity in the visual cortex of kittens (Hubel and Wiesel, 1963; Hirsch and Spinelli, 1970; Blakemore and Cooper, 1970), these studies will be mentioned here for three reasons: (a) they represent a substantial effort to reconstruct the development of a sensory system and thus complement the review of motor and association systems; (b) they are uniquely illustrative of the issues that arise in the study of the impact that environmental stimulation has on the maturation of the nervous system; and (c) sensory systems, in particular the visual system, are often put forth as models for analyses of structure—function relationships in the central nervous system.

1. Properties of Visual Cortical Neurons in the Adult

As with other ontogenetic analyses, the study of the visual system proceeds against a background of what is known about the organization and functions of this system in the adult. For the geniculostriate system, the background information is rich, both the anatomy and physiology of visual structures having been extensively investigated. Of particular interest from a developmental point of view are those receptive-field properties of individual cells in the retina (Kuffler, 1953), lateral geniculate body (Hubel and Wiesel, 1961), and visual cortex (Hubel and Wiesel, 1959, 1962) that have been described so well in elegant electrophysiological mapping studies of the adult cat brain.

The receptive field of a neuron in the visual system, of course, is that region of the visual field which can influence the firing of that nerve cell. Two types of cells have been identified in the retina (Kuffler, 1953) and lateral geniculate body (Hubel and Wiesel, 1961): (a) those which respond with increased firing rates to stimuli presented in the center of their fields and with decreased firing rates to stimuli presented in the periphery of these fields; and (b) the converse. The excitatory and inhibitory regions of these receptive fields are arranged concentrically (see Fig. 10), with either the excitatory or inhibitory region being in the center of the field. In contrast, the receptive fields of cortical neurons are much more varied and individualized in their predilection for specific features of the visual world. Instead of cells with concentric "on" or "off" center fields, cortical neurons transform the afferent information coming to them from geniculate neurons and have receptive fields whose areas of excitation and inhibition are arranged side by side, separated not by circular boundaries but by straight lines. As illustrated in Fig. 10, some cells have receptive fields with a long narrow excitatory region bounded by inhibitory regions on either side, or the reverse; others have only one excitatory and one inhibitory region separated by a straight line. A particularly interesting feature of cortical neurons is that they fire preferentially to linear stimuli of a particular orientation: some cells respond maximally to slits, edges, and contours oriented vertically; others, to similar stimuli oriented horizontally; and still others, to oblique stimuli. The visual cortex of a normal adult cat contains cells for virtually every orientation. Another feature of cortical neurons in the adult cat is that the great majority of them (84%) are binocular, i.e., they respond to stimulation of either eye (Hubel and Wiesel, 1962). A much smaller percentage of them can be driven by only one or the other eye. In this respect also cortical neurons differ from lateral geniculate neurons, which are primarily monocular. The orientation specificity and binocularity of cortical cells presumably provide the central mechanisms for pattern recognition and stereoscopic vision.

2. Development of Receptive Field Properties

No part of the brain would seem to afford a better opportunity to analyze the contributions of innate and experiential factors to the development of structure and function in the central nervous system than the primary visual cortex. Since earlier studies on visual deprivation (e.g., Chow et al., 1957; Gyllenstein, 1959; Riesen, 1960, 1961; Wiesel and Hubel, 1963a, b; Gyllenstein et al., 1965; Valverde, 1967, 1968) established beyond question that visual experience is essential for normal development, the central issue is not whether such experience modulates development but when and how it does so. Thus, experience could play an inductive role and be absolutely necessary for the initial establishment of visual structure and function. On the other hand, the information-processing capacities of the visual cortex could arise prefunctionally but require experience or "functional validation" (Jacobson, 1969, 1970) for their maintenance.

A first step toward resolving this issue is to determine when in ontogeny cells in the visual cortex exhibit adult properties. The presence of such properties in the neonate, or at least prior to eye opening or in animals deprived from birth of

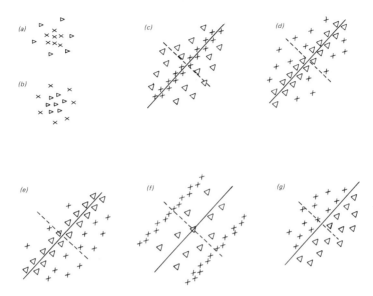

Fig. 10. Common arrangements of lateral geniculate and cortical receptive fields: (a) "On" center geniculate receptive field. (b) "Off" center geniculate receptive field. (c–g) Various arrangements of simple cortical receptive fields. Key: ×, areas giving excitatory ("on") responses; △, areas giving inhibitory ("off") responses. Receptive-field axes are shown by continuous lines through field centers; in this illustration these are all oblique, but each arrangement occurs in all orientations. (Reproduced with permission from Hubel and Wiesel, 1962.)

visual experience, would strongly indicate that they had developed prefunctionally. Accordingly, Hubel and Wiesel (1963) applied the electrophysiological techniques that had been worked out so beautifully in the adult cat to studies of the receptive field properties of visual cortical neurons in two immature and visually deprived kittens. One of the kittens was examined at 9 days of age, prior to eye opening; the other, which had its eyes occluded before eye opening, was examined at 16 days of age. Although by adult standards the cortical cells in the two visually inexperienced kittens were "sluggish" in their spontaneous activity and in their responsiveness to patterned stimuli, and also were easily fatigable, nevertheless they exhibited preferential firing rates to elongated straight-line stimuli presented only in particular orientations, much as is found in the normal adult. Other characteristics of adult cortical neurons were also exhibited by the immature and visually inexperienced kittens. The proportion of cells that could be driven by both eyes and the spatial organization of cells into columns with similar orientation specificities were not unlike those observed in the mature cat. In this now famous but preliminary study, Hubel and Wiesel (1963) concluded that the "highly organized behavior of cells in the striate cortex must be present at birth or within a few days of it" and, further, that the development of receptive field properties occurs in the absence of patterned visual experience.

Some of Hubel and Wiesel's findings have been amply confirmed. There is some basis for thinking, for example, that the main outlines of retinotopic organization of the feline visual system are present at or not long after birth since: (1) the major afferent and efferent connections between thalamus and cortex are present at birth (Anker and Cragg, 1974); (2) immature cortical neurons can be activated in newborn kittens by both electrical and exteroceptive sensory stimuli (Marty and Scherrer, 1964; Huttenlocher, 1967; Rose and Lindsley, 1968; Rose et al., 1972); (3) prior to eye opening, cortical units have receptive fields, albeit often larger ones than in adults, and the proportion of cells exhibiting monocular and binocular activation does not differ greatly from that of the adult (Hubel and Wiesel, 1963; Pettigrew, 1974); and (4) the capacity of visual cortical neurons to respond selectively to stimuli moving in a particular direction, i.e., direction specificity, appears well developed in young inexperienced kittens (Pettigrew, 1974; Blakemore and Van Sluyters, 1975). However, controversy surrounds other of Hubel and Wiesel's findings. Thus, it has been questioned whether cortical neurons are fully adultlike in their orientation specificities at or soon after birth and, if not, whether this property of individual neurons, which presumably forms the basis of pattern recognition and visual discrimination abilities, depends upon visual experience. Also in question is whether or not, in spite of the presence of binocularly driven cortical neurons in the immature cortex, the central mechanisms for stereoscopic vision are entirely developed prefunctionally. The original study of Hubel and Wiesel (1963) did not specifically address this issue.

A number of more extensive reports on visual cortical development in the kitten have now appeared, and the results are conflicting. Pettigrew (1974) studied the neuronal specificities for orientation, direction of motion, and binocular disparity in both normal and visually deprived kittens at 1 to 6 weeks of age (see also Barlow and Pettigrew, 1971; Pettigrew, 1972). As mentioned, there is little disagreement that immature and visually inexperienced neurons respond selectively to directions of motion of a target, and Pettigrew's findings are in accord with this conclusion. However, using criteria somewhat different and by some standards more stringent than those of Hubel and Wiesel for evidence of orientation specificity, Pettigrew failed to detect visual cortical cells that responded selectively to stimuli of particular orientations in normally reared kittens under 4 weeks of age, whereas after this age the orientation specificity of such cells increased toward adult levels. Since in this study evidence for true orientation specificity did not emerge until well after eye opening (around 9 days of age), the clear implication is that visual experience after the time of eye opening normally plays some role in the development of this feature-extracting mechanism. Studies in the rabbit, whose visual system is organized somewhat differently from that of the cat, also support this concept, since in this species the evidence is quite good that functional properties (including orientation specificity) characteristic of the adult are not present before the time of eye opening and develop normally after considerable visual experience (Grobstein and Chow, 1975). Additional evidence that the development of orientation specificity requires visual input was provided by Pettigrew's finding that visual deprivation produced by bilateral lid suture prevented the normal increase in the proportion of cells exhibiting orientation specificities; this finding was in accord with the results of a related experiment (Imbert and Buisseret, 1975) in which no orientation specificity could be detected at all in kittens reared in total darkness until 5 weeks of age.

Pettigrew's analysis of binocular interaction also indicated considerable immaturity of visual cortical mechanisms in the first few weeks of the kittens' life. Binocular interaction is not to be confused with binocularity per se, a property of immature cortical neurons which indicates only that they can be driven by stimuli presented to either eye alone, without specifying the nature of that cell's ability to integrate simultaneous binocular input. In the adult cat, 68% of visual cortical neurons exhibit "disparity selectivity," i.e., they respond optimally only when a stimulus presented to both eyes falls near or upon corresponding points in the two eyes (Pettigrew, 1972). By contrast, binocular cells in immature cortex respond vigorously to stimuli over a wide range of retinal disparities (Barlow and Pettigrew, 1971; Pettigrew, 1972, 1974). According to Pettigrew (1974), the ability to detect retinal disparities, the presumed basis of stereoscopic vision, apparently also does not develop in normal kittens until about the fourth week of life and fails to develop at all in kittens whose eyelids had been sutured prior to the time of eye opening.

A possible resolution of the discrepancy between Pettigrew's findings on orientation specificity and those of Hubel and Wiesel (1963) is that it arose from differences in methodology. Barlow and Pettigrew (1971), for example, obtained response curves of individual units both with spot stimuli as well as with elongated stimuli. By comparing the unit's responses to each type of stimulus, they were able to dissociate the neuron's ability to fire preferentially to target movement as opposed to target orientation and to show that only the former was clearly present in visually inexperienced animals. Pettigrew (1974) raised the possibility that Hubel and Wiesel had measured the directional rather than the orientation specificities of immature and visually deprived neurons, since they varied the orientation of an elongated stimulus and its direction of motion simultaneously. Responding to this argument in a recent paper on the visually naive monkey, Wiesel and Hubel (1974a) mentioned that they had extended their investigations on visually naive kittens and had succeeded to their satisfaction in finding cortical neurons that responded preferentially only to stationary

lines of a particular orientation, thus eliminating the objection of target movement artifact. Unfortunately, none of the data obtained in the kitten was
presented in support of their claim. However, additional information pertinent
to this issue has recently been obtained by Stryker (1975) in another study of
cortical physiology in visually deprived kittens. In this study, many cells were
found in kittens reared in the dark for 22–29 days that responded to moving bar
stimuli in a variety of orientations with a degree of selectivity similar to that
found in the adult cat. When individual neurons which responded to only one
direction of movement of an elongated bar were tested with moving spot stimuli
equal in area to the elongated stimulus, the majority of those tested responded
more strongly to the moving bar than to the moving spot. Stryker concluded
that the response of these cells depended on the shape of the stimulus and not
merely on its direction of movement. Still another approach to this problem has
been taken by Blakemore and Van Sluyters (1975). They compared responses of
units in the visual cortex of immature and visually deprived kittens to moving
edges or bars, moving spots, and flashed bars. They had no difficulty in
obtaining visual units that met the criteria of responding more strongly to a
moving bar than to a moving spot and, in addition, responded to a nonmoving
flashed bar. Although fewer such units could be found with increasing durations
of visual deprivation, their presence in a 9-day-old kitten tested before its eyes
opened completely and in a kitten reared in the dark until it was tested at 19
days of age seems to provide strong support for the position that orientation
specificity develops prefunctionally. However, even this evidence may not be as
compelling as it first appears. Stryker (1975) has noted that small errors in
centering a flashed stimulus on the receptive field of a neuron can make a cell
that is not selective for orientation appear to be so.

3. Comments on Development of Orientation-Selective
Neurons in Kittens

It would appear that there is as yet no agreement in the literature as to the role
of experience on the development of orientation specificity and other features
of adult cortical physiology, nor at the same time is their unequivocal evidence
that the information-processing capacity of visual cortical neurons are fully
developed at birth. The difficulties in this area stem from problems inherent to
the study of immaturity in any system. This review has focused on only certain
methodological difficulties, namely, those involved in establishing adequate
criteria for determining the maturity of orientation-specific cells. In addition to
the criteria already mentioned, it should be noted that other standards could
also be applied to the developing visual cortex. For example, one may ask
whether neurons which exhibit orientation specificity are primarily monocular
or binocular. Blakemore and Van Sluyters (1975) and Stryker (1975) found that

many of the neurons which met their criteria for orientation specificity were monocular, and since orientation specificity and binocularity are probably interdependent in normal function, the degree to which orientation selective neurons are monocular or binocular is also a useful measure of their maturity. Other types of methodological issues exist. For example, Blakemore and Van Sluyters (1975) found a majority of their orientation-specific neurons in layer IV of the cortex, a fact which they interpreted as significant in accounting for some of the discrepancies in the literature. They reasoned that Pettigrew (1974) and Imbert and Buisseret (1975) may have obtained negative results in young visually deprived kittens because they had perhaps not recorded sufficiently from the deeper layers of the cortex. Finally, it is interesting that few studies in this area directly compare the cortical physiology of immature and fully mature animals. Given the differences in methodology among studies and the vagaries associated with electrophysiological studies of this kind, it might be helpful for each study to have its own adult controls—even though the adult physiology has been rather well elucidated.

Whatever the outcome of future studies in this area, the results will have to harmonize with other information about the developing feline visual system. For example, it is not until the third or fourth week of life that visual placing reactions (Warkentin and Smith, 1937) and behavioral evidence of depth perception (Karmel et al., 1970) first appear. Clearly, if the feature detecting and binocularity of visual cortical neurons are fully mature before this time, as indicated by electrophysiological criteria, they are not at the same time functionally ready, since their electrophysiological maturity would antedate the emergence of adult behavioral function. Also, it is not until about the fourth week of life that synaptogenesis is complete. At 8 days of age, very near the time of eye opening, the visual cortex contains only 1.5% of the adult complement of synapses (Cragg, 1972b). Ninety percent or more of the synapses that will arise in the following weeks are thought to be intrinsic to the cortex (Colonnier and Rossignol, 1969; Cragg, 1971; Garey and Powell, 1971). Thus, neurons exhibiting orientation specifity and other mature properties in 9-day-old kittens must depend mainly on extrinsic geniculostriate connections which are present at birth (Anker and Cragg, 1974). Some other function would have to be assigned to the intrinsic circuitry of the visual cortex which undergoes such extraordinary development during the next 3–4 weeks of life. Finally, critical periods for the effects of visual deprivation (Hubel and Wiesel, 1970) and selective stimulation (Blakemore and Cooper, 1970; Hirsch and Spinelli, 1970, 1971) have been claimed, and these critical periods extend well beyond 4 weeks of age. The existence of a critical period spanning the fourth week of life implies a degree of physiological immaturity after the time when most investigators agree that orientation and binocular specifities are developed to adult levels, even though many may disagree about genetic and environmental determinism.

4. Environmental Modification of Orientation Selectivity during Development

In this section we consider efforts to examine the influence of visual experience on visual cortical development in the kitten, not by depriving animals of light or patterned vision but by exposing them to restricted and specified visual input. Hirsch and Spinelli (1970, 1971) reared kittens in total darkness for the first 3 months of life except for daily sessions, beginning at 3 weeks of age, when the kittens wore special masks that exposed one eye to vertical stripes and the other to horizontal stripes. At the end of the 3-month rearing period, the investigators recorded from single units of the visual cortex in their specially reared animals and discovered that the cortical neurons of these kittens differed from those of normal kittens in two ways: they were predominantly monocular rather than binocular, and they responded selectively to line orientations that corresponded to the orientation of lines presented during rearing, i.e., units activated by the eye exposed to vertical lines tended to have receptive fields of essentially the same vertical organization, whereas units activated by the eye exposed to horizontal lines had horizontal receptive fields. These findings have recently been replicated by Leventhal and Hirsch (1975). Similar results were also obtained by Blakemore and Cooper (1970), whose method differed from that of Hirsch and Spinelli (1970) in allowing kittens concordant binocular exposure to either horizontal or vertical lines rather than discordant monocular stimulation during the beginning months of life. Accordingly, in the Blakemore and Cooper experiment, the stimulus orientation preferences of cortical neurons were similarly biased by the conditions of their early experience, but most of them could be activated binocularly. Pettigrew and Freeman (1973) then reported analagous experiments in two kittens that were exposed to point sources of light ("like bright stars in a dark sky") rather than to linear stimuli. In contrast to findings in both normal adults and kittens reared with line stimuli, only 2 of 69 cells studied in one animal and none out of 40 cells studied in another could be classified as edge detectors. Rather, a large proportion of cells responded optimally to moving, circumscribed bright targets less than 0.5° in diameter, i.e., to spots of light corresponding to those seen by the kittens in their controlled visual experience. Similar findings had been reported by Spinelli and Hirsch (1971) and more recently by Blakemore and Van Sluyters (1975) for similar conditions of rearing. Since these studies seem to provide strong evidence that the normal preference of visual cortical neurons for straight-line stimuli can be changed to a preference for spots by environmental means, they have received close scrutiny. One objection that can be raised is that these studies involved rearing kittens essentially in the dark. There is need for clarification of the influence on orientation specificity that dark rearing itself may have had. Finally, some investigations have provided evidence for the existence of a critical period lasting from 3 to 14 weeks of age with peak sensitivity at 4–5 weeks, during which the receptive fields of cortical neurons can be influenced by controlled exposure to particular stimuli. Exposure to a particular stimulus for as little as 1 hour on day 28 has been claimed to be sufficient to affect cortical orientation specificity, whereas the same amount of stimulation either before or after this period has so far proven to be less effective (Blakemore and Mitchell, 1973; Blakemore, 1973, 1974; Blakemore and Van Sluyters, 1974).

There is now controversy surrounding some of these findings, just as there is about timetables of development of mature cortical physiology in normal and visually deprived kittens. Specifically, Stryker and Sherk (1975) have attempted a replication—without success—of the Blakemore and Cooper (1970) study in which kittens were reared in striped cylinders and found to have neuronal specificities which matched their visual experience. On the other hand, they did obtain positive evidence for the modifying influence of selective exposure to visual stimuli by rearing kittens fitted with special goggles after the method of Hirsch and Spinelli (1970). While it is too early to determine how the conflicting results will eventually be resolved, Stryker and Sherk's study is notable for its careful methodology and should contribute to the over-all development of the field.

It should be noted that selective exposure to a given visual stimulus spanning the critical period need not always result in increased sensitivity of the visual system for that stimulus. Maffei and Fiorentini (1974) recorded multiunit activity from lateral geniculate neurons in kittens exposed during the first 10 weeks of life to vertical gratings of a particular spatial frequency. The neurons showed a diminished amplitude of response to the grating to which they had been exposed as compared to spatial gratings of lower or higher periodicity. It is not yet clear whether this instance of decreased sensitivity at the thalamic level involves mechanisms complementary to or independent of those by which experience modifies cortical development.

The controversy surrounding the age of appearance of adult properties of cortical neurons in developing kittens, previously discussed, together with the conflicting evidence just reviewed for the modifiability of neuronal specificities by selective stimulation or "environmental surgery" (Hirsch, 1972), thus leaves open the question of whether visual cortical neurons are at birth largely uncommitted to the particular features of the environment to which they will preferentially respond. An alternative interpretation of this same evidence is that the selective properties of cortical neurons are specified prefunctionally; that the full expression of these properties, however, requires the maturation with age of the necessary synaptic connections; and, finally, that in the absence of normal visual input such neurons degenerate through disuse. Evaluation of these alternatives can be aided by information on the columnar organization of the cortex in kittens raised under conditions of selective visual exposure. Normally, the adult visual cortex is organized so that neurons which have a common receptive-field axis orientation are aligned in discrete columns extending from the cortical surface to the white matter. Neurons in an adjacent column share responsiveness to another receptive-field axis orientation, and so on (Hubel and Wiesel, 1962). Recording electrodes that penetrate the cortex normal to its surface thus generally encounter cells with common orientations at successive distances along the electrode tract. By contrast, electrodes which penetrate the cortex at an oblique angle or parallel to the cortical surface encounter frequent shifts in axis orientation as the recording electrode cuts across the boundaries of adjacent columns. If visual neurons degenerate as a function of disuse, then oblique or parallel penetrations of the visual cortex in a cat raised under conditions of restricted visual input should encounter many "silent" areas which would correspond to columns of cells deprived of their normal sensory input between responsive areas corresponding to columns of cells that had not been so deprived. A preliminary experiment of this nature has recently been done (Pettigrew et al., 1973). These investigators reported that they encountered responsive units no less frequently in a selectively reared cat than in normal cats. However, in contrast to normal cats, in which electrode penetrations parallel to the cortical surface encounter a high proportion of binocular cells with a broad range of preferred stimulus orientations, in the selectively reared cat the cells encountered along the parallel trajectory were primarily monocular and preferred either vertical or horizontal stimulus orientations corresponding to their early experience. These results, though preliminary, support the idea that visual neurons are pluripotential at birth and become tuned to specific features of the environment through experience, though the precise mechanism or guiding principles by which this is accomplished in normal development remain obscure.

This discussion would be incomplete without mentioning the interesting structural changes in the visual cortex that have recently been briefly described (Spencer and Coleman, 1974). These investigators made quantitative measurements of the length and orientation of neurons in the visual cortex (layers III and IV) of normal kittens and of kittens raised in environments consisting either of vertical or horizontal stripes. In four kittens exposed to vertical stripes, cortical dendritic fields were longer than normal and oriented along the anteroposterior axis, corresponding to the topographical projection of the vertical meridian; an equal number of kittens exposed to horizontal stripes also had elongated cortical dendrites, but these were preferentially oriented in the dorsoventral axis, a direction corresponding to the projection of the horizontal meridian. The dendrites of normal kittens showed no such orientation preferences; further, the cortical dendritic fields of dark-reared kittens were shorter than normal and also exhibited no spatial biases. These findings imply a measure of anatomical plasticity in the visual system that had not been anticipated, and the findings cannot be adequately evaluated until they are more fully reported.

Equally striking anatomical changes have also been found following the removal of one eye, but in the monkey (Wiesel and Hubel, 1974b). These investigators found that anatomically defined ocular-dominance columns (discrete regions of the visual cortex from surface to white matter, containing cells that are driven preferentially by one eye) related to the normal eye enlarged at the expense of the columns that would have received input through the extirpated eye. A more extensive discussion of anatomical reorganization is contained in Section V.

5. Effects on Behavior

Of special concern to a chapter on the development of structure and function is the question of whether animals whose cortical neurons are altered by environmental exposures such as those just described exhibit concomitantly altered behavioral capacities.

Blakemore and Cooper (1970) commented upon the free-moving behavior of the dark-reared kittens that had been given intermittent binocular experience with either vertical or horizontal lines when these kittens were first observed under normal conditions of illumination and visual stimulation at about 5 months of age. At first, these kittens were clumsy and showed no visual placing responses nor startle reactions to visual challenge. After 10 hours in a normal visual environment, however, most of these symptoms were ameliorated. Blakemore and Cooper also reported effects which did not disappear over the time course of their experiments: bumping into objects as the kittens engaged in "active, and as time went on increasingly frenzied, visual exploration of the room." Furthermore, they reported that the kittens were "virtually blind" to linear stimuli perpendicular to the orientations they had earlier experienced—showing no placing response nor startle reaction to the sudden approach of such stimuli. Blakemore and Cooper provided a vivid behavioral description of a vertically experienced and a horizontally experienced kitten to a vertically held rod. If the rod were shaken, the "one cat would follow it, run to it and play with it. Now if it was held horizontally, the other cat was attracted and its fellow completely ignored it" (Blakemore and Cooper, 1970).

More formal behavioral studies on the consequences of selective visual stimulation have recently been conducted, though with less dramatic results. In one of these (Hirsch, 1972), four animals that had been reared from 3 to 12 weeks with the discordant method of providing vertical stripes to one eye and horizontal stripes to the other and two normally reared controls were studied when they were between 11 and 26 weeks of age. The animals were compared in their abilities to learn flux, form, line-orientation, and mirror-image discriminations under monocular viewing conditions in a two-choice discrimination apparatus. In addition, equivalence data, line-orientation thresholds and measures of interocular transfer were obtained. The thrust of the findings is best illustrated by considering the animals' performance in the discrimination of orientation differences. On the basis of Blakemore and Cooper's (1970) observations, it could be predicted that when the animal discriminates between a horizontal line (the positive stimulus) and a line at a 45° angle (the negative stimulus), performance should be better through the eye that had been earlier exposed to horizontal stripes than through the eye that had viewed vertical lines. For a discrimination of verticality, the converse could be expected. After achieving criterion on this initial discrimination, the animals were further tested for their ability to make finer and finer discriminations by narrowing the difference in the orientations of the positive and negative stimuli. As shown in Fig. 11, in accord with the prediction, the performance on the horizontal discriminations was better through the horizontally experienced eye, whereas the vertical discriminations were performed better through the vertically experienced eye, though neither was quite as good as the normal eye. However, none of the differences was statistically significant, and in absolute terms each eye performed well on either horizontal- or vertical-orientation discriminations. Similarly, slight deficits were present on most of the other tests employed by Hirsch (1972), but again, overall, the experimental animals performed well on the various measures of visual function. In a related experiment, Muir and Mitchell (1973) reared three kittens under conditions similar to those employed by Blakemore and Cooper (1970) to produce altered electrophysiological properties. Two of the kittens were exposed 5 hours daily to either vertical or horizontal stripes from the age of 20 days until 5 months. The exposure of a third kitten to vertical stripes was confined to a 2-week period when it was between 3 and 5 weeks of age. At 6 months of age the kittens were brought out of their dark-rearing environment, experienced normal lighting conditions for 3–6 months, and then were tested for their ability to discriminate vertical and horizontal gratings of graded spatial frequencies from a blank field of matched luminance. Each animal was tested on both vertical and horizontal gratings. Normally reared adult cats discriminated vertical and horizontal gratings equally well; however, the acuity of cats reared under special conditions depended upon the orientation of contours to which they had been exposed. Cats exposed to vertical stripes during the first 5 months of life showed virtually normal acuity for vertical stripes but were deficient on gratings of the orthogonal orientation, especially at high spatial frequencies; the cat reared with horizontal stripes displayed the converse pattern of results, namely, near normal acuity on horizontal gratings and deficits in vertical gratings. Again, these findings were less dramatic than the informal observations reported by Blakemore and Cooper (1970), but [together with the findings of Hirsch (1972)] they provide evidence that visual discriminative capacity may be altered by early restricted sensory experience. Moreover, these effects are long lasting in that the acuity deficits were still present nearly 2 years after the animals had been introduced to a normal visual environment.

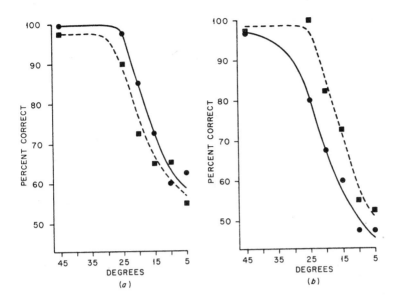

Fig. 11. Orientation discrimination thresholds: effect of changing the orientation of the test stimuli. Mean percentage correct scores are plotted as a function of the orientation differences between the positive and negative stimuli. (*a*) Vertical orientation threshold (left-hand side). For all but the 10° orientation difference, experimental subjects performed better when tested with the vertical eye (VE, •) than when tested with the horizontal eye (HE, ■). (*b*) Horizontal orientation threshold (right-hand side). For all but the 45° orientation difference, experimental subjects performed better when tested with the HE than when tested with the VE. (Reproduced with permission from Hirsch, 1972.)

The likelihood that some of the effects of selective visual stimulation during the critical period were reversed by the subsequent normal visual experience should be taken into account in evaluating the absolute magnitude of effect in these studies. Spinelli *et al.* (1972) have shown that though the biased receptive field properties that characterize visual cortical neurons after an early period of exposure to selective stimulation persisted up to 19 months following normal vision, other types of cells could be recorded that were not detectable prior to normal viewing experience. Significantly, these cells, whose properties were presumably acquired during the normal binocular viewing period, could be driven by either eye and had disk-shaped receptive fields. Considering the counteracting influence of normal visual experience, the findings of Hirsch (1972) and of Muir and Mitchell (1973) are the more important in pointing to a small but definite effect on discrimination, attributable to sensory experience in development.

6. Environmental Modification of Binocularity during Development

Raising kittens from birth or soon after with discordant visual input to the two eyes not only appears to narrow the range of orientation-specific cells in the visual cortex (from the full complement of orientation specificities to a subset of orientation specificities), it also drastically reduces the population of cortical neurons that can be driven by both eyes (Hirsch and Spinelli, 1970, 1971). A similar reduction in binocular, orientation-selective cells occurs also if kittens are reared under conditions of monocular deprivation (Wiesel and Hubel, 1963a, 1965; Ganz et al., 1968). Morphological changes in the lateral geniculate body accompany the electrophysiological alterations of monocularly deprived cortical neurons: the cells in the layers of the geniculate that receive input from the deprived eye are reduced in volume, and in some layers the decrease in mean cross-sectional area of cell bodies amounts to 30–40% (Wiesel and Hubel, 1963b; Guillery and Stelzner, 1970). As in the case of discordant or restricted sensory exposure, there is also a critical or sensitive period during development for susceptibility to the effects of monocular deprivation, in this case both to the cortical electrophysiological and the subcortical morphological effects. Furthermore, the onset and duration of these critical periods are virtually identical. Thus, the sensitive period to the consequences of monocular deprivation also begins rather abruptly near the fourth week of life and declines about the end of the third month, with a period of maximum susceptibility in the fourth and fifth weeks (Hubel and Wiesel, 1970). Monocular eye closure for as little as 6 days during this time of peak sensitivity can produce a picture of alteration as severe as that following monocular visual deprivation lasting from birth until 3 months of age, whereas monocular closure for more than 1 year in an adult cat produces no such changes (Hubel and Wiesel, 1970).

Paradoxically, binocular visual deprivation over the same period of developmental vulnerability, rather than producing greater abnormalities in cortical physiology, actually has less severe consequences: although the number of unresponsive units in the visual cortex is increased over that of the normal, a large proportion of cells retain binocular innervation, and many of these exhibit orientation specificity (Wiesel and Hubel, 1965; Ganz et al., 1968).

The different effects of monocular and binocular deprivation provide still another opportunity to assess the functional significance of binocular orientation-selective cells in the visual cortex. To the extent that such cells are part of a physiological mechanism for pattern recognition and discrimination, then animals reared monocularly who have lost these cells in large numbers should exhibit greater deficits in discrimination of visual patterns than binocularly deprived animals who have not. Furthermore, monocularly reared animals should have greater difficulty learning through their deprived than through their experienced eye.

The general behavioral effects of a long period of monocular visual deprivation are not unlike those described for dark-reared cats exposed to selective stimulation. When such animals were observed after the deprivation period had ceased, with only their deprived eye open, "they walked in a cautious and irresolute way, they bumped frequently against the walls of the room and the objects in it, and they fell off when placed on a table, apparently unaware of the borders. Moreover they were unable to follow objects moved in front of their eyes and to localize objects or pieces of food abruptly introduced in different parts of their visual field" (Rizzolatti and Tradardi, 1971, p. 184). With their experienced eye open, such cats behaved normally. Ganz and Fitch's (1968, p. 643) description is further illuminating:

> ... with only their normal eye open the cats typically ran toward the front of the cage when the experimenter opened their cage door and jumped onto his shoulder. With only their deprived eye open, they ran to the back of the cage and stayed there.

The authors regarded this and other similar responses as evidence of failure of the subject to recognize the experimenter when using the deprived eye though recognition was normal with the experienced eye. Many though not all of these initial symptoms of visual deprivation are alleviated with time and normal visual experience (Wiesel and Hubel, 1965; Ganz and Fitch, 1968; Rizzolatti and Tradardi, 1971).

Using more formal methods of assessment, Ganz et al. (1972) compared the learning ability of monocularly and binocularly deprived kittens at 13–25 weeks of age, just after the conclusion of deprivation, on discriminations of flux, grid orientations, and form (upright versus inverted triangles). On the flux and grid-orientation problems, the binocular group performed as well as normal and significantly better than the monocular group tested with its deprived eye. On the discrimination of inverted and upright triangles, the binocular group exhibited some impairment compared both to normal animals and to monocular animals using their experienced eye, but the binocular animals were clearly able to learn the discrimination. The monocular animals using their deprived eyes did not evidence this ability. Similarly, Ganz and Fitch (1968) had shown that monocularly deprived kittens were unable to discriminate between vertical and horizontal lines with the deprived eye even though they could do so with their experienced eye. This loss in visual discriminative capacity persisted even after the animals had been forced to use their deprived eye (when the normal eye was sutured) or after binocular vision of several months duration. Dews and Wiesel (1970) also found that monocularly reared cats were impaired in discriminating continuous and horizontal lines with 1.5- or 30-mm gaps, with the degree of impairment related to the duration of deprivation within the first 16 weeks of life. Animals with 16 weeks of monocular deprivation were unable to learn the pattern discrimination, though such animals retained the ability to discriminate luminous flux. Likewise, Ganz *et al.* (1972) reported that monocularly reared kittens could not learn to discriminate upright versus inverted triangles and were markedly impaired in flux and horizontal/vertical discriminations. On the other hand, Rizzolatti and Tradardi (1971) were able to train monocularly deprived kittens on a variety of pattern discriminations. However, the number of trials necessary to achieve this success was about seven times that required by the nondeprived eye, in spite of the use of punishment for incorrect responses. Significantly, the animals in this study employed head movements to scan the discriminanda when learning with the deprived eye, suggesting that mechanisms other than purely visual ones may have aided in learning the discrimination.

7. Summary and Comments on the Effects of Deprivation and Restricted Sensory Experience

The bulk of anatomical, electrophysiological, and behavioral evidence points to a period beginning in the fourth week of the cat's life when significant maturational events are taking place, events that can be substantially altered by the nature of the visual environment. It should be added, however, that this conclusion is supported more strongly by deprivation studies, which on the whole have generated more consistent results, than by selective stimulation experiments, which have yielded somewhat conflicting evidence. Perhaps this state of affairs reflects the relative ease of duplicating deprivation procedures and evaluating the degree to which cortical neurons can be driven by one or both eyes, on the one hand, and the relative difficulty of controlling individual experience and assessing orientation specificity, on the other. Since binocularity and orientation specificity are often concomitantly affected by the range of abnormal visual environments that have been studied, it is somehow difficult to believe that each of these indices of central nervous system organization has a different susceptibility to perturbation by experience. Again it should be emphasized that the results obtained in the work on kittens is inconclusive with respect to the main issue of whether experience affects the normal developmental process itself or whether experience simply prevents degradation of genetically programmed instructions.

It is likely that future research will continue to evaluate the many attractive hypotheses that have been offered with respect to the precise mechanisms by which sensory experience alters the structure and function of the nervous system (e.g., Guillery and Stelzner, 1970; Sherman, 1972; Spinelli *et al.,* 1972; Blakemore, 1973; Pettigrew, 1974; Blakemore and Van Sluyters, 1975). Probably there will need to be more work on the behavioral or functional implications of abnormal visual experience. For example, the effects of various rearing conditions (concordant and discordant restricted visual stimulation; monocular and binocular deprivation) on discrimination behavior of cats have been studied in a number of different experiments. For reasons not totally clear, the degree of impairment is extremely severe following monocular deprivation and much less severe following binocular discordant stimulation, though both conditions of rearing produce a similar pattern of abnormal cortical physiology (e.g., reduction in the number of binocular, orientation-selective cells). Furthermore, there is a discrepancy between the long-term electrophysiological consequences of selective visual experience and some of the behavioral effects which appear to be transient. Blakemore and Cooper (1970), for example, reported that rearing kittens in selective visual environments rendered them "blind" to orientations of lines that were orthogonal to those experienced. However, this blindness abates quickly while the electrophysiological changes are long lasting. Furthermore, the long-term impairments on discrimination of orientations (Hirsch, 1972) and acuity deficits are surprisingly slight. Thus, although there is a clear relationship between loss in discriminative ability and abnormal visual experience, on the one hand, and cortical pathophysiology and abnormal visual experience, on the other, the precise ways in which the structural and functional events are causally linked remain to be further elucidated.

V. LIMBIC SYSTEM STRUCTURES: ILLUSTRATIONS OF NEURONAL PLASTICITY IN DEVELOPMENT

In preceding sections of this chapter, the goal has been to draw inferences about normal development. The studies reviewed highlight in a number of different ways and at a number of different levels of analysis the functional disadvantages that result from the disruption or elimination of specific elemental constituents of the nervous system at special times in development. In many instances, blocking the development of cellular components irreversibly blocks some aspect of functional development. It may be inferred, however, particularly from work on the immature visual cortex, that the nervous system normally possesses a considerable measure of plasticity. The binocular specificity of a neuron in the visual cortex is, for a period of time at least, open to the influence of experience; and the pattern of ocular dominance seen in the normal adult cat presumably reflects the concordant binocular visual input to which that cat had been exposed in normal development. Numerous other studies, reviewed elsewhere, also attest to the inductive and modifying influence on brain development of early stimulation and experience (e.g., Riesen, 1966; Shapiro and Vukovich, 1970; Geller, 1971; Rosensweig, 1971). The concept of plasticity suggested by such studies is carried a step further in the present section. Not only are CNS neurons plastic to the effects of experience, their structure and function can be altered in a dramatic way by hormones and by injury.

Relative to other CNS structures, limbic system structures are generally considered to have remained quite stable over evolutionary history. Paradoxically, however, they provide some of the most remarkable instances of CNS plasticity. We shall here be concerned with three of these structures: the hypothalamus and related structures, as examples of plasticity in the neural basis of sex differences; and the hippocampus, as an example of neuronal plasticity in response to injury.

A. THE HYPOTHALAMUS

It is now widely accepted that hormones exert an inductive or organizing influence on the development of the brain (e.g., Harris, 1964; Young et al., 1964; Barraclough, 1967; Valenstein, 1968; Whalen, 1968; Goy, 1970a; Flerko, 1967; Gorski, 1971; Levine, 1972). It is important to emphasize that although the hormonal environment can be altered by experimental means or by "experiments" of nature, the fact that the nature and function of the endocrine glands are themselves under genetic control simply indicates that there is a modifiable link in the chain by which the action of genes is normally expressed. Indeed, the expression of genetic control through hormonal conditions is nowhere more evident than in comparisons of individuals with XX or XY chromosomes, i.e., in the comparison between normal males and females.

1. Gonadal Hormones and Neural Mechanisms in the Adult

It is well known that marked differences exist between normal males and females in gonadal morphology, in the pattern of gonadotrophin release from the pituitary gland, in body growth, and in a variety of reproductive and nonreproductive behaviors. Many of these sex-dependent characteristics can either be modified or reversed by the presence or absence of the androgen testosterone propionate, at early critical or sensitive periods in development (Phoenix et al., 1959; Barraclough, 1961; Harris and Levine, 1962, 1965; Gorski and Wagner, 1965; Grady et al., 1965; Gerall and Ward, 1966; Neumann and Kramer, 1967; Nadler, 1968; Flerko et al., 1969; Goy and Resko, 1972).

Major advances have been made in understanding the neural control of sex-dependent characteristics, particularly with respect to the role that the hypothalamus plays in the regulation of gonadotrophin release in mature males and females. Since the classical studies of Goodman (1934) and Pfeiffer (1936), it has been known that the female of spontaneously ovulating species exhibits cyclic fluctuations of hormonal secretions in relation to ovulation, whereas the male pattern of gonadotrophin release is more tonic (Everett and Sawyer, 1950; Everett, 1964; Harris, 1964; Davidson, 1966; Goldman et al., 1969; Gay et al., 1970; Brown-Grant, 1971). These differences in neuroendocrine function are accompanied, at least in many infrahuman mammals, by differences in sexual receptivity: sexual receptivity of the female is cyclical and peaks just before ovulation, whereas that of the male is more constant (e.g., Lisk, 1967; Michael *et al.*, 1972).

The specific regions of the hypothalamus that are responsible for gonado-trophin release have now been reasonably well identified. Considerable evidence suggests that the tuberal hypothalamus is a neural locus necessary for the maintenance of basal or tonic levels of gonadotrophin release in both normal males and females, whereas the preoptic area of the anterior hypothalamus mediates the cyclic surge of gonadotrophin secretion associated with ovulation (Everett, 1964, 1969; Halász, 1969; Terasawa and Sawyer, 1969; Kawakami *et al.*, 1970; Holsinger and Everett, 1970; Gorski, 1971; Moss and Law, 1971; Dyer *et al.*, 1972).

Although it has been known for some time that the preoptic area of the hypothalamus is a probable site of control for cyclic release of hormones, only recently has evidence been obtained for an anatomical difference in the synaptology of this region in adult males and females. Raisman and Field (1971, 1973) used ultrastructural methods to study the hypothalamus of normal male and female rats. Serial sections taken from the preoptic area and from the ventromedial nucleus (part of the tuberal hypothalamus) were examined for the frequency of certain classes of synaptic contacts, i.e., axons terminating on the main shafts of dendrites, or axons terminating on the finer protuberances of the dendritic apparatus—the spines. In addition, they were able to further classify these synapses in terms of where their presynaptic afferents arose. At an appropriate time prior to the anatomical analysis, the pathways connecting the amygdala with the hypothalamus were severed, thus allowing Raisman and Field to discriminate between synapses of nonamygdaloid origin and those formed by axons originating in the amygdala (since the latter appeared more opaque in the electromicrographs due to the onset of degenerative processes). They found no differences between males and females in any of the four types of synaptic arrangements in the ventromedial hypothalamus; but there was a significant difference in the incidence of one of the types in the preoptic area—synapses on dendritic spines of nonamygdaloid origin. This finding together with earlier evidence of sex differences in the neural organization of the hypothalamus (Dorner and Staudt, 1968, 1969; Pfaff, 1966) offer the possibility of an anatomical basis for the differential regulation of gonadotrophin release in males and females.

2. Development of Sexual Dimorphism in Hypothalamic Mechanisms

Raisman and Field also studied whether gonadal hormones play a role in the development of these sex-dependent morphological differences. In addition to analyzing the relative frequency of various types of synapses in normal adult

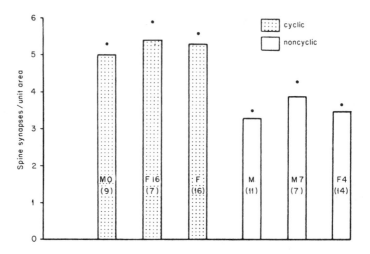

Fig. 12. A bar diagram showing the mean incidences (the dot represents one standard error) of nonstrial synapses per grid square in each of six groups of animals. The number in parentheses is the number of animals in each group. Abbreviations: F, normal females; F16, females treated with androgen on day 16; M0, males castrated within 12 hours of birth; M7, males castrated on day 7; F4, females androgenized on day 4; M, normal males. (Reproduced with permission from Raisman and Field, 1973.)

males and females, they also examined the brains of adult males that had been gonadectomized and those of females that had been exposed to androgens before the end of or subsequent to the critical period for hypothalamic differentiation. As illustrated in Fig. 12, the incidence of spine synapses of non-amygdaloid origin in genetic males deprived of androgen before the end of the critical period was similar to that of the normal genetic female; conversely, the incidence of such synapses in females subject to injections of testosterone propionate within the critical time resembled that of the genetic male. Alteration of the hormonal milieu after the critical period failed to produce any significant morphological changes in either males or females, as would be expected. Thus, neurons in the preoptic area of the hypothalamus are essentially bipotential at early stages of development and will develop certain of their synaptic connections depending upon the presence or absence of androgen. It is not yet clear, however, whether the preoptic region in males and females contains different numbers of dendritic spines or whether the number of spines is the same but there are differences in the number of axonal contacts. Nor is the source of afferents terminating upon the dendritic spines known, except that it appears that they do not originate in the amygdala. These anatomical findings nevertheless suggest that sexual dimorphism in endocrine and behavioral functions may come about through the directive influence of hormones on the neural circuitry of the differentiating brain.

B. PATHWAYS TO THE HYPOTHALAMUS

Although the hypothalamus represents the most thoroughly documented example of sexual dimorphism in the central nervous system, there is ample evidence to indicate that sex differences in structure and function may be a pervasive characteristic of brain organization. The evidence is of three kinds. First, there are the classical studies of Beach (1940, 1944), which indicate that the cerebral cortex plays an important role in copulatory behavior, perhaps more so in the male than the female. Unfortunately, insufficient attention has been given to research designed to follow up this important finding (but see Larsson, 1962, 1964). Second, there are reports of differences between males and females in hypothalamic mechanisms that are not especially related to reproductive behaviors but rather to taste preferences, food intake, and water regulation (Valenstein, 1968; Valenstein et al., 1967, 1969; Wade and Zucker, 1969a, b; Zucker, 1969). Finally, there is substantial evidence for sex differences in nonreproductive behaviors such as aggression (e.g., Edwards, 1969), emotionality (e.g., Gray et al., 1965; Phillips and Deol, 1973), learning (e.g., McDowell et al., 1960), and play (e.g., Goy, 1970a; Goy and Phoenix, 1972), and also in reaction to the effects of isolation rearing (Sackett, 1972). These various sexually dimorphic behaviors and reactions likely depend on neural structures other than, or in addition to, the hypothalamus.

1. Behavioral Consequences of Septal Lesions in the Adult

Septal lesions in the adult rat result in a dramatic syndrome of emotional hyperreactivity, deterioration of conditioned emotional reactions (Brady and Nauta, 1953), an enhancement of two-way active avoidance learning (King, 1958; Meyer et al., 1970), and a paradoxical increase in social cohesiveness (Jonason and Enloe, 1971). Brady and Nauta's (1953, p. 343) early description of the emotional behavior of septal rats included reference to "a picture of striking alertness with limbs rigidly extended and eyes intently following the movements of the observer approaching the cage," explosive startle reactions to auditory stimuli, and the substitution of normal exploratory behavior by "freezing." In addition, such rats fiercely resisted the experimenter's attempt to capture them and when placed together engaged in continuous and vigorous fights. To this picture may be added the observations of Jonason and Enloe (1971, p. 293) on social cohesiveness in an open field situation: "The typical first reaction of these hyperreactive rats when placed into the open field was an explosive retreat to opposite edges of the field. Subsequently, septal animals cautiously approached each other until contact was established. Having made this initial contact, these subjects spent virtually the entire remaining test session in direct physical contact." It now appears that these effects may not be entirely specific to septal lesions but may be due rather to the inadvertant damage that such lesions produce in the adjacent tracts and nuclei of the stria terminalis which connects the amygdala with the hypothalamus (Turner, 1970). The neural focus for the affective behavior associated with septal lesions is not, however, critical for the present account. What is important is that affectivity is influenced by lesions in extrahypothalamic structures.

2. Development of the Septal Syndrome

Recently, several studies have examined the effects of septal lesions in infancy on the subsequent development of hyperemotionality (Johnson, 1972; Phillips and Deol, 1973). Phillips and Deol reported that females exhibited a greater degree of emotionality on a number of measures than did males. In order to test the hypothesis that the septum (or adjacent structures), may be a part of the neural basis for sex differences in emotionality and, as such, might develop under the influence of gonadal hormones in a manner analogous to hypothalamic mechanisms, Phillips and Deol (1973) compared the effects of septal lesions in males castrated on the second day of life with that of such lesions in females given injections of testosterone propionate on the same day. Sham-operated males and oil-injected females served as controls. Four parallel groups were not subjected to septal surgery, though all animals in the study were anesthetized at the time of CNS surgery. They found that the lesions induced the same degree of hyperemotionality in castrated males as they did in normal females, while the effects of septal lesions in androgenized females resembled those observed in normal genetic males. This reversal of sex differences in affective behavior provides further evidence that there may be an extrahypothalamic locus for the control of sex differences in emotional behavior; and like the hypothalamus with respect to sexual behavior, this limbic locus (septum or adjacent neural structures) differentiates under the control of gonadal hormones at critical stages in development.

C. FUNCTIONAL DIMORPHISMS IN SEARCH OF STRUCTURAL SUBSTRATES

As indicated earlier, the hypothalamus and its afferent inputs are not likely to be the only sexually dimorphic structures in the central nervous system. In particular, studies on primates have provided indirect though compelling reason to suspect that sexual dimorphism may extend to other limbic system structures and perhaps even beyond the limbic system. For example, genetic female monkeys exposed to testosterone propionate *in utero* not only develop masculinized external genitalia but also display masculine patterns of play behavior as they mature (Young *et al.,* 1964; Phoenix *et al.,* 1968; Goy, 1970a, b; Peretz *et al.,* 1971; Goy and Resko, 1972; Goy and Phoenix, 1972). Specifically, these pseudohermaphroditic monkeys engage in more play initiation, pursuit play, rough-and-tumble play, threats, and mounting behavior than do normal females. Indeed, the pseudohermaphroditic females resemble normal males in their behavioral propensities. Although these studies do not investigate the neural substrates that might mediate these expressions of sex differences in juvenile play behavior, it is unlikely that the complex social skills and interactions which evolve slowly over the first few years of life do not also entail equally complex neural mechanisms.

In a most intriguing set of papers, Gray and Buffery have reviewed a massive amount of evidence for human and infrahuman gender differences in a wide variety of cognitive as well as emotional capacities (Gray, 1971; Gray and Buffery, 1971; Buffery and Gray, 1972). Having approached their subject from an evolutionary perspective, they came to the idea that the prefrontal cortex, among other structures, may form part of the neural basis of sex-dependent differences in a wide variety of behaviors. The theory proposes a continuity in the neural basis of sex differences from monkey to man, in whom, of course, there is the additional factor of lateralization of function.

Gray and Buffery's ideas receive some support from three sources. A recent series of studies in primates has produced striking evidence of the critical role that the anterior association cortex (prefrontal or anterior temporal cortex) plays in the appreciation of social signals and in species survival (Franzen and Myers, 1973a, b; Myers *et al.,* 1973). These investigators made detailed observations of the social performance of monkeys over long periods of time (preoperatively and postoperatively) as these monkeys interacted with their family members and peers in long-standing group-living arrangements. In one study (Franzen and Myers, 1973a) the monkeys lived in groups of 6–12 members in large compounds that assured continued interaction among the monkeys. Under these conditions, prefrontal or anterior temporal cortical lesions resulted in drastic alterations of social competence. Monkeys with such lesions, but not those given either cingulate or posterior inferotemporal cortical lesions, exhibited impoverishment of facial expressions, vocalizations, and social communicative gestures, decreased aggressiveness, a depression of grooming, a decrease in physical proximity to other animals, including that involved in the care of infants and in sexual receptivity when approached by interested males. In general, the animals behaved inappropriately to the social signals of the group, which in turn produced asocial counterreactions from the group and ultimately resulted in the loss of social contact and, hence, social isolation. These findings were dramatically amplified in a separate study of a 103-member troop of free-ranging macaques on Cayo Santiago (Myers *et al.,* 1973). Nineteen monkeys were trapped from this natural social group during a 16-month period of preoperative observations. Five of these received bilateral prefrontal lobectomies, while the remaining animals were given other cortical lesions or sham procedures. Upon their return to the island within a few days of the surgery, all four of the adult-operated monkeys passed through or did not rejoin their social group, disappeared, remained solitary, and eventually died (apparently from failure to obtain food and water) within a 12-day period. This drastic picture of ultimate social agnosia was not evidenced by animals whose cingulate gyrus had been removed or who had undergone pinealectomies or sham procedures. The authors concluded that "their failure to return to lifelong patterns of social interactions and their taking up of solitary existences suggested the prefrontal cortex normally plays a role of major importance in primate social behavior" (Myers et al., 1973, pp. 265–266). This group of studies thus adds a dimension to earlier studies that were limited to the involvement of frontal cortex in the purely reproductive aspects of social behavior (Beach et al., 1955; Larsson, 1964). Further, they provide a basis for the following suggestion: to the extent that prefrontal and anterior temporal cortical structures are critical for normal social interaction in the adult, they may also be an important component of the neural basis for socialization of the young, and in particular for the playful behavior that has been shown to be sexually dimorphic.

The second line of evidence to support Gray and Buffery's general approach comes from work in the author's laboratory (Goldman and Brown, 1975). Recently, performance on an object discrimination reversal task, a cognitive task known to depend upon the integrity of the orbital prefrontal cortex in the adult monkey, was studied in normal 75-day-old male and female monkeys and in 75-day-old females that were administered small doses of testosterone propionate in multiple injections from birth through 46 days of age. Normal males performed the task at significantly higher levels than did normal females at this age. Postnatal injections of testosterone propionate enhanced the performance of the androgenized females to the level of normal males. Additional groups of males and androgenized females were subjected to orbital prefrontal lesions. These groups exhibited deficits on the object reversal task at 75 days of age, whereas nontreated females given identical lesions did not differ from unoperated females at this age and did not exhibit similar deficits until nearly a year later, at 15–18 months of age (Goldman et al., 1974). These results suggest that the orbital prefrontal cortex normally develops its functions earlier in males than in females. They further indicate that gonadal hormones may play an inductive role in the postnatal differentiation of cortical mechanisms similar to that played in the differentiation of hypothalamic mechanisms, though the nature and time course of the critical period for modifying the development of these different structures and functions may differ. The results thus provide further and more direct evidence for the view that cortical mechanisms may be sexually dimorphic and that such dimorphism may account in part for the broad spectrum of social, psychological, and cognitive traits that differentiate the sexes. It is of interest that the orbital prefrontal cortex is often included as a part of the limbic system (Kaada, 1960), to which, in any case, it is anatomically closely related (Nauta, 1972).

Finally, evidence has been obtained from *in vitro* studies of newborn rat brain that the cortex as well as the hypothalamus may contain target cells for testosterone. For example, Weisz and Philpott (1971) found that both the cortex and the hypothalamus of 5-day-old male and female rats converted testosterone to dihydrotestosterone and did so to a greater extent than the same structures in adults. Such findings are in line with the possibility that differentiation of cortex may be directly influenced by gonadal hormones at critical periods in development.

D. THE HIPPOCAMPUS

In his 1928 monograph, "Degeneration and Regeneration of the Nervous System," Ramón y Cajal distinguished between *normal histogenesis* and *pathological regeneration*. In practice, it is very difficult to disentangle studies of normal development from those whose primary goal is to understand abnormal development. Rarely can such a classification be based on methodological approaches since experiments which involve the use of lesions, X irradiation, sensory deprivation, or genetic mutation—conditions that induce disordered development—are precisely those that have given the clearest insights into mechanisms of normal development. In this section, consideration is given to mechanisms that might never be expressed in the normal case and arise only in connection with neuropathology. Yet it is distinctly possible, as many have pointed out, that mechanisms for anatomical restructuring following brain injury may be an extension of inherent growth processes underlying normal development (Guth and Windle, 1970; Sotelo and Palay, 1971; Goodman *et al.*, 1973; Schneider, 1973; Teuber, 1974).

1. Organization of the Adult Hippocampus

The hippocampus has been implicated in a variety of functions, including memory (Scoville, 1954; Penfield and Milner, 1958; Iversen, 1973), various aspects of learning (Douglas and Pribram, 1966; Correll and Scoville, 1967), and arousal (Kimble, 1968; Campbell *et al.*, 1971; Altman *et al.*, 1973). As mentioned, this structure forms an important component of circuits involving the septum and hypothalamus and also possesses a cellular and synaptic organization equaled only by the cerebellar cortex in its suitability for structure/function analysis.

Figure 13 presents a diagrammatic representation of the main features of

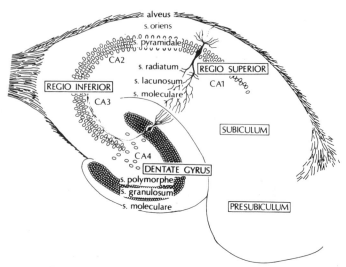

Fig. 13. Schematic diagram of the hippocampal formation. The layers of the dentate gyrus and Ammon's horn (CA 1–4) are indicated together with a drawing of a granule cell and a pyramidal cell. (Reproduced with permission from Altman *et al.*, 1973.)

hippocampal architecture in the adult rat. For present purposes, attention is drawn to two interlocking horseshoe-shaped formations, the smaller dentate gyrus and the larger cornu ammonis. A double layer of pyramidal cells constitute the major neurons of both the superior and inferior arms of the cornu ammonis, whereas granule cells form the major cellular component of the dentate gyrus. The dentate gyrus has three layers: a granular layer composed of the aforementioned granule cells; a polymorph layer internal to the granular layer; and a molecular layer external to the granule cells. The axons of the granule cells project into the polymorph layer, where, together with processes from polymorph cells located there, they enter the cornu ammonis and form synapses with the dendrites of pyramidal neurons, the primary efferent neurons of the hippocampal complex. The dendrites of the granule cells, on the other hand, project into the molecular layer, where they become engaged in a variety of synaptic contacts (as schematized in Fig. 14). The dendritic branches of granule cells reaching into roughly the outer one-half to two-thirds portion of the molecular layer receive projections from the medial and lateral areas of the ipsilateral entorhinal cortex (Blackstad, 1958; Raisman *et al.*, 1965; Hjorth-Simonsen and Jeune, 1972), a transitional form of cortex in the anterior part of the temporal lobe. This same region of the molecular layer also receives a projection from the homotypical contralateral cortex, but this crossed pathway is much less dense than its uncrossed counterpart (Zimmer and Hjorth-Simonsen, 1975; Goldowitz *et al.*, 1975). In the inner one-fourth to one-third portion of the molecular layer, granule cell dendrites receive afferents mainly from the contralateral hippo-

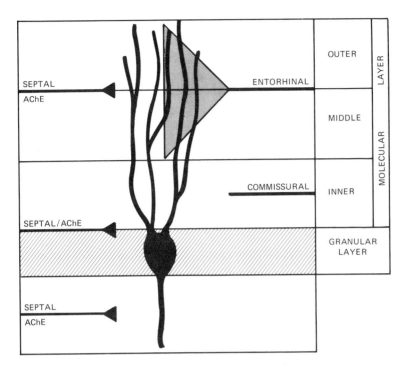

Fig. 14. Schematic representation of the distribution of afferents to a granule cell of the dentate gyrus. (Reproduced with permission from Lynch *et al.*, 1973c.)

campus through the ventral ramus of the hippocampal commissure (Blackstad, 1956; Raisman *et al.*, 1965; Laatsch and Cowan, 1966; Gottlieb and Cowan, 1972). This same region also receives projections, not illustrated in Fig. 14, from the association fibers of the ipsilateral hippocampus (Raisman *et al.*, 1965; Zimmer, 1971; Gottlieb and Cowan, 1972). The distribution of septal inputs to the granule cell dendrites are illustrated here but may be ignored in the interests of simplicity. It is the granule cell and its spatially separated and precisely ordered synaptic relationships that is of special interest in the context of CNS plasticity.

The normal afferent pathways to the dentate gyrus have been described as an aid to understanding how they can be rearranged following selective elimination of one or another of them consequent to lesions in the developing rat. Two types of reorganization will be described: (1) the spreading or sprouting of afferent fibers into areas of the dendritic field adjacent to areas they would normally occupy; and (2) the development of an expanded afferent projection onto dendritic fields that it would normally innervate only sparsely.

2. Effects of Entorhinal Lesions in Infancy on Reorganization of Connections in the Dentate Gyrus: Spreading or Sprouting of Commissural Afferents

Because it is known that entorhinal afferents to the dentate gyrus terminate in the outer two-thirds portion of the molecular layer (thus innervating the distal portion of the granule cell dendritic tree), it was of some interest to determine what happens to that portion of the dendritic field when it is deafferented (by degeneration of the entorhinal fibers) consequent to entorhinal cortical lesions. Lynch *et al.* (1973b) addressed this question by removing the entorhinal cortex in one hemisphere of 11-day-old rats and then allowed time for complete degeneration to ensue and for the products of the degeneration to be removed by the normal process of phagocytosis. Patterning their experimental approach on that originally established by Edds (1953) in studies of regeneration in the peripheral nervous system, Lynch *et al.* then interrupted the commissural pathway to the hippocampus and compared its anatomical distribution in animals given early entorhinal lesions with that of normal animals. They obtained evidence that the commissural pathway had expanded from its normal location in the inner one-third portion of the molecular layer to occupy sites of termination along that region of the dendritic field that would normally have been occupied by entorhinal afferents. The fibers of commissural origin now occupied more than 90% of the molecular layer in the dentate gyrus on the side deafferented by the entorhinal lesion. This distribution was in sharp contrast to the pattern of findings in the normal hemisphere of the early-lesioned animals and in both hemispheres of the normal controls, where the commissural projection was strictly confined to a narrow zone just above the granule cell bodies. Consistent with the anatomical findings, Lynch *et al.* (1973a) recorded extracellular potentials from various depths of the molecular layer in response to commissural stimulation in normal adult rats and in rats in whom the entorhinal afferents had been destroyed at 11 days of age. In normal rats, commissural stimulation produces characteristic short-latency negative responses in the inner molecular layer (to which the commissure projects) and short-latency positive potentials in the outer molecular layer (innervated by entorhinal fibers). In rats with preexisting entorhinal lesions, short-latency negative responses occurred to commissural stimulation in both the inner and outer molecular layer. These results provided electrophysiological support for the idea that the commissural afferents had spread into the region of the dendritic field normally occupied by entorhinal fibers and additionally showed that these newly acquired anomalously placed connections could be activated electrophysiologically.

3. Effects of Entorhinal Lesions in Infancy on Reorganization of Connections in the Dentate Gyrus: Substitution of Ipsilateral Entorhinal Afferents by Contralateral Entorhinal Afferents

Another example of neuronal plasticity is provided by the demonstration of anomalous projections from the contralateral entorhinal cortex following ipsilateral entorhinal lesions in the infant rat (Steward *et al.*, 1973). Normally, as indicated previously, each entorhinal area sends a heavier projection to the dentate gyrus of the same hemisphere than to the corresponding region of the opposite hemisphere (Zimmer and Hjorth-Simonsen, 1975; Goldowitz *et al.*, 1975). Following unilateral entorhinal lesions at 10–11 days of age, however, a subsequent lesion in the opposite entorhinal cortex reveals that it has developed an anomalous expanded pattern of connections. The crossed afferent projections from the remaining homotypical contralateral region, which are normally sparse, become more dense; that is, the entorhinal cortex in the intact hemisphere not only projects to the ipsilateral dentate gyrus, it also now projects more heavily to those regions of the contralateral dentate molecular layer that had been deafferented by the original injury.

The new connections support synaptic transmission, since stimulation of the contralateral entorhinal cortex in animals that received unilateral entorhinal lesions in infancy produces short-latency activation of granule cell dendrites both contralaterally as well as ipsilaterally, whereas normally such activation is restricted only to the ipsilateral dentate gyrus. This electrophysiological activation is presumably mediated by the new synaptic contacts formed by the anomalously expanded crossed projection and the granule cell dendrites deprived since infancy of their normal ipsilateral input. It is doubtful, however, that these new connections are functionally adaptive, since rats given unilateral entorhinal lesions in infancy are just as impaired in spontaneous alternation performance as animals given identical lesions as adults but, unlike the adults, do not exhibit recovery of spontaneous alternation behavior with time (Smith *et al.*, 1975). In this particular instance, the anomalous connections may be functionally maladaptive and impede recovery.

4. Relationship of Postlesion Neuronal Plasticity to Age

The capacity to respond to injury by reorganization of connections surviving the injury is not an exclusive property of the developing nervous system. Many examples of structural reorganization have been reported in adult animals (Liu and Chambers, 1958; Goodman and Horel, 1966; Raisman, 1969; Moore *et al.*, 1971; Wall and Egger, 1971; Lynch *et al.*, 1972; Stenevi *et al.*, 1972; Steward *et al.*, 1974). As pointed out by Lynch *et al.* (1973c), however, most studies have used either neonatal *or* adult animals and only a few studies have made direct comparisons between the two. Lynch and associates compared the effects of entorhinal lesions on the distribution of commissural projections to the dentate gyrus and hippocampus in immature and mature rats. As just described, entorhinal lesions in 11-day-old rats caused the commissural projections to fill almost the entire molecular layer in the rostrodorsal portion of the hippocampus; similar lesions in adult rats also result in some expansion of the dentate commissural system but to a quantitatively lesser degree, at the most 50% of the molecular layer. On the other hand, unilateral entorhinal lesions appear to stimulate the growth of anomalous crossed projections from the contralateral entorhinal area to a greater extent in adults than in infants (Steward *et al.*, 1974). This result should be somewhat cautiously interpreted, however, since the anatomical methods employed to assess postlesion growth in adult-operated animals differed from that used in the case of early-operated animals.

Lund *et al.* (1973) studied patterns of degeneration in the superior colliculus and lateral geniculate body consequent to eye removal in adulthood in animals whose other eye had earlier been removed at varying ages from birth to 100 days of age. The removal of an eye in newborn rats resulted in an increased projection from the remaining eye to the ipsilateral subcortical visual centers that had been deafferented by the original enucleation. The increased projection did not occur in animals enucleated at 10 days of age or older. Similar age-dependent alterations in retinogeniculate connections have been reported by Guillery (1972). Also, Hicks and D'Amato (1970) presented evidence of the development of an uncrossed primordial corticospinal tract in young rats that had been subjected to motor cortex ablation, but not in older rats given the same lesion. Schneider (1970, 1973) has provided evidence of dramatic alteration of visual system connections following lesions of the superior colliculus in neonate hamsters that, so far as is known, do not result from similar lesions in the adult. Thus, when direct comparisons of anatomical changes following early and late lesions are made, on the whole the evidence seems to indicate that the developing nervous system has a quantitatively greater capacity for reorganization than does the mature nervous system, i.e., neuronal plasticity declines with age.

Mechanisms for neuronal plasticity are far from understood. Similar processes may underlie anatomical reorganization in cases where young and mature animals exhibit similarities, and different mechanisms may be responsible for those cases just mentioned in which the immature animal exhibits a unique capacity for injury-induced repair. The greater degree of anatomical restructuring following some lesions in neonates may be due in part to incomplete neuronal and synaptic development at the time of injury. For example, in the case of the dentate gyrus in the 11-day-old rat, many granule cells have not yet been generated (Altman, 1966), and owing to incomplete outgrowth of axons or of dendrites, or both, synaptogenesis is not complete until 25–30 days of age

(Crain *et al.*, 1973). Indeed, differences in the normal time at which afferents from different sources arrive at the dentate gyrus have been postulated (Gottlieb and Cowan, 1972) as the basis for differences in the ratio of ipsilateral to contralateral afferents in different regions of the hippocampus. Thus, it is possible that some restructuring may be accomplished following early lesions by still-growing axonal processes altering their normal course. Similar suggestions have been made by Lund *et al.* (1973), Lynch *et al.* (1973c), and Steward *et al.* (1974), to mention only a few.

5. Comment on Functional Consequences of Postlesion Neuronal Plasticity

An extensive body of evidence indicates that behavioral functions are spared to a far greater degree following brain injury at earlier ages than at later ages. Review of this literature would entail a chapter of its own. Reference to this evidence may be found in several recent publications resulting from conferences and symposia (Isaacson, 1968; Stein *et al.*, 1974; Eidelberg and Stein, 1974). An hypothesis that continues to be attractive to many workers in the field is that the greater preservation of behavioral capacity following lesions in neonates is related to their greater capacity for neuronal plasticity. Some evidence for this hypothesis has been provided by Schneider (1970), who showed that Syrian hamsters given bilateral lesions of the superior colliculus in infancy exhibited recovery of visual-motor behavior and anomalous retinofugal projections, whereas hamsters operated upon as adults showed neither. Much more work needs to be done before a causal link can be established between behavioral and neuronal plasticity, but the prospects have never been more promising. Some of the difficulties surrounding this issue have been discussed previously (see Goldman, 1974).

VI. FINAL COMMENTS

It would be inappropriate to conclude this chapter by drawing overly general conclusions about the nature of development, particularly as our understanding of this complex subject is expanding rapidly. Indeed, the intent of this review has been only to sample the rich and fertile territory waiting to be cultivated by behaviorally oriented scientists, for it is evident that the challenge of future research is to define more precisely the neural basis of psychological processes, e.g., perception, memory, cognition, and socialization. However, in reviewing the material contained here, one cannot help but gain some impressions, some prejudices, and some insights, which, though they in no way represent original formulations, yet might serve as guideposts for the future.

It is widely acknowledged that the development of the nervous system is strongly influenced by the external environment and the opportunities that it provides for experience and learning. It is possible that this chapter has under-emphasized this omnipresent regulator of development, the influence of function on structure, and has instead stressed effects in the opposite direction, that of structure on function. This emphasis is merely an abstraction of convenience and not meant to minimize or deny the mutual and bidirectional effects of structural and functional variables. We hope, however, that the concentration here on structural determinants of development may serve to correct an imbalance in the literature of psychology, in general, and of developmental psychology, in particular.

Indeed, a major premise of this chapter is that a full understanding of behavioral development cannot be attained without cognizance of the development of that organ of the body without which there would be no behavior. There is ample evidence throughout this review of an orderliness and uniformity in the unfolding of the structural features of the nervous system. Cells destined to become neurons are generated at specific days in specific places on the embryonic neural plate. These cells migrate, again according to precise timetables, to their ultimate destinations. They then continue to expand in size and to develop their specific morphological characteristics. All evolve their axonal and dendritic processes and form synapses with the processes of other neurons located in the near vicinity and quite far away. Whether particular synaptic arrangements within an area of the brain are governed strictly by chemical specificities, by spatial constraints, or by other factors is an issue yet to be resolved. Once formed, however, synapses support neural transmission and thus become the functional building blocks for behavioral capacity. It is unlikely that any element in this chain of events can be broken or altered without some consequences for behavioral development. It seems inescapable that many of these aspects of structural development, which are set in motion in embryonic life and continue well into the postnatal period, are largely under the control of genetic mechanisms and regulated or modified by environmental and experiential events.

Development is by definition a sequential process. One function of a stepwise maturational progression may be to regulate the order and impact of internal and external stimuli and experience on the developmental process itself. Entrance into the world at birth may not so drastically alter the environment of the infant as is often supposed. The biological constraints that are involved, for example, in the delay of eye opening, in the lateness of puberty, or in the hypofunctional status of certain neocortical mechanisms—all manifestations of immaturity—may be ways of regulating *when* as well as *what* features of the environment will be "effective" stimuli for an organism. A particularly useful statement of this position may be found in the insightful writings of S. Shapiro (1971a, b; Shapiro and Vukovich, 1970). Shapiro suggested that the immaturity of the adrenal cortical response to stress in infant rats protected the neonate from wide variations in circulating hormones. As also noted by Shapiro, the immaturity of other neuroregulatory mechanisms may similarly protect the developing organism: "As the primary responsibility of nature is to ensure survival of the newborn, it does not seem unreasonable to assume that absence of certain of these regulatory systems is in itself an adaptive device which contributed to survival of the neonate or perhaps lays the foundation for effective survival at later stages of the life cycle" (Shapiro, 1971a, p. 307). The immaturity of the infant nervous system may, for example, explain why, in a recent study of Guatemalan children (Kagan, 1975), mild to moderate social and physical deprivation during the first 1 to 2 years of life placed no serious constraints on their eventual intellectual competence, providing remedial experiences followed the period of deprivation. Thus, although a potentially infinite variety of both positive and aversive stimuli would seem to be available in the external world, the maturational status of the organism provides a filter through which only a subset can be effective at particular times. Uniformity and orderliness in the sequence of exposure to the environment may be governed and programmed by the developmental timetables of different parts of the nervous system.

At the same time that there may be insensitive periods in early life designed to protect the developing organism from wide fluctuation in the conditions of development, there is also abundant evidence for the existence of particularly sensitive or critical periods. Work described earlier on the inductive influence of hormones in the perinatal period on differentiation of hypothalamic mechanisms and on the effects of visual deprivation on visual cortical function clearly indicated that the nervous system is especially vulnerable to environmental conditions only at certain times in development, a situation that probably extends to man (e.g., Money and Ehrhardt, 1972; Mitchell et al., 1973). These episodes presumably have the opposite effect of insensitive periods, i.e., insuring that particular stimuli and experiences will be effective at a time when they are required for the promotion of normal development.

Orderliness seen in normal development must also obtain in pathological development. The rules and mechanisms for regenerative phenomena in the developing nervous system are not yet well understood, but it is most unlikely that, when discovered, they will overturn basic concepts of CNS structure and function. It would now appear that the anomalous connections which develop in response to CNS injury, though they develop under abnormal circumstances, nonetheless possess structure-function specificities of their own.

Acknowledgments

I thank B. Dow, H. Kaplan, J. Petras, J. Semmes, B. Slotnick, M. Snyder, P. Rakic, and H. E. Rosvold for reading all or part of this manuscript and for offering helpful suggestions

72   PATRICIA S. GOLDMAN

which contributed greatly to its improvement. Thanks are also due to Candy Moore for excellent secretarial support and Thelma Galkin and Robert Powell for bibliographic assistance.

For permission to reproduce certain figures, I thank the authors, the editors, and the publishers.

References

Addison, W. H. F. 1911. The development of the Purkinje cells and of the cortical layers in the cerebellum of the albino rat. *J. Comp. Neurol.* **21**, 459–488.
Ades, H. W., and Raab, D. H. 1946. Recovery of motor function after exterpation of area 4 in monkeys. *J. Neurophysiol.* **9**, 55–60.
Adinolfi, A. M. 1972a. The organization of paramembranous densities during postnatal maturation of synaptic junctions in the cerebral cortex. *Exp. Neurol.* **34**, 383–393.
Adinolfi, A. M. 1972b. Morphogenesis of synaptic junctions in layers 1 and 11 of the somatic sensory cortex. *Exp. Neurol.* **34**, 372–382.
Aghajanian, G. K., and Bloom, F. E. 1967. The formation of synaptic junctions in developing rat brain: a quantitative electron microscopic study. *Brain Res.* **6**, 716–727.
Akert, K. 1964. Comparative anatomy of the frontal cortex and thalamocortical connections. *In* "The Frontal Granular Cortex and Behavior" (J. M. Warren and K. Akert, eds.), pp. 372–396. McGraw-Hill, New York.
Akert, K., Orth, O. S., Harlow, H. F., and Schiltz, K. A. 1960. Learned behavior of rhesus monkeys following neonatal bilateral prefrontal lobotomy. *Science* **132**, 1944–1945.
Alexander, G. E., and Fuster, J. M. 1973. Effects of cooling prefrontal cortex on cell firing in the nucleus medialis dorsalis. *Brain Res.* **61**, 93–105.
Altman, J. 1966. Autoradiographic and histological studies of postnatal neurogenesis. II. A longitudinal investigation of the kinetics, migration and transformation of cells incorporating tritiated thymidine in infant rats, with special reference to postnatal neurogenesis in some brain regions. *J. Comp. Neurol.* **128**, 431–474.
Altman, J. 1969a. DNA metabolism and cell proliferation. *In* "Handbook of Neurochemistry" (A. Lajtha, ed.), Vol. 2, pp. 137–182. Plenum, New York.
Altman, J. 1969b. Autoradiographic and histological studies of postnatal neurogenesis. III. Dating the time of production and onset of differentiation of cerebellar microneurons in rats. *J. Comp. Neurol.* **136**, 269–294.
Altman, J. 1972a. Postnatal development of the cerebellar cortex in the rat. I. The external germinal layer and the transitional molecular layer. *J. Comp. Neurol.* **145**, 353–398.
Altman, J. 1972b. Postnatal development of the cerebellar cortex in the rat. II. Phases in the maturation of Purkinje cells and of the molecular layer. *J. Comp. Neurol.* **145**, 399–464.
Altman, J. 1972c. Postnatal development of the cerebellar cortex in the rat. III. Maturation of the components of the granular layer. *J. Comp. Neurol.* **145**, 465–514.
Altman, J. 1975. Effects of interference with cerebellar maturation on the development of locomotion. *In* "Brain Mechanisms in Mental Retardation" (N. A. Buchwald and M. A. B. Brazier, eds.), pp. 41–91. Academic Press, New York.
Altman, J., and Anderson, W. J. 1971. Irradiation of the cerebellum in infant rats with low level x-ray: histological and cytological effects during infancy and adulthood. *Exp. Neurol.* **30**, 492–509.
Altman, J., Anderson, W. J., and Wright, K. A. 1967. Selective destruction of precursors of microneurons of the cerebellar cortex with fractionated low-dose x-rays. *Exp. Neurol.* **17**, 481–497.
Altman, J., Anderson, W. J., and Strop, M. 1971. Retardation of cerebellar and motor development by focal x-irradation during infancy. *Physiol. Behav.* **7**, 143–150.

Altman, J., Brunner, R. L., and Bayer, S. A. 1973. The hippocampus and behavioral maturation. *Behav. Biol.* 8, 557–596.

Angevine, J. B., Jr. 1970a. Critical cellular events in the shaping of neural centers. *In* "The Neurosciences, Second Study Program" (F. O. Schmitt, ed.), pp. 62–72. Rockefeller Univ. Press, New York.

Angevine, J. B., Jr. 1970b. Time of neuron origin in the diencephalon of the mouse. An autoradiographic study. *J. Comp. Neurol.* 139, 129–188.

Angevine, J. B., Jr., and Sidman, R. L. 1961. Autoradiographic study of cell migration during histogenesis of cerebral cortex in the mouse. *Nature (London)* 192, 766–768.

Anker, R. L., and Cragg, B. G. 1974. Development of the extrinsic connections of the visual cortex in the cat. *J. Comp. Neurol.* 154, 29–42.

Balazs, R., Kovacs, S., Cocks, W. A., Johnson, A. L., and Eayrs, J. T. 1971. Effect of thyroid hormone on the biochemical maturation of rat brain: Postnatal cell formation. *Brain Res.* 25, 555–570.

Barlow, H. B., and Pettigrew, J. D. 1971. Lack of specificity of neurons in the visual cortex of young kittens. *J. Physiol. (London)* 218, 98–100.

Barnes, D., and Altman, J. 1973. Effects of two levels of gestational-lactational undernutrition on the postweaning growth of the rat cerebellum. *Exp. Neurol.* 38, 420–428.

Barraclough, C. A. 1961. Production of anovulatory, sterile rats by single injections of testosterone proprionate. *Endocrinology* 68, 62–67.

Barraclough, C. A. 1967. Modifications in reproductive function after exposure to hormones during the prenatal and early postnatal period. *In* "Neuroendocrinology" (L. Martini and W. F. Ganong, eds.), Vol. 2, pp. 61–99. Academic Press, New York.

Beach, F. A. 1940. Effects of cortical lesions upon the copulatory behavior of male rats. *J. Comp. Psychol.* 29, 193–244.

Beach, F. A. 1944. Effects of injury to the cerebral cortex upon sexually-receptive behavior in the female rat. *Psychosomat. Med.* 6, 40–55.

Beach, F. A., Zitrin, A., and Jaynes, J. 1955. Neural mediation of mating in male cats: II. Contributions of the frontal cortex. *J. Exp. Zool.* 130, 381–402.

Beck, C. H., and Chambers, W. W. 1970. Speed, accuracy, and strength of forelimb movement after unilateral pyramidotomy in rhesus monkeys. *J. Comp. Physiol. Psychol. Monogr.* 70, 1–22.

Bernhard, C. G., and Bohm, E. 1954. Cortical representation and functional significance of the corticomotoneuronal system. *Arch. Neurol. Psychiat.* 72, 473–502.

Berry, M., and Rogers, A. W. 1965. The migration of neuroblasts in the developing cerebral cortex. *J. Anat.* 99, 691–709.

Birch, H. G. 1971. Levels, categories, and methodological assumptions in the study of behavioral development. *In* "The Biopsychology of Development" (E. Tobach, L. R. Aronson, and E. Shaw, eds.), pp. 503–513. Academic Press, New York.

Blackstad, T. W. 1956. Commissural connections of the hippocampal region in the rat, with special reference to their mode of termination. *J. Comp. Neurol.* 105, 417–538.

Blackstad, T. W. 1958. On the termination of some afferents to the hippocampus and fascia dentata. An experimental study in the rat. *Acta Anat.* 35, 202–214.

Blakemore, C. 1973. Environmental constraints on development in the visual system. *In* "Constraints on Learning: Limitations and Predispositions" (R. A. Hinde and J. Stevenson-Hinde, eds.), pp. 51–73. Academic Press, London.

Blakemore, C. 1974. Developmental factors in the formation of feature extracting neurons. *In* "The Neurosciences: Third Study Program" (F. O. Schmitt and F. G. Worden, eds.), pp. 105–113. MIT Press, Cambridge, Massachusetts.

Blakemore, C., and Cooper, G. F. 1970. Development of the brain depends on the visual environment. *Nature (London)* 228, 477–478.

Blakemore, C., and Mitchell, D. E. 1973. Environmental modification of the visual cortex and the neural basis of learning and memory. *Nature (London)* **241**, 467–468.

Blakemore, C., and Van Sluyters, R. C. 1974. Reversal of the physiological effects of monocular deprivation in kittens: further evidence for a sensitive period. *J. Physiol. (London)* **237**, 195–216.

Blakemore, C., and Van Sluyters, R. C. 1975. Innate and environmental factors in the development of the kitten's visual cortex. *J. Physiol. (London)* **248**, 663–716.

Bodian, D. 1970. A model of synaptic and behavioral ontogeny. *In* "The Neurosciences. Second Study Program" (F. O. Schmitt, ed.), pp. 129–140. Rockefeller Univ. Press, New York.

Boulder Committee. 1970. Embryonic vertebrate central nervous system: revised terminology. *Anat. Rec.* **166**, 257–262.

Brady, J. V., and Nauta, W. J. H. 1953. Subcortical mechanisms in emotional behavior: Affective changes following septal lesions in the albino rat. *J. Comp. Physiol. Psychol.* **46**, 596–602.

Brindley, G. S. 1964. The use made by the cerebellum of the information it receives from sense organs. *Int. Brain Res. Org. Bull.* **3**, 80.

Brinkman, J., and Kuypers, H. G. J. M. 1972. Splitbrain monkeys: cerebral control of ipsilateral and contralateral arm, hand, and finger movements. *Science* **176**, 536–539.

Brinkman, J., and Kuypers, H. G. J. M. 1973. Cerebral control of contralateral and ipsilateral arm, hand and finger movements in the split-brain rhesus monkey. *Brain* **96**, 653–674.

Brown-Grant, K. 1971. The role of steroid hormones in the control of gonadotrophin secretion in adult female mammals. *U.C.L.A. Forum Med. Sci.* **15**, 269–288.

Brunner, R. L., and Altman, J. 1973. Locomotor deficits in adult rats with moderate to massive retardation of cerebellar development during infancy. *Behav. Biol.* **9**, 169–188.

Buffery, A. W. H., and Gray, J. A. 1972. Sex differences in the development of spatial and linguistic skills. *In* "Gender Differences in Developmental Medicine" (C. Ounsted and D. C. Taylor, eds.), pp. 123–157. Churchill, London.

Butters, N., Rosen, J., and Stein, D. 1973. Recovery of behavioral functions after sequential ablation of the frontal lobes of monkeys. *In* "Plasticity and Recovery of Function in the Central Nervous System" (D. G. Stein, J. J. Rosen, and N. Butters, eds.), pp. 429–466. Academic Press, New York.

Buxton, D. F., and Goodman, D. C. 1967. Motor function and the corticospinal tracts in the dog and raccoon. *J. Comp. Neurol.* **129**, 341–360.

Campbell, B. A., Ballantine, P., and Lynch, G. 1971. Hippocampal control of behavioral arousal: duration of lesion effects and possible interactions with recovery after frontal cortical damage. *Exp. Neurol.* **33**, 159–170.

Caveness, W. F., Echlin, F. A., Kemper, T. L., and Kato, M. 1973. The propagation of focal paroxysmal activity in the *Macaca mulatta* at birth and at 24 months. *Brain* **96**, 757–764.

Caviness, V. S., Jr., and Sidman, R. L. 1972. Olfactory structures of the forebrain in the reeler mutant mouse. *J. Comp. Neurol.* **145**, 85–104.

Caviness, V. S., Jr., and Sidman, R. L. 1973. Retrohippocampal, hippocampal, and related structures of the forebrain in the reeler mutant mouse. *J. Comp. Neurol.* **147**, 235–254.

Chambers, W. W., and Liu, C. N. 1957. Cortico-spinal tract of the cat. An attempt to correlate the pattern of degeneration with the deficits in reflex activity following neocortical lesions. *J. Comp. Neurol.* **108**, 23–56.

Cheek, D. B., Graystone, J. E., and Rowe, R. D. 1969. Hypoxia and malnutrition in newborn rats: Effects on RNA, DNA and protein in tissues. *Amer. J. Physiol.* **217**, 642–645.

Chow, K. L., Riesen, A. H., and Newell, F. W. 1957. Degeneration of retinal ganglion cells in infant chimpanzees reared in darkness. *J. Comp. Neurol.* **107**, 27–42.

Coghill, G. E. 1929. "Anatomy and the Problem of Behavior." Cambridge Univ. Press, London and New York.

Colonnier, M., and Rossignol, S. 1969. Heterogeneity of the cerebral cortex. *In* "Basic Mechanisms of the Epilepsies" (H. Jasper, A. Ward, and A. Pope, eds.), pp. 26–40. Little, Brown, Boston, Massachusetts.

Correll, R. E., and Scoville, W. B. 1967. Significance of delay in performance of monkeys with medial temporal lobe resections. *Exp. Brain Res.* **4**, 85–96.

Coyle, J. T., and Axelrod, J. 1972. Tyrosine hydroxylase in rat brain: developmental characteristics. *J. Neurochem.* **19**, 1117–1123.

Coyle, J. T., and Henry, D. 1973. Catecholamines in fetal and newborn rat brain. *J. Neurochem.* **21**, 61–67.

Cragg, B. G. 1971. The fate of axon terminals in visual cortex during transsynaptic atrophy of the lateral geniculate nucleus. *Brain Res.* **34**, 53–60.

Cragg, B. G. 1972a. The development of cortical synapses during starvation in the rat. *Brain* **95**, 143–150.

Cragg, B. G. 1972b. The development of synapses in cat visual cortex. *Invest. Ophthalmol.* **11**, 377–385.

Crain, B., Cotman, C., Taylor, D., and Lynch, G. 1973. A quantitative electron microscopic study of synaptogenesis in the dentate gyrus of the rat. *Brain Res.* **63**, 195–204.

Dadoune, J. P. 1966. Contribution a l'étude de la differenciation de la cellule de Purkinje et du cortex cerébélleux chez le rat blanc. *Arch. Anat. Hist. Embryol.* **49**, 383–393.

Davidson, J. M. 1966. Control of gonadotropin secretion in the males. *In* "Neuroendocrinology" (L. Martini and W. F. Ganong, eds.), Vol. 1, pp. 565–611. Academic Press, New York.

del Cerro, M. P., and Snider, R. S. 1972. Studies on the developing cerebellum. II. The ultrastructure of the external granular layer. *J. Comp. Neurol.* **144**, 131–164.

Dews, P. B., and Wiesel, T. N. 1970. Consequences of monocular deprivation on visual behavior in kittens. *J. Physiol. (London)* **206**, 437–455.

Divac, I., Rosvold, H. E., and Szwarcbart, M. K. 1967. Behavioral effects of selective ablation of the caudate nucleus. *J. Comp. Physiol. Psychol.* **63**, 184–190.

Dobbing, J., and Sands, J. 1970. Timing of neuroblast multiplication in developing human brain. *Nature (London)* **226**, 639–640.

Dobbing, J., Hopewell, J. W., and Lynch, A. 1971. Vulnerability of developing brain. VII. Permanent deficit of neurons in cerebral and cerebellar cortex following early mild undernutrition. *Exp. Neurol.* **32**, 439–447.

Dorner, G., and Staudt, J. 1968. Structural changes in the preoptic anterior hypothalamic area of the male rat following neonatal castration and androgen substitution. *Neuroendocrinology* **3**, 136–140.

Dorner, G., and Staudt, J. 1969. Structural changes in the hypothalamic ventromedial nucleus of the male rat following neonatal castration and androgen treatment. *Neuroendocrinology* **4**, 278–281.

Douglas, R. J., and Pribram, K. H. 1966. Learning and limbic lesions. *Neuropsychologia* **5**, 197–220.

Dyer, R. G., Pritchett, C. J., and Cross, B. A. 1972. Unit activity in the diencephalon of female rats during the oestrous cycle. *J. Endocrinol.* **53**, 151–160.

Eccles, J. C., Ito, M., and Szentagothai, J. 1967. "The Cerebellum as a Neuronal Machine." Springer-Verlag, Berlin and New York.

Edds, M. V. 1953. Collateral nerve regeneration. *Quart. Rev. Biol.* **28**, 260–276.

Edwards, D. A. 1969. Early androgen stimulation and aggressive behavior in male and female mice. *Physiol. Behav.* 4, 333–338.

Eidelberg, E., and Stein, D. G., eds. 1974. Functional recovery after lesions of the nervous system. *Neurosci. Res. Progr. Bull.* 12, 191–303.

Eisenberg, L. 1971. Persistent problems in the study of behavioral development. *In* "The Biopsychology of Development" (E. Tobach, L. R. Aronson, and E. Shaw, eds.), pp. 515–529. Academic Press, New York.

Everett, J. W. 1964. Central neural control of reproductive functions of the adenohypophysis. *Physiol. Rev.* 44, 373–431.

Everett, J. W. 1969. Neuroendocrine aspects of mammalian reproduction. *Annu. Rev. Physiol.* 31, 383–416.

Everett, J. W., and Sawyer, C. H. 1950. A 24-hour periodicity in the "LH-release apparatus" of female rats disclosed by barbiturate sedation. *Endocrinology* 47, 198–218.

Falconer, D. S. 1951. Two new mutants "trembler" and "reeler" with neurological actions in the house mouse (*Mus musculus*). *J. Genet.* 50, 192–201.

Felix, D., and Wiesendanger, M. 1971. Pyramidal and non-pyramidal motor cortical effects on distal forelimb muscles of monkeys. *Exp. Brain Res.* 12, 81–91.

Finger, S., Walbran, B., and Stein, D. G. 1973. Brain damage and recovery: serial lesion phenomena. *Brain Res.* 63, 1–18.

Fish, I., and Winick, M. 1969. Effect of malnutrition on regional growth of the developing rat brain. *Exp. Neurol.* 25, 534–540.

Flerkó, B. 1967. Brain mechanisms controlling gonadotrophin secretion and their sexual differentiation. *In* "Symposium on Reproduction" (K. Lissak, ed.), pp. 11–37. Akadémiai Kiadó, Budapest.

Flerkó, B., Mess, B., and Illei-Donhoffer, A. 1969. On the mechanism of androgen sterilization. *Neuroendocrinology* 4, 164–169.

Fox, C. A. 1962. The structure of the cerebellar cortex. *In* "Correlative Anatomy of the Nervous System" (E. C. Crosby, T. Humphrey, and E. W. Lauer, eds.), pp. 193–198. Macmillan, New York.

Fox, M. W., and Spencer, J. W. 1967. Development of the delayed response in the dog. *Anim. Behav.* 15, 162–168.

Franzen, E. A., and Myers, R. E. 1973a. Neural control of social behavior: prefrontal and anterior temporal cortex. *Neuropsychologia* 11, 141–157.

Franzen, E. A., and Myers, R. E. 1973b. Age effects on social behavior deficits following prefrontal lesions in monkeys. *Brain Res.* 54, 277–286.

Fujita, S. 1967. Quantitative analysis of cell proliferation and differentiation in the cortex of the postnatal mouse cerebellum. *J. Cell Biol.* 32, 277–288.

Fujita, S., Shimada, M., and Nakamura, T. 1966. H^3 thymidine autoradiographic studies on the cell proliferation and differentiation in the external and internal layers of the mouse cerebellum. *J. Comp. Neurol.* 128, 191–208.

Fuster, J. M., and Alexander, G. E. 1970. Delayed response deficit by cryogenic depression of frontal cortex. *Brain Res.* 20, 85–90.

Fuster, J. M., and Alexander, G. E. 1971. Neuron activity related to short-term memory. *Science* 173, 652–654.

Fuster, J. M., and Alexander, G. E. 1973. Firing changes in cells of the nucleus medialis dorsalis associated with delayed response behavior. *Brain Res.* 61, 79–91.

Ganz, L., and Fitch, M. 1968. The effect of visual deprivation on perceptual behavior. *Exp. Neurol.* 22, 638–660.

Ganz, L., Fitch, M., and Satterberg, J. A. 1968. The selective effect of visual deprivation on receptive field shape determined neurophysiologically. *Exp. Neurol.* 22, 614–637.

Ganz, L., Hirsch, H. V. B., and Tieman, S. B. 1972. The nature of perceptual deficits in visually-deprived cats. *Brain Res.* 44, 547–568.

Garey, L. J., and Powell, T. P. S. 1971. An experimental study of the termination of the lateral geniculo-cortical pathway in the cat and monkey. *Proc. Roy. Soc., Ser. B* 179, 41–63.

Gay, V. L., Midgley, A. R., and Niswender, G. D. 1970. Patterns of gonadotrophin secretion associated with ovulation. *Fed. Proc.* 29, 1880–1887.

Geller, E. 1971. Some observations on the effects of environmental complexity and isolation on biochemical ontogeny. *In* "Brain Development and Behavior" (M. B. Sterman, D. J. McGinty, and A. M. Adinolfi, eds.), pp. 277–305. Academic Press, New York.

Gerall, A. A., and Ward, I. I. 1966. Effects of prenatal exogenons androgen on the sexual behavior of the female albino rat. *J. Comp. Physiol. Psychol.* 62, 370–375.

Gesell, A. 1942. The documentation of infant behavior in relation to cultural anthropology. *In* "Proceedings of the 8th American Scientific Congress Held in Washington, 1940," Vol. II: Anthropological Sciences, pp. 279–289. U.S. Dept. of State, Washington, D.C.

Glees, P., and Cole, J. 1950. Recovery of skilled motor functions after small repeated lesions of motor cortex in macaque. *J. Neurophysiol.* 13, 137–148.

Goldman, B. D., Kamberi, I., Siiteri, P. K., and Porter, J. C. 1969. Temporal relationship of progestin secretion, LH release and ovulation in rats. *Endocrinology* 85, 133–142.

Goldman, P. S. 1971. Functional development of the prefrontal cortex in early life and the problem of neuronal plasticity. *Exp. Neurol.* 32, 366–387.

Goldman, P. S. 1972. Developmental determinants of cortical plasticity. *Acta Neurobiol. Exp.* 32, 495–511.

Goldman, P. S. 1974. An alternative to developmental plasticity: heterology of CNS structures in infants and adults. *In* "Plasticity and Recovery of Function in the Central Nervous System" (D. G. Stein, J. J. Rosen, and N. Butters, eds.), pp. 149–174. Academic Press, New York.

Goldman, P. S. 1975. Age, sex, and experience as related to the neural basis of cognitive development. *In* "Brain Mechanisms in Mental Retardation" (N. A. Buchwald and M. A. B. Brazier, eds.), pp. 379–392. Academic Press, New York.

Goldman, P. S., and Brown, R. M. 1975. The influence of neonatal androgen on the development of cortical function in the rhesus monkey. *Abstr. Soc. Neurosci.* 1, 494.

Goldman, P. S., and Rosvold, H. E. 1970. Localization of function within the dorsolateral cortex of the rhesus monkey. *Exp. Neurol.* 27, 291–304.

Goldman, P. S., and Rosvold, H. E. 1972. The effects of selective caudate lesions in infant and juvenile rhesus monkeys. *Brain Res.* 43, 53–66.

Goldman, P. S., Rosvold, H. E., and Mishkin, M. 1970. Evidence for behavioral impairment following prefrontal lobectomy in the infant monkey. *J. Comp. Physiol. Psychol.* 70, 454–463.

Goldman, P. S., Rosvold, H. E., Vest, B., and Galkin, T. W. 1971. Analysis of the delayed-alternation deficit produced by dorsolateral prefrontal lesions in the rhesus monkey. *J. Comp. Physiol. Psychol.* 77, 212–220.

Goldman, P. S., Crawford, H. T., Stokes, L. P., Galkin, T. W., and Rosvold, H. E. 1974. Sex-dependent behavioral effects of cerebral cortical lesions in the developing rhesus monkey. *Science* 186, 540–542.

Goldowitz, D., White, W. F., Steward, O., Lynch, G., and Cotman, C. 1975. Anatomical evidence for a projection from the entorhinal cortex to the contralateral dentate gyrus of the rat. *Exp. Neurol.* 47, 433–441.

Goldstein, K. 1939. "The Organism," 533 pp. Beacon Press, Boston, Massachusetts.

Goodman, D. C., and Horel, J. A. 1966. Sprouting of optic tract projections in the brain stem of the rat. *J. Comp. Neurol.* 127, 71–88.

Goodman, D. C., Bogdasorian, R. S., and Horel, J. A. 1973. Axonal sprouting of ipsilateral optic tract following opposite eye removal. *Brain, Behav. Evol.* 8, 27–50.

Goodman, L. 1934. Observations on transplanted immature ovaries in the eyes of adult male and female rats. *Anat. Rec.* 59, 223–252.

Gorska, T., and Czarkowska, J. 1973. Motor effects of stimulation of the cerebral cortex in the dog. An ontogenetic study. *In* "Motor Control" (N. T. Tankov and D. S. Kosarov, eds.), pp. 147–166. Plenum, New York.

Gorski, R. A. 1971. Gonadal hormones and the perinatal development of neuroendocrine function. *In* "Frontiers in Neuroendocrinology" (L. Martini and W. Ganong, eds.), pp. 237–290. Oxford Univ. Press, London and New York.

Gorski, R. A., and Wagner, J. W. 1965. Gonadal activity and sexual differentiation of the hypothalamus. *Endocrinology* 76 226–239.

Gottlieb, D. I., and Cowan, W. M. 1972. Evidence for a temporal factor in the occupation of available synaptic sites during the development of the dentate gyrus. *Brain Res.* 41, 452–456.

Goy, R. W. 1970a. Early hormonal influences on the development of sexual and sex-related behavior. *In* "The Neurosciences: Second Study Program" (F. O. Schmitt, ed.), pp. 196–207. Rockefeller Univ. Press, New York.

Goy, R. W. 1970b. Experimental control of psychosexuality. *Phil. Trans. Roy. Soc. London, Ser. B* 259, 149–162.

Goy, R. W., and Phoenix, C. H. 1972. The effects of testosterone proprionate administered before birth on the development of behavior in genetic female rhesus monkeys. *U.C.L.A. Forum Med. Sci.* 15, 193–201.

Goy, R. W., and Resko, J. A. 1972. Gonadal hormones and behavior of normal and pseudohermaphroditic nonhuman female primates. *Rec. Progr. Horm. Res.* 28, 707–733.

Grady, K. L., Phoenix, C. H., and Young, W. C. 1965. Role of the developing rat testis on differentiation of the neural tissue mediating sexual behavior. *J. Comp. Physiol. Psychol.* 59, 176–182.

Gray, J. A. 1971. Sex differences in emotional behaviour in mammals including man: Endocrine bases. *Acta Psychol.* 35, 29–46.

Gray, J. A., and Buffery, A. W. H. 1971. Sex differences in emotional and cognitive behavior in mammals including man: Adaptive and neural bases. *Acta Psychol.* 35, 89–111.

Gray, J. A., Levine, S., and Broadhurst, P. L. 1965. Gonadal hormone injections in infancy and adult emotional behaviour. *Anim. Behav.* 13, 33–43.

Grobstein, P., and Chow, K. L. 1975. Receptive field development and individual experience. *Science* 190, 352–358.

Guillery, R. W. 1972. Experiments to determine whether retinogeniculate axons can form translaminar collateral sprouts in the dorsal lateral geniculate nucleus of the cat. *J. Comp. Neurol.* 146, 407–420.

Guillery, R. W., and Stelzner, D. J. 1970. The differential effects of unilateral lid closure upon the monocular and binocular segments of the dorsal lateral geniculate nucleus in the cat. *J. Comp. Neurol.* 139, 413–422.

Guth, L., and Wendle, W. F. 1970. The enigma of central nervous regeneration. *Exp. Neurol. Suppl.* 5, 1–43.

Gyllenstein, L. 1959. Postnatal development of the visual cortex in darkness (mice). *Acta Morphol. Neerl.-Scand.* 2, 331–345.

Gyllenstein, L., Malmfors, T., and Norrlin, M.-L. 1965. Effect of visual deprivation on the optic centers of growing and adult mice. *J. Comp. Neurol.* 124, 149–160.

Hajós, F., Patel, A. J., and Balázs, R. 1973. Effect of thyroid deficiency on the synaptic organization of the rat cerebellar cortex. *Brain Res.* 50, 387–401.

Halász, B. 1969. The endocrine effects of isolation of the hypothalamus from the rest of the brain. *In* "Frontiers in Neuroendocrinology" (L. Martini and W. F. Ganong, eds.), pp. 307–342. Oxford Univ. Press, London and New York.

Harlow, H. F. 1959. The development of learning in the rhesus monkey. *Amer. Sci.* 47, 459–479.

Harlow, H. F., Blomquist, A. J., Thompson, C. I., Schiltz, K. A., and Harlow, M. K. 1968. Effects of induction age and size of prefrontal lobe lesions on learning in rhesus monkeys. *In* "The Neuropsychology of Development" (R. Isaacson, ed.), pp. 79–120. Wiley, New York.

Harlow, H. F., Thompson, C. I., Blomquist, A. J., and Schiltz, K. A. 1970. Learning in rhesus monkeys after varying amounts of prefrontal lobe destruction during infancy and adolescence. *Brain Res.* 18, 343–353.

Harris, G. W. 1964. Sex hormones, brain development and brain function. *Endocrinology* 75, 627–648.

Harris, G. W., and Levine, S. 1962. Sexual differentiation of the brain and its experimental control. *J. Physiol. (London)* 163, 42P–43P.

Harris, G. W., and Levine, S. 1965. Sexual differentiation of the brain and its experimental control. *J. Physiol. (London)* 181, 379–400.

Hebb, D. O. 1949. "Organization of Behavior" John Wiley and Sons, Inc., New York.

Herndon, R. M., Margolis, G., and Kilham, L. 1971. The synaptic organization of the malformed cerebellum induced by perinatal infection with the feline panleukopenia virus (PLV). II. The Purkinje cell and its afferents. *J. Neuropathol. Exp. Neurol.* 30, 557–570.

Hicks, S. P., and D'Amato, C. J. 1968. Cell migration to the isocortex in the rat. *Anat. Rec.* 160, 619–634.

Hicks, S. P., and D'Amato, C. J. 1970. Motor-sensory and visual behavior after hemispherectomy in newborn and mature rats. *Exp. Neurol.* 29, 416–438.

Hicks, S. P., D'Amato, C. J., Klein, S. J., Austin, L. L., and French, B. C. 1969. Effects of regional irradiation or ablation of the infant rat cerebellum on motor development. *In* "Radiation Biology of the Fetal and Juvenile Mammal" (M. R. Sekov and D. D. Mahlum, eds.), U.S. At. Energy Comm. Publ., pp. 739–916. Washington, D.C.

Himwich, W. A. 1972. Developmental changes in neurochemistry during the maturation of sleep behavior. *In* "Sleep and the Maturing Nervous System" (C. D. Clemente, D. P. Purpura, and F. E. Mayer, eds.), pp. 125–140. Academic Press, New York.

Hines, M. 1942. The development and regression of reflexes, postures, and progression in the young macaque. *Contr. Embryol. Carnegie Inst.* 30, 153–209.

Hirano, A., Dembitzer, H. M., and Jones, M. 1972. An electronmicroscopic study of cycasin-induced cerebellar alterations. *J. Neuropathol. Exp. Neurol.* 31, 113–125.

Hirsch, H. V. B. 1972. Visual perception in cats after environmental surgery. *Exp. Brain Res.* 15, 405–423.

Hirsch, H. V. B., and Spinelli, D. N. 1970. Visual experience modifies distribution of horizontally and vertically oriented receptive fields in cats. *Science* 168, 869–871.

Hirsch, H. V. B., and Spinelli, D. N. 1971. Modification of the distribution of receptive field orientation in cats by selective visual exposure during development. *Exp. Brain Res.* 13, 509–527.

Hjorth-Simonsen, A., and Jeune, B. 1972. Origin and termination of the hippocampal perforant path in the rat studied by silver impregnation. *J. Comp. Neurol.* **144**, 215–232.

Holsinger, J. W., and Everett, J. W. 1970. Thresholds to preoptic stimulation at varying times in the rat estrous cycle. *Endocrinology* **86**, 251–256.

Hubel, D. H., and Wiesel, T. N. 1959. Receptive fields of single neurons in the cat's striate cortex. *J. Physiol. (London)* **148**, 574–591.

Hubel, D. H., and Wiesel, T. N. 1961. Integrative action in the cat's lateral geniculate body. *J. Physiol. (London)* **155**, 385–398.

Hubel, D. H., and Wiesel, T. N. 1962. Receptive fields, binocular interaction and functional architecture in the cat's visual cortex. *J. Physiol. (London)* **160**, 106–154.

Hubel, D. H., and Wiesel, T. N. 1963. Receptive fields of cells in striate cortex of very young, visually inexperienced kittens. *J. Neurophysiol.* **26**, 994–1002.

Hubel, D. H., and Wiesel, T. N. 1970. The period of susceptibility to the physiological effects of unilateral eye closure in kittens. *J. Physiol. (London)* **206**, 419–436.

Hunter, W. S. 1913. The delayed reaction in animals and children. *Behav. Monogr.* **2** (Whole No. 1).

Huttenlocher, P. R. 1967. Development of cortical neuronal activity in the neonatal cat. *Exp. Neurol.* **17**, 247–262.

Huttenlocher, P. R. 1975. Synaptic and dendritic development and mental defect. *In* "Brain Mechanisms in Mental Retardation" (N. A. Buchwald and M. A. B. Brazier, eds.), pp. 123–140. Academic Press, New York.

Imbert, M., and Buisseret, P. 1975. Receptive field characteristics and plastic properties of visual cortical cells in kittens reared with or without visual experiences. *Exp. Brain Res.* **22**, 25–36.

Isaacson, R., ed. 1968. "The Neuropsychology of Development," pp. 1–177. Wiley, New York.

Iversen, S. D. 1973. Brain lesions and memory in animals. *In* "The Physiological Basis of Memory" (J. A. Deutsch, ed.), pp. 305–364. Academic Press, New York.

Jacobsen, C. F. 1936. Studies of cerebral function in primates. *Comp. Psychol. Monogr.* **13**, 1–68.

Jacobson, M. 1969. Development of specific neuronal connections. *Science* **163**, 543–547.

Jacobson, M. 1970. Development, specification and diversification of neuronal connections. *In* "The Neurosciences: Second Study Program" (F. O. Schmitt, ed.), pp. 116–128. Rockefeller Univ. Press, New York.

Johnson, D. A. 1972. Developmental aspects of recovery of function following septal lesions in the infant rat. *J. Comp. Physiol. Psychol.* **78**, 331–348.

Johnson, T. N., and Rosvold, H. E. 1971. Topographic projections on the globus pallidus and the substantia nigra of selectively placed lesions in the precommissural caudate nucleus and putamen in the monkey. *Exp. Neurol.* **33**, 584–596.

Johnson, T. N., Rosvold, H. E., and Mishkin, M. 1968. Projections from behaviorally-defined sectors of the prefrontal cortex to the basal ganglia, septum, and diencephalon of the monkey. *Exp. Neurol.* **21**, 20–34.

Johnson, T. N., Rosvold, H. E., Galkin, T. W., and Goldman, P. S. 1976. Postnatal maturation of subcortical projections from the prefrontal cortex in the rhesus monkey. *J. Comp. Neurol.* **166**, 427–444.

Jonason, K. R., and Enloe, L. J. 1971. Alterations in social behavior following septal and amygdaloid lesions in the rat. *J. Comp. Physiol. Psychol.* **75**, 286–301.

Jones, E. G., and Powell, T. P. S. 1970. An anatomical study of converging sensory pathways within the cerebral cortex of the monkey. *Brain* **93**, 793–820.

Kaada, B. R. 1960. Cingulate, posterior orbital, anterior insular and temporal pole cortex. *In* "Handbook of Physiology" (J. Field, ed.), Vol. II, Section I, pp. 1345–1372. Amer. Physiol. Soc., Washington, D.C.

Kagan, J. 1975. Resilience and cognitive development. *Ethos* **3**, 231–247.

Karmel, B. Z., Miller, P. N., Dettweiler, L., and Anderson, G. 1970. Texture density and normal development of visual depth avoidance. *Develop. Psychobiol.* **3**, 73–90.

Kawakami, M., Terasawa, E., and Ibuki, T. 1970. Changes in multiple unit activity of the brain during the estrous cycle. *Neuroendocrinology* **7**, 54–64.

Kemp, J. M., and Powell, T. P. S. 1970. The cortico-striate projection in the monkey. *Brain* **93**, 525–546.

Kemper, T. L., Caveness, W. F., and Yakovlev, P. I. 1973. The neuronographic and metric study of the dendritic arbours of neurons in the motor cortex of *Macaca mulatta* at birth and at 24 months of age. *Brain* **96**, 765–782.

Kennard, M. A. 1936. Age and other factors in motor recovery from precentral lesions in monkeys. *Amer. J. Physiol.* **115**, 138–146.

Kennard, M. A. 1938. Reorganization of motor function in the cerebral cortex of monkeys deprived of motor and premotor areas in infancy. *J. Neurophysiol.* **1**, 477–496.

Kennard, M. A. 1940. Relation of age to motor impairment in man and in subhuman primates. *Arch. Neurol. Psychiat.* **44**, 377–397.

Kennard, M. 1942. Cortical reorganization of motor function: studies on series of monkeys of various ages from infancy to maturity. *Arch. Neurol. Psychiat.* **48**, 227–240.

Kimble, D. P. 1968. Hippocampus and internal inhibition. *Psychol. Bull.* **70**, 285–295.

King, F. A. 1958. Effects of septal and amygdaloid lesions on emotional behavior and conditioned avoidance response in the rat. *J. Nerv. Ment. Dis.* **126**, 57–63.

Kirk, G. R., and Breazile, J. E. 1972. Maturation of the corticospinal tract in the dog. *Exp. Neurol.* **35**, 394–397.

Kling, A., and Tucker, T. J. 1967. Effects of combined lesions of frontal granular cortex and caudate nucleus in the neonatal monkey. *Brain Res.* **6**, 428–439.

Kling, A., and Tucker, T. J. 1968. Sparing of function following localized brain lesions in neonatal monkeys. *In* "The Neuropsychology of Development" (R. Isaacson, ed.), pp. 121–145. Wiley, New York.

Kornhuber, H. H. 1974. Cerebral cortex, cerebellum, and basal ganglia: An introduction to their motor functions. *In* "The Neurosciences, Third Study Program" (F. O. Schmitt and F. G. Worden, eds.), pp. 267–280. MIT Press, Cambridge, Massachusetts.

Krauthamer, G., Liebeskind, J., and Salmon-Legagneur, A. 1967. Reversible deficit on a delayed alternation task during subcortical cooling. *J. Physiol. (London)* **190**, 18P–19P.

Kubota, K., and Niki, H. 1971. Prefrontal cortical unit activity and delayed alternation performance in monkeys. *J. Neurophysiol.* **34**, 337–347.

Kuffler, S. W. 1953. Discharge patterns and functional organization of mammalian retina. *J. Neurophysiol.* **16**, 37–68.

Kuypers, H. G. J. M. 1956. Cortical projections to the pons and the medulla oblongata in cat and man. *Anat. Rec.* **124**, 322–323.

Kuypers, H. G. J. M. 1960. Central cortical projections to motor and somatosensory cell groups. *Brain* **83**, 161–184.

Kuypers, H. G. J. M. 1962. Corticospinal connections: postnatal development in the rhesus monkey. *Science* **138**, 678–680.

Kuypers, H. G. J. M. 1974. Recovery of motor function in rhesus monkeys. *In* "Functional Recovery after Lesions of the Nervous System" (E. Eidelberg and D. G. Stein, eds.), *Neurosci. Res. Prog. Bull.* **12**, 240–244.

Kuypers, H. G. J. M., and Brinkman, J. 1970. Precentral projections to different parts of the spinal intermediate zone in the rhesus monkey. *Brain Res.* **24**, 29–48.

Laatsch, R. H., and Cowan, W. M. 1966. Electron microscopic studies of the dentate gyrus of the rat. I. Normal structure with special reference to synaptic organization. *J. Comp. Neurol.* **128**, 359–396.

Landis, D., and Sidman, R. L. 1975. Electronmicroscopic analysis of postnatal histogenesis in the cerebellar cortex of staggerer mutant mice. Cited in Sidman (1972).

Lane, P. 1964. Quoted in Sidman *et al.* (1965).

Langworthy, O. R. 1927. Histological development of cerebral motor areas in young kittens correlated with their physiological reaction to electrical stimulation. *Contrib. Embryol.* **104**, Carnegie Inst. Washington, Publ. 380, 177–207.

Larramendi, L. M. H. 1969. Analysis of synaptogenesis in the cerebellum of the mouse. *In* "Neurobiology of Cerebellar Evolution and Development" (R. Llinás, ed.), pp. 803–843. AMA, Chicago, Illinois.

Larsson, K. 1962. Mating behavior in male rats after cerebral cortical ablation. I. Effects of lesions in the dorsolateral and the median cortex. *J. Exp. Zool.* **151**, 167–176.

Larsson, K. 1964. Mating behavior in male rats after cerebral cortical ablation. II. Effects of lesions in the frontal lobes compared to lesions in the posterior half of the hemispheres. *J. Exp. Zool.* **155**, 203–214.

Lashley, K. S. 1941. Coalescence of neurology and psychology. *Proc. Amer. Phil. Soc.* **84**, 461–470.

Lawrence, D. G., and Hopkins, D. A. 1972. Developmental aspects of pyramidal motor control in the rhesus monkey. *Brain Res.* **40**, 117–118.

Lawrence, D. G., and Kuypers, H. G. J. M. 1968a. The functional organization of the motor system in the monkey. I. The effects of bilateral pyramidal lesions. *Brain* **91**, 1–14.

Lawrence, D. G., and Kuypers, H. G. J. M. 1968b. The functional organization of the motor system in the monkey. II. The effects of lesions of the descending brain-stem pathways. *Brain* **91**, 15–36.

Legrand, J. 1971. Comparative effects of thyroid deficiency and undernutrition on maturation of the nervous system and particularly on myelination in the young rat. *In* "Hormones in Development" (M. Hamburgh and E. J. W. Barrington, eds.), pp. 381–390. Appleton-Century-Crofts, New York.

Lehrman, D. S. 1970. Semantic and conceptual issues in the nature-nurture problem. *In* "Development and Evolution of Behavior" (L. R. Aronson *et al.,* eds.), pp. 17–52. Freeman, San Francisco, California.

Leonard, C. M. 1973. A method for assessing stages of neural maturation. *Brain Res.* **53**, 412–416.

Leonard, C. M. 1974. Degeneration argyrophilia as an index of neural maturation: studies on the optic tract of the golden hamster. *J. Comp. Neurol.* **156**, 435–458.

Leventhal, A. G., and Hirsch, H. V. B. 1975. Cortical effect of early selective exposure to diagonal lines. *Science* **190**, 902–904.

Levine, S. 1972. Introduction and basic concepts. *In* "Hormones and Behavior" (S. Levine, ed.), pp. 1–9. Academic Press, New York.

Lisk, R. D. 1967. Sexual behavior: hormonal control. *In* "Neuroendocrinology" (L. Martini and W. F. Ganong, eds.), Vol. 2, pp. 197–239. Academic Press, New York.

Liu, C. N., and Chambers, W. W. 1958. Intraspinal sprouting of dorsal root axons. *Arch. Neurol. Psychiat.* **79**, 46–61.

Liu, C. N., and Chambers, W. W. 1964. An experimental study of the corticospinal system in the monkey (*Macaca mulatta*). *J. Comp. Neurol.* **123**, 257–283.

Llinás, R., ed. 1969. "Neurobiology of Cerebellar Evolution and Development," Proc. 1st Int. Symp. Inst. Biomed. Res. AMA Educ. Res. Found., Chicago, Illinois.

Llinás, R., Hellman, D. E., and Precht, W. 1973. Neuronal circuit reorganization in mammalian agranular cerebellar cortex. *J. Neurobiol.* **4**, 69–94.

Lund, R. D., Cunningham, T. J., and Lund, J. S. 1973. Modified optic projections after unilateral eye removal in young rats. *Brain, Behav. Evol.* **8**, 51–72.

Lynch, G., Matthews, D., Mosko, S., Parks, T., and Cotman, C. 1972. Induced acetyl-cholinesterase-rich layer in rat dentate gyrus following entorhinal lesions. *Brain Res.* **42**, 311–318.

Lynch, G., Deadwyler, S., and Cotman, C. 1973a. Postlesion axonal growth produces permanent functional connections. *Science* **180**, 1364–1366.

Lynch, G. S., Mosko, S., Parks, T., and Cotman, C. W. 1973b. Relocation and hyperdevelopment of the dentate gyrus commissural system after entorhinal lesions in immature rats. *Brain Res.* **50**, 174–178.

Lynch, G., Stanfield, B., and Cotman, C. W. 1973c. Developmental differences in post-lesion axonal growth in the hippocampus. *Brain Res.* **59**, 155–168.

Lynn, R., and Compton, V. 1966. The role of internal inhibition and the frontal lobes in child development. *Conditional Reflex* **1**, 195–198.

McDowell, A. A., Brown, W. L., and McLee, A. C. 1960. Sex as a factor in spatial delayed response performance by rhesus monkeys. *J. Comp. Physiol. Psychol.* **52**, 429–432.

Maffei, L., and Fiorentini, A. 1974. Geniculate neural plasticity in kittens after exposure to periodic gratings. *Science* **186**, 447–449.

Magoun, H. W., and Ranson, S. W. 1938. The behavior of cats following bilateral removal of the rostral portion of the cerebral hemispheres. *J. Neurophysiol.* **1**, 39–44.

Manning, F. J., and Mishkin, M. 1975. Nonspatial memory after selective prefrontal lesions in monkeys. Paper read at Eastern Psychol. Ass., U.S.

Marin-Padilla, M. 1974. Structural organization of the cerebral cortex (motor area) in human chromosomal aberrations. A Golgi Study. I. D, (13–15) trisomy, Patau syndrome. *Brain Res.* **66**, 375–391.

Marty, R., and Scherrer, J. 1964. Criteres de maturation des systemes afferents corticaux. *Progr. Brain Res.* **4**, 222–236.

Meyer, P. M., Johnson, D. A., and Vaughn, D. W. 1970. The effect of septal and cortical ablations upon the acquisition of a two way conditioned avoidance response in rats. *Brain Res.* **22**, 113–120.

Miale, I. L., and Sidman, R. L. 1961. An autoradiographic analysis of histogenesis in the mouse cerebellum. *Exp. Neurol.* **4**, 277–296.

Michael, R. P., Zumpe, D., Keverne, E. B., and Bonsall, R. W. 1972. Neuroendocrine factors in the control of primate behavior. *Rec. Prog. Horm. Res.* **28**, 665–706.

Milner, B. 1964. Some effects of frontal lobectomy in man. *In* "The Frontal Granular Cortex and Behavior" (J. M. Warren and K. Akert, eds.), pp. 313–334. McGraw-Hill, New York.

Mishkin, M. 1964. Perseveration of central sets after frontal lesions in monkeys. *In* "The Frontal Granular Cortex and Behavior" (J. M. Warren and K. Akert, eds.), pp. 219–241. McGraw-Hill, New York.

Mitchell, D. E., Freeman, R. D., Millodot, M., and Haegerstrom, G. 1973. Meridianal amblyopia: evidence for modification of the human visual system by early visual experience. *Vision Res.* **13**, 535–558.

Money, J., and Ehrhardt, A. 1972. "Man and Woman, Boy and Girl: The Differentiation and Dimorphism of Gender Identity from Conception to Maturity," Johns Hopkins Univ. Press, Baltimore, Maryland.

Moore, R. Y., Bjorkland, A., and Stenevi, U. 1971. Plastic changes in the adrenergic innervation of the rat septal area in response to denervation. *Brain Res.* **33**, 13–35.

Morest, D. K. 1969. The growth of dendrites in the mammalian brain. *Z. Anat. Entwicklungsgesch.* **128**, 290–317.

Morest, D. K. 1970. A study of neurogenesis in the forebrain of opposum pouch young. Z. Anat. Entwicklungsgesch. 130, 265–305.

Moss, R. L., and Law, O. T. 1971. The estrous cycle: its influence on single unit activity in the forebrain. Brain Res. 30, 435–438.

Mugnaini, E. 1969. Ultrastructural studies on the cerebellar histogenesis. II. In "Neurobiology of Cerebellar Evolution and Development" (R. Llinás, ed.), pp. 749–782. AMA, Chicago, Illinois.

Mugnaini, E., and Forstrønen, P. F. 1967. Ultrastructural studies on the cerebellar histogenesis. I. Differentiation of granule cells and development of glomeruli in the chick embryo. Z. Zellforsch. 77, 115–143.

Muir, D. W., and Mitchell, D. E. 1973. Visual resolution and experience: acuity deficits in cats following early selective visual deprivation. Science 180, 420–422.

Myers, R. E., Swett, C., and Miller, M. 1973. Loss of social group affinity following prefrontal lesions in free-ranging macaques. Brain Res. 64, 257–269.

Nadler, R. D. 1968. Masculinization of female rats by intracranial implantation of androgen in infancy. J. Comp. Physiol. Psychol. 66, 157–167.

Nathanson, N., Cole, G. A., and Van der Loos, H. 1969. Heterotopic cerebellar granule cells following administration of cyclophosphamide to suckling rats. Brain Res. 15, 532–536.

Nauta, W. J. H. 1964. Some efferent connections of the prefrontal cortex in the monkey. In "The Frontal Granular Cortex and Behavior" (J. M. Warren and K. Akert, eds.), pp. 397–409. McGraw-Hill, New York.

Nauta, W. J. H. 1972. Neural associations of the frontal cortex. Acta Neurobiol. Exp. 32, 125–140.

Neumann, F., and Kramer, M. 1967. Female brain differentiation of male rats as a result of early treatment with an androgen antagonist. In "Hormonal Steroids" (L. Martini, F. Fraschini, and M. Motta, eds.), pp. 932–941. Excerpta Medica, Amsterdam.

Nicholson, J. L., and Altman, J. 1972. The effects of early hypo- and hyper-thyroidism on the development of the rat cerebellar cortex. II. Synaptogenesis in the molecular layer. Brain Res. 44, 25–36.

Paley, S. L., and Chan-Paley, V. 1973. "Cerebellar Cortex: Cytology and Organization," Springer-Verlag, Berlin and New York.

Pandya, D. N., and Kuypers, H. G. J. M. 1969. Cortico-cortical connections in the rhesus monkey. Brain Res. 13, 13–36.

Pandya, D. N., Dye, P., and Butters, N. 1971. Efferent cortico-cortical projections of the prefrontal cortex in the rhesus monkey. Brain Res. 31, 35–46.

Passingham, R. 1975. Delayed matching after selective prefrontal lesions in monkeys (Macaca mulatta). Brain Res. 92, 89–102.

Penfield, W., and Milner, B. 1958. Memory deficit produced by bilateral lesions in the hippocampal zone. A.M.A. Arch. Neurol. Psychiat. 79, 475–497.

Peretz, E., Goy, R. W., Phoenix, C. H., and Resko, J. A. 1971. Influence of gonadal hormones on the development and activation of the nervous system of the rhesus monkey. In "Influence of Hormones on the Nervous System," Proc. Int. Soc. Psychoendocrinol., Brooklyn, 1970, pp. 401–411. Karger, Basel.

Petras, J. M. 1969. Some efferent connections of the motor and somatosensory cortex of simian primates and felid, canid and procyonid carnivores. Ann. N. Y. Acad. Sci. 167, 469–505.

Pettigrew, J. D. 1972. The importance of early visual experience for neurons of the developing geniculostriate system. Invest. Ophthalmol. 11, 386–394.

Pettigrew, J. D. 1974. The effect of visual experience on the development of stimulus specificity by kitten cortical neurons. J. Physiol. (London) 237, 49–74.

Pettigrew, J. D., and Freeman, R. D. 1973. Visual experience without lines: effect on developing cortical neurons. *Science* 182, 599–601.

Pettigrew, J. D., Olson, C., and Hirsch, H. V. B. 1973. Cortical effect of selective visual experience: degeneration or reorganization. *Brain Res.* 51, 345–351.

Pfaff, D. W. 1966. Morphological changes in the brains of adult male rats after neonatal castration. *J. Endocrinol.* 36, 415–416.

Pfeiffer, C. A. 1936. Sexual differences of the hypophyses and their determination by the gonads. *Amer. J. Anat.* 58, 195–225.

Phillips, A. G., and Deol, G. 1973. Neonatal gonadal hormone manipulation and emotionality following septal lesions in weanling rats. *Brain Res.* 60, 55–64.

Phillips, C. G., and Porter, R. 1964. The pyramidal projection to motoneurons of some muscle groups of the baboon's forelimb. *Prog. Brain Res.* 12, 222–242.

Phoenix, C. H., Goy, R. W., Gerall, A. A., and Young, W. C. 1959. Organizing action of prenatally administered testosterone proprionate on the tissues mediating mating behavior in the female guinea pig. *Endocrinology* 65, 369–382.

Phoenix, C. H., Goy, R. W., and Resko, J. A. 1968. Psychosexual differentiation as a function of androgenic stimulation. *In* "Reproduction and Sexual Behavior" (M. Diamond, ed.), pp. 33–49. Indiana Univ. Press, Bloomington, Indiana.

Purpura, D. P. 1975. Dendritic differentiation in human cerebral cortex; normal and aberrant developmental patterns. *Advan. Neurol.* 12, 91–116.

Raisman, G. 1969. Neuronal plasticity in the septal nuclei of the adult rat. *Brain Res.* 14, 25–48.

Raisman, G., and Field, P. M. 1971. Sexual dimorphism in the preoptic area of the rat. *Science* 173, 731–733.

Raisman, G., and Field, P. M. 1973. Sexual dimorphism in the neuropil of the preoptic area of the rat and its dependence on neonatal androgen. *Brain Res.* 54, 1–29.

Raisman, G., Cowan, W. M., and Powell, T. P. S. 1965. The extrinsic afferent commissural and association fibers of the hippocampus. *Brain* 88, 963–996.

Rakic, P. 1971a. Neuron-glia relationship during granule cell migration in developing cerebellar cortex. A Golgi and electronmicroscopic study in Macacus rhesus. *J. Comp. Neurol.* 141, 283–312.

Rakic, P. 1971b. Guidance of neurons migrating to the fetal monkey neocortex. *Brain Res.* 33, 471–476.

Rakic, P. 1972. Mode of cell migration to the superficial layers of fetal monkey neocortex. *J. Comp. Neurol.* 145, 61–84.

Rakic, P. 1973. Kinetics of proliferation and latency between final cell division and onset of differentiation of cerebellar stellate and basket neurons. *J. Comp. Neurol.* 147, 523–546.

Rakic, P. 1974a. Neurons in rhesus monkey visual cortex: systematic relation between time of origin and eventual disposition. *Science* 183, 425–427.

Rakic, P. 1974b. Embryonic development of the pulvinar-LP complex in man. *In* "The Pulvinar-LP Complex" (I. S. Cooper, M. Riklan, and P. Rakic, eds.), pp. 3–35. Thomas, Springfield, Illinois.

Rakic, P. 1975. Timing of major ontogenetic events in the visual cortex of the rhesus monkey. *In* "Brain Mechanisms and Mental Retardation" (N. A. Buchwald and M. A. B. Brazier, eds.), pp. 3–40. Academic Press, New York.

Rakic, P., and Sidman, R. L. 1969. Telencephalic origin of pulvinar neurons in the fetal human brain. *Z. Anat. Entwicklungsgesch.* 129, 53–82.

Rakic, P., and Sidman, R. L. 1970. Histogenesis of cortical layers in human cerebellum, particularly the lamina dissecans. *J. Comp. Neurol.* 139, 473–500.

Rakic, P., and Sidman, R. L. 1973a. Weaver mutant mouse cerebellum: defective neuronal migration secondary to abnormality of Bergmann glia. *Proc. Nat. Acad. Sci.. U.S.* 70, 240–244.

Rakic, P., and Sidman, R. L. 1973b. Sequence of developmental abnormalities leading to granule cell deficit in cerebellar cortex of weaver mutant mice. *J. Comp. Neurol.* 152, 103–132.

Rakic, P., and Sidman, R. L. 1973c. Organization of cerebellar cortex secondary to deficit of granule cells in weaver mutant mice. *J. Comp. Neurol.* 152, 133–162.

Ramón y Cajal, S. 1911. "Histologie du Système Nerveux de l'Homme et des Vertebrés." Maloine, Paris. Reprinted by Consejo Superior de Investigationes Cientificas, 1955. Vol. II, Madrid.

Ramón y Cajal, S. 1928. "Degeneration and Regeneration of the Nervous System" (R. M. May, transl. and ed.), Vol. 1. Oxford Univ. Press, London and New York.

Ramón y Cajal, S. 1960. "Studies on Vertebrate Neurogenesis" (L. Guth, transl.). Thomas, Springfield, Illinois.

Rezai, Z., and Yoon, C. H. 1972. Abnormal rate of granule cell migration in the cerebellum of "weaver" mutant mice. *Develop. Biol.* 29, 17–26.

Riesen, A. H. 1960. Effects of stimulus deprivation on the development and atrophy of the visual sensory system. *Amer. J. Orthopsychiat.* 30, 23–36.

Riesen, A. H. 1961. Stimulation as a requirement for growth and function in behavioral development. *In* "Functions of Varied Experience" (I. W. Fiske and S. R. Maddi, eds.), pp. 57–105. Dorsey Press, Homewood, Illinois.

Riesen, A. 1966. Sensory deprivation. *Progr. Psychol.* 117–147.

Rizzolatti, G., and Tradardi, V. 1971. Pattern discrimination in monocularly reared cats. *Exp. Neurol.* 33, 181–194.

Rose, G. H., and Lindsley, D. B. 1968. Development of visually evoked potentials in kittens: specific and nonspecific responses. *J. Neurophysiol.* 31, 607–623.

Rose, G. H., Gruenau, S. P., and Spencer, J. W. 1972. Maturation of visual electrocortical responses in unanesthetized kittens: effects of barbiturate anesthesia. *Electroenceph. Clin. Neurophysiol.* 33, 141–158.

Rosensweig, M. R. 1971. Effects of environment on development of brain and of behavior. *In* "The Biopsychology of Development" (E. Tobach, L. R. Aronson, and E. Shaw, eds.), pp. 303–342. Academic Press, New York.

Rosvold, H. E. 1968. The prefrontal cortex and caudate nucleus: a system for effecting correction in response mechanisms. *In* "Mind as a Tissue" (C. Rupp, ed.), pp. 21–38. Harper and Row, New York.

Sackett, G. P. 1972. Exploratory behavior of rhesus monkeys as a function of rearing experiences and sex. *Devel. Psychol.* 6, 260–270.

Sauer, M. E., and Walker, B. E. 1959. Radioautographic study of interkinetic nuclear migration in the neural tube. *Proc. Soc. Exp. Biol. Med.* 101, 557–560.

Scheibel, M. E., and Scheibel, A. B. 1972. Maturing neuronal subsystems: the dendrites of spinal motoneurons. *In* "Sleep and the Maturing Nervous System" (C. D. Clemente, D. P. Purpura, and F. E. Mayer, eds.), pp. 49–75. Academic Press, New York.

Schmechel, D. E., and Rakic, P. 1973. Evolution of fetal radial glial cells in rhesus monkey telencephalon: A golgi study. *Anat. Rec.* 175, 436.

Schneider, G. E. 1970. Mechanisms of functional recovery following lesions of visual cortex or superior colliculus in neonate and adult hamsters. *Brain, Behav. Evol.* 3, 295–323.

Schneider, G. E. 1973. Early lesions of superior colliculus: factors affecting the formation of abnormal retinal projections. *In* "Neuromorphological Plasticity" (J. J. Bernstein and D. C. Goodman, eds.). *Brain, Behav. Evol.* 8, 73–109.

Schneirla, T. C. 1957. The concept of development in comparative psychology. In "The Concept of Development" (D. B. Harris, ed.), pp. 78–108. Univ. of Minnesota Press, Minneapolis, Minnesota.

Schulman, S. 1964. Impaired delayed response from thalamic lesions. Arch. Neurol. 11, 477–499.

Scoville, W. B. 1954. The limbic lobe in man. J. Neurosurg. 11, 64–66.

Shapiro, S. 1971a. Hormonal and environmental influences on rat brain development and behavior. In "Brain Development and Behavior" (M. B. Sterman, D. J. McGinty, and A. M. Adinolfi, eds.), pp. 307–334. Academic Press, New York.

Shapiro, S. 1971b. Influence of hormones and environmental stimulation on brain development. In "Influence of Hormones on the Nervous System," Proc. Int. Soc. Psychoneuroendocrinol., Brooklyn, 1970, pp. 63–73. Karger, Basel.

Shapiro, S., and Vukovich, K. R. 1970. Early experience effects upon cortical dendrites: a proposed model for development. Science 167, 292–294.

Sherman, S. M. 1972. Visual development in cats. Invest. Ophthalmol. 11, 394–401.

Shimada, M., and Langman, J. 1970. Cell proliferation, migration and differentiation in the cerebral cortex of the golden hamster. J. Comp. Neurol. 139, 227–244.

Sidman, R. L. 1968. Development of interneuronal connections in brains of mutant mice. In "Physiological and Biochemical Aspects of Nervous Integration" (F. D. Carlson, ed.), pp. 163–193. Prentice-Hall, Englewood Cliffs, New Jersey.

Sidman, R. L. 1970. Cell proliferation, migration and the interaction in the developing mammalian central nervous system. In "The Neurosciences, Second Study Program" (F. O. Schmitt, ed.), pp. 100–107. Rockefeller Univ. Press, New York.

Sidman, R. L. 1972. Cell interactions in developing mammalian central nervous system. In "Cell Interaction" (L. G. Silvestri, ed.), pp. 1–13. North-Holland Publ., Amsterdam.

Sidman, R. L. 1974. Cell-cell recognition in the developing central nervous system. In "The Neurosciences, Third Study Program" (F. O. Schmitt and F. O. Worden, eds.), pp. 743–758. MIT Press, Cambridge, Massachusetts.

Sidman, R. L., and Rakic, P. 1972a. Cell distribution and orientation in the cerebellar cortex of postnatal reeler mutant mice. Cited in Sidman (1972).

Sidman, R. L., and Rakic, P. 1972b. Synaptic organization in the cerebellar cortex of reeler mutant mice. Cited in Sidman (1972).

Sidman, R. L., and Rakic, P. 1973. Neuronal migration, with special reference to developing human brain: a review. Brain Res. 62, 1–35.

Sidman, R. L., Miale, I. I., and Feder, N. 1959. Cell proliferation in the primitive ependymal zone: an autoradiographic study of histogenesis in the nervous system. Exp. Neurol. 1, 322–333.

Sidman, R. L., Lane, P., and Deckie, M. 1962. Staggerer, a new mutation in the mouse affecting the cerebellum. Science 137, 610.

Sidman, R. L., Green, M. C., and Appel, S. H. 1965. "Catalogue of the Neurological Mutants of the Mouse." Harvard Univ. Press, Cambridge, Massachusetts.

Smith, R. L., Steward, O., Cotman, C. W., and Lynch. G. 1975. Evidence for the role of post-lesion neuronal growth in the recovery of spontaneous alternation behavior following entorhinal cortex damage in young and adult rats. In preparation.

Soltmann, O. 1876. Experimentelle studien über die functionen des grossherns der neugeborenen. Jb. Kinderheilk. 9, 106–148.

Sotelo, C., and Palay, S. L. 1971. Altered axons and axon terminals in the lateral vestibular nucleus of the rat. Possible example of axonal remodeling. Lab. Invest. 25, 653–671.

Spencer, R. F., and Coleman, P. D. 1974. Influence of selective visual experience upon the morphological maturation of the visual cortex. Anat. Rec. 178, 469.

Sperry, R. W. 1945. The problem of central nervous reorganization after nerve regeneration and muscle transposition. *Quart. Rev. Biol.* **20**, 311–369.

Sperry, R. W. 1971. How a developing brain gets itself properly wired for adaptive function. *In* "The Biopsychology of Development" (E. Tobach, L. R. Aronson, and E. Shaw, eds.), pp. 27–44. Academic Press, New York.

Sperry, R. W., Gazzaniga, M. S., and Bogen, J. E. 1969. Interhemispheric relationships: the neocortical commissures; syndromes of hemisphere disconnection. *In* "Handbook of Clinical Neurology" (P. J. Venken and G. W. Bruyn, eds.), pp. 273–290. North-Holland Publ., Amsterdam.

Spinelli, D. N., and Hirsch, H. V. B. 1971. Genesis of receptive field shapes in single units of cats' visual cortex. *Fed. Proc.* **30**, 615. (Abstr. No. 2348.)

Spinelli, D. N., Hirsch, H. V. B., Phelps, R. W., and Metzler, J. 1972. Visual experience as a determinant of the response characteristics of cortical receptive fields in cats. *Exp. Brain Res.* **15**, 289–304.

Stein, D. G., Rosen, J. J., Graziadei, J., Mishkin, D., and Brink, J. J. 1969. Central nervous system recovery of function. *Science* **166**, 528–530.

Stein, D. G., Rosen, J. J., and Butters, N., eds. 1974. "Plasticity and Recovery of Function in the Central Nervous System." Academic Press, New York.

Stenevi, U., Bjorkland, A., and Moore, R. Y. 1972. Growth of intact central adrenergic axons in the denervated lateral geniculate body. *Exp. Neurol.* **35**, 290–299.

Steward, O., Cotman, C. W., and Lynch, G. S. 1973. Re-establishment of electrophysiologically functional entorhinal cortical input to the dentate gyrus, deafferented by ipsilateral entorhinal lesions: innervation by the contralateral entorhinal cortex. *Exp. Brain Res.* **18**, 396–414.

Steward, O., Cotman, C. W., and Lynch, G. S. 1974. Growth of a new fiber projection in the brain of adult rats: re-innervation of the dentate gyrus by the contralateral entorhinal cortex following ipsilateral entorhinal lesions. *Exp. Brain Res.* **20**, 45–66.

Stryker, M. P. 1975. Experiments on the development and maintenance of orientation selectivity in the cat's visual cortex. Ph.D. Dissertation, Dept. of Psychology, MIT, Cambridge, Massachusetts.

Stryker, M. P., and Sherk, H. 1975. Modification of cortical orientation selectivity in the cat by restricted visual experience: A reexamination. *Science* **190**, 904–906.

Szabo, J. 1962. Topical distribution of the striatal efferents in the monkey. *Exp. Neurol.* **5**, 21–36.

Szabo, J. 1970. Projections from the body of the caudate nucleus in the rhesus monkey. *Exp. Neurol.* **27**, 1–15.

Taber Pierce, E. 1966. Histogenesis of the nucleus griseum pontis, corporis ponto-bulbaris and reticularis tegmenti pontis (Bechterew) in the mouse. *J. Comp. Neurol.* **126**, 219–240.

Terasawa, E., and Sawyer, C. H. 1969. Electrical and electrochemical stimulation of the hypothalamo-hypophysial system with stainless steel electrodes. *Endocrinology* **84**, 918–925.

Teuber, H-L. 1964. The riddle of frontal lobe function in man. *In* "The Frontal Granular Cortex and Behavior" (J. M. Warren and K. Akert, eds.), pp. 410–444. McGraw-Hill, New York.

Teuber, H-L. 1974. Recovery of function after lesions of the central nervous system: History and prospects. *In* "Functional Recovery after Lesions of the Nervous System" (E. Eidelberg and D. G. Stein, eds.), *Neurosciences Res. Progr. Bull.* **12**, 197–209.

Tinbergen, N. 1974. Ethology and stress disease. *Science* **185**, 20–27.

Tower, S. S. 1940. Pyramidal lesion in the monkey. *Brain* **63**, 36–90.

Travis, A. M., and Woolsey, C. N. 1956. Motor performance of monkeys after bilateral partial and total cerebral decortications. *Amer. J. Phys. Med.* **35**, 273–310.

Tucker, T. J., and Kling, A. 1967. Differential effects of early and late lesions of frontal granular cortex in the monkey. *Brain Res.* **5**, 377–389.

Turner, B. H. 1970. Neural structures involved in the rage syndrome of the rat. *J. Comp. Physiol. Psychol.* **71**, 103–113.

Valenstein, E. S. 1968. Steroid hormones and the neuropsychology of development. *In* "The Neuropsychology of Development" (R. L. Isaacson, ed.), pp. 1–39. Wiley, New York.

Valenstein, E. S., Kakolewski, J. W., and Cox, V. C. 1967. Sex differences in taste preference for glucose and saccharin solutions. *Science* **156**, 942–943.

Valenstein, E. S., Cox, V. C., and Kakolewski, J. W. 1969. Sex differences in hyperphagia and body weight following hypothalamic damage. *Ann. N. Y. Acad. Sci.* **157**, 1030–1046.

Valverde, F. 1967. Apical dendritic spines of the visual cortex and light deprivation in the mouse. *Exp. Brain Res.* **3**, 337–352.

Valverde, F. 1968. Structural changes in the area striata of the mouse after enucleation. *Exp. Brain Res.* **5**, 274–292.

Voeller, K., Pappas, G. D., and Purpura, D. P. 1963. Electron microscope study of development of cat superficial neocortex. *Exp. Neurol.* **7**, 107–130.

Wade, G. N., and Zucker, I. 1969a. Taste preferences of female rats: modification by neonatal hormones, food deprivation and prior experience. *Physiol. Behav.* **4**, 935–943.

Wade, G. N., and Zucker, I. 1969b. Hormonal and developmental influences on rat saccharin preferences. *J. Comp. Physiol. Psychol.* **69**, 291–300.

Walker, A. E., and Fulton, J. F. 1938. Hemi-decortication in chimpanzee, baboon, macaque, potto, cat and coati. A study of encephalization. *J. Nerv. Ment. Dis.* **87**, 677–700.

Wall, P. D., and Egger, M. D. 1971. Formation of new connections in adult rat brains after partial deafferentation. *Nature (London)* **232**, 542–545.

Warkentin, J., and Smith, K. U. 1937. The development of visual acuity in the cat. *J. Genet. Psychol.* **50**, 371–399.

Watson, J. B. 1924. "Behaviorism." Norton, New York.

Weisz, J., and Philpott, J. 1971. Uptake and metabolism of testosterone by the brain of the newborn rat. *In* "Influence of Hormones on the Nervous System," Proc. Int. Soc. Psychoneuroendocrinol., Brooklyn, 1970, pp. 282–295. Karger, Basel.

Welker, W. I., Benjamin, R. M., Miles, R. C., and Woolsey, C. N. 1957. Motor effects of stimulation of cerebral cortex of squirrel monkey *(Saimiri sciureus)*. *J. Neurophysiol.* **20**, 347–364.

Whalen, R. E. 1968. Differentiation of the neural mechanisms which control gonado-tropin secretion and sexual behavior. *In* "Perspectives in Reproductive and Sexual Behavior" (M. Diamond, ed.), pp. 303–340. Indiana Univ. Press, Bloomington, Indiana.

Wiesel, T. N., and Hubel, D. H. 1963a. Single-cell responses in striate cortex of kittens deprived of vision in one eye. *J. Neurophysiol.* **26**, 1003–1017.

Wiesel, T. N., and Hubel, D. H. 1963b. Effects of visual deprivation on morphology and physiology of cells in the cat's lateral geniculate body. *J. Neurophysiol.* **26**, 978–993.

Wiesel, T. N., and Hubel, D. H. 1965. Comparison of the effects of unilateral and bilateral eye closure on cortical unit responses in kittens. *J. Neurophysiol.* **28**, 1029–1040.

Wiesel, T. N., and Hubel, D. H. 1974a. Ordered arrangement of orientation columns in monkeys lacking visual experience. *J. Comp. Neurol.* **138**, 307–318.

Wiesel, T. N., and Hubel, D. H. 1974b. Reorganization of ocular dominance columns in monkey striate cortex. *Program Abstr. Soc. Neurosci.* **478**.

Wikmark, R. G. E. 1974. Maturation of spatial delayed responses to auditory cues in kittens. *J. Comp. Physiol. Psychol.* **86**, 322–327.

Wirth, F. P., O'Leary, J. L., Smith, J. M., and Jenny, A. B. 1974. Monosynaptic corticospinal-motoneuron path in the raccoon. *Brain Res.* **77**, 344–348.

Woolsey, C. N. 1958. Organization of somatic sensory and motor areas of the cerebral cortex. *In* "Biological and Biochemical Basis of Behavior" (H. F. Harlow and C. N. Woolsey, eds.), pp. 63–81. Univ. of Wisconsin Press, Madison, Wisconsin.

Woolsey, C. N., Settlage, P. H., Meyer, D. R., Spencer, W., Pinto-Hamuy, T., and Travis, A. M. 1952. Patterns of localization in precentral and "supplementary" motor areas and their relation to the concept of a premotor area. *Res. Publ. Ass. Nerv. Ment. Dis.* **30**, 238–264.

Young, W. C., Goy, R. W., and Phoenix, C. H. 1964. Hormones and sexual behavior. *Science* **143**, 212–218.

Zimmer, J. 1971. Ipsilateral afferents to the commissural zone of the fascia dentata demonstrated in decommissurated rats by silver impregnation. *J. Comp. Neurol.* **142**, 393–416.

Zimmer, J., and Hjorth-Simonsen, A. 1975. Crossed pathways from the entorhinal area to the fascia dentata II. Provokable in rats. *J. Comp. Neurol.* **161**, 71–102.

Zucker, I. 1969. Hormonal determinants of sex differences in saccharin preference, food intake and body weight. *Physiol. Behav.* **4**, 595–602.

Functional Analysis of Masculine
Copulatory Behavior in the Rat

BENJAMIN D. SACHS

DEPARTMENT OF PSYCHOLOGY
THE UNIVERSITY OF CONNECTICUT
STORRS, CONNECTICUT

AND

RONALD J. BARFIELD

DEPARTMENT OF BIOLOGY
LIVINGSTON COLLEGE
RUTGERS UNIVERSITY
NEW BRUNSWICK, NEW JERSEY

I. INTRODUCTION

For 20 years the prevailing framework for the discussion of data on the masculine copulatory behavior of animals has been the model proposed by Frank A. Beach (1956; Beach and Jordan, 1956). In reaction to the prevailing tendency at that time to treat "sex drive" as a unitary motivational system, Beach pointed out that the data on the male rat's copulatory behavior could not be adequately handled without postulating at least two underlying factors—one for initiation of copulation, the other for maintenance of copulation and achievement of ejaculation. No one, least of all Beach himself, believed the model he proposed at that time could explain everything, nor have investigators hesitated to revise or add hypothetical factors (e.g., Beach *et al.,* 1966; Beach and Whalen, 1959a, b; Cherney and Bermant, 1970; Clemens, undated; McGill, 1965). Yet the form of the theory that continues to be most frequently cited is the original, commonly referred to as the *dual-factor model.* The durability of the dual-factor approach no doubt has derived in part from its precedence, its parsimony, and to a certain extent its plasticity. In view of recent renewed interest in models of copulatory behavior (Carlsson and Larsson, 1974; Freeman and McFarland, 1974; Karen, 1973, 1975; Kurtz and Adler, 1973; Malsbury and Pfaff, 1974; Pollak, 1974; Sachs and Barfield, 1974), it seemed timely for a thorough reconsideration of this behavior. In this chapter we shall analyze the masculine copulatory behavior of the rat. Our major concern is with the behavioral elements, the temporal patterning of the elements, and the functional relations among the elements. Another goal of this chapter is to indicate how this functional analysis speaks to some of the models that have been developed. We can not at this stage present a comprehensive model, but we shall call attention to phenomena that models, whether based upon hypothetical or physiological mechanisms, must account for, and we shall indicate some characteristics that such models are likely to have.

II. DESCRIPTION OF COPULATION

A. BRIEF DESCRIPTION

Copulation in rats consists of a series of intermittent mounts, during which the male briefly inserts his penis into the female's vagina. During the last insertion of the series the male ejaculates. An inactive period follows, and then the male resumes copulation; he may ejaculate several times in a 1-hour period. Such a brief description masks numerous complex processes. Analysis of these processes and their organization requires more precise description and measurement of the behavior.

We should emphasize that it is not just the behavioral scientist who counts mounts, intromissions, and ejaculations, or who measures the time intervals between them. The neuroendocrine system of the mating female also makes these counts and measures these intervals. For example, pregnancy in female rats does not result simply from transfer of live sperm from penis to vagina. Rather, the female requires a minimal number of intromissions (Adler, 1969), an optimal range of intervals between intromissions (Edmonds et al., 1972), and a minimal period of sexual inactivity after she receives an ejaculation (Adler and Zoloth, 1970). Similar effects have been described for other rodent species (Davis et al., 1974; Gray et al., 1974; McGill, 1974; Diamond, 1970, 1972). In general, the requirements of the female for maximizing pregnancy coincide with the behavioral tendencies of the male of the species. Thus, the discovery of this metric capacity of females has led to significant contributions to our understanding of reproductive biology and of species-isolating mechanisms (Dewsbury, 1972; Diakow, 1974; Diamond, 1970, 1972; McGill, 1974) and has demonstrated again the value of precision in behavioral description and measurement.

A more complete description of a copulatory sequence is necessary in order to point out the behavioral features that allow one to distinguish among copulatory acts and to introduce the measures that are commonly applied to the behavior.[1] In subsequent sections we shall present more precise morphological and behavioral descriptions of specific elements in the copulatory sequence as a means of arriving at a thorough analysis. It should be emphasized that we are

---

[1] Indeed, the development of behavioral criteria for distinguishing among mounts without insertion, mounts with insertion, and mounts with insertion and ejaculation was a major landmark in the subsequent analysis of copulatory behavior. Stone and Ferguson (1940) made these distinctions, but not entirely correctly. They assumed that all mounts with thrust were insertions. It is not certain who discovered the correct basis for the distinctions.

focusing on the behavior of the male laboratory rat as it is commonly studied. We shall not be describing the female's behavior in any detail, nor the synchronization of her behavior with the male's. These are important problems which have received attention recently in a number of reports (Diakow, 1975; Doty, 1974; McClintock and Adler, 1974; Pfaff and Lewis, 1974; Pfaff *et al.*, 1972), but they are beyond the scope of the present review.

B. EXTENDED DESCRIPTION

1. Initiation of Copulation

In the usual testing situation, a male is placed in a testing cage for about 5 minutes, and then a receptive female is placed with him. After a period of mutual investigation, often with sexual solication by the female, the male mounts her from the rear, palpates her flanks with his forelegs, and thrusts his penis rapidly and repeatedly (10 to 40 msec intervals between thrusts). If no insertion occurs the act is referred to as a *mount*. Following a mount the male dismounts, usually grooms his penis with his mouth, and then mounts again. Penile insertion, or *intromission*, is identifiable by one or more of the following acts: a long (200 to 400 msec), deep thrust after the rapid shallow thrusts; a rapid kick with one hindleg; a marked lateral withdrawal of the male's forelimbs from the female's flanks; and a short-stepped rapid posterior withdrawal of the male from the female. Genital grooming follows an intromission almost invariably; but since grooming also follows most mounts, grooming cannot be used to distinguish reliably between mounts with and without intromissions. The time from the introduction of the female to the first sexual act (mount or intromission) is the *mount latency*. The interval from introduction of the female to first intromission is termed the *intromission latency*.

2. Pacing of Copulation

After the initial latency, mounts and intromissions recur at fairly regular intervals. The most common measure of copulatory rate is the *interintromission* (or intercopulatory) *interval* (III), the average interval between intromissions. There are occasions, however, when this measure is misleading or useless. For example, some years ago we observed that in castrated male rats that were incapable of achieving intromission there was still a clear periodicity in their *attempts* to copulate. They exhibited clusters, or bouts, of 1 to 5 mounts within a short period (2 to 10 sec), separated by longer periods (30 to 90 sec) free of mounts. The intervals between clusters were similar to the males' precastration interintromission intervals.

These observations suggested to us that the temporal organization of bouts of mounting might be basic to the male's mating behavior. In order to test this hypothesis an operational definition of a mount bout was needed. The observed periodicity could obviously not be described by the interintromission interval, and the average interval between mounts misrepresented the substantial clustering of mounts. We noted that within clusters of mounts males rarely engaged in any activity other than genital grooming or some female-oriented activity. This observation gave us a behavioral basis for defining a *mount bout* as a sequence of one or more mounts, with or without intromission, that is not interrupted by any noncopulatory behavior except genital grooming or orientation of the male toward the female. A mount bout was ruled to be terminated by the last sexual act preceding any "extraneous" activity such as grooming other parts of the body, cage exploration, digging, and lying down. Mount periodicity could then be measured by: (1) the *mount-bout period,* the average time from the first sexual act (mount or intromission) of one bout to the first act of the next bout; and (2) *time out,* the time from the last act of one bout to the first act of the next bout. Later (Section V,B,1) we shall review some studies demonstrating the utility of these measures, but in general they are useful, even necessary, whenever the number of intromissions per mount bout differs significantly from 1.0. Recently Larsson (1973) tethered receptive females in an arena with copulating

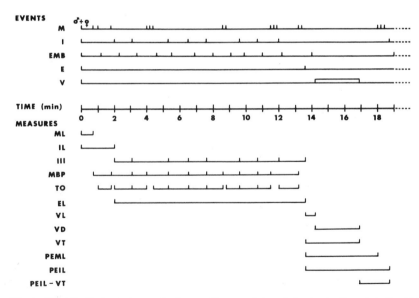

Fig. 1. Hypothetical event record of masculine copulatory behavior in the rat, indicating the major events and measures of their temporal patterning. Abbreviations: M, mount; I, intromission; EMB, end-of-mount-bout behavior; E, ejaculation; V, vocalization; ML, mount latency; IL, intromission latency; III, interintromission interval; MBP, mount-bout period; TO, time out; EL, ejaculation latency; VL, vocalization latency; VD, vocalization duration; VT, vocalization termination; PEML, postejaculatory mount latency; PEIL, postejaculatory intromission latency. Temporal measures would be taken as the intervals (or the average of the intervals) between connected vertical ticks.

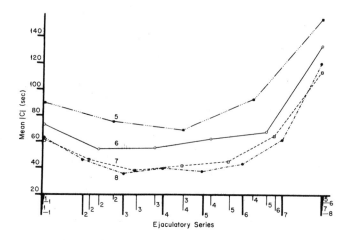

Fig. 2

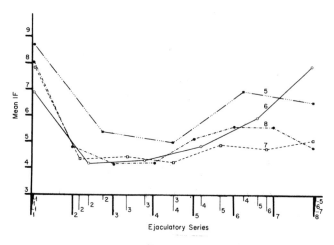

Fig. 3

Figs. 2–5. Intercopulatory interval (ICI, Fig. 2), number of intromissions (IF, Fig. 3), ejaculation latency (EL, Fig. 4), and postejaculatory intromission latency (PEI, Fig. 5) in each ejaculatory series for male rats tested to a criterion of sexual exhaustion. The four curves represent groups of males attaining 5, 6, 7, and 8 ejaculations prior to reaching criterion (N = 11, 7, 12, and 6, respectively). The abscissas are drawn so that the course of exhaustion for all groups may be depicted full scale. [From Karen and Barfield (1975). Copyright 1975 by the American Psychological Association. Reprinted by permission.]

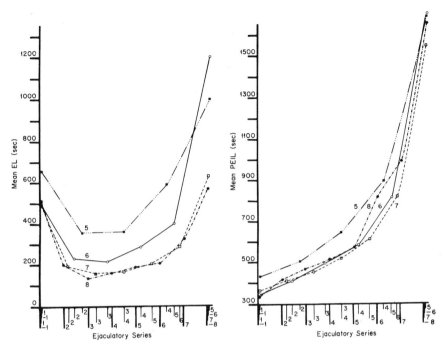

Figs. 4 and 5. See facing page for legend.

males. The time intervals between "visits" of the male to the female seem to correspond closely to the periodicity of mount bouts as we have measured them.

3. Ejaculation and Postejaculatory Behavior

After a number of intromissions the male mounts again, gains penile insertion, and ejaculates sperm and a coagulated seminal "plug" into the vagina. Ejaculation is identifiable by a terminal pelvic thrust that is slower and deeper than that of an intromission, a reduction in the elevation of the hindleg (Hart, 1968), a lateral removal of the arms that is slower than after mounts and intromissions and is held for a moment at the apex, and an absence of backstepping before genital grooming. The time from first intromission to ejaculation is the *ejaculation latency.* The number of intromissions preceding ejaculation is commonly termed the *intromission frequency,* but since that sounds like a rate measure rather than a count, we shall use *number of intromissions* in this chapter.

It should be emphasized that from the lateral view it is rarely possible to see the genitalia during a copulatory event. Therefore, the observer must usually rely on the animal's body movements to distinguish among mounts, intromissions, and ejaculations. In some experimental preparations the movements of the body belie the genital events occurring, and in these cases it is proper to refer to *intromission pattern* and *ejaculation pattern,* rather than to intromission and ejaculation per se.

After the first ejaculation there is a 4- to 8-minute period with no copulatory activity, but this time is not devoid of behavior. Dewsbury (1967a) has described some of the activities occurring during this interval, but we should like to emphasize one behavior of the male. Beginning about 30 seconds after ejaculation, the male begins to vocalize (Barfield and Geyer, 1972, 1975). The vocalization is a phasic, relatively pure tone beyond the range of most humans' hearing, at 22–23 kHz. When the animal is still, a bellows-like breathing movement of the flanks occurs synchronously with vocalization. The vocalization continues for about 3 to 4 minutes after the first ejaculation. We shall return to postejaculatory behavior later (Section VII).

The time from ejaculation to the next mount is the *postejaculatory mount latency* (PEML), and the interval between ejaculation and the next intromission is the *postejaculatory intromission latency* (PEIL). Each sequence from mount to ejaculation is called a *copulatory series,* and the measures for each series may be identified by the number of series (e.g., III-2, PEML-3).

Tests may continue until no copulatory acts occur for an arbitrary period, usually 30 to 60 minutes. At this point the male is referred to as *sexually exhausted.* Males commonly reach this state after 6 to 10 ejaculations.

A summary of copulatory events and their measurement is depicted in Fig. 1. Figures 2–5 present data on four measures of males copulating to sexual exhaustion (Karen and Barfield, 1975).

III. INITIATION OF COPULATION

A. INITIATION LATENCIES AND AROUSABILITY

Why does a male start copulating when he does? That is, what factors in the male determine the duration of the mount and intromission latencies in mating tests? Most models have dealt with this question only tangentially (Kurtz and Adler, 1973) or not at all (Freeman and McFarland, 1974; Sachs and Barfield, 1974). Beach (1942a, 1956) considered this question in considerable detail, and we may begin this analysis with a summary of his early formulations.

Beach (1956) postulated that the period prior to mating is under the control of a process called the "sexual arousal mechanism" (SAM). The SAM had its origin in the earlier concept of the "central excitatory mechanism" (Beach, 1942a), and later (Beach and Jordan, 1956) it was simply called the "arousal mechanism." This process was viewed as bringing the male to the threshold for initiation of copulation. The rate of approach to that threshold was believed to be determined by the male's intrinsic arousability and by extrinsic sources of stimulation (Beach, 1942a). Thus, highly arousable males will mount immobilized females, whereas less arousable males will require considerable stimulation from highly proceptive[2] females before starting copulation.

A central question here concerns the potential distinction between sexual arousability, as measured primarily by mount and intromission latencies, and nonsexual arousability, however that might be measured. We use the terms *arousability* and *excitability* interchangeably to refer to the animal's rate of approach to a threshold. That rate will vary among individuals, and from time to time within individuals, e.g., circadian rhythms of excitability. By *arousal* we mean the animal's momentary level of excitation relative to a threshold. These definitions differ somewhat from those of Whalen (1966). For a discussion of the many uses of these terms, see Andrew (1974).

In most studies of copulatory behavior no measures are made of noncopulatory activity. However, in a series of studies on the effects of pharmacological agents, Malmnäs (1973) evaluated each drug for its effect on motor activity as well as on sexual behavior. Several treatments yielded opposite effects on these variables. For example, *para*-chlorophenylalanine (a chemical that reduces the levels of certain neurotransmitters, especially serotonin) sharply depressed locomotion and sharply potentiated copulation. In other cases drugs affected locomotion and copulation in the same direction. An unusually short period was allowed for the males to begin mounting in these tests, so the data must be viewed with some caution. Still, the fact that one can observe heightened sexual activity in an animal that shows reduced nonsexual locomotor activity suggests that sexual arousal can be dissociated from other kinds of arousal. It would appear appropriate to retain the modifying word *sexual* when discussing the arousal mechanism underlying the initiation of copulation, rather than assume it reflects a *general* arousal mechanism.

Another approach to the question of the relation of sexual arousal to other forms of arousal would be to evaluate the effects of nonsexual motivational states upon copulatory behavior. There are surprisingly few relevant studies. It had been expected that food deprivation would reduce sexual arousability (Herberg, 1963; Olds, 1958). Sachs (1965) found that mount latencies increased when males were starved for up to 9 days before a mating test, but few other variables were affected among those males that copulated at all. The delay in mating could be interpreted in terms of competing attention to food cues in the test cage, e.g., shavings, boluses (Hinde, 1970). However, in a subsequent study (Sachs and Marsan, 1972) males were tested with simultaneous access to a

[2] Proceptive behavior refers to the seeking of copulation by such acts as darting and hopping that potentiate mounting by males. This behavior is usefully distinguished from *receptive* behavior, which refers to the acceptance of mounts by appropriate postures, and from *attractivity*, which refers to the desirability of the female to the male (Beach, 1976).

receptive female and to food which was spread over the cage floor. Again, longer periods of prior starvation led to longer mount latencies, but of the males that copulated at all few ate during this extended latency. In fact, most males copulated to at least one ejaculation before eating any food. Larsson (1956) has observed similar effects. Copulation appears to have precedence over eating in males capable of copulation.

Studies of noncopulating males offer further evidence on the question of the separability of sexual arousability from nonsexual arousability. Noncopulators are males that do not mate within an arbitrary time limit. Many of these males can become copulators, and so we may ask why such males do not copulate within the time limit allowed. Their deficiency may result from inadequate sexual arousability, reduced "general" arousability, inability to overcome competing activities during the latency period, or other factors. We are discussing here only persistent noncopulators. Many males may not copulate during their first sex test, although from their behavior they appear to be highly aroused: they actively investigate the female, climb over and under her, and run around the cage. Such males commonly copulate with short latencies in subsequent tests. Other males do little exploring of the female or the cage, and it is these males that are likely to be persistent nonmaters.

According to the formulation of Beach (1942a), noncopulators may be males of very low arousability. Is the reduced arousability a general condition, or is it specific to sexual stimuli? Pottier and Baran (1973) compared persistent noncopulators (a stringent criterion was used) with copulators in a number of nonsexual behavior tests, such as open-field activity and exploration of novel objects in the home cage. The noncopulators were also less reactive in these tests, indicating a more general syndrome of reduced arousability than simply sexual hyporeactivity. Presumably even highly attractive and proceptive females are inadequate stimuli to bring such males to the copulatory threshold within a reasonable time. However, additional extrinsic arousing stimuli can cause such males to start mating. Beach (1942a, p. 175) reported that a sluggish male "can sometimes be aroused to renewed copulatory activity if he is batted sharply about the cage by the experimenter." Years later this observation was formalized in several experimental studies. A higher percentage of males copulated in their first sex test when intermittent tail shock was applied than when no additional arousal was induced (Caggiula, 1972; Caggiula and Eibergen, 1969; Goldfoot and Baum, 1972), and copulation was induced in persistent noncopulators by painful peripheral shock (Caggiula and Eibergen, 1969; Malsbury, 1972; Malsbury and Pfaff, 1974). Crowley et al. (1973) carried these findings a step further. A neutral stimulus that did not itself affect mating in noncopulators gained the potential to induce and pace mating by being paired first with painful shock outside the testing situation. Thus, pain and stimuli associated with pain can effectively reduce mount latencies below the supracriterion levels characteristic of noncopulators. Later (Section V,B,2,a) we shall consider the effects of painful stimulation on copulation itself.

A common procedure is to place male rats into the testing cage a few minutes before the female is introduced. This treatment is commonly described as an adaptation period. If nonsexual stimuli can potentiate copulation, why should the male benefit from a period during which the male is presumably becoming less aroused by the novel cues in the cage? Presumably, after a period of cage exploration, cues from an estrous female would be more salient, reducing the chance that exploration would compete with copulation. In that case males tested in their home cage, already thoroughly explored, should have faster mount latencies, and this hypothesis has been confirmed (Bemmels, 1971). The adaptation period may also give time for the male to be sexually aroused by cues in the test cage, and therefore to mount more quickly when the female enters. Some of the cage cues may be unconditioned olfactory stimuli, since the cages are rarely cleaned between mating tests. Other cues from the cage, and from the handling that precedes placement in the cage, may become associated with copulation and act as conditioned arousers. Such a conditioned arousal to the test cage has been demonstrated (Beach and Fowler, 1959) and may contribute to an understanding of the common observation that mount latencies are shorter for experienced males than for inexperienced males (Dewsbury, 1969).

Beach (1956, p. 22) analyzed the underlying processes in the initiation of sexual behavior as follows:

> It is as though two opposing processes were occurring simultaneously. On the one hand, the male is reacting positively to the stimuli associated with the receptive female. Continuous exposure to these stimuli tends to produce increasing excitement until the copulatory threshold is reached. . . . At the same time, there is a tendency for the male to become habituated or adapted to the visual, olfactory, and tactile cues provided by the female, and therefore they gradually lose their power to evoke excitement. If mating is to occur, the trend toward increasing arousal must reach the copulatory threshold before the habituation produces too great a reduction in reactivity to erotic stimuli.

In fact, males have been exposed to copulating females for 40 minutes without changing the intromission latency, once access to the females was allowed (Härd and Larsson, 1970). Still, some such process as Beach postulated may account for the effectiveness of another method commonly used to induce males to begin copulating. A male that has not copulated with one female will often start copulating soon after the stimulus female is changed (Stone and Ferguson, 1940). Presumably, a change in the female can simultaneously increase sexual arousal and reduce habituation, thereby potentiating copulation. An alternative explanation, namely, that individual differences exist among females in their attractiveness to males, can not account for all of this effect because simply removing the female and replacing her is often also effective (Beach, 1942b). Numerous studies have examined the effectiveness of female changes after one or more ejaculations, but to our knowledge none has systematically explored the effects of change of female prior to the start of copulation.

B. GATING FROM PRECOPULATORY TO COPULATORY BEHAVIOR

Prior to reaching the copulatory threshold the male may display a variety of precopulatory actions, but as described by Beach (1956, p. 23): "This behavior disappears with dramatic suddenness as soon as one or two successful copulations have occurred. Now the male proceeds rather calmly and methodically to mount and penetrate the female at regular intervals until ejaculation occurs. It looks very much as though the behavior has come under the control of a new mechanism which is here designated the *IEM* [intromission and ejaculatory mechanism]."

This dramatic shift, from precopulatory behavior to copulation itself, was part of the reason Beach rejected a unitary "sex drive" and hypothesized a minimum of two relatively independent mechanisms, with the sexual arousal mechanism controlling initiation and ejaculation. Since an intromission requires well-aimed thrusting, well-timed erection, and cooperation on the part of the female, the mount latency may be considered a "purer" measure of motivation, and the intromission latency a measure that reflects motivational and performance components (Cherney and Bermant, 1970; Pfaff and Zigmond, 1971). We should like to emphasize here, however, that activity prior to the first mount is necessarily performance as well. As we noted, inexperienced males may spend substantial time investigating stimulus females, often with more intensity than experienced males. On the other hand, some experienced males may do little investigating, may even remain lying down for a long period before suddenly getting up and mounting the female with few preliminaries. For such experienced males, it is as if copulation were suddenly "switched on," or "gated." For actively investigating, inexperienced males, the deficit is clearly not in arousal itself, nor in copulation itself, but may be in gating the copulatory patterns: if such a male is pinched on the tail he will often start mounting immediately. Again, it is as if the pinch gated copulation. Similarly, males with lesions in the medial forebrain bundle stop copulating. With such males changing the female, tail shock, and other forms of stimulations will induce approach to the female and anogenital investigation but rarely mounts with thrust (Caggiula *et al.*, 1973). Such a deficit may be viewed as inadequate net sexual arousal, but it may also indicate an inability to gate adequate arousal into appropriate copulatory behavior. In a related preparation, Malsbury (1971) placed electrodes into the preoptic region (an area of the forebrain) of inexperienced males. Other investigators had shown that electrical stimulation of this region in experienced males potentiated copulation (Malsbury, 1971; Van Dis and Larsson, 1971; Vaughan and Fisher, 1962). Malsbury found that preoptic stimulation was ineffective in sexually naive males. They appeared aroused and approached the females but did not mount. Painful stimulation to the skin, however, rapidly led to mounts, and only then was preoptic stimulation also effective. Malsbury and Pfaff (1974) suggested that preoptic stimulation may cause genital sensations that are like those received during copulation, and such stimulation may lead to copulation only in animals which have experienced these sensations during copulation. This is an intriguing hypothesis but leaves unanswered the question as to why painful peripheral stimulation can gate copulation without prior experience. Unfortunately, we cannot yet answer this question. It is clear, however, that once copulation is gated, once one or two intromissions have occurred spontaneously or have been induced with extrinsic stimuli like painful shock, then the probability of subsequent intromissions occurring is greatly increased. Such a situation suggests a positive feedback loop. Positive feedback was implicit in Beach's view (1956; Beach and Jordan, 1956) and was made explicit in the recent model of Freeman and McFarland (1974).

C. RELATION OF INITIATION LATENCIES TO OTHER
MEASURES OF COPULATORY BEHAVIOR

The proposition that the processes controlling initiation and maintenance of copulation are relatively independent is supported by studies showing that damage to a number of central nervous system structures may increase initiation latencies while leaving unaffected or potentiating other copulatory variables. Partial decortication (Larsson, 1962, 1964), hippocampal lesions (Dewsbury et al., 1968), and destruction of various posterior hypothalamic areas (Caggiula et al., 1973) all have been found to increase mount or intromission latencies without producing inhibitory effects on other variables of copulatory behavior. Destruction of the olfactory bulbs also tends only to delay the start of copulation (Heimer and Larsson, 1967; Larsson, 1969).[3]

Beach (1956) used intercorrelations among variables as one means for inferring

[3] This effect is relatively small in sexually experienced males, but the effect is magnified when the surgery is done upon mature inexperienced males (Bermant and Taylor, 1969) or prepubertally, especially if the males are then raised in social isolation (Wilhelmsson and Larsson, 1974). When the bulbectomy is done during the neonatal period (day 5), however, no reliable effects upon copulatory behavior are detectable (Pollak and Sachs, 1975b; A. Lumia, personal communication, 1975).

which variables might be controlled by the same hypothetical mechanism. To our knowledge no one has published a factor analysis of a set of normative data from exhaustion tests. Such an analysis could potentially inform us about which measures are redundant (e.g., those which correlate 0.90 or more), and the minimum number of hypothetical factors might be inferred from the number of clusters of variables.

Inferences about dependence or independence among the processes underlying certain variables may also be based upon correlations among measures for the behavior of several inbred strains, in a way analogous to the correlations among individuals. This type of analysis for mouse strains was used for this purpose by McGill (1965; see also Section VII,A). Data on rats have recently become available (Dewsbury, 1975b) for four strains and their reciprocal crosses. Among the parental strains, the F344 had the longest mean initiation latencies (mount latency, 239 sec; intromission latency, 359 sec), but males of this strain also had the shortest mean interintromission intervals and postejaculatory latencies. This inverse relation between preintromission and postintromission variables was not, however, characteristic among the twelve F_1 genotypes resulting from the reciprocal crosses. For these genotypes the rank-order correlation between mount latency and interintromission interval was +0.64 ($t = 2.66$; $df = 10$; $p < 0.05$). From other data we have reviewed we agree that initiation and main-tenance of copulation may result from relatively independent processes, as Beach (1956) indicated, but these interstrain correlational data suggest that some more general process may be reflected in all phases of copulatory behavior.

IV. GENITAL EVENTS DURING COPULATION

MACDUFF: What three things does drink especially provoke?
PORTER: Marry, sir, nose-painting, sleep, and urine. Lechery, sir, it provokes, and unprovokes; it provokes the desire, but it takes away the performance; therefore much drink may be said to be an equivocator with lechery: it makes him, and it mars him; it sets him on, and it takes him off; it persuades him, and disheartens him; makes him stand to, and not stand to; in conclusion, equivocates him in a sleep, and, giving him the lie, leaves him. (*Macbeth,* Act II, Scene 2)

In this passage Shakespeare documented his recognition that impotence is not synonymous with inadequate sexual desire. The genital events associated with erection and ejaculation may be dissociated from other behavioral signs of sexual arousal, and this means that they are at least partially under independent control. When a male rat mounts a receptive female he usually gains insertion. What controls the occurrence of erection and intromission? What exactly are the genital events associated with mounts, intromissions, and ejaculations?

A. DESCRIPTION FROM VISUAL AND ELECTRICAL
   MONITORING OF COPULATION

As we noted earlier, the genitals are rarely visible during copulation, and so one must generally rely upon other body movements to discriminate among genital events. This level of description is adequate for many purposes, but incomplete description necessarily leads to incomplete understanding.

The limitations of our normal perspective of copulating rats have been overcome with a number of techniques that have answered some questions and raised others. Analyses of genital events have been based upon slow-motion photography (Stone and Ferguson, 1940; Bermant, 1965; Diakow, 1975; Pfaff and Lewis, 1974), ventral viewing (Larsson, 1956; Larsson and Södersten, 1973), electrical detection of moist genital contacts (Peirce and Nuttall, 1961a; Bermant et al., 1969), and combinations of these techniques. These analyses have revealed that mounts are accompanied by an average of 3 or 4 brief shallow thrusts during which vaginal penetration does not occur. These thrusts may be followed by a single deep ballistic thrust which marks intromission itself. The total duration of vaginal penetration is 200 to 350 msec. Bermant (1965) endorsed Beach's (1942d) suggestion that the shallow thrusts serve a detection function, whereas the penile-vaginal contact during the deep thrust provides the stimulation that ultimately causes the male to ejaculate. It would seem obvious that it is the penis itself that detects the location of the vagina during the preliminary thrusts, especially since application of topical anesthetics to the penis prevents intromission (Carlsson and Larsson, 1964; Adler and Bermant, 1966; Sachs and Barfield, 1970). However, Larsson and Södersten (1973) tested male rats with the dorsal penile nerve cut and an anesthetic (5% lidocaine) applied to the glans. Such males continued to display a high rate of intromission patterns, higher even than intact males with lidocaine applied. Larsson and Södersten concluded that nonpenile sources of stimulation contribute to triggering the intromission thrust. However, Lodder and Zeilmaker (1976) severed the pudendal nerve, of which the dorsal penile nerve is a branch, and found that this deafferentation eliminated intromission patterns. They concluded that the penile nerves of the intromitting rats of Larsson and Södersten (1973) had regenerated prior to postsurgical testing.

During the preliminary thrusts the penis is generally visible outside its sheath, but its length is rather variable (Fig. 6). When the male withdraws from the female after intromission, the extension of the penis is quite marked (Fig. 7), and it has commonly been assumed that this extension represents maximum erection of the penis. (As we shall see shortly, this conclusion is unwarranted on several grounds.) During the male's postcopulatory genital grooming, the penis becomes withdrawn into its sheath (Fig. 8). Hart and Haugen (1971) demonstrated that if the male is prevented from engaging in genital autogrooming

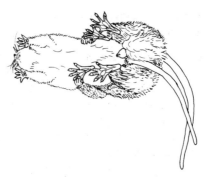

Fig. 6. Ventral view of copulating rats during preintromissive thrusts, traced from a projection of a single "frame" of videotape. The male's pelage has been emphasized to help distinguish him from the female. The head and most of the anterior portion of the male are above, and obscured by, the female. The male's forepaws are gripping the female's flanks, and the penis is partially extended.

during copulation, then the penis does not withdraw fully and shows repeated "flips" between intromissions. (Other parameters of copulatory behavior remain unaffected. Apparently the oral-genital contact does not contribute to ejaculatory excitement, as had sometimes been suspected.)

B. DESCRIPTION BASED ON OSCILLOSCOPIC MONITORING

The precise measurement of the timing and patterning of genital events occurring prior to or during intromission has been accomplished with the inertia-free system of a cathode ray tube. Thus the lag time of conventional relay circuits was avoided, and clear evidence on the number and duration of preliminary thrusts as well as the intromission itself has been obtained.

Fig. 7. Ventral view of rats immediately after intromission, traced from a projection of a single "frame" of videotape. The male's forepaws have moved up and away from the female. The penis is partially retracted by the time it is withdrawn from the vagina.

Fig. 8. Ventral view of male rat grooming his penis after intromission, traced from a projection of a single "frame" of videotape. The act of grooming stimulates the full withdrawal of the penis into its sheath.

Karen (1975) utilized a circuit in which opposing poles of a 100-μA, 1.0-V (*max.*) constant current source were connected so that current flowed only when the male and female were in physical contact. Since the voltage changes in the current are inversely proportional to the electrical resistance between the male and female, the contact of the moist genital membranes can be easily monitored on an oscilloscope. This technique indicates that an intromission is composed of a series of shallow thrusts at 20- to 40-msec intervals, followed by an insertion of 200 to 350 msec. The typical number of preinsertion thrusts is 1 to 3, although it can range from 0 to at least 6.

The oscilloscopic technique was employed in an effort to analyze the stimulus determinants of intromission duration (Karen, 1975). The penis was anesthetized with tetracaine, and the male was permitted to recover to a point where the ability to obtain intromission just returned. Under these conditions both the number of thrusts and the duration of insertions were elevated. During this period of partial anesthetization the male may have been compensating for reduced genital sensation by prolonging the duration of his intromissions. This effect however was quite transitory. Once the ability to copulate successfully returned the durations declined by the fifth intromission to control levels, and the total duration of penis-vaginal contact occurring prior to an ejaculation did not differ significantly between control and partial anesthesia conditions. The same steep decline in anesthesia effectiveness was also noted by Adler and Bermant (1966).

A similar technique was employed to analyze 92 intromissions and 12 ejaculations displayed by 3 males (B. Sachs and M. Milkovic, unpublished data, 1974). Approximately 20% of the recorded intromissions occurred without preliminary thrusts. Since some moist contact was required for triggering, it is possible that some perivaginal thrusts went undetected, but later analysis of videotapes of ventral views supports the conclusion that intromissions do not require preliminary thrusting. Most intromissions followed one or two detectable thrusts. With only three exceptions, successive thrusts lasted progressively longer. Typically the first thrust had a 30-msec duration, the second a 40-msec duration, and so on. The duration of the deep thrust was, on the average, 251, 257, and 287 msec for the three males. In two of the males the deep thrust bore a reliable negative relation to the number and duration of the preliminary thrusts ($r = -0.70$, -0.44, and -0.26 for the three males). It is as if time or effort invested in preliminary thrusts is "deducted" from the time of the deep thrust. On the other hand, in none of the males was there a reliable relation between intromission duration and the duration of the preceding or following interintromission interval.

C. EXTRAVAGINAL INTROMISSION PATTERNS AND EJACULATIONS

Another approach to understanding the genital events associated with copulation is by analysis of extravaginal intromission patterns and ejaculations (Pollak and Sachs, 1973, 1976). Extravaginal ejaculations have frequently been observed and reported. For example, Larsson (1956) noted that ejaculation outside, rather than within, the vagina was potentiated when longer-than-normal intervals between intromissions were imposed by the experimenter. Extravaginal intromission patterns (XVIPs) have also been observed, but they have not previously been recognized for what they are, owing to the normal lateral perspective. The XVIP has the normal distinctive features of intromission, except that ventral viewing reveals that penetration of the vagina does not occur.

In a study on the sensory basis of temporal patterning of copulation (Sachs and Barfield, 1970), males attempted copulation with females that had their vaginas surgically closed. (The receptive and proceptive behavior of such females appears undiminished. In contrast, females often spend a good deal of time trying to remove tape when that material has been used to prevent penetration.) We were astonished that some males would still display intromission patterns. Additional surgical closure did not effectively reduce these apparent intromissions. Hård and Larsson (1968a) tested males with females that had their vaginas sewn shut, and they discarded some male subjects that displayed intromission patterns.

It is now clear that the display of the intromission pattern is not a completely reliable indicator that penile insertion has occurred. Pollak and Sachs (1973, 1976) analyzed slow-motion videotape records of ventral views of normal copulation and discovered that some responses that were scored as intromissions were unaccompanied by vaginal penetration. For more systematic study, 5 males were assigned to each of 3 groups. In one group the males' penes were swabbed with 5% lidocaine. A second group of males was untreated, but the vaginas of their stimulus females were surgically closed. The third group served as untreated controls. All responses were monitored laterally and ventrally by eye and by videotape record for subsequent analysis.

None of the control males exhibited the XVIP, and among the lidocaine-treated males only one exhibited a single XVIP. However, 4 of the 5 males mating with closed-vagina females displayed a total of 10 XVIPs in the 15-minute test, and one of these males showed an additional 12 XVIPs during a 60-minute ad hoc extension of the test.

The XVIP is characterized by penile extension more than twice that seen during preliminary thrusting or after withdrawal from insertion (Fig. 9). The full extension is estimated to be 30 to 33 mm. This penile extension is temporally coordinated with the pelvic thrust that accompanies intromission, although the musculature controlling the hips is different from that controlling the penis. (Extension of the penis in rats and other rodents is accomplished primarily by muscular action as in rhesus monkeys and most ungulates, for example, rather than by vascular engorgement, as in horses and humans. Some of the penile swelling in the rat results from engorgement, but extension and retraction during XVIPs usually occur without swelling.) The deep penile thrust associated with intromission has been described as having a ballistic quality, that is, it does not appear to be controlled once it has been initiated (e.g., Bermant, 1965). However, the intromission thrust may occur without any short thrusts preceding it (Stone and Ferguson, 1940; Bermant, 1965; Pollak and Sachs, 1973). This observation leads us to infer, not that the male can achieve insertion without first detecting the vagina, but rather that at least the initial portion of the insertion thrust has a nonballistic detection component. If "not vagina" is

Fig. 9. Ventral view of extravaginal intromission pattern, traced from a projection of a single "frame" of videotape. The penis is at maximum extension along the female's ventral surface. The male's forepaws are tightly grasping the female, and his right hindpaw is elevated.

detected, then the thrust is "aborted," the hips withdraw, and another thrust is initiated 2 to 5 msec later. In the absence of a "not vagina" cue the thrust continues smoothly and the penis simultaneously extends maximally. XVIPs and extravaginal ejaculations presumably occur when a "not vagina" cue is not received or not processed. The movement of fingers on typewriter keys is a convenient analogy. Correct strikes, analogous to intromission thrusts, tend to be smooth and continuous. Most incorrect strikes are aborted before completion, analogously to preintromission thrusts. Typographical errors, similar to XVIPs, occur when the error of the strike is detected too late or not at all.

After the forward hip thrust, the hips withdraw from the female and most of the penis withdraws into its sheath. Penile retraction is synchronized with hip withdrawal. The time from the beginning to the end of the long penile extension during XVIPs was estimated at 238 msec ($\pm$ 33 msec) by videotape analysis. This value is in very close agreement with the estimate for ad lib intromissions of Bermant et al. (1969), but somewhat shorter than the estimates (300 msec) of Peirce and Nuttall (1961a). This substantial temporal agreement leads us to believe that what the penis does inside the vagina during normal intromissions is very similar to what it does during an XVIP. The reliability of measurement of intromission duration, with different procedures and different strains of rats, seems all the more surprising when one considers that intromission duration is a function of insertion speed, insertion depth, duration of maximum penetration, and withdrawal speed.

Fig. 10. Ventral view of extravaginal ejaculation, traced from a projection of a single "frame" of videotape. The male's forepaw clasp is intense, and the penis is at maximum extension along the female's ventral surface. The tip of the penis has flared, forming the "penile cup." The ejaculate is expelled into this cup a few milliseconds later, and as the penis retracts the ejaculate is exposed at the tip. Normally the ejaculate adheres inside the vagina where it is left as a plug.

Analysis of videotapes revealed that during extravaginal ejaculations the penis is extended to about the same length, but for almost a second longer, than during intromission patterns (Fig. 10). At maximum extension the end of the penis flares into a cup-shaped structure, into which the ejaculate is projected. The cup retracts as the penis retracts, revealing the coagulated plug at the end of the penis. Normally, of course, this plug is deposited against the cervix. McGill and Coughlin (1970) have reported that a similar penile cup is formed during ejaculation by *Mus musculus.*

D. PENILE REFLEXES

In a rather different approach to the understanding of penile responses, Hart (1968) and Rodgers and Alheid (1972) have observed the penile reflexes of male rats supine on a laboratory table. When males are lightly restrained on their backs and the prepuce held retracted so the penis extends well beyond it, there occur clusters of penile responses which Hart (1968) identified as erections, short flips, and long flips (Fig. 11).

Pollak and Sachs (1973) used a similar technique to compare penile reflexes with the penile events they had observed during extravaginal intromission and ejaculation patterns. Many of the reflexes were similar in form to those seen during copulation, but the sequencing was variable. For example, full extension, partial distal swelling, flips, and the formation of penile cups occurred repeatedly within response clusters. We know the cup to be associated with ejaculation, and successive ejaculatory cups are normally several minutes apart during copulation. Apparently the control of reflexes in the supine male is rather different from that of a normally copulating animal. It should be added that no one who has studied the reflexes of supine males has reported ejaculation of a seminal plug (emission), even after 2 hours of reflexes.

Finally, it should be noted here that the sensory basis of penile reflexes is different in the natural and supine situations. To obtain penile reflexes from supine male rats the penis must be constantly extended. Prolonged penile extension is not a necessary condition for triggering intromission and ejaculation in copulating males. Hart (1972a) applied 5% lidocaine to the glans of spinally transected males, and this treatment reduced but did not eliminate reflexes in supine tests. Hart concluded that the receptors which evoke the reflexes are on the shaft rather than the glans. Some intromission-relevant receptors must be on the glans, and some direct effect of lidocaine upon the muscles of erection is conceivable. However, Hart's conclusion is supported by the finding of Spaulding and Peck (1974) that males whose glans had been amputated at weaning were nonetheless able as adults to achieve intromission and ejaculation.

Later (Section VII,B,3) we shall consider further the interactions between

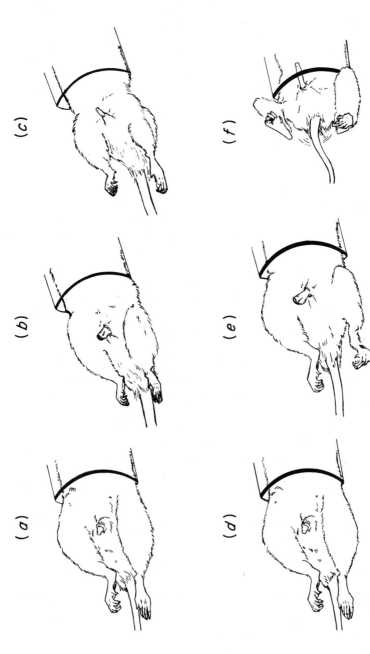

Fig. 11. Penile responses in a representative cluster of a spinally transected male (drawn from motion picture prints). The tube enclosing the anterior portion of the supine male is shown, but the mechanical retention of the sheath in retracted position is not depicted. The stages illustrated are the following: (a) quiescent stage before onset of a response cluster; (b) response cluster beginning with a brief penile erection; (c) a quick flip which generally followed several erections; (d) brief quiescent stage within a response cluster; (e) another erection within a response cluster; and (f) a long flip which generally occurred near the end of a response cluster. [From Hart (1968). Copyright 1968 by the American Psychological Association. Reprinted by permission.]

penile reflexes and copulation, but clearly the analysis of penile events during copulation is incomplete. At this stage we can only say that there is more to copulation than meets the eye, by whatever perspective. As we shall see (in Section VI,B,6) estimation of intromission duration and analysis of its causes and effects constitute a significant exercise in microanalysis. In fact, this analysis may lie at the heart of understanding just what stimulation brings the male rat to his ejaculatory threshold.

V. TEMPORAL PATTERNING OF COPULATION

A. PRELIMINARY DATA AND INTERPRETATION

We have considered what brings the male to start copulation and what the genital events associated with copulation are. We turn now to the question of what controls the intervals between copulatory acts prior to ejaculation. The duration of the intervals between intromissions is one of the more reliable features of the male rat's copulatory behavior. Beach (1956) reported a test-retest reliability of +0.94 for the average interintromission interval of 101 males. Within a single ejaculatory series intromissions also recur at fairly regular intervals, but there is a reliable change in rate during the series. When the ejaculation latency is divided into fifths, the intromission rate slows from the first to the second fifth and then accelerates monotonically until ejaculation (Dewsbury, 1967b).

Beach (1956) attributed the interval between intromissions to two factors. First, intromissions were assumed not to follow one upon the other because of the precedence of an incompatible response, namely, genital autogrooming, which follows after almost every intromission. Secondly, the intromission was thought to reduce sexual excitement temporarily below a hypothetical copulatory threshold, in a way similar in kind but not in degree to the way in which ejaculation depresses sexual arousal. Evidence that Beach adduced in support of some commonality between the postintromission (III) and postejaculatory interval (PEI) was a correlation of +0.50 between their average durations.

The hypothetical mechanisms underlying the temporal patterning were unspecified. As we have seen, on the one hand Beach suggested that the initiation of copulation (intromission latency) is under the control of the sexual arousal mechanism, but after one or two intromissions copulation is regulated by a relatively independent copulatory mechanism. On the other hand, the postejaculatory interval was believed to be, like the intromission latency, under the control of the sexual arousal mechanism. Therefore the correlation between interintromission interval and postejaculatory interval might indicate some role for the sexual arousal mechanism in the control of the interval between intromissions.

B. FURTHER ANALYSIS AND INTERPRETATION

1. Limitations of Traditional Measures of Copulatory Rate

In almost all the literature to be reviewed here, the only measure of copulatory rate was the average interval between intromissions. For reasons already discussed, these measures are unreliable whenever the number of intromissions per mount bout is significantly different from 1.0. In those studies reporting an acceleration in the intromission rate as the result of some treatment, it may be that the number of intromissions per mount bout was increased, while the time out between mount bouts was actually unchanged. In studies reporting an increased interintromission interval the behavior may have been better described as a reduced probability of intromissions occurring during a mount bout and not necessarily a retardation in the rate of mount bouts. Finally, those experiments in which no significant change in intromission rate was detected may reflect, for example, an accelerated rate of mount bouts but a normal rate of intromissions. In some reports data on the average interval between mounts, or the total number of mounts, or the average number of mounts per intromission, are also presented. These figures may aid in interpretation, but they neglect the temporal clustering of mounts that is basic to the male rat's copulatory behavior. These pitfalls may usually be avoided by rate measures based upon mount bouts, such as mount-bout period and time out (Sachs and Barfield, 1970; Larsson, 1973; Dewsbury, 1975a).

2. Relation of Arousal to Copulatory Rate

a. *Physiological and Psychological Manipulations.* In general it appears that treatments that increase arousal act to accelerate copulation, whereas reduced sensory input or arousal tends to retard the copulatory rate. For example, the interintromission interval (III) may be reduced by amphetamines (Butcher *et al.*, 1969; Bignami, 1966), *para*-chlorophenylalanine (Ahlenius *et al.*, 1971; Salis and Dewsbury, 1971), intermittent mildly painful shocks (Barfield and Sachs, 1968; Sachs and Barfield, 1974; Caggiula and Vlahoulis, 1974), and a course of electroconvulsive shocks (Beach *et al.*, 1955). Conversely, cannabis (Merari *et al.*, 1973), olfactory bulb lesions (Heimer and Larsson, 1967), and dorsal penile nerve section (Larsson and Södersten, 1973) all act to increase III. In these cases the effect on III is consistent with the probable effect on arousal and arousability, although none of these studies had independent measures of arousal.

A similar picture emerges when the stimulus situation is manipulated. The III has been reduced by changing the female (Bermant *et al.*, 1968), withholding the female for longer-than-normal intervals after intromission or ejaculation (Beach and Whalen, 1959a,b; Dewsbury and Bolce, 1968; Härd and Larsson, 1970; Larsson, 1959b; Bermant, 1964), or by exposing the male to a pair of copulating rats before allowing him access to the female (Härd and Larsson, 1969). All these treatments may be viewed as tending to increase arousal. The data indicating an abbreviated III after restricted access to the female may offer a basis for understanding the long-vexing problem of the nonmonotonic shape of the III function during the ejaculation latency as reported by Dewsbury (1967b) and depicted in Fig. 12. In this study, as usual, experienced males were placed in the testing cage for 5 minutes before the female was admitted. There is reason to believe that sexual arousal may increase during this time due to unconditioned sexual cues (odors) in the cage as well as a conditioned expectancy that the female will soon make her appearance. Such anticipatory arousal may accelerate the first few intromissions but may also be diminished by those intromissions. The copulatory rate would then slow for a time. Subsequent acceleration during the last three-fifths of the ejaculation latency might then be attributable to the excitement from approach to ejaculation. According to this hypothesis, the III function would be a monotonic declining function if males were tested in their home cages.

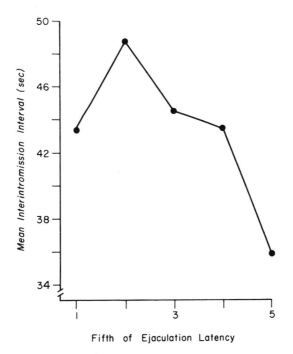

Fig. 12. Mean interintromission interval in successive fifths of the ejaculation latency period (N = 79). [From Dewsbury (1967b). Copyright 1967 by The Psychonomic Society. Reprinted by permission.]

Normative data are also consistent with the view that the III varies inversely with arousability. Assuming that more arousable males are capable of more ejaculations prior to sexual exhaustion, it is significant that males with a faster copulatory rate achieve more ejaculations prior to exhaustion (Karen and Barfield, 1975).

These examples of the possible relation of III to arousability tend to oversimplify a rather complex picture. There are many treatments that do not yield reliable effects on III where such effects might well be expected. Ventral midbrain stimulation (Eibergen and Caggiula, 1973), certain hypothalamic lesions (Caggiula et al., 1973) cerebral cortex ablation (Larsson, 1962, 1964), induction of anxiety (Beach and Fowler, 1959), and variation in room illumination (Härd and Larsson, 1968b) are among the treatments that might be expected to affect arousal levels but did not change III reliably, though other variables were affected in most of these studies.

b. *Diurnal Rhythm of Copulatory Rate.* One of the more illuminating determinants of copulatory rate is the time of day at which the copulatory test is given. The III is longest during the light phase of the photoperiod and decreases monotonically through the dark phase (Larsson, 1958; Dewsbury, 1968a). There may be a 100% difference in the rate at the two ends of the dark phase. Yet, strikingly, there is no associated change in the number of intromissions preceding ejaculation. The importance of the regularity of intromission number despite substantial differences in intromission rate will become clear later. Suffice it to say here that this dissociation in affected variables may indicate that the variables are controlled by relatively different processes, and an effect on III with no associated effect on intromission number has been commonly observed (Larsson, 1966, 1971; Butcher et al., 1969; Ahlenius et al., 1971; Sachs and Barfield, 1974).

c. *Pacing by Periodic Shock.* When mildly painful shocks are administered to the skin of male rats at regular intervals, each shock is almost invariably soon followed by a copulatory attempt; that is, periodic shocks can pace and accelerate the copulatory attempts of the males (Barfield and Sachs, 1968; Sachs and Barfield, 1974). A neutral stimulus that has been paired with shock can also serve this pacing function (Crowley et al., 1973). The shocks act directly on the sexual proclivity of the male, rather than through some indirect effect produced by the female's response to the male's jump when he is shocked. This conclusion follows from a study (Sachs et al., 1974) in which the female was removed from the test cage after each mount bout, and the male was required to press a bar to regain access to the female. Just as shock led to immediate copulation when the female was present, in this study the shocks led to immediate bar pressing and then copulation when the female dropped into the cage.

Reductions in III approaching 50% have been achieved by periodic shocks, but there are apparently limits to the potential acceleration, depending in part on the normal copulatory rate of individual males. For example, shocks administered at the rate of 10 per minute to males with ad lib IIIs of more than 60 seconds did not increase the copulatory rate beyond that obtained when the males were shocked once per minute (Caggiula and Vlahoulis, 1974). On the other hand, "fast" rats, with ad lib IIIs less than 30 seconds, showed reductions in IIIs of at least 50% when they were shocked within 6 seconds of the previous intromission (Karen, 1975; Karen and Barfield, unpublished, 1976). One limiting factor in the pacing of copulation by shocks is that shocks may have inhibitory aftereffects that decay more slowly than the facilitative effects (Pollak, 1974; Pollak and Sachs, 1975a).

3. Kinesthetic and Somesthetic Determination of Copulatory Rate: Evidence for a Copulatory Clock

a. Prevention of Intromissions by Males. It has generally been assumed that feedback from intromissions and from genital autogrooming after intromission is primarily responsible for the ensuing period of sexual quiescence. Accumulating evidence suggests that neither intromissions nor genital grooming are necessary for the normal pacing of copulation.

First, we may cite again the study of Hart and Haugen (1971), described previously, which showed no effect on the pacing of copulation from prevention of genital grooming. Sachs and Barfield (1970) prevented males from gaining intromission by anesthetizing the penes, or by occluding the vagina of the stimulus female. These males had a temporal patterning of mount bouts that was not distinguishable from the normal copulatory rate. Apparently mount bouts with or without intromission could induce a time out, and the duration of the time out was the same in the two conditions. Similarly, Lodder and Zeilmaker (1976) determined that mount-bout periods and time outs were unaffected by pudendal nerve cuts, although intromissions were eliminated by this surgery.

b. Masculine Copulatory Behavior of Female Rats. Female rats exhibit high levels of masculine copulatory behavior when they are treated with androgen perinatally and in adulthood (e.g., Ward, 1969; Whalen and Robertson, 1968). The temporal patterning of their mount bouts is indistinguishable from that of males (Sachs *et al.*, 1973). Such an equivalence is interesting enough in genetic females that, due to prenatal androgen treatment, have a hypertrophied phallus and therefore achieve insertion (Pollak and Sachs, 1975c). When the same temporal patterning is also displayed by normally reared females which, with their normal clitorides, presumably do not achieve insertion (Schoelch-Krieger and Barfield, 1975), then it becomes clear that the duration of the periods between bouts of sexual activity is not solely dependent upon stimulation arising from intromissions.

c. Time Out Following Mounts, Intromissions, and Extravaginal Intromission Patterns. Mounts without intromission differ from intromissions in the somesthetic and the kinesthetic consequences for the male. Extravaginal intromission patterns appear motorically identical to intromissions, but there is no penile insertion. Therefore XVIPs should offer the male the same kinesthetic feedback as intromissions but different somesthetic feedback. To analyze the relative contributions of these forms of feedback one may compare the probability and duration of time out after mounts, XVIPs, and intromissions.

The results from two sets of data are summarized in Table I (Pollak and Sachs, 1976). The different copulatory acts vary considerably in the probability that they will be followed by a time out (i.e., that they will be the last act in a mount bout). Approximately 25% of mounts, 50% of XVIPs, and 90% of intromissions are followed by time out. However, once a time out begins, its duration is independent of the event that preceded it. This means that the kinesthetic and somesthetic feedback from copulation is relevant only to the probability that a time out will begin and irrelevant to the duration of time out. Together with the other data considered in this section, these results suggest that neither the somatosensory nor the kinesthetic feedback from intromissions is a requisite for normal temporal patterning of mount bouts. It is as if there is a copulatory clock (Schoelch-Krieger and Barfield, 1975) which can be started in a number of ways but which runs at a constant rate independently of how it is started.

The behavioral evidence for a copulatory clock may be a useful context in which to consider some data from electroencephalographic recordings of male rats during copulation. Kurtz and Adler (1973) noted that the frequency of the hippocampal theta rhythm decreased after intromissions and ejaculations. However, following 73% of mounts without intromission theta frequency increased. The percentage of mounts that led to a decrease in theta frequency (27%) is similar to the 26% and 23% of mounts that terminated mount bouts in the two replications in the Pollak and Sachs study just reported (Table I). It may be that the mounts that led to a lasting reduction in the theta frequency in the study of Kurtz and Adler were the last sexual acts of mount bouts, just as intromissions and ejaculations almost always are. Confirmation of a reliable relation between theta frequency and mount bouts would provide a physiological definition of this unit of copulatory activity and might ultimately lead to the discovery of the physiological basis of the hypothetical copulatory clock.

4. Is There a Refractory Period After Intromissions?

For some time after ejaculation the male is unresponsive to stimuli which otherwise would cause him to copulate. Is there a similar refractory period after intromissions? Pollak (1974) shocked males 2 or 5 seconds after alternate intromissions. The groups did not differ in their probability of mounting within 5 seconds after shock, but males in the 2-second group were less likely to gain intromission.

TABLE I
Probability and Duration of Time Outs Following Mounts,
Extravaginal Intromission Patterns (XVIP), and Intromissions[a]

| | | Preceding event | | | N | P |
		Mount	XVIP	Intromission		
Probability	Replication 1	0.26	0.41	0.93	14	<0.001
of time out[b]	Replication 2	0.23	0.58	0.86	7	<0.025
Duration of	Replication 1	20.6	19.0	26.0	7	>0.20
time out (seconds)	Replication 2	27.8	24.7	30.4	5	>0.20

[a]Data from Pollak and Sachs (1976).
[b]Probability scores are based on arc sine transformations of the raw data.

Karen (1975) shocked males 3, 6, 12, or 24 seconds after intromissions. Faster subjects (those with IIIs of less than 30 seconds in control tests) showed significantly shorter response latencies and decreased IIIs following all shocks. Slower subjects, however, were unresponsive to shocks administered 3 seconds after a prior intromission and only marginally responsive after 6 seconds. Following shocks that occurred 12 or 24 seconds after an intromission, there was an increased percentage of immediate copulatory responses within 6 seconds of the shock. It appears that a brief period of profound unresponsiveness follows an intromission but that it occupies no more than 10% of the normal III; during the remainder of the III, responsiveness increases progressively. Taken together, these studies offer tentative support for Beach's (1956) idea that the male's time out after intromissions is a minor version of his postejaculatory refractory period, but conclusive research is lacking.

5. Pacing by Females

Up to this point we have emphasized that the control of time out is relatively independent of the control of other copulatory processes, but we have omitted the other half of the copulating pair and the social milieu in which copulation normally occurs. Studies in which the female has been given control of the rate of copulation (Peirce and Nuttall, 1961b; Bermant, 1961; McClintock and Adler, 1974) have demonstrated that the female also takes a time out after copulatory contacts, with mounts, intromissions, and ejaculations leading, respectively, to longer and longer time outs. The longer time out following ejaculation is attributable to the coagulated plug in the female's vagina (Bermant and Westbrook, 1966). Under quasi-naturalistic conditions in which the female, by going into and emerging from a "burrow," determines the timing of the male's access to her, it is clear that the female sets limits on the male's rate of copulation (McClintock and Adler, 1974). This finding is fundamental to a complete understanding of the control of copulation, but we must keep in mind that the female and male are acting upon each other's endogenous processes. In this connection, it has been noted that there is a surprising concordance between the postintromission time out of the mounting male and that of the mounted female (Schoelch-Krieger and Barfield, 1975; Doty, 1974). This correspondence has raised the possibility that the copulatory clocks of the male and female are similar in mechanism and not only in period. Synchronization of the pair's clocks may not pose a problem under natural conditions for the rat, since the pacing of copulation is largely determined by the female's emergence from her burrow, and several males may compete to mount her during each brief emergence (Calhoun, 1962; McClintock and Adler, 1974).

VI. ACCUMULATION OF EJACULATORY POTENTIAL

A. NORMATIVE DATA

What is it that brings the male to ejaculate when he does? The motor pattern of ejaculation is commonly associated with seminal emission, but not always. Except where we have specified otherwise, we shall use the term *ejaculation* synonymously with the display of the gross motor pattern that observers use to identify and score the occurrence of ejaculation.

Male rats do not ejaculate until they have repeatedly gained insertion, and the number of such intromissions is the most widely used index of the amount of stimulation needed for ejaculation. Indeed, this measure may define the ejaculatory threshold (Freeman and McFarland, 1974). This requisite level of stimulation, as measured by the number of intromissions, varies as a function of the ejaculatory series. At least as long ago as the study of Stone and Ferguson (1940) it has been recognized that the first ejaculation of a test is preceded by more intromissions than are the subsequent ejaculations. In some earlier sets of normative data it appeared that the number of intromissions declines monotonically over several copulatory series (Beach and Jordan, 1956; Larsson, 1956), but there is now reliable evidence of an upturn in number of intromissions as exhaustion approaches, yielding a backward J-shaped function (Brown, 1974; Dewsbury, 1968b; Karen and Barfield, 1975).

The number of intromissions tends to be rather stable from one test to another, yet Beach (1956) reported a lower test-retest reliability for number of intromissions (+0.58) than for interintromission interval (+0.94), ejaculation latency (+0.82), or postejaculatory intromission latency (+0.82). The relatively low correlation for number of intromissions, however, may not be due to a true lower reliability, but rather to the restricted range among males. In a sample of

20 of our Long-Evans males, the ratio of standard error to mean was only 0.06 for number of intromissions, compared with 0.17 for the interintromission interval and 0.29 for the ejaculation latency. Only the postejaculatory intromission latency, with a ratio of 0.05, had a coefficient of variation as small as for number of intromissions. (Such low variances within a population of animals may indicate that one is measuring species-typical characteristics.)

B. HYPOTHESES FOR THE TRIGGERING OF EJACULATION

1. The Quantal Hypothesis

The reflexes associated with ejaculation are organized at the spinal level, but they are under inhibitory influence from higher neural systems. The stimulation derived from intromissions may serve to reduce this inhibition, perhaps by exciting a system that itself inhibits the ejaculation-inhibiting system (Beach, 1967; Beach *et al.,* 1966). The form of the hypothetical function that relates intromissions to ejaculatory excitation has received considerable attention.

The simplest assumption is that intromissions result in instantaneous, stepwise, but not necessarily equal increments of ejaculatory excitement. This straw-man hypothesis, which may be termed the "quantal" hypothesis, has been considered and rejected repeatedly because it cannot account for certain phenomena, especially the so-called enforced-interval effect. The enforced interval refers to the time between intromissions. When male and female are separated for intervals longer than the ad lib rate of copulation, then the number of intromissions that precede ejaculation is affected in a J-shaped function [Larsson (1956) and many other studies since then] ; that is, at enforced intervals moderately longer than the ad lib intervals there is a significant reduction in number of intromissions. As the intervals are further increased the number of intromissions increases exponentially until, with enforced intervals of 10 minutes or more, the male rat may never ejaculate (Fig. 13). Single enforced intervals of optimal duration may be as effective as several enforced intervals in reducing both the number of intromissions and the interintromission interval (Bermant, 1964). Without additional assumptions, the quantal hypothesis would predict no effect of enforced intervals. Making a simple additional assumption of a gradual decay from the maximum excitation received from each intromission, one could explain the above-normal number of intromissions with long enforced intervals, but one could not explain the reduced number of intromissions with moderate enforced intervals.

2. The Temporal Hypothesis

Two alternatives to the quantal hypothesis have been developed to account for the enforced-interval effect. The first of these, which may be called the "tem-

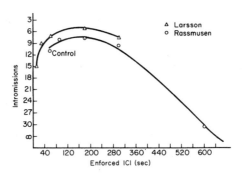

Fig. 13. Effects of enforced intercopulatory intervals (ICI) of various durations on the number of intromissions required for ejaculation. Data from Larsson (1956) and Rassmusen [unpublished, cited in Larsson (1956)]. Note the inverted ordinate. (Unpublished figure, printed by permission of F. A. Beach.)

poral" hypothesis, was the alternative preferred by Beach (1956; see Figure 14). In this view the initial intromission triggers a time-dependent accumulation of excitation, and ejaculation occurs when this excitation is maintained above threshold for a fixed amount of time. The role of intromissions after the first is only to maintain excitation above threshold, and it is assumed that suprathreshold maintenance can be accomplished by intromissions at a rate moderately slower than ad libitum. At rates much slower than ad lib, more intromissions than normal would be needed before the total suprathreshold time became long enough to trigger ejaculation.

Part of the attractiveness of this hypothesis, besides its accounting for the enforced-interval data, stems from the high reliability noted earlier for the ejaculation latency. Many researchers regard the ejaculation latency and the number of intromissions as fundamental and consider the interintromission interval as derived. After all, the average interintromission interval may be derived by dividing the number of intromissions into ejaculation latency. However, arithmetic operations should not be confused with functional operations. In the previous sections we considered the reasons for believing that the pacing of copulation, as measured by the mount-bout period or the interintromission interval, reflects a basic functional rhythmicity in the male. For reasons to be considered shortly, we believe that number of intromissions is also functionally important. We are therefore inclined to view ejaculation latency as a derived measure, the product of two functional processes: the copulatory clock which paces copulation, and an excitation processor with input from the number of intromissions.

3. The Nonquantal Hypothesis

There is another hypothesis that was developed specifically to account for the enforced-interval effect and that has been widely accepted. This hypothesis,

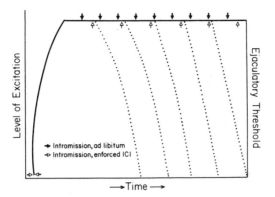

Fig. 14. Depiction of the "temporal" hypothesis of accumulation of ejaculatory potential. The initial intromission is presumed to increase excitation to a maximum for some period of time (solid line), after which excitation declines (dotted line). Subsequent ad lib intromissions (solid arrows) maintain excitation at this maximum, but the intromissions occur at a rate greater than that necessary for this purpose. Hence, enforcing a longer period between intromissions allows excitation to be maintained at maximum with fewer intromissions (open arrows). When excitation has been maintained at maximum level for some threshold duration, then ejaculation will occur during the next insertion. (Unpublished figure, printed by permission of F. A. Beach.)

which may be termed "nonquantal," assumes in common with the quantal hypothesis that the ejaculatory excitement from each intromission is additive with the level from preceding intromissions; but it uniquely assumes that the excitation from each intromission does not reach maximum until some time after intromission (Fig. 15). The postintromission increase of excitation from one intromission is stopped by the occurrence of the next intromission (Freeman and McFarland, 1974). That enforced interval which yields the greatest reduction in the number of intromissions is believed to be the interval required for intromission-induced excitation to reach a maximum. After reaching a maximum, excitation declines at a relatively rapid rate. This latter assumption accounts for the exponential increase in number of intromissions as greater-than-optimal intervals are enforced between intromissions. The outlines of the nonquantal hypothesis were presented by Larsson (1959b) and Beach and Whalen (1959b), and depicted most explicitly by Bermant (1967; see also Bermant and Davidson, 1974).

4. Predictions from the Temporal and Nonquantal Hypotheses

For different reasons both the temporal and the nonquantal alternatives to the simple quantal hypothesis lead to the following prediction: acceleration of the intromission rate should result in an increased number of intromissions prior to

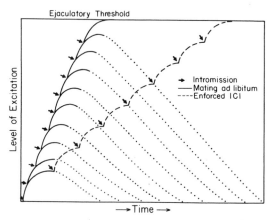

Fig. 15. Depiction of the "nonquantal" hypothesis of accumulation of ejaculatory potential. Solid line represents growth of excitation under ad lib conditions of copulation. Ten intromissions are depicted as bringing the male to the ejaculatory threshold; ejaculation would occur during the next insertion. The dashed line represents ejaculatory excitation when each intercopulatory interval is enforced, i.e., extended beyond its normal duration. Under this condition each intromission summates with a higher level of excitation consequent upon the preceding intromission. Hence, a reduced number of intromissions, in this case eight, brings the male to the ejaculatory threshold. (Unpublished figure, printed by permission of F. A. Beach.)

ejaculation. The temporal hypothesis requires this conclusion because intromissions after the first do not add ejaculatory excitement—they only function to maintain excitement for the needed time. The nonquantal hypothesis leads to this inference because each intromission would be building upon a lower level of ejaculatory excitation accumulated from the previous intromission.

A wide variety of treatments have led to an acceleration of copulatory rate, but in our search of the literature we have encountered no experiments in which such an acceleration was associated with an increase in the number of intromissions. Typically, there has been no change in number of intromissions (e.g., Beach *et al.*, 1956; Bermant, 1964; Caggiula, 1972; Dewsbury, 1968a), or there was a significant decrease (e.g., Beach *et al.*, 1955; Caggiula and Vlahoulis, 1974; Larsson, 1963). Sachs and Barfield (1974) reported three separate experiments in which intercopulatory intervals were significantly reduced by periodic shock, and in none of these studies was there a significant change in number of intromissions. It should also be noted that interintromission interval accelerates from the first to the second copulatory series, and intromission number also declines rather than increasing.

Of particular interest is the study by Dewsbury (1968a), cited earlier, in which male rats were tested at various times during the dark phase of the photoperiodic cycle. The intervals between intromissions varied from 28 to 83 sec ($p < 0.001$), but number of intromissions did not change significantly (range 9.2–10.7) and was not correlated with the direction of change in the intervals between intromissions. Larsson (1958), comparing daytime with nighttime copulation in rats, noted a similar acceleration in nocturnal copulation without an attendant change in number of intromissions. And in another study (Larsson, 1966), male rats were castrated at different ages and then tested following androgen replacement in adulthood. The later the castration, the faster the intromission rate (range of 0.3 per min for day-7 castrates to 1.6 per min for day-19 castrates; $p <$ 0.001), but in all four groups the median number of intromissions was 8.0.

Such constancy in intromission number despite wide variations in intromission rate cannot be accounted for by the temporal or nonquantal hypotheses in their present form. Yet any alternative hypothesis must also account for existing data, and particularly the enforced-interval effect that gave rise to the temporal and nonquantal hypotheses.

5. Quantal Increments and Nonquantal Decay?

To account for the existing data we merged certain elements of the quantal hypothesis with elements of the nonquantal hypothesis (Sachs and Barfield, 1974). That is, we assumed that each intromission yielded a quantal increment in excitation, followed by a nonquantal, time-dependent decay. The assumptions of stepwise increase and slow decay account for the relative constancy of number of intromissions despite wide variations in intromission rate. The assumption of ultimate decay is required, as in the other models, to explain why the male may never ejaculate when intercopulatory intervals are too long. Additional assumptions are still required to explain why the number of intromissions is reduced with optimal enforced intervals, and we turn now to these.

6. Intromission Duration

As we noted earlier, the number of intromissions is the most common index of the requisite stimulation for ejaculation, but it has long been recognized that the duration of an intromission may give some clue to its excitatory value (Stone and Ferguson, 1940; Carlsson and Larsson, 1962; Peirce and Nuttall, 1961a; Bermant et al., 1969). The working assumption has been that longer insertions have greater excitatory value. Most data are consistent with this view, as we shall see, but in principle the reverse relation could hold. Until other techniques offer more direct methods of assessing the quantity of excitation from intromissions, we must be careful about drawing conclusions.

On the average, intromission duration during the first ejaculatory series is shorter than in the second series (Peirce and Nuttall, 1961a; Carlsson and Larsson, 1962). If ejaculatory excitement is a multiplicative function of the number of intromissions and their durations, then the reduced number of intromissions typical of the second series may be compensated by the increased duration of each intromission. If compensation were complete, that is, if total intromission duration were constant from one series to another, and total intromission duration rather than number were the better measure of ejaculatory threshold, then the threshold may not change from series to series as much as is commonly believed.

Evidence in support of the importance of intromission duration comes from a study of intromission following enforced intervals of various durations [see Fig. 16 (Bermant, *et al.,* 1969)]. Contact times between penis and vagina were found to be shortest when males were copulating ad libitum, and contacts became progressively longer as longer intervals were enforced. However, multiplication of average intromission duration by average number of intromissions yielded a total contact time of 2385, 1804, 1528, 1525, 1530, and 1815 msec for, respectively, ad libitum, 1-, 2-, 3-, 4-, and 5-minute interintromission intervals. The variability among these multiples indicates that compensation may not have been complete. These estimates of total intravaginal time may be misleading, since the multiple of the average for several animals may not equal the average of

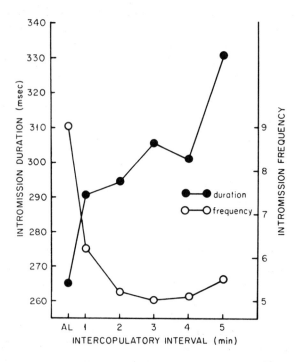

Fig. 16. Changes in intromission frequency (number of intromissions) and intromission duration as a function of intercopulatory interval. [From Bermant *et al.* (1969). Copyright 1969 by The Psychonomic Society. Reprinted by permission.]

the multiple for those animals. Furthermore, estimates based on contact times, rather than some exponential function of such times, may also be misleading.

Finally, it should be said that previous estimates of intromission duration may not be as accurate as necessary to evaluate the role of this variable in the accumulation of ejaculatory potential. Some estimates have been based upon cinematography, with its attendant problems of errors in frame speed and judgments about onset and termination of insertion; others have been derived from electrical detection of insertion. The latter technique also has at least two problems. The first is that the relay switches in circuits that have been used have a time lag for closing and opening that may itself yield an error in estimate. A greater potential problem is the setting of triggering level for the resistance drop that will signal the start of intromission. Since some of the preliminary thrusts yield wet contacts with the vagina, the onset of an intromission may be signaled before insertion actually beings, but the relay circuit may not reopen during the very brief interval between detection thrusts (2 to 5 msec). Oscilloscopes have the response speed to distinguish reliably between intromission and preintromission thrusts, and oscilloscopy may be the current method of choice for measuring intromission duration (see Section IV,B).

7. Frustration-Induced Arousal

Our hypothesis that ejaculatory excitement increases suddenly at intromission and declines slowly after intromission accounts only for the normal stability of intromission number despite wide fluctuations in intromission rate and for the approach of intromission number toward infinity when supraoptimal interintromission intervals are enforced. For the below-normal number of intromissions obtained from optimal enforced intervals we need an additional hypothesis, and one possibility is frustration-induced arousal (Gerall, 1958; Sachs and Barfield, 1974).

In considering the enforced-interval effect, a useful analogy may be human premature ejaculation, that is, ejaculation with little or no vaginal contact. Commonly, arousal from precoital stimulation as well as from anxiety about copulation may summate with minimal copulatory stimulation to bring the male prematurely to his ejaculatory threshold.

This analogy was suggested by Beach and Fowler (1959) to account for data obtained from male rats which had been shocked, strongly and repeatedly, in a certain chamber. After repeated shocks in that chamber the males were placed in it again, but they received no shocks. Instead, receptive females were placed with the males. In these circumstances males ejaculated after significantly fewer intromissions, while the average interval between intromissions was unchanged. Beach and Fowler suggested that the autonomic consequences of anxiety potentiated ejaculation by sensitizing the underlying mechanism, and they hypothesized that the sensitizing effect was similar to that normally produced by the first ejaculation, i.e., the reduction from the first series number of intromissions to that of the second series.

Enforced intervals moderately longer than ad lib may constitute a frustration for the male rat. Frustration, like anxiety, may generate arousal, and the frustration-induced arousal may potentiate ejaculation. This hypothesis was suggested by Gerall (1958) to account for the enforced-interval effect when he demonstrated its occurrence in guinea pigs, but it has received only one indirect test (Gerall and Berg, 1964).

According to this hypothesis, frustration results from interference with the normal pattern of a bout of consummatory activity, for example, by delaying access of the male to the female. The male apparently has expectations of resuming copulation after each mount bout, even when the female is not continuously present. Expectations may not be seen, but they may be inferred from behavior (Krechevsky, 1932; Cofer and Appley, 1964). The arousal of the male during enforced intervals of optimal duration is readily apparent from his behavior during that time, namely, exploration of the cage with increased rearing up, sniffing, and digging (Larsson, 1956). Production of high-frequency (50–100 kHz), short-duration pulses also increases during enforced intervals (R. J. Barfield, unpublished observation, 1974). Evidence from recent studies in which the male had to press a bar to gain access to a female is relevant in this context (Jowaisas et al., 1971; Sachs et al., 1974). In the study of Sachs et al., the intervals between mount bouts were about 50% longer when the female was not continuously present, but the males did press the bars at regular intervals. With intervals between intromissions 50% or more longer than ad lib, previous interpretations of the enforced-interval effect would have predicted a reduced number of intromissions. However, since the males had free access to the females, frustration would presumably be absent, and therefore a frustration-based interpretation of the enforced-interval effect would have predicted no significant change in number of intromissions. The mean intromission frequency in the ad lib condition was 9.4, and in the bar-press condition was 7.9 ($t = 1.96$; $0.10 > p > 0.05$). Jowaisas et al. (1971) also reported fewer intromissions before ejaculation in the bar-press condition than in the free-access condition, but the reliability of the difference was not evaluated statistically. The female was present in a vented container throughout the bar-press test, and two to four presses were required to gain access to the female. These factors may have generated frustration, as we have defined it here. The data from both these studies are equivocal relative to the two hypotheses.

To have credence, a hypothesis should not invoke a phenomenon to account only for a single data set. In the present instance, credibility for the notion of frustration-induced potentiation of ejaculation would be improved if the concept could be applied to data other than those from enforced-interval studies. There are two other experiments that may be usefully considered here because their procedures involved apparent frustration (as we have defined it).

Härd and Larsson (1968a) sought to test the possibility that mounts without intromission contributed some excitation toward ejaculation. They arranged for males to be placed with females that had their vaginas sewn shut, thus allowing the males to mount but preventing them from gaining insertion. Control males were placed in a cage with females that were enclosed in a vented container, offering olfactory and auditory stimulation only. After 40 min in the appropriate condition, both groups of males were given fresh females and allowed to copulate ad libitum. Relative to the control males, the experimental males had significantly fewer intromissions before ejaculating. This difference was interpreted as confirming some stimulatory value of mounts toward ejaculation. However, if mounts without intromission were more frustrating than partial exposure to a female without opportunity to mount, then a frustration-induced-arousal hypothesis could account for the data. If the arousal induced by frustration were general, and not limited to the potentiation of ejaculation, then one would expect frustration to accelerate copulation as well as ejaculation. In the experiment just described the intercopulatory interval was not significantly reduced.

An opposite relation was obtained in the other relevant study by Härd and Larsson (1969). Control males were contained inside a vented box inside an empty experimental chamber. Experimental males were similarly contained, but during the male's confinement another pair of rats copulated in the chamber. After 40 minutes the males were released and given access to receptive females. The experimental males had significantly shorter interintromission intervals than the control males (0.51 versus 0.82 min), but the median number of intromissions was identical in the two conditions. Exposure to the copulating animals, and its presumed attendant frustration, clearly increased the copulatory rate but had no effect on ejaculatory potential. Until some studies are performed that are specifically designed to test the frustration hypothesis, we cannot resolve these discrepencies.

C. DISSOCIATION OF NUMBER OF INTROMISSIONS FROM INTERINTROMISSION INTERVAL

A secondary outcome in the studies just reviewed, an outcome that we have seen before and that is central to our discussion, is that number of intromissions and interintromission interval are commonly affected differently by an experimental treatment. As we suggested before, such a dissociation of variables implies control by at least partially separate processes. Although number of intromissions and intromission rate have commonly been assumed to reflect activity within a single copulatory mechanism, the possible plurality of this mechanism was stated explicitly by Beach (1956, p. 20). If there are multiple processes controlling copulation, then these processes may be distinguishable by physiological analysis. A modest beginning has been made in that direction.

Beach *et al.* (1966) reviewed substantial evidence that the control of ejaculation is relatively independent of the control of other copulatory processes. Some more recent studies have lent additional support to this conclusion. Hart (1972b) treated neonatal castrated male rats with testosterone propionate, fluoxymesterone (another androgen), or nothing. At maturity all males were tested under the influence of testosterone. The most important result for our purposes was that the fluoxymesterone-treated animals were not distinguishable from the other males in most aspects of copulatory behavior: their initiation latencies and interintromission intervals were normal. However, they had a reduced potential for ejaculation: only 3/16 of these males displayed the ejaculatory pattern, despite showing more than an adequate number of intromission patterns. Unfortunately, we can not know how many of the intromission patterns were actually accompanied by insertion. Hart also tested the penile reflexes of these males following spinal transection, and these reflexes were normal. Hart (1972b, p. 845) concluded that fluoxymesterone in the dose used, "although leaving unorganized some brain structure, did organize the spinal cord along with sensitizing the penis to later development. . . . Some cranial neural system mediating the control of ejaculation would require the presence of neonatal androgen for complete development." That is, the supraspinal system controlling ejaculation is functionally different from those controlling the initiation of copulation and the triggering and pacing of intromissions.

Studies on part of the limbic system suggest one possible locus for a neural system in which information about copulatory stimulation is processed in bringing the male to his ejaculatory threshold (Harris *et al.*, 1974; Harris and Sachs, 1975; Emery and Sachs, 1976b). Lesions were made in the corticomedial nuclei of the amygdala of experienced male rats, or in the bed nucleus of the stria terminalis, which is reciprocally connected with the corticomedial nuclei. Relative to sham-operated control males, the experimental males had a severe impairment in achieving ejaculation, strikingly similar to Hart's fluoxymesterone-treated males. Bed nucleus and corticomedial males achieved as many as 40–60 intromissions and still did not ejaculate. Males that did ejaculate often had 50–100% more intromissions prior to ejaculation than control males. Some males with lesions also had deficits in the initiation and pacing of copulation, but others copulated at a normal rate and still displayed many more intromissions. Furthermore, slower pacing of copulation is commonly associated with a reduction, not an increase, in the number of intromissions preceding ejaculation. It appears that the neural system investigated is involved in the male's achievement of ejaculation, as well as in controlling other aspects of sexual excitability.

One striking feature of these studies was that sometimes a male that had accumulated more than 50 intromissions without showing signs of impending ejaculation (these signs are clear to the experienced observer) could be made to ejaculate on the next intromission by the simple expedient of pinching his tail.

As we noted, many males that did not get pinched never ejaculated. The very quick induction of ejaculation by a pinch has led us to think that the effective lesions blocked ejaculation, not by reduced sensory afference from each intromission, nor by reduced accumulation of ejaculatory potential, but by a reduced potential for the ultimate gating of the ejaculatory pattern. Such a gating system has been incorporated into the model of Freeman and McFarland (1974) for very different reasons.

D. EJACULATORY PATTERN DISPLAYED BY FEMALE RATS

Some recent developments have complicated our long-held assumption that intromissions are a prerequisite for the accumulation of ejaculatory potential and the ultimate gating of the ejaculatory pattern. It has been known for decades that normal female rats have the potential for the display of the masculine mount and intromission patterns (Beach, 1942d; Beach and Rasquin, 1942). A considerable literature has been amassed on the conditions that predispose females to display these patterns, as well as on the reasons that normal females do not display the ejaculatory pattern. In an exhaustive review of the problem, Beach (1971) aptly summarized the available evidence as indicating that female rodents will not display the ejaculatory pattern unless they have been treated with androgen some time in the perinatal period.

A controversy surrounding these data has concerned the origin of this sexual dimorphism in behavioral potential. Reduced to their simplest terms, the question has been whether a sex difference in the anatomy or hormone sensitivity of the nervous system is responsible or whether the behavioral difference is attributable to differences in phallic size, sensitivity, and insertability. Now it seems we may have to reexamine not only these hypotheses but also the very phenomenon they were supposed to explain.

Very simply, we have discovered that some female rats will indeed display the ejaculatory pattern even though they were not treated with androgen in the perinatal period. The ejaculatory pattern displayed by these females is unmistakable—in the force and duration of the ejaculatory thrust and arm clasp it is a considerable exaggeration of the normal male's response. (In fact, the stimulus female may cry out and throw off the "ejaculating" female. This result raises the possibility that the cry of pain often heard from a female during the male's ejaculatory thrust is not, as has been assumed, due entirely to painful vaginal penetration, but possibly also to pain from grasping forepaws.)

Space does not allow detailed presentation of these experiments here, but, briefly, we have learned that chronic estrogen treatment, intermittent electric shocks, injection of *para*-chlorophenylalanine, or occasional tail pinches may in various combinations sharply potentiate the ejaculatory response of females that never received exogenous androgen, or received it only in adulthood. For example, seven females that received implants of estradiol benzoate reliably displayed intromission but not ejaculatory patterns. After injection with *para*-chlorophenylalanine all seven displayed ejaculatory patterns. [For additional details of these experiments, see Emery and Sachs (1975, 1976a); Krieger and Barfield (1976).]

One question is central to the present context. What stimulation brings these females to the ejaculatory threshold? The ejaculation pattern is displayed after an approximately normal number and rate of intromission patterns, but we do not yet know whether insertion is achieved. Even if there is insertion of the sheath-covered clitoris into the vagina, the penetration would be shallow. It would seem unlikely that the resultant stimulation would be equivalent to that resulting from penile insertion, but this possibility cannot be ruled out. The clitorides of the ejaculating females appear macroscopically indistinguishable from those of normal females, but hypersensitivity may be present in the estrogen-treated females (Komisaruk *et al.*, 1972; Kow and Pfaff, 1973/74). If insertion is not achieved by the females, then it is possible that during the thrust accompanying the intromission patterns there is adequate friction between clitoris and sheath to provide excitation toward the ejaculatory threshold. In any case, it seems clear that the behavioral dimorphism that had been assumed between male and female rats may be less marked than had been thought. Perhaps there is a more marked sexual dimorphism in the nature of the genital stimulation that potentiates the ejaculatory pattern.

VII. THE POSTEJACULATORY INTERVAL

A. PREVIOUS INTERPRETATIONS: EMPHASIS ON AROUSAL

After a male rat's first ejaculation, 4 to 6 minutes elapse before he is likely to resume copulation, and successive postejaculatory intervals are progressively longer (see Fig. 5). What controls the duration of those intervals?

It has generally been assumed that arousal is depressed during the period following ejaculation. Recovery of copulatory potential after ejaculation was considered by Beach (1956; Beach and Jordan, 1956) to be a function of the sexual arousal mechanism. "The two indicators of excitability of the AM [sexual arousal mechanism] are the intromission latency and the postejaculatory refractory periods" (Beach and Jordan, 1956, p. 131). Evidence from later experiments led to the conclusion that most or all of the control of the postejaculatory interval could not be referred to the same arousal mechanism that controlled the intromission latency. Rather, control was referred to a general fatigue process (Beach and Whalen, 1959a). This conclusion has been questioned (Boland and Dewsbury, 1971; Dewsbury, 1968b; Dewsbury and

Bolce, 1968, 1970; McGill, 1965), but the emphasis on reduced arousal in the postejaculatory interval has generally been retained. McGill (1965) noted that among strains of domestic mice and their crosses the correlation between ejaculation latencies and duration of postejaculatory refractoriness was poor. Other evidence too was inconsistent with a fatigue concept, and McGill posited instead a relatively independent mechanism controlling the rate of recovery from ejaculation. (McGill called this an "ejaculatory mechanism," but that term would seem best reserved to the processes controlling ejaculation itself. McGill's concept might better be referred to as a "refractory mechanism" to reduce confusion.)

The emphasis on reduced arousal and arousability during the postejaculatory interval, especially during its early portion, has seemed justifiable on the basis of the male rat's behavior after ejaculation. After a short period of postejaculatory grooming, the male is likely to lie down and show tonic immobility, although he may appear to rest or even to sleep (Dewsbury, 1967a). That is, he appears to be in a state of reduced arousal. According to Soulairac (1952, p. 99): "La période réfractaire semble ainsi représenter une phase de dé-afférentation sensori-motrice, sans posséder toutefois les caracteristiques d'un comportement hypnique." [The refractory period thus appears to represent a phase of sensory-motor deafferentation, but without having the characteristics of a hypnotic state (translation by the present authors).] Treatments that increase arousal or arousability have the effect of shortening the postejaculatory interval. Thus, nonspecific arousing stimuli such as handling (Larsson, 1963) or mildly painful electric shocks (Barfield and Sachs, 1968; Caggiula, 1972; Sachs and Barfield, 1974) shorten the postejaculatory interval. Treatment with pharmacological agents known to potentiate arousal are similarly effective (Bignami, 1966; Salis and Dewsbury, 1971). Electrical stimulation of neural systems that mediate copulatory behavior is similarly capable of reducing the postejaculatory interval (Van Dis and Larsson, 1971; Caggiula and Szechtman, 1972; Eibergen and Caggiula, 1973). All such treatments seem to be more effective in animals with less intrinsic arousability, as indicated by longer ad libitum postejaculatory intervals. In addition, handling (Larsson, 1963) and shock (Sachs and Barfield, 1974; Sharma and Hays, 1974) were more effective in older than younger males, and shock was more effective in later postejaculatory intervals than in earlier ones.

B. A ROLE FOR ACTIVE INHIBITION IN THE POSTEJACULATORY INTERVAL

1. Evidence from Neural and Vocal Activity

Recent evidence suggests that the postejaculatory interval can not be adequately considered in terms of an arousal process. Rather, this evidence points to the existence of an active inhibitory process that can be measured independently of the excitation process. This inhibition is especially detectable after ejaculation, but it may also be active prior to ejaculation.

Kurtz and Adler (1973) discovered that soon after the male rat ejaculates, and for some time after that, his electroencephalogram (EEG) is characterized by high-amplitude slow-wave activity such as that of sleeping males. The male is not simply resting during the period that his EEG reflects a sleeplike state. Rather, the male emits an ultrasonic vocalization, often at a considerable intensity (Barfield and Geyer, 1972, 1975). Furthermore, the male's posture tends not to be that of a relaxed sleep state, but rather one of tonic, that is, active, immobility (cf. Dewsbury, 1967a). The immobility of a vocalizing male is less like that of a sleeping rat than like a rat suffering defeat from a conspecific (Seward, 1945). (The combination of active behavior—i.e., vocalization, tonic immobility—coincident with a sleeplike EEG has led us to designate this state as *paradoxical wakefulness.*)

2. *Arousal and Inhibition as Opponent Processes*

From the EEG and related behavioral data on males during copulation and after ejaculation, Kurtz and Adler (1973) developed a model of the regulation of sexual arousal and refractoriness (Fig. 17). The basic assumption of this model is that the generation of arousal in a system results in a simultaneous increase of activity in an opposing inhibitory system, whereas a waning of inhibition depends upon a waning of excitation.

When a male and receptive female rat are placed together, stimuli from the female generate sexual arousal in the male until his copulatory threshold is exceeded. At this point copulatory stimulation begins to summate with other sexual stimuli, causing an increased rate of growth of excitation. With the increase in excitation there is a proportional growth of inhibition. When excitation reaches another hypothetical threshold value, the male ejaculates upon his next intromission. Ejaculation causes excitation to return to base level, which in turn allows a decay in excitation. Since the female is still present, stimuli from her result in a regeneration of arousal during the postejaculatory interval. This interval ends, that is, copulation resumes, when excitation exceeds both the copulatory threshold and the level of inhibition. With the resumption of copulation, the rate of growth of arousal and inhibition again increases. This pattern is repeated over successive copulatory series. Sexual exhaustion sets in when the level of inhibition exceeds the ejaculatory threshold and cannot be surpassed by the level of arousal within a criterion time.

The Kurtz-Adler model is a creative departure from previous models, particularly in formally incorporating arousal and inhibitory processes throughout copulation and refractoriness. It seems likely that attention to interactions among excitation and inhibition will be a prominent feature in any new model of copulatory behavior. This model also accounts for a good many of the normal

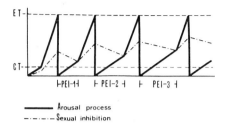

Fig. 17. An opponent-process model of sexual behavior. At the origin of the abscissa an estrous female is placed with a male. Cues from the female generate sexual arousal in the male, and sexual inhibition is induced simultaneously but at a lower rate. When arousal exceeds the copulatory threshold (CT), the male begins to copulate. Stimuli arising from coitus increase the rate of growth of arousal, which in turn increases the rate of growth of inhibition. When arousal reaches the ejaculatory threshold (ET), the male ejaculates, thereby depressing arousal to its original level and allowing inhibition to dissipate. During the postejaculatory interval (PEI), arousal is again generated by cues from the female, and copulation resumes when arousal exceeds both the CT and the level of inhibition. Resumption of copulation renews the growth of inhibition. For further explanation and analysis, see text. [From Kurtz and Adler (1973). Copyright 1973 by the American Psychological Association. Reprinted by permission.]

changes in copulatory behavior that occur over the course of an exhaustion test, as indeed it was designed to do. By being explicitly depicted, some of its liabilities as a model are clearer than those of some previous, less explicitly stated models.

Some of these problems are relatively minor and could possibly be dealt with by minor changes. For example, the model was developed to account for a monotonically decreasing ejaculation latency over series, but we know now (Brown, 1974; Dewsbury, 1968b; Karen and Barfield, 1975) that the function is J-shaped, possibly reaching a minimum as early as the second series. Another minor problem is that the generation and regeneration of arousal is assumed to depend only on extrinsic stimulation and not on endogenous changes, but this assumption does not seem to be necessary to the model.

Some other problems seem to be more fundamental. For example, the account of what happens during postejaculatory intervals seems to violate the basic assumption of the model. During these times arousal is depicted as increasing while inhibition wanes. However, an increase in excitation should generate growth of inhibition after ejaculation, just as it does during the mount latency and the ejaculation latency.

Another difficulty is that the temporal patterning of copulation prior to ejaculation is not accounted for. Since arousal is described as exceeding inhibition throughout the ejaculation latency, the male should pursue and mount the female continuously until he ejaculates. In fact few males behave in this way. Rather, bouts of mounting activity tend to be separated by longer periods of sexual inactivity. It is this phasic nature of copulation that led us (Sachs and Barfield, 1974) to depict each mount bout as acting to depress net sexual arousal (arousal minus inhibition) below the copulatory threshold. Were such a change to be superimposed upon the Kurtz-Adler model, the ejaculatory threshold could not be reached, since a single arousal-inhibition mechanism with two thresholds is employed. This problem was part of what motivated us to separate the copulatory mechanism with its threshold from the ejaculatory mechanism with its threshold. Additional motivation for this separation was the data reviewed earlier indicating that the pacing of copulation is the same in animals not approaching ejaculation [e.g., androgenized females (Schoelch-Krieger and Barfield, 1975); pudendectomized males (Lodder and Zeilmaker, 1976)] as it is in those that are approaching ejaculation. In the model of Freeman and McFarland (1974) the control of pacing is linked to the approach to ejaculation, and thus this model would also seem unable to deal with the apparently normal pacing of nonejaculating animals. On the other hand our model did not speak to such questions as the changes in copulation over the course of exhaustion tests, a prominent concern of the other models (Beach, 1956; Freeman and McFarland, 1974; Kurtz and Adler, 1973).

3. Hypothetical Neural Basis of Inhibitory Mechanism

A plausible candidate for part of the neural basis of the sexual inhibitory system derives in part from a study of Heimer and Larsson (1964). They made massive lesions in the posterior hypothalamic–midbrain junction of male rats. The average first PEIL of these males was as short as the average interintromission interval, about 1 minute. Successive PEILs were longer, but still very short. Barfield et al. (1975) observed drastic abbreviations of the PEIL after more discrete lesions within the same area and noted further that the postejaculatory vocalization was abolished in most operated animals and reduced significantly in the others (Table II). These data were interpreted as indicating that the lesions effectively destroyed the cerebral portion of the inhibitory system that controls the early portion of postejaculatory refractoriness, while leaving unaffected the arousal system which is responsible for the residual portion of the postejaculatory interval. In this context, the drastic reductions of PEIL sometimes resulting from brain stimulation (Caggiula, 1970; Caggiula and Hoebel, 1966; Malsbury, 1971; Van Dis and Larsson, 1971; Vaughan and Fisher, 1962) may be viewed as overriding this cerebral inhibitory system. Extreme reductions in the PEIL also were seen after more dorsal lesions that interrupted a major noradrenergic pathway (Clark et al., 1975). These lesions, though different anatomically from the lesions of Barfield et al. (1975), may have been similar neurochemically.

TABLE II

Postejaculatory Intromission Latencies (PEIL) during a Single Test of a
Male Rat Bearing Bilateral Lesions in the Ventral Tegmental Area
of the Rostral Midbrain[a]

Series number	PEIL	(PEML)[b]	Series number	PEIL	(PEML)[b]
1	90		10	145	(135)[c]
2	130	(75)	11	390	
3	90	(80)	12	330	
4	255	(145)	13	390	(320)
5	245		14	230	
6	205	(135)	15	360	
7	255	(130)	16	260	
8	330	(320)	17	300	(290)[d]
9	300				

[a]Postejaculatory mount latencies (PEML) are indicated in parentheses when these differed from the PEIL. [Unpublished data from the study of Barfield et al. (1975).]

[b]In seconds.

[c]The tail was pinched briefly 60 seconds after the preceding ejaculation.

[d]The test was terminated at this time. The male was evidently not approaching a point of self-termination of copulation.

In the study of Clark et al. (1975) the experimental animals also exhibited a reduction in the interintromission interval prior to the first ejaculation, but the interintromission intervals prior to subsequent ejaculations were unaltered, as were the number of intromissions and the ejaculation latency in all series. There were also no significant changes in the preejaculatory behavior of the experimental animals of Barfield et al. (1975). These data, considered in the context of the effect of the lesions on the PEILs, suggest that the mechanism involved in postejaculatory inhibition is not significantly involved in the pacing of copulation before ejaculation or in the accumulation of ejaculatory potential.

There is some evidence of endocrine involvement in the activation, and possibly the organization, of this inhibitory system. Female rats that have been androgenized perinatally and in adulthood display copulatory behavior that is indistinguishable from that of males. Relevant here is the fact that their PEILs and their postejaculatory vocalizations have the same duration as those of normal males (Sachs et al., 1973; Pollak and Sachs, 1975c). Female rats may display the ejaculatory pattern after only long-term estrogen treatment in adulthood; such females have much shorter PEILs than normal males, and they do not vocalize after the ejaculatory pattern (Emery and Sachs, 1975). It may be that androgen is needed to activate the inhibitory system, or it could be that estrogen is more effectively arousing than androgen. We cannot with certainty attribute the effect in long-term estrogenized females to endocrine actions because in many of these females pituitary hypertrophy and tumors resulted in lesions of or pressure upon the brain in about the area where lesions were found to drastically reduce the postejaculatory interval. On the other hand, female rats treated with 8 or 32 μg estradiol benzoate daily for 2 or 3 weeks and subjected to electrical shock have also displayed ejaculatory patterns; and although these animals had abbreviated refractory periods with little or no vocalization, no pituitary or hypothalamic pathology was evident upon autopsy. Like-treated male rats also exhibited little vocalization, but had normal refractory periods (Barfield and Krieger, submitted), and treatment of castrate male rats with estradiol (in combination with dihydrotestosterone) reduced or eliminated postejaculatory vocalization, but did not reduce the PEIL (Parrott and Barfield, 1975). Thus, there may be a fundamental sex difference in postejaculatory responses of male and female rats subjected to estradiol treatment.

The possible role of a spinal component in postejaculatory refractoriness has been investigated (Hart, 1967, 1968; Sachs and Garinello, 1975). Male rats held in supine position with their penis extended display clusters of penile reflexes that consist of erections, cups (distal flaring of the penis), and dorsal flips of the penis. [Hart (1968) observed no plug ejaculation in spinally transected males and concluded that separation of the spine from higher neural areas was responsible for the absence of plugs. However, intact males rarely display ejaculation of a plug either (Sachs and Garinello, 1975).] The interval between clusters of reflexes is about 2 to 3 minutes at the start of a test and gets progressively longer. These increasing intervals between clusters are characteristic even of males with transected spinal cords (Hart, 1968), and therefore there must be a spinal basis for the development of this genital refractoriness.

How much of postejaculatory refractoriness and ultimate exhaustion can be attributed to changes in the potential for elicitation of penile reflexes required for natural copulation? The relation between penile reflexes of supine males and of copulating males is by no means clear (Hart, 1968; Pollak and Sachs, 1973; Sachs and Garinello, 1975), but the former may tell us something about the latter.

Hart (1968) tested the penile reflexes of spinal males for 2 hours and noted a significant reduction in all classes of reflexes. When the males were retested 24 hours later, all reflexes had returned to normal levels. Hart concluded that recovery from sexual exhaustion does not depend upon recovery of sexual reflexes presumably controlled entirely at the spinal level.

Hart did not test the effects of copulatory behavior on penile reflexes, and it seemed conceivable that such effects would demonstrate a greater relation between penile reflexes and sexual exhaustion. To answer this question, Sachs and Garinello (1975) tested the penile reflexes of intact, unanesthetized male rats immediately after sexual exhaustion, as well as 4, 8, and 16 hours after exhaustion. The results, summarized in Table III, indicated a substantial reduction in the reflexes of exhausted males. The display of penile cups such as those seen during the ejaculatory pattern were especially depressed. Within 8 hours of sexual exhaustion all penile reflexes had returned to the levels of well-rested males, although few males copulate to ejaculation until 3 days after sexual exhaustion (Beach and Jordan, 1956).

These data support the conclusion of Hart (1968) that recovery from presumed spinal refractoriness plays little role in regulating the recovery from sexual exhaustion, but the data do not rule out an important role for spinal systems in regulating postejaculatory refractoriness, especially in the early portion of the postejaculatory interval during which the hypothetical inhibitory system predominates (Barfield and Geyer, 1975). In a second experiment (Sachs and Garinello, 1975), sexual reflexes were tested in the usual way in well-rested males and exhausted males. The significant decline in reflex elicitability in exhausted males was confirmed. Males were also tested after two and four ejaculations. After two ejaculations the number of all reflexes was statistically indistinguishable from the reflexes of well-rested males. However, after four ejaculations reflexes were depressed to the level characteristic of exhausted

TABLE III

Median Number of Erections (E), Cups (C), and Flips (F) during Supine Tests Following Sexual Exhaustion in Rats[a]

Group	Test 1[b]			Test 2			Test 3			Test 4		
	E	C	F	E	C	F	E	C	F	E	C	F
Experimental (N = 5)	5^a	0^c	0^c	10	1^c	1^c	17	9	4	16	8	7
Control (N = 3)	28^d	10^d	11^d	22^e	7^d	9	20	9	6	14	8	7

[a]Data from Sachs and Garinello (1975).

[b]Males in the control group had not copulated for at least 1 week prior to testing. Males in the experimental group received Test 1 upon reaching a criterion of sexual exhaustion, i.e., 45 minutes after ejaculation without additional sexual activity. Tests 2, 3, and 4 followed Test 1 by 4, 8, and 16 hours, respectively. Test duration was 15 minutes.

[c]Value significantly different from Test 4 value by paired-t test; $p < 0.01$.

[d]Value significantly different from experimental value by independent-t test; $p < 0.02$.

males, that is, essentially to zero. Immediately after the 15-minute reflex test, these males were placed with a receptive female and all copulated to ejaculation with short latency and without apparent difficulty. In a further experiment, well-rested males had their reflexes elicited for 1 hour in supine tests. In subsequent copulation to exhaustion, no variables exhibited significant changes from control levels. Clearly the role, if any, of spinal neural systems in the functioning of the hypothetical inhibitory mechanism bears further analysis.

C. ABSOLUTE AND RELATIVE PHASES OF THE POSTEJACULATORY REFRACTORY PERIOD

In 1949 Beach and Holz-Tucker suggested that the postejaculatory interval should not be treated as a unitary period. They proposed that there were two phases: an absolute refractory phase (ARP) during which the male is incapable of being aroused to renewed copulation; followed by a relative refractory phase (RRP) during which supranormal levels of stimulation are required to bring about resumption of copulation. This distinction was presumably made on the basis of behavioral changes that Beach and Holz-Tucker observed, but no measure was suggested that could discriminate these phases. Later, Larsson (1959a) proposed a similar distinction based upon the consequences of extending the postejaculatory interval beyond its normal time, but there was no way of measuring the phases in an ad libitum copulation test.

Recently, the combined outcomes of a number of studies have lent considerable support to the concepts of the ARP and RRP and have indicated ways in which the phases may be measured.

Painful shocks are unlikely to be effective in bringing the male to resume copulation until about 75% of the normal PEIL has elapsed (Barfield and Sachs, 1968; Sachs and Barfield, 1974), and gentle handling has a similar lower limit (Larsson, 1963). Electrical stimulation of the brain may occasionally result in much earlier resumption, but even with this treatment the PEIL is reduced on the average by only 25–35% (Malsbury, 1971; Caggiula and Szechtman, 1972), or even less (Eibergen and Caggiula, 1973). On the average, the male vocalizes during 65–75% of his PEIL, and the sleeplike EEG extends through the same period (Barfield and Geyer, 1972, 1975). Even when females are hormonally treated so that they display the full masculine copulatory pattern, their vocalization extends through 65–75% of the PEIL. Taken together, these data have led us to conclude that the ARP extends through 65–75% of the first PEIL and the RRP occupies the balance of the PEIL.

Evidence for the separateness of the processes controlling the ARP and the RRP derives from a study of the pre- and postejaculatory behavior of male rats when tested to exhaustion (Karen and Barfield, 1975). Plotted as an undivided

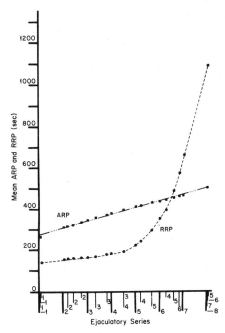

Fig. 18. Change in duration of absolute refractory period (ARP) and relative refractory period (RRP) of the postejaculatory interval in each ejaculatory series for male rats tested to a criterion of sexual exhaustion. The ARP is computed as the time from ejaculation to termination of vocalization. The RRP is the balance of the postejaculatory interval, from termination of vocalization to the resumption of copulation. The curves are based upon weighted averages for 4 groups of males attaining 5, 6, 7, and 8 ejaculations prior to reaching criterion. The abscissa is drawn so that the course of exhaustion for all groups may be depicted full scale. [From Karen and Barfield (1975). Copyright 1975 by the American Psychological Association. Reprinted by permission.]

variable, the PEIL shows a positively accelerated function as exhaustion approaches (see Fig. 5). A rather different picture is obtained when the PEIL is divided into its ARP (measured as time from ejaculation to termination of vocalization) and RRP (measured as the balance of the PEIL after vocalization termination). Then the ARP is revealed to increase slowly and linearly as exhaustion approaches, while RRP increases exponentially (Fig. 18). The ARP is believed to derive from activity in an inhibitory system, whereas the RRP derives from inactivity in an arousal system. Thus, sexual exhaustion would appear to be due to a failure of sufficient arousal, a conclusion that supports the earlier views of Beach (1956) and many others. By this view, only the initial portion of postejaculatory sexual inactivity is attributable to excessive inhibition.

D. EFFECTS OF EXTRINSIC STIMULI ON THE PEIL AND ITS
   COMPONENTS

1. The Effect of Painful Shocks

In the refractory period prior to the time that shocks to the skin cause the male to mount the receptive female, successive shocks may yield successively stronger reactions of the male toward the female. Soon after ejaculation there may not even be an alerting reaction, but later with successive shocks the male may orient to the female but not approach, approach but not touch, touch with a forepaw but not mount, and then mount but not thrust (Barfield and Sachs, 1968; Sachs and Barfield, 1970, 1974). Similar successive approaches to copulation have been reported when direct brain stimulation was used (Caggiula, 1970; Eibergen and Caggiula, 1973). This type of reaction led to the formulation of a model (Fig. 19) in which the arousing effects of extrinsic stimulation upon the male were viewed as having a very brief duration (Sachs and Barfield, 1974). The magnitude of the arousal increment was depicted as sufficient to induce copulation only when it acted upon an adequate base of intrinsic arousal, presumed to come after the ARP. However, as Soulairac (1952) and others have implied, after ejaculation the male is not simply in a state of reduced *arousal*; his insensitivity to strong environmental stimuli, sexual and nonsexual, bespeaks a state of reduced *arousability* as well. This characteristic could be represented in the

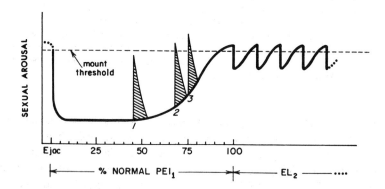

Fig. 19. Model of change in net sexual arousal (arousal − inhibition) of male rats during the first postejaculatory interval (PEI₁) and, by extension, during copulation prior to a second ejaculation (EL₂). The effects of applying fixed amounts of shock are shown at *1, 2,* and *3*. Only at *3* does shock increase sexual arousal above threshold for a long enough time to allow the resumption of copulation, thereby shortening the postejaculatory interval to about 75% of its normal duration. "Ejac" represents ejaculation. [From Sachs and Barfield (1974). Copyright 1974 by the American Psychological Association. Reprinted by permission.]

model by indicating progressively larger increments in stimulation-induced arousal as a function of time since ejaculation.

Recent data require additional modification of the model. In particular, it is now clear that painful stimuli prior to the end of the ARP actually extend the ARP; that is, they appear to enhance the inhibitory process.

Barfield and Geyer (1975) applied skin shock to males every 30 seconds in order to investigate the effects of this treatment on the ARP and the RRP. As expected, shock shortened the total PEIL, primarily by shortening the RRP (i.e., PEIL − VT). Unexpectedly, intermittent shocks, and even the presetting of shock levels in the control condition, acted to increase the duration of the ARP: not only did the males continue vocalization later into the PEIL, they also started vocalizing sooner after ejaculation. In a further experiment it was determined that if a single shock were applied immediately after vocalization ended, then copulation was immediately resumed. Thus the male is capable of being stimulated to copulation immediately after the end of activity in the presumed inhibitory process.

But what of the extension of the ARP by application of shocks prior to the spontaneous termination of the ARP? Pollak (1974; Pollak and Sachs, 1975a) applied intermittent shocks to males during the ARP only, during the RRP only, or during the presumed time of transition between ARP and RRP. When shocks were started soon after ejaculation (the ARP), the latency to the onset of vocalization was shortened, and the time to the end of vocalization was increased. Stimulation during the postvocalization period (the RRP) shortened that phase. Shocks during the transitional period between ARP and RRP acted to prolong the PEIL, but that effect was overcome if shocks continued into the RRP. On the whole these data confirmed the picture from the study of Barfield and Geyer (1975) and, together with other evidence, led to the following conclusion: shock does indeed have transient excitatory effects, as indicated by Sachs and Barfield (1974), but it also has inhibitory effects which decay more slowly. Similar effects upon interintromission intervals resulted from shocks administered prior to ejaculation. Both sets of effects were interpreted in the context of Solomon and Corbit's (1974) opponent process theory (Pollak, 1974). A similar biphasic influence was noted by Caggiula and Szechtman (1972) for the effects of brain stimulation upon copulation.

2. Role of the Female

a. Effects of Removing the Female. The female is, of course, an extrinsic stimulus for the male, and yet her role in regulating the resumption of copulation after ejaculation is questionable. Sachs *et al.* (1974) tested males in two conditions. In one condition males copulated ad libitum with the female continuously present before and after copulation. In the other condition, the female was removed from the cage after each mount bout before ejaculation, as well as immediately after ejaculation. The male was required to press a bar for the female to be returned to the cage. When she was not in the cage, no immediate cues from her were available to the male, although of course stimuli from the cage continued to be present.

As we have seen (Section VI,B,7), the absence of the female between mount bouts prior to ejaculation slowed the pace of copulation considerably. However, her absence after ejaculation appeared to have no effect: the postejaculatory intervals in the two conditions were statistically indistinguishable. Also of interest was the timing of the first bar press after ejaculation. Some males (designated Type A) pressed the bar and gained access to the female after 50–75% of their PEIL. Other males (Type B) pressed the bar and then copulated as soon as the female was available. If the female were to make a difference in the rearousal of the male's copulatory potential, one would expect the Type A males to have shorter PEILs than the Type B males. In fact the intervals were almost equivalent.

The intervals from ejaculation to bar press were consistent with the view that Type B males did not press the bar until the end of their relative refractory period, whereas the Type A males pressed the bar after their absolute refractory period. The equivalence of their postejaculatory intervals lead to the conclusion that the rate of recovery from ejaculation is primarily an endogenous process (but see Larsson, 1973). In this study the behavior of the females was not systematically recorded. All were highly receptive, but it is not clear how actively they solicited copulation. Still, the data suggest that the more distant cues from a receptive female, such as sight and smell and sound, can not effectively shorten the postejaculatory interval.

b. The Coolidge Effect. This conclusion about the role of the female may seem at variance with what is commonly known as the Coolidge effect: the resumption of copulation by a sexually exhausted male following a change in the stimulus female. It will be recalled that sexual exhaustion is defined as a very long period, usually 30 minutes or more, without an attempted mount. Usually this long interval follows an ejaculation rather than a mount or intromission, and so it is natural to view sexual exhaustion as an ultralong postejaculatory interval and to view changing the female as a way of shortening that interval. By that view receptive females have a potentially significant role in the recovery from postejaculatory refractoriness.

Several lines of evidence suggest this view is wrong. The most direct evidence is the uniform failure to observe a Coolidge effect in male rats prior to sexual exhaustion. If a novel female can shorten the terminal (exhaustion) PEIL dramatically, then she ought to be able to shorten preexhaustion PEILs significantly. All attempts to demonstrate such an effect on the PEIL (Hsiao, 1965; Dewsbury, 1968b; Pollak, 1974) or its component parts (Barfield and Geyer, 1975) have failed. [However, see Westbrook (1974).]

One possible reason for the failure of these attempts is that the female has usually been changed immediately after ejaculation. In the earlier demonstrations of the Coolidge effect the female was almost certainly changed during the RRP, at a time when the male may be presumed to be more sensitive to novelty cues than he is during the ARP. Changing the female immediately after ejaculation in preexhaustion tests for the Coolidge effect may have given time for the male to become adapted to whatever cues to novelty the female has. It would therefore be instructive to change the female immediately after the ARP (i.e., after termination of vocalization).

It could be further argued that changing the female after each ejaculation allowed the male to become habituated to change itself. However, even when the novel female was introduced only after the ARP of the second series, no change in the PEIL was evident although, as in similar experiments by Dewsbury (1968b), the number of intromissions in the next series was reduced (Pollak, 1974; Pollak and Sachs, 1975a). This reduction in number of intromissions was evident whether the female was changed during the ARP, the RRP, or even after the first intromission of the next series.

The weight of this evidence suggests that a sexually exhausted male is not just in a very long postejaculatory interval. Rather, there appears to be a qualitative difference between a sexually exhausted male and a male in a preexhaustion postejaculatory interval. The nature of this difference remains to be discovered.

VIII. CONCLUSION

In this chapter we have analyzed the masculine copulatory behavior of the rat. Many measures of copulatory behavior—initiation latencies, copulatory rate, number of intromissions, etc.—were found to vary rather independently of each other, and this evidence was taken as support for the view that sexual arousal is not unitary. We reviewed data showing that some or all of the arousal systems have inhibitory counterparts. This is particularly clear with respect to the absolute and relative postejaculatory refractory periods, but probably it is also true of systems controlling behavior prior to ejaculation. Considerable emphasis was given to the neglected problem of the pacing of copulation prior to ejaculation. We reviewed evidence that this patterning is often best described by measures based upon mount bouts and that mount bouts without intromission have the same effect upon copulatory pace as do mount bouts with intromission. In describing the regularity of the temporal patterning we used the metaphor of a "copulatory clock," and we summarized evidence that the number of intromissions needed for ejaculation is substantially independent of the speed of this copulatory clock.

Our primary concern in this chapter was to describe how the elements of copulatory behavior were "wired together," rather than how the nervous system controlling that behavior is "wired together." Nevertheless, behavioral and physiological analysis must proceed in parallel, and our consideration of the physiological evidence reminded us forcefully how little is known about the physiological mechanisms underlying sexual behavior. Potential neural and chemical (including hormonal) correlates of some of the hypothetical excitatory and inhibitory systems have begun to be explored. We know that manipulation of certain parts of the central nervous system can dramatically influence initiation latencies and postejaculatory latencies, but we have little idea of the physiological basis of the pacing of copulation, or of the accumulation of ejaculatory potential, or of the gating functions that behavioral analysis suggests must be present. Some of the spinal mechanisms controlling erection and ejaculation have been identified for decades, but we still have little idea how these spinal systems become integrated into the behavior pattern of the whole organism. Even in some instances in which the physiological evidence is overwhelming, the common interpretation of that evidence may be suspect. For example, in every mammalian species tested, lesions in the medial preoptic area–anterior hypothalamus have largely eliminated copulatory behavior. The effects have been variously attributed to sexual motivational or performance deficits. Now J. Slimp, B. Hart, and R. Goy (personal communication, 1976) have determined that male rhesus monkeys bearing such lesions also are unlikely to copulate, but these animals continue to masturbate to ejaculation at their characteristically high rate. These males are clearly predisposed toward, and capable of, sexual arousal and ejaculation, but not with female partners. The evidence suggests that the lesions interfered with the processing of cues from the female or with the decision to copulate, but a definitive conclusion awaits further analysis.

One goal of this chapter was to relate the behavioral analysis to a number of theoretical models of copulatory behavior. These models have varied in complexity from the "dual-factor" approach of Beach (1956) to the manifold variables and interactions employed in the control systems approach (Freeman and McFarland, 1974; Karen, 1975). There are clearly substantial correlations among the variables by which we measure copulatory behavior, but we have also been impressed with the experimental dissociability of many of the variables, and we believe that this potential independence reflects a substantial functional independence among the multiple systems that control copulatory behavior. The prevailing tendency to obey the Law of Parsimony should not compel us, in the face of apparent complexity, to "make things easy by leaving out the hard parts."[4] We believe the behavioral data will best be described by a theoretical model that emerges from a recognition of the plurality of arousal and inhibitory

[4] Rheem Jarrett of the University of California, Berkeley, is responsible for keeping alive this quotation of Sylvanus P. Thompson.

systems and their complex interaction. If such a model is also founded in biological reality, then the model can serve as a valuable integrating framework for behavioral data and as a guide for the search for underlying physiological mechanisms.

Acknowledgments

This chapter is dedicated to Frank A. Beach, whose creative ideas and research paved the way for much of the work reviewed in this paper, and to the late Daniel S. Lehrman, who provided the atmosphere of open inquiry that fostered the beginning of our collaboration at the Institute of Animal Behavior, Rutgers University.

The research and writing of this chapter were supported by USPHS research grants HD-04484 (to RJB) and HD-04048 and HD-08933 (to BDS), and grants from the University of Connecticut Research Foundation (to BDS). Final preparation of the chapter was assisted by the hospitality of Julian M. Davidson and the Department of Physiology, Stanford University, during a sabbatical leave by BDS. We are indebted to Anthony R. Caggiula, Donald A. Dewsbury, Donna E. Emery, Valerie S. Harris, Edward I. Pollak, and the editors of this series for their valuable critiques of earlier drafts of this chapter. Figure 1 was drawn by Dorothy Tallentire; Figs. 6–10 by Barbara Vinopal.

References

Adler, N. T. 1969. Effects of the male's copulatory behavior on successful pregnancy of the female rat. *J. Comp. Physiol. Psychol.* **69**, 613–622.

Adler, N. T., and Bermant, G. 1966. Sexual behavior of male rats: effects of reduced sensory feedback. *J. Comp. Physiol. Psychol.* **61**, 240–243.

Adler, N. T., and Zoloth, S. R. 1970. Copulatory behavior can inhibit pregnancy in female rats. *Science* **168**, 1480–1482.

Ahlenius, S., Eriksson, H., Larsson, K., Modigh, K., and Södersten, P. 1971. Mating behavior in the male rat treated with *p*-chlorophenylalanine methyl ester alone or in combination with pargyline. *Psychopharmacologia* **20**, 383–388.

Andrew, R. J. 1974. Arousal and the causation of behaviour. *Behaviour* **51**, 135–165.

Barfield, R. J., and Geyer, L. A. 1972. Sexual behavior: ultrasonic postejaculatory song of the male rat. *Science* **176**, 1349–1350.

Barfield, R. J., and Geyer, L. A. 1975. The ultrasonic postejaculatory vocalization and the postejaculatory refractory period of the male rat. *J. Comp. Physiol. Psychol.* **88**, 723–734.

Barfield, R. J., and Krieger, M. S. Ejaculatory and postejaculatory behavior of male and female rats: Effects of sex hormones and electric shock. Submitted to *J. Comp. Physiol. Psychol.*

Barfield, R. J., and Sachs, B. D. 1968. Sexual behavior: stimulation by painful electrical shock to skin in male rats. *Science* **161**, 392–396.

Barfield, R. J., Wilson, C., and McDonald, P. G. 1975. Sexual behavior: extreme reduction of the postejaculatory refractory period by posterior hypothalamic lesions in male rats. *Science* **189**, 147–149.

Beach, F. A. 1942a. Analysis of factors involved in the arousal, maintenance and manifestation of sexual excitement in male animals. *Psychosomat. Med.* **4**, 173–198.

Beach, F. A. 1942b. Analysis of the stimuli adequate to elicit mating behavior in the sexually inexperienced male rat. *J. Comp. Psychol.* **33**, 163–207.

Beach, F. A. 1942c. Effects of testosterone propionate upon the copulatory behavior of sexually inexperienced male rats. *J. Comp. Psychol.* **33**, 227–247.

Beach, F. A. 1942d. Execution of the complete masculine copulatory pattern by sexually receptive female rats. *J. Genet. Psychol.* **60**, 137–142.

Beach, F. A. 1956. Characteristics of masculine "sex drive." *In* "The Nebraska Symposium on Motivation" (M. R. Jones, ed.), pp. 1–32. Univ. of Nebraska Press, Lincoln, Nebraska.

Beach, F. A. 1967. Cerebral and hormonal control of reflexive mechanisms involved in copulatory behavior. *Physiol. Rev.* **47**, 289–316.

Beach, F. A. 1971. Hormonal factors controlling the differentiation, development, and display of copulatory behavior in the ramstergig and related species. *In* "The Biopsychology of Development" (E. Tobach, L. Aronson, and E. Shaw, eds.), pp. 249–296. Academic Press, New York.

Beach, F. A. 1976. Sexual attractivity, proceptivity, and receptivity in female mammals. *Horm. Behav.* **7**, 105–138.

Beach, F. A., and Fowler, H. 1959. Effects of "situational anxiety" on sexual behavior in male rats. *J. Comp. Physiol. Psychol.* **52**, 245–248.

Beach, F. A., and Holz-Tucker, A. M. 1949. Effects of different concentrations of androgen upon sexual behavior in castrated male rats. *J. Comp. Physiol. Psychol.* **42**, 433–453.

Beach, F. A., and Jordan, L. 1956. Sexual exhaustion and recovery in the male rat. *Quart. J. Exp. Psychol.* **8**, 121–133.

Beach, F. A., and Rasquin, P. L. 1942. Masculine copulatory behavior in intact and castrated female rats. *Endocrinology* **31**, 393–409.

Beach, F. A., and Whalen, R. E. 1959a. Effects of ejaculation on sexual behavior in the male rat. *J. Comp. Physiol. Psychol.* **52**, 249–254.

Beach, F. A., and Whalen, R. E. 1959b. Effects of intromission without ejaculation upon sexual behavior in male rats. *J. Comp. Physiol. Psychol.* **52**, 476–481.

Beach, F. A., Goldstein, A. C., and Jacoby, O. 1955. Effects of electroconvulsive shock on sexual behavior in male rats. *J. Comp. Physiol. Psychol.* **48**, 173–179.

Beach, F. A., Conovitz, M. W., Steinberg, F., and Goldstein, A. C. 1956. Experimental inhibition and restoration of mating behavior in male rats. *J. Genet. Psychol.* **89**, 165–181.

Beach, F. A., Westbrook, W. H., and Clemens, L. G. 1966. Comparisons of the ejaculatory response in men and animals. *Psychosomat. Med.* **28**, 749–763.

Bemmels, B. 1971. The effect of cage environment on the sexual behavior of the male rat. Master's Thesis, Rutgers University.

Bermant, G. 1961. Response latencies of female rats during sexual intercourse. *Science* **133**, 1771–1773.

Bermant, G. 1964. Effects of single and multiple enforced intercopulatory intervals on the sexual behavior of male rats. *J. Comp. Physiol. Psychol.* **57**, 398–403.

Bermant, G. 1965. Rat sexual behavior: photographic analysis of the intromission response. *Psychon. Sci.* **2**, 65–66.

Bermant, G. 1967. Copulation in rats. *Psychol. Today* **1** (July), 52–60.

Bermant, G., and Davidson, J. M. 1974. "Biological Bases of Sexual Behavior." Harper and Row, New York.

Bermant, G., and Taylor, L. 1969. Interactive effects of experience and olfactory bulb lesions in male rat copulation. *Physiol. Behav.* **4**, 13–17.

Bermant, G., and Westbrook, W. 1966. Peripheral factors in the regulation of sexual contact by female rats. *J. Comp. Physiol. Psychol.* **61**, 244–250.

Bermant, G., Lott, D., and Anderson, L. 1968. Temporal characteristics of the Coolidge Effect in male rat copulatory behavior. *J. Comp. Physiol. Psychol.* **65**, 447–452.

Bermant, G., Anderson, L., and Parkinson, S. R. 1969. Copulation in rats: Relations among intromission duration, frequency, and pacing. *Psychon. Sci.* 17, 293–294.

Bignami, G. 1966. Pharmacologic influences on mating behavior in the male rat. Effects of *d*-amphetamine, LSD-25, strychnine, nicotine, and various anticholinergic agents. *Psychopharmacologia* 10, 44–58.

Boland, D. B., and Dewsbury, D. A. 1971. Characteristics of sleep following sexual activity and wheel running in male rats. *Physiol. Behav.* 6, 145–149.

Brown, R. 1974. Rat copulatory behavior. *In* "Motivational Control Systems Analysis" (D. J. McFarland, ed.), pp. 461–479. Academic Press, New York.

Butcher, L. L., Butcher, S. G., and Larsson, K. 1969. Effects of apomorphine, (+)-amphetamine, and nialimide on tetrabenazine-induced suppression of sexual behavior in the male rat. *Eur. J. Pharmacol.* 7, 283–288.

Caggiula, A. R. 1970. Analysis of the copulation-reward properties of posterior hypothalamic stimulation in male rats. *J. Comp. Physiol. Psychol.* 70, 399–412.

Caggiula, A. R. 1972. Shock-elicited copulation and aggression in male rats. *J. Comp. Physiol. Psychol.* 80, 393–397.

Caggiula, A. R., and Eibergen, R. 1969. Copulation of virgin male rats evoked by painful peripheral stimulation. *J. Comp. Physiol. Psychol.* 69, 414–419.

Caggiula, A. R., and Hoebel, B. G. 1966. "Copulation-reward site" in the posterior hypothalamus. *Science* 153, 1284–1285.

Caggiula, A. R., and Szechtman, H. 1972. Hypothalamic stimulation: A biphasic influence on copulation of the male rat. *Behav. Biol.* 7, 591–598.

Caggiula, A. R., and Vlahoulis, M. 1974. Modifications in the copulatory performance of male rats produced by repeated peripheral shock. *Behav. Biol.* 11, 269–274.

Caggiula, A. R., Antelman, S. M., and Zigmond, M. J. 1973. Disruption of copulation in male rats after hypothalamic lesions: a behavioral, anatomical, and neurochemical analysis. *Brain Res.* 59, 273–287.

Calhoun, J. B. 1962. "Ecology and Sociology of the Norway Rat." U.S. Dept. of Health, Education, and Welfare, Public Health Service, Bethesda, Maryland.

Carlsson, S. G., and Larsson, K. 1962. Intromission frequency and intromission duration in the male rat mating behavior. *Scand. J. Psychol.* 3, 189–191.

Carlsson, S. G., and Larsson, K. 1964. Mating in male rats after local anesthetization of the glans penis. *Z. Tierpsychol.* 21, 854–856.

Carlsson, S., and Larsson, K. 1974. Comments on the RATSEX model. *In* "Motivational Control Systems Analysis" (D. J. McFarland, ed.), pp. 504–507. Academic Press, New York.

Cherney, E. F., and Bermant, G. 1970. Role of stimulus female novelty in the rearousal of copulation in male laboratory rats (*Rattus norvegicus*). *Anim. Behav.* 18, 567–574.

Clark, T. K., Caggiula, A. R., McConnell, R. A., and Antelman, S. M. 1975. Sexual inhibition is reduced by rostral midbrain lesions in the male rat. *Science* 190, 169–171.

Clemens, L. G. Undated. Mechanism of male sexual behavior. Unpublished manuscript.

Cofer, C. N., and Appley, M. A. 1964. "Motivation: Theory and Research." Wiley, New York.

Crowley, W. R., Popolow, H. B., and Ward, O. B., Jr. 1973. From dud to stud: Copulatory behavior elicited through conditioned arousal in sexually inactive male rats. *Physiol. Behav.* 10, 391–394.

Davis, H. N., Gray, G. D., Zerylnick, M., and Dewsbury, D. A. 1974. Ovulation and implantation in montane voles (*Microtus montanus*) as a function of varying amounts of copulatory stimulation. *Horm. Behav.* 5, 383–388.

Dewsbury, D. A. 1967a. A quantitative description of the behaviour of rats during copulation. *Behaviour* 29, 154–178.

Dewsbury, D. A. 1967b. Changes in inter-intromission interval during uninterrupted copulation in rats. *Psychon. Sci.* 7, 177–179.

Dewsbury, D. A. 1968a. Copulatory behavior of rats—variations within the dark phase of the cycle. *Commun. Behav. Biol., Part A* 1, 373–377.

Dewsbury, D. A. 1968b. Copulatory behavior in rats: changes as satiety is approached. *Psychol. Rep.* 22, 937–943.

Dewsbury, D. A. 1969. Copulatory behaviour of rats (*Rattus norvegicus*) as a function of prior copulatory experience. *Anim. Behav.* 17, 217–223.

Dewsbury, D. A. 1972. Patterns of copulatory behavior in male mammals. *Quart. Rev. Biol.* 47, 1–33.

Dewsbury, D. A. 1975a. The normal heterosexual pattern of copulatory behavior in male rats: Effects of drugs that alter monoamine levels. *In* "Sexual Behavior: Pharmacology and Biochemistry" (M. Sandler and G. L. Gessa, eds.), pp. 169–179. Raven Press, New York.

Dewsbury, D. A. 1975b. A diallel cross analysis of genetic determinants of copulatory behavior in rats. *J. Comp. Physiol. Psychol.* 88, 713–722.

Dewsbury, D. A., and Bolce, S. K. 1968. Sexual satiety in rats: Effects of prolonged post-ejaculatory intervals. *Psychon. Sci.* 13, 25–26.

Dewsbury, D. A., and Bolce, S. K. 1970. Effects of prolonged postejaculatory intervals on copulatory behavior of rats. *J. Comp. Physiol. Psychol.* 72, 421–425.

Dewsbury, D. A., Goodman, E. D., Salis, P. J., and Bunnell, B. N. 1968. Effects of hippocampal lesions on the copulatory behavior of male rats. *Physiol. Behav.* 3, 651–656.

Diakow, C. 1974. Male-female interactions and the organization of mammalian mating patterns. This series, pp. 227–268.

Diakow, C. 1975. Motion picture analysis of rat mating behavior. *J. Comp. Physiol. Psychol.* 88, 704–712.

Diamond, M. 1970. Intromission pattern and species vaginal code in relation to induction of pseudopregnancy. *Science* 169, 995–997.

Diamond, M. 1972. Vaginal stimulation and progesterone in relation to pregnancy and parturition. *Biol. Reprod.* 6, 281–287.

Doty, R. L. 1974. A cry for the liberation of the female rodent: courtship and copulation in *Rodentia. Psychol. Bull.* 81, 159–172.

Edmonds, S., Zoloth, S. R., and Adler, N. T. 1972. Storage of copulatory stimulation in the female rat. *Physiol. Behav.* 8, 161–164.

Eibergen, R. D., and Caggiula, A. R. 1973. Ventral midbrain involvement in copulatory behavior in the male rat. *Physiol. Behav.* 10, 435–441.

Emery, D. E., and Sachs, B. D. 1975. Ejaculatory pattern in female rats without androgen treatment. *Science* 190, 484–486.

Emery, D. E. and Sachs, B. D. 1976a. Hormonal and monoaminergic influences on masculine copulatory behavior in the female rat. *Horm. Behav.* (in press).

Emery, D. E., and Sachs, B. D. 1976b. Copulatory behavior of male rats with lesions in the bed nucleus of the stria terminalis. *Physiol. Behav.* (in press).

Freeman, S., and McFarland, D. J. 1974. RATSEX—an exercise in simulation. *In* "Motivational Control Systems Analysis" (D. J. McFarland, ed.), pp. 479–504. Academic Press, London.

Gerall, A. A. 1958. Effect of interruption of copulation on male guinea pig sexual behavior. *Psychol. Rep.* 4, 215–221.

Gerall, A. A., and Berg, W. S. 1964. Effect of novel situation and modification in sexual drive on rate of oxygen consumption in guinea pigs. *Psychol. Rep.* 15, 311–317.

Goldfoot, D. A., and Baum, M. J. 1972. Initiation of mating behavior in developing male rats following peripheral electric shock. *Physiol. Behav.* 8, 857–863.

Gray, G. D., Zerylnick, M., David, H. N., and Dewsbury, D. A. 1974. Effects of variations in male copulatory behavior on ovulation and implantation in prairie voles, *Microtus ochrogaster*. *Horm. Behav.* 5, 389–396.

Härd, E., and Larsson, K. 1968a. Effects of mounts without intromission upon sexual behaviour in male rats. *Anim. Behav.* 16, 538–540.

Härd, E., and Larsson, K. 1968b. Visual stimulation and mating behavior in male rats. *J. Comp. Physiol. Psychol.* 66, 805–807.

Härd, E., and Larsson, K. 1969. Effects of precoital exposure of male rats to copulating animals upon subsequent mating performances. *Anim. Behav.* 17, 540–541.

Härd, E., and Larsson, K. 1970. Effects of delaying intromission on the male rat's mating behavior. *J. Comp. Physiol. Psychol.* 70, 413–416.

Harris, V. S., and Sachs, B. D. 1975. Copulatory behavior in male rats following amygdaloid lesions. *Brain Res.* 86, 514–518.

Harris, V. S., Emery, D. E., Yutzey, D. A., and Sachs, B. D. 1974. Limbic lesions and ejaculatory potential in the male rat. Paper presented at the Eastern Conference on Reproductive Behavior, Atlanta, Georgia.

Hart, B. L. 1967. Testosterone regulation of sexual reflexes in spinal male rats. *Science* 155, 1283–1284.

Hart, B. L. 1968. Sexual reflexes and mating behavior in the male rat. *J. Comp. Physiol. Psychol.* 65, 453–460.

Hart, B. L. 1972a. Sexual reflexes in the male rat after anesthetization of the glans penis. *Behav. Biol.* 7, 127–130.

Hart, B. L. 1972b. Manipulation of neonatal androgen: Effects on sexual responses and penile development in male rats. *Physiol. Behav.* 8, 841–845.

Hart, B. L., and Haugen, C. M. 1971. Prevention of genital grooming in mating behaviour of male rats (*Rattus norvegicus*). *Anim. Behav.* 19, 230–232.

Heimer, L., and Larsson, K. 1964. Drastic changes in the mating behaviour of male rats following lesions in the junction of diencephalon and mesencephalon. *Experientia* 20, 460–461.

Heimer, L., and Larsson, K. 1967. Mating behavior of male rats after olfactory bulb lesions. *Physiol. Behav.* 2, 207–209.

Herberg, L. J. 1963. Seminal ejaculation following positively reinforcing electrical stimulation of the rat hypothalamus. *J. Comp. Physiol. Psychol.* 56, 679–685.

Hinde, R. 1970. "Animal Behaviour." McGraw-Hill, New York.

Hsiao, S. 1965. Effects of female variation on sexual satiation in the male rat. *J. Comp. Physiol. Psychol.* 60, 467–479.

Jowaisas, D., Taylor, J., Dewsbury, D. A., and Malagodi, E. F. 1971. Copulatory behavior of male rats under an imposed operant requirement. *Psychon. Sci.* 25, 287–290.

Karen, L. M. 1973. Sexual exhaustion in the male rat. Paper presented at Eastern Conference on Reproductive Behavior, Chicago, Illinois.

Karen, L. M. 1975. Male rat sexual behavior: a theoretical interpretation of experiments on its organization. Doctoral dissertation. Rutgers University.

Karen, L. M., and Barfield, R. J. 1975. Differential rates of exhaustion and recovery of several parameters of male rat sexual behavior. *J. Comp. Physiol. Psychol.* 88, 693–703.

Komisaruk, B. R., Adler, N. T., and Hutchison, J. 1972. Genital sensory field: Enlargement by estrogen treatment in female rats. *Science* 178, 1295–1298.

Kow, L.-M., and Pfaff, D. W. 1973/74. Effects of estrogen treatment on the size of receptive field and response threshold of pudendal nerve in the female rat. *Neuroendocrinology* 13, 299–313.

Krechevsky, I. 1932. "Hypotheses" in rats. *Psychol. Rev.* **39**, 516–532.

Krieger, M. S., and Barfield, R. J. 1976. Masculine sexual behavior: Pacing and ejaculatory patterns in female rats induced by electrical shock. *Physiol. Behav.* (in press).

Kurtz, R. G., and Adler, N. T. 1973. Electrophysiological correlates of copulatory behavior in the male rat: Evidence for a sexual inhibitory process. *J. Comp. Physiol. Psychol.* **84**, 225–239.

Larsson, K. 1956. Conditioning and sexual behaviour in the male albino rat. *Acta Psychol. Gothoburgensia* **1**, 1–269.

Larsson, K. 1958. Age differences in the diurnal periodicity of male sexual behavior. *Gerontologia* **2**, 64–72.

Larsson, K. 1959a. Effects of prolonged postejaculatory intervals in the mating behaviour of the male rat. *Z. Tierpsychol.* **16**, 628–632.

Larsson, K. 1959b. The effect of restraint upon copulatory behaviour in the rat. *Anim. Behav.* **7**, 23–25.

Larsson, K. 1962. Mating behavior in male rats after cerebral cortex albations: I. Effects of lesions in the dorsolateral and the median cortex. *J. Exp. Zool.* **151**, 167–176.

Larsson, K. 1963. Non-specific stimulation and sexual behaviour in the male rat. *Behaviour* **20**, 110–114.

Larsson, K. 1964. Mating behavior in male rats after cerebral cortex ablation: II. Effects of lesions in the frontal lobes compared to lesions in the posterior half of the hemispheres. *J. Exp. Zool.* **155**, 203–213.

Larsson, K. 1966. Effects of neonatal castration upon the development of the mating behavior of the male rat. *Z. Tierpsychol.* **23**, 867–873.

Larsson, K. 1969. Failure of gonadal and gonadotrophic hormones to compensate for an impaired sexual function in anosmic male rats. *Physiol. Behav.* **4**, 733–738.

Larsson, K. 1971. Impaired mating performances in male rats after anosmia induced peripherally or centrally. *Brain, Behav. Evol.* **4**, 463–471.

Larsson, K. 1973. Sexual Behavior: The result of an interaction. *In* "Contemporary Sexual Behavior: Critical Issues in the 1970s" (J. Zubin and J. Money, eds.), pp. 33–51. Johns Hopkins Univ. Press, Baltimore, Maryland.

Larsson, K., and Södersten, P. 1973. Mating in male rats after section of the dorsal penile nerve. *Physiol. Behav.* **10**, 567–571.

Lodder, J., and Zeilmaker, G. H. 1976. Effects of pelvic nerve and pudendal nerve transection upon mating behavior in the male rat. *Physiol. Behav.* (in press).

McClintock, M. K., and Adler, N. T. 1974. The role of the female rat during copulatory behavior. Paper presented at the meeting of the Eastern Psychological Association, Philadelphia, Pennsylvania.

McGill, T. E. 1965. Studies of the sexual behavior of male laboratory mice: effects of genotype, recovery of sex drive, and theory. *In* "Sex and Behavior" (F. A. Beach, ed.), pp. 76–88. Wiley, New York.

McGill, T. E. 1974. Reproductive isolation, behavioral genetics, and functions of sexual behavior in rodents. Paper presented at Symposium on Reproductive Behavior and Evolution, Newark, New Jersey.

McGill, T. E., and Coughlin, R. C. 1970. Ejaculatory reflex and luteal activity induction in *Mus musculus. J. Reprod. Fertil.* **21**, 215–220.

Malmnnäs, C. O. 1973. Monoamine precursors and copulatory behavior in the male rat. *Acta Physiol. Scand.* (Suppl. 395), 47–114.

Malsbury, C. W. 1971. Facilitation of male rat copulatory behavior by electrical stimulation of the medial preoptic area. *Physiol. Behav.* **7**, 797–805.

Malsbury, C. W. 1972. Effects of preoptic area and peripheral stimulation in sexually inactive male rats. Paper presented at the meeting of the Eastern Psychological Association, Boston, Massachusetts.

Malsbury, C. W., and Pfaff, D. W. 1974. Neural and hormonal determinants of mating behavior in adult male rats. A review. *In* "The Limbic and Autonomic Nervous System: Advances in Research" (L. DiCara, ed.), pp. 85–136. Plenum, New York.

Merari, A., Barak, A., and Plaves, M. 1973. Effects of $\Delta^{1(2)}$-tetrahydrocannabinol on copulation in the male rat. *Psychopharmacologia* 28, 243–246.

Olds, J. 1958. Effects of hunger and male sex hormone on self-stimulation of the brain. *J. Comp. Physiol. Psychol.* 51, 320–324.

Parrott, R. F., and Barfield, R. J. 1975. Post-ejaculatory vocalization in castrated rats treated with various steroids. *Physiol. Behav.* 15, 484–486.

Peirce, J. T., and Nuttall, R. L. 1961a. Duration of sexual contacts in the rat. *J. Comp. Physiol. Psychol.* 54, 585–587.

Peirce, J. T., and Nuttall, R. L. 1961b. Self-paced sexual behavior in the female rat. *J. Comp. Physiol. Psychol.* 54, 310–313.

Pfaff, D. W., and Lewis, C. 1974. Film analyses of lordosis in female rats. *Horm. Behav.* 5, 317–335.

Pfaff, D. W., and Zigmond, R. E. 1971. Neonatal androgen effects on sexual and non-sexual behavior of adult rats tested under various hormone regimes. *Neuroendocrinology* 7, 129–145.

Pfaff, D. W., Lewis, C., Diakow, C., and Keiner, M. 1972. Neurophysiological analysis of mating behavior responses as hormone-sensitive reflexes. *Prog. Physiol. Psychol.* 5, 253–297.

Pollak, E. I. 1974. Temporal patterning of copulation in male *Rattus norvegicus:* Endogenous and exogenous control. Doctoral Dissertation. Univ. of Connecticut, Storrs, Connecticut.

Pollak, E. I., and Sachs, B. D. 1973. Mounts, intromissions, and ejaculations: A ventral view. Paper presented at the Eastern Regional Conference on Reproductive Behavior, Chicago, Illinois.

Pollak, E. I., and Sachs, B. D. 1975a. Excitatory and inhibitory effects of stimulation applied during the postejaculatory interval of the male rat. *Behav. Biol.* 15, 449–461.

Pollak, E. I., and Sachs, B. D. 1975b. Male copulatory behavior and female maternal behavior in neonatally bulbectomized rats. *Physiol. Behav.* 14, 337–343.

Pollak, E. I., and Sachs, B. D. 1975c. Masculine sexual behavior and morphology: Paradoxical effects of perinatal androgen treatment in male and female rats. *Behav. Biol.* 13, 401–411.

Pollak, E. I., and Sachs, B. D. 1976. Penile movements and the sensory control of copulation in the rat. *Behav. Biol.* (in press).

Pottier, J. J. G., and Baran, D. 1973. A general behavioral syndrome associated with persistent failure to mate in the male laboratory rat. *J. Comp. Physiol. Psychol.* 83, 499–509.

Rodgers, C. H., and Alheid, G. 1972. Relationship of sexual behavior and castration to tumescence in the male rat. *Physiol. Behav.* 9, 581–584.

Sachs, B. D. 1965. Sexual behavior of male rats after one to nine days without food. *J. Comp. Physiol. Psychol.* 60, 144–146.

Sachs, B. D., and Barfield, R. J. 1970. Temporal patterning of sexual behavior in the male rat. *J. Comp. Physiol. Psychol.* 73, 359–364.

Sachs, B. D., and Barfield, R. J. 1974. Copulatory behavior of male rats given intermittent electric shocks: theoretical implications. *J. Comp. Physiol. Psychol.* 86, 607–615.

Sachs, B. D., and Garinello, L. D. 1975. Exhaustion and recovery of penile reflexes following exhaustion of copulatory behavior in the male rat. Paper presented at meeting of the Eastern Psychological Association, New York City.

Sachs, B. D., and Marsan, E. 1972. Male rats prefer sex to food after 6 days of food deprivation. *Psychon. Sci.* **28**, 47–49.

Sachs, B. D., Pollak, E. I., Krieger, M. S., and Barfield, R. J. 1973. Sexual behavior: Normal male patterning in androgenized female rats. *Science* **181**, 770–772.

Sachs, B. D., Macaione, R., and Fegy, L. 1974. Pacing of copulatory behavior in the male rat: Effects of receptive females and intermittent shocks. *J. Comp. Physiol. Psychol.* **87**, 326–331.

Salis, P. J., and Dewsbury, D. A. 1971. *p*-Chlorophenylalanine facilitates copulatory behavior in male rats. *Nature (London)* **232**, 400–401.

Schoelch-Krieger, M., and Barfield, R. J. 1975. Independence of temporal patterning of male mating behavior from the influence of androgen during the neonatal period. *Physiol. Behav.* **14**, 251–254.

Seward, J. P. 1945. Aggressive behavior in the rat. I. General characteristics, age, and sex differences. *J. Comp. Psychol.* **38**, 175–197.

Sharma, O. P., and Hays, R. L. 1974. Increasing copulatory behaviour in ageing male rats with an electrical stimulus. *J. Reprod. Fertil.* **39**, 111–113.

Solomon, R. L., and Corbit, J. D. 1974. An opponent process theory of motivation: I. Temporal dynamics of affect. *Psychol. Rev.* **81**, 119–145.

Soulairac, A. 1952. La signification physiologique de la période réfractoire dans le comportement sexuel du rat mâle. *J. Physiol.* **44**, 99–113.

Spaulding, W. D., and Peck, C. K. 1974. Sexual behavior of male rats following removal of the glans penis at weaning. *Develop. Psychobiol.* **7**, 43–46.

Stone, C. P., and Ferguson, L. W. 1940. Temporal relationships in the copulatory acts of adult male rats. *J. Comp. Psychol.* **30**, 419–433.

Van Dis, H., and Larsson, K. 1971. Induction of sexual arousal in the castrated male rat by intracranial stimulation. *Physiol. Behav.* **6**, 85–86.

Vaughan, E., and Fisher, A. E. 1962. Male sexual behavior induced by intracranial electrical stimulation. *Science* **137**, 758–760.

Ward, I. L. 1969. Differential effect of pre- and postnatal androgen on the sexual behavior of intact and spayed female rats. *Horm. Behav.* **1**, 25–36.

Westbrook, W. H. 1974. The effect of female change on the copulatory behavior of the male rat. Doctoral Dissertation, Univ. of California, Berkeley, California.

Whalen, R. E. 1966. Sexual motivation. *Psychol. Rev.* **73**, 151–163.

Whalen, R. E., and Robertson, R. T. 1968. Sexual exhaustion and recovery of masculine copulatory behavior in virilized female rats. *Psychon. Sci.* **11**, 319–320.

Wilhelmsson, M., and Larsson, K. 1974. The development of sexual behavior in anosmic male rats reared under various social conditions. *Physiol. Behav.* **11**, 227–232.

Sexual Receptivity and Attractiveness
in the Female Rhesus Monkey

Eric B. Keverne

DEPARTMENT OF ANATOMY
UNIVERSITY OF CAMBRIDGE
CAMBRIDGE, ENGLAND

I. INTRODUCTION

The early observations that catarrhine monkeys and apes did not show well-circumscribed periods of estrus but could copulate throughout their menstrual cycle led to the view that the primate's brain was somewhat emancipated from gonadal hormone influences (Ford and Beach, 1951). While it is certainly true that, in contrast to infraprimate mammals, sexual activity is not exclusively dependent on gonadal steroids, evidence has accumulated in the last decade which suggests that endocrine variables play an important role in sexual interactions. Much of this evidence comes from investigations of primates carried out in the laboratory, where accurate and quantitative observations are more easily made and endocrine changes can be altered in a readily controllable manner.

155

This is not to imply that field work has made no contribution: indeed, long before most laboratory colonies were established, Zuckerman (1932) and Carpenter (1942) observed that sexual interaction varied between phases of the female primate's menstrual cycle. In recent years, a number of field studies have indicated that primates of several species appear to have periods of heightened sexual activity, usually around mid-cycle, when the females are more ready to permit the male to mount [in *Presbytis entellus* (Jay, 1965); in *Papio ursinus* and *Papio anubis* (Bolwig, 1959; Hall and DeVore, 1965; Saayman, 1970); in *Papio hamadryas* (Kummer, 1968); in *Cercocebus albigenea* (Chalmers, 1968); in *Cercopithecus aethiops* (Gartlan, 1969); in *Pan troglodytes* (van Lawick-Goodall, 1968)].

While no field study has refuted the existence of periodic estrous behavior during the breeding season, many have failed to demonstrate consistencies between copulations and the stage of the female's menstrual cycle (reviewed by Rowell, 1972). This has led to the suggestion that there is no reliable hormonal correlate of estrus in intact group-living primates. Since this view contrasts with recent laboratory findings, how can the differences between field and laboratory studies be reconciled? Clearly, there are limits to the extrapolations one can make from the pair test of the laboratory to the complexities of group living seen in feral primates. That is not to say that the cyclic behavior observed in primate dyads is an artifact of laboratory testing. Indeed, a number of laboratory investigations have reported that catarrhine monkeys and apes copulate throughout their entire menstrual cycle (Eckstein and Zuckerman, 1956; Maslow, 1936; Yerkes, 1939; Rowell, 1963; Michael and Zumpe, 1970b), which is not at odds with certain field observations. Given, however, a limited degree of social interaction in the laboratory, even such a simplistic measure of sexual behavior as copulatory activity shows some cyclicity in a number of primate species [in the baboon (Rowell, 1967a); in the talapoin monkey (Scruton and Herbert, 1970); in the pigtail macaque (Goldfoot, 1971)]. Most laboratory studies agree that, although copulations may occur throughout the menstrual cycle, the numbers of mounts, intromissions, and ejaculations by male primates progressively increase in frequency during the follicular phase, reaching a peak around the expected time of ovulation. These components of the copulatory sequence then diminish during the luteal phase of the cycle in the chimpanzee (Young and Orbison, 1944), in the rhesus monkey (Ball and Hartman, 1935; Michael, Herbert, and Welegalla, 1967), and in the pigtail macaque (Bullock, Paris, and Goy, 1972).

In the study of primate sexual behavior the macaques have received particular attention, perhaps because of their widespread laboratory use, while their terrestrial mode of living also makes them readily observable in the field. Rowell (1972) drew attention to the variability in duration of behavioral estrus as reported by field workers for the rhesus macaque, but since menstrual flow is rarely visible in this species and changes in sex-skin coloration are an unreliable index of menstrual cycle stage, the endocrine basis of such variability is unknown. Moreover, the observation that certain aggressive behaviors can alter the plasma levels of sex hormones, at least in the male rhesus monkey (Bernstein, Rose, and Gordon, 1974), points to the complex nature of the reciprocal relationship between hormones and behavior and may account for some of this variability. On the other hand, in those species of Old World primates which exhibit sexual skin swellings as visible indicators of endocrine status, there is little doubt even from field studies that copulation is maximal at mid-cycle swelling [in the anubis baboon (Rowell, 1967a); in the mangabey (Rowell and Chalmers, 1970); in the chacma baboon (Saayman, 1970); in the chimpanzee (van Lawick-Goodall, 1968); and in the pigtail macaque (Bernstein, 1967)].

In our understanding of the contribution which hormones make to the expression of sexual behavior, the question at issue is not whether sexual rhythmicity in relationship to the primate's menstrual cycle is common both to field and laboratory studies, since at best such rhythmical changes only provide an indicator. To rest the case for the proposition that hormones regulate sexual behavior on observations of menstrual cycle rhythmicity is not at all convincing, and even the strongest advocates for such a proposal grant that rhythmicity is not found in all pairs (Michael and Welegalla, 1968). Even in those menstrual cycles where behavioral changes are observed to occur, the best one can do to understand the role which hormones play is attempt to correlate behavior with the underlying endocrine changes. In field studies determination of these changes is invariably indirect, while direct estimates of plasma hormone titers show the complex nature of concurrent changes in the secretion patterns of more than one hormone. As far as sexual behavior and sex hormones are concerned, the estrogens, androgens, and progesterones are all undergoing rhythmic fluctuation during the female's menstrual cycle. It is not until the influence of each of these hormones on behavior has been determined that attempts can be made to understand their combined role in the intact animal and eventually the group living situation.

Hormones may influence behavior patterns through either peripheral or central mechanisms, and it was in trying to distinguish these that the terms *attractiveness* and *receptivity* were introduced (Herbert and Trimble, 1967; Michael, Saayman, and Zumpe, 1967). By analyzing primate sexual behavior, it was possible to differentiate between, on the one hand, the sexual motivation of the female (expressed by the number of her sexual invitations) and, on the other hand, the female's value as a stimulus for the male (expressed by her success in stimulating the male to mount). Thus it appeared that two distinct mechanisms might underlie diminished sexual interactions during the luteal phase of the female's menstrual cycle. The first depended on a decrease in the attractiveness of the female, indicated by the failure of her sexual invitations to stimulate mounting. The second depended on a decrease in the receptivity of the female, indicated by the number of female refusals seen at this time (Michael, Saayman, and Zumpe, 1967). In experiments carried out on ovariectomized females it was found that sexual receptivity and attractiveness are affected differentially by estradiol and testosterone. These studies attributed the role of estrogen principally to peripheral action on the female's genitalia, whereas androgen had its behavioral effects principally on the central nervous system (Herbert and Trimble, 1967). The purpose of the present review is to consider in more detail the role of hormones in sexual attraction and receptivity and to discuss the merits and limitations of applying such concepts to primate sexual behavior.

II. SCORING OF BEHAVIOR

Adult, sexually active male and mature female rhesus monkeys were used in all studies, but only after they had undergone 3 months of acclimatization to laboratory conditions. It was during this period that intact females had their fallopian tubes ligated to prevent conceptions. Observations were made of pairs of animals of opposite sexes in an acoustically isolated room from behind a one-way vision mirror. Tests were conducted, usually for 60 minutes, in large observation cages into which first the male and then the female were introduced at the beginning of each test session. Animals were housed singly between observations in a communal monkey house.

Sexual attractiveness can be differentiated from sexual receptivity in the laboratory by behavioral criteria. High sexual receptivity is characterized by high levels of female sexual invitations, the absence of refusals of male mounting attempts, and to a lesser extent by the presence of a female clutching reaction during the male's ejaculatory mount. These components of sexual receptivity, and also the rates of female lever pressing for access to males in an operant situation, fit Beach's concept of proceptivity (Beach, 1976); that is, they represent a degree of active participation rather than passive receptivity. Low levels of sexual receptivity, or unreceptive behavior, are characterized by high levels of female refusals and low levels of sexual invitations. Simply quantifying such scores does not, in itself, allow reliable inferences to be made about changes in female receptivity. The behavior of the male towards the female has also to be accounted for, and both female refusals and sexual invitations depend not only on the female's receptive condition but also on the frequency of the male's attempts to mount. It was in overcoming problems such as these that the terms *male success ratio* (Michael, Herbert, and Welegalla, 1967) or *female acceptance ratio* (Everitt and Herbert, 1971) were introduced, both referring to the proportion of male mounts accepted by the female. The *male acceptance ratio* (also called *female success ratio*), on the other hand, represents the proportion of female presentations accepted by the male and reflects female attractiveness. Also of importance in the context of attractiveness are *male mounting attempts and ejaculations* (Keverne and Michael, 1971), the *male sexual performance index* (Herbert and Trimble, 1967), and the *proportion of mounts initiated by the male*.

Because of the confusion that has arisen because different groups have used different terminologies, a table of behavior and behavioral indices indicating female receptivity and attractiveness is presented here (Table I). It will at once be recognized that no one behavior component is in itself satisfactory in defining receptivity or attractiveness. A number of dependent variables have been found to be necessary as the phenomena were analyzed in more detail, and it should soon be apparent that while such concepts as receptivity and attractiveness may help our understanding of the mechanisms involved in hormonal influences on behavior, by no means do they provide the complete picture.

The scoring of female receptive behavior differs between field and laboratory studies. Field observers use the term *receptive period* to describe a limited number of successive days on which a particular female engages in copulation or shows other behavioral manifestations of willingness to mate. In addition to copulations, the behavioral patterns interpreted as indications of receptivity have included male following, female approaches and solictations, formation of consort pairs, and increased frequency of grooming episodes both by and of adult males (Carpenter, 1942; Lindburg, 1967; Loy, 1971). Some of these variables indicate female attractiveness as it is defined in the laboratory.

III. CHANGES IN RECEPTIVITY
DURING THE MENSTRUAL CYCLE

Assessing changes in female receptive behavior during the menstrual cycle is not without its problems, although such changes have been reported to occur in rhesus monkeys during the mating season in northern India (Southwick, Beg, and Siddiqi, 1965; Lindburg, 1967), and Cayo Santiago (Conaway and Koford, 1964; Kaufmann, 1965; Loy, 1971). Cyclical receptive behavior is observed at intervals of around 29–33 days (20 days if perimenstrual estrus is taken into account) and in most instances lasts for approximately 8–11 days. Females may experience up to six periods of receptive behavior during a breeding season, but most frequently observed are one to three such periods of receptivity before conception. Field workers, however, score a number of behaviors as receptive which are, in all probability, indicators of female attractiveness.

Laboratory workers also have experienced difficulties in assessing changes in female receptivity during the menstrual cycle, although many are in agreement that female acceptance of male mounting attempts and ejaculations reaches its

TABLE I

Scoring of Behavior

Behavior	Description	References
Female receptivity		
Proceptive behavior		
Female sexual invitations	Includes head-ducks, hand reaches, head bobs, and presentations; collectively grouped as one unit—"presentations"	Michael and Zumpe (1970a); Everitt and Herbert (1971)
Female clutching reaction	The female turns backwards to look at the male during his ejaculatory mount, and reaches back to grasp at him	Zumpe and Michael (1968)
Female operant responding	The female has 30 minutes in which to press a lever (FR schedule 250:1)[a] in order to gain access to the male partner	Michael *et al.* (1972)
Unreceptive behavior		
Female refusals	The female does not respond to the male's attempts to mount and may pull away from the male	Michael and Welegalla (1968)
Male success ratio } Female acceptance ratio }	The proportion of the male's attempts to mount accepted by the females	Michael *et al.* (1967); Everitt and Herbert (1971)
Female attractiveness		
Male mounting attempts	Total mounts plus attempts at mounting	Michael *et al.* (1967)
Male ejaculations and sexual performance index (SPI)	SPI is the product of the rate (total mounts over ejaculation time) that successive mounts occur and the mean number of thrusts delivered at each mount	Herbert and Trimble (1967)
Male acceptance ratio } Female success ratio }	The proportion of female mounting invitations eliciting a male mount	Everitt and Herbert (1971); Michael and Welegalla (1968)
Proportion of mounting attempts initiated by the male	With increased attractiveness, males initiate most of the sexual interactions	Herbert (1970)
Male operant response	The male has 30 minutes to press a lever 250 times to gain access to his female partner; fast rates of responding with short latencies to first press indicates maximal female attractiveness	Michael and Keverne (1968)

[a] FR, fixed ratio.

maximum at or near the middle of the menstrual cycle and diminishes shortly after ovulation during the luteal phase. Such changes have been observed in the chimpanzee (Yerkes & Elder, 1936; Young and Orbison, 1944), rhesus monkey (Ball and Hartman, 1935; Michael, Herbert, and Welegalla, 1967), pigtail macaque (Bullock, Paris, and Goy, 1972), lowland gorilla (Hess, 1973) and talapoin monkey (Scruton and Herbert, 1971). Changes in sexual invitations are most commonly used as indicators of female receptivity, but fluctuations in female sexual invitations are inconsistent [observed in 36% of those pairs studied by Michael and Welegalla (1968)]. Moreover at mid-cycle, when it is generally assumed the female is maximally receptive, her sexual invitations may para-doxically decrease (Herbert, 1970; Michael and Welegalla, 1968). The sexual invitations of female rhesus monkeys in paired situations are also influenced by such factors as male dominance and the threat of male aggression, and so changes in the frequency of presentations may not reflect true alterations in receptivity. Female refusals of male mounting attempts have also been used as a major indicator of female sexual receptivity (Michael, Saayman, and Zumpe, 1968; Everitt and Herbert, 1971). However, only one study has to date reported the regular occurrence of female refusals of the male during the menstrual cycle (Michael and Welegalla, 1968). The females involved in this study showed refusals in 7 out of 22 menstrual cycles, and although refusals were observed in four out of five females, these were all paired with the same male. Since these same females were not refusing other males at this time, there is at least a suggestion that refusals on these occasions were more a reflection of partner preference than receptivity changes.

The female's clutching reaction depends on the male achieving ejaculation, and since unreceptiveness in females influences this event, it is unlikely that an unreceptive female has much occasion to display her clutching reaction. During the menstrual cycle females clasp back at the male in the vast majority of ejaculatory mounts (97%), with no significant differences between follicular or luteal phases of the cycle (Zumpe and Michael, 1968).

In order to overcome some of these problems in assessing receptive behavior during the menstrual cycle, use has been made of an operant conditioning situation whereby the female, pressing a lever 250 times, opened a door between two cage compartments, thus gaining access to a male partner. Males were untrained and therefore not able to open the door. Following access, a 50-minute period of behavioral interaction was observed, but on those occasions when females failed to press for access in the 30 minutes provided, they were given a separate behavioral test some 2 hours later in a free cage situation.

Observations on five intact females with their fallopian tubes ligated ranged from 7 to 18 months, but only menstrual cycle data from cycles between 26–35 days duration will be considered here initially. Thirty-two such menstrual cycles were observed with a mean duration of 29.7 ± 0.8 days and behavioral observations were made during 733 50-minute tests with two male partners. Confirming what was said above, females were rarely observed to refuse male mounting attempts (52 in 733 tests), and fluctuations in sexual invitations by these females were restricted to only a few cycles. Of the behavioral indices reflecting changes in sexual activity, male mounting rate and ejaculation times did show significant changes during the menstrual cycle, but it was the number of ejaculations per test that gave consistent changes in all paired combinations [see also Michael and Zumpe (1970b)]. The females' performance at lever pressing for the males and the males' sexual activity are shown in Fig. 1. Rhythmic changes in both the operant performance (reciprocal of access latency) and male ejaculations were observed with all pairs in relation to the menstrual cycle. A peak in operant responding occurred 16–17 days prior to menstruation, and this was followed by a marked decline during the luteal phase of the menstrual cycle. A secondary but smaller peak in female operant performance occurred in the luteal phase of the menstrual cycle the day before menstruation. This pre-menstrual increase in female level pressing for access to her male partner did not occur in all cycles and is therefore somewhat masked in the group data but can be readily seen in certain individuals' cycles (see Figs. 5 and 6 in Section VI). The cyclicity in male sexual behavior was also noteworthy in relation to the female's menstrual cycle, and maximum ejaculations synchronized with the peak in female pressing for access and occurred during the expected period of ovulation.

IV. CHANGES IN RECEPTIVITY
DURING LONG SUMMER CYCLES

The occurrence of menstruation in female rhesus monkeys is difficult to assess reliably under field conditions, but quantitative data obtained in the laboratory have indicated that menstruation in this species is infrequent and irregular during the summer months (Hartman, 1932; van Wagenen, 1945; Kerber and Reese, 1969; Keverne and Michael, 1970). Such long cycles during the summer months are thought to be anovulatory (Josimovich and Knobil, 1961; Riesen, Meyer, Wolf, 1971), and although mating has been observed during all months of the year in feral females which did not become pregnant (Loy, 1971), little is known about behavior during such long cycles. Observations throughout the summer months were made on the five females used in the operant situation described in the previous section. Data were recorded on 13 menstrual cycles of duration longer than 40 days; of these, 9 were between 40 to 50 days and 4 periods of amenorrhea lasting 63, 81, 107, and 109 days were recorded between April and July. Indeed, most of these long cycles occurred during the summer months of April to July, the exceptions being 3 cycles of 41, 46, and 80 days that occurred

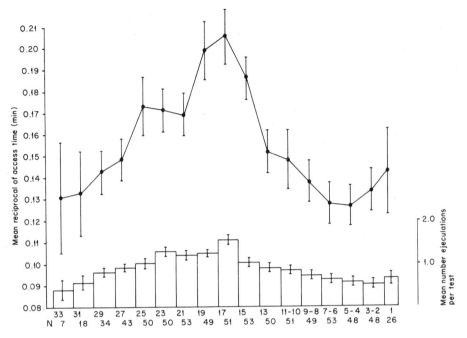

Fig. 1. The operant behavior of five female rhesus monkeys (upper curve) and the sexual behavior of their two male partners throughout the course of 32 normal menstrual cycles (mean cycle length 29.7 ± 0.8 days). plotted as days from menstruation. (N equals number of observations; access time equals latency to first response plus pressing time.)

in the months October–November, September–October, and February–March, respectively.

During the long cycles and periods of amenorrhea, females continued to lever press for access to their male partners, although responding in fewer tests than during normal cycles of 26–35 days (no pressing occurred in 21.5% of tests during long cycles and in 4.7% tests in normal cycles). Moreover, these females took significantly longer to achieve access (13.13 ± 0.42 minutes) than during the cycles of normal length (mean access time was 8.94 ± 0.19 minutes).

During these long cycles there were slightly fewer female sexual invitations, although differences among individuals were more marked, with a decrease in six pairs and an increase in invitations in four pairs. Refusals by females of mounting attempts by males were rare in both long and short cycles: only 52 female refusals were observed in 733 tests during normal cycles, and 19 were observed during 538 tests during long cycles and periods of amenorrhea.

Although sexual behavior continued throughout the summer months, the rhythmicity in behavior seen in normal cycles disappeared during the long cycles and amenorrhea. The most marked behavioral changes in relation to these long cycles were those seen prior to menstruation, when females pressed faster for access and made more sexual invitations; this activity is a possible correlate of the perimenstrual estrus described for feral females (Loy, 1970). Although no data are available for these females, it seems likely that during the summer months ovulation did not occur (Riesen, Meyer, and Wolf, 1971). This being the case, then the absence of any mid-cycle peak in either sexual behavior or female lever pressing for access is probably due to the absence of the changes in hormone levels that accompany ovulation.

V. HORMONAL CORRELATES
OF SEXUAL RECEPTIVITY

Rhythmic changes in female operant performance in relation to the menstrual cycle would appear to be under the influence of ovarian hormones. A direct test of this proposition might be achieved by looking at the effects of ovariectomy on both female lever pressing and interactions of the pair. Following ovariectomy there is usually a marked decline in sexual interactions, especially male mounting and ejaculations. To what extent changes in female receptivity are responsible for this decline in sexual interactions is difficult to determine. There are decreases in female sexual invitations (Michael and Welegalla, 1968; Michael and Zumpe, 1970a), provided that sufficient time is allowed to elapse after ovariectomy. Some 35 days after ovariectomy sexual invitations actually increased in sexually experienced females, and although significant decreases in female sexual invitations were observed 110 days after ovariectomy, it is unlikely that these reflected the absence of the hormonal effects which normally act upon brain mechanisms mediating the behavior. A more plausible interpretation would be that prolonged absence of ovarian hormones on the female's genital tract resulted in painful sexual intromission, a factor borne out by the decrease in male success ratio in such long-term ovariectomized females (Michael, Herbert, and Welegalla, 1967). Certainly, administration of low doses of estrogen (stilbestrol) directly into the vagina bring about cornification and reduce the incidence of female withdrawing at ejaculation (Michael and Saayman, 1968). In those pairs where mounting and ejaculation continue after ovariectomy, a decrease in the female's clutching reaction has been recorded (Zumpe and Michael, 1968). Although this clutching reaction is recorded in only 64% of ejaculations after ovariectomy, the fact that it continued for the majority of ejaculations and indeed that the female permitted the male to mount and ejaculate at all brings into question the proposition that the absence of ovarian hormones makes the female unreceptive.

Studies by the present author, using the operant situation in Richard P.

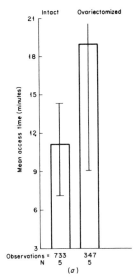 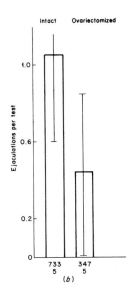

Fig. 2. (*a*) Effects of ovariectomy on the operant responding of five female rhesus monkeys and (*b*) the sexual behavior of their two male partners. Data are included from the first test after ovariectomy until females stopped pressing for access in eight tests. The first 30 tests after ovariectomy are included for the female which did not stop pressing. (*N* equals number of females.)

Michael's laboratory, indicate that ovariectomy reduces female receptivity if lever pressing for access may be considered a measure of receptivity, but marked individual differences are observed. Considering the combined data for all 10 pairs of animals, ovariectomy resulted in an over-all increase in the time taken for females to lever press for access to their male partners, and their subsequent sexual behavior decreased markedly (Fig. 2). Pressing for access stopped after ovariectomy with four of the five females, and while this occurred within 2 weeks for two females, the remaining three continued to press for the male for 90, 180, and more than 200 days. The number of sexual invitations made by these females decreased after ovariectomy (1.42 ± 0.1 to 0.97 ± 0.2), but there was little change in the number of female refusals of male mounting attempts (a total of 20 in 317 tests after ovariectomy). This behavior pattern remained infrequent.

A. ESTROGEN AND FEMALE RECEPTIVITY

When lever pressing by the female for access to the male eventually stopped after ovariectomy, estradiol replacement in graded doses was administered daily to the female. The amount of estradiol required to restore lever pressing depended upon both the individual female and in certain cases the male with which she was partnered. Nevertheless, all estrogenized females (5–10 μg estradiol daily) pressed for access to their male partners at rates similar to those when they were intact, taking into account the complete menstrual cycle. However, the speed at which access was obtained did not nearly reach those levels recorded only in the mid-cycle ovulatory period (days 14 to 18 from menstruation). The mean access time on 5–10 μg estradiol replacement was 11.7 ± 0.6 minutes compared with 7.2 ± 0.6 min during the ovulatory period for these same pairs (Fig. 3). This dosage of estrogen did, however, bring about a return of female attractiveness equivalent to that found at the mid-cycle ovulatory period. Hence, with these estrogenized females males achieved higher ejaculation scores than the over-all scores throughout the menstrual cycle but not significantly different from those recorded during the ovulatory phase of the menstrual cycle (Fig. 3).

B. EFFECTS OF TESTOSTERONE ON FEMALE RECEPTIVITY

Lever pressing for access to males was faster when estrogen treated females received low doses of testosterone. The mean access time for all estrogenized females prior to testosterone administration was 12.2 ± 1.3 min, which decreased to 7.4 ± 0.5 min when the androgen was administered (Fig. 4). Withdrawal of testosterone, on the other hand, brought about a marked and significant increase in the time taken to press for access to the male (15.1 ± 4.3 min). Behavior indicative of receptivity apart from operant performance was infrequent; however, in those pairs where it occurred, testosterone administration increased receptivity but was without effect on female attractiveness. In other words, there was no over-all increase in male mounting attempts and the incidence of ejaculation remained unchanged when the females received testosterone. Withdrawal of testosterone in the estrogenized females resulted not only in a loss of female interest in the males but also in a decrease in the males' sexual interest in the females. Both male mounting attempts and ejaculations decreased considerably following withdrawal of testosterone in the female, and these changes occurred in the absence of any behavioral signs of females becoming unreceptive (Fig. 4).

What then is the role played by the ovarian hormones in determining receptivity in the female primate? Since the tendency is, in the main, for the female rhesus monkey to press for access to her male partner throughout the menstrual cycle and rarely to refuse mounting attempts, it could be argued that she is receptive throughout the menstrual cycle. That is to say, she is both willing to work for access to the male (and to accept his mounts and ejaculations) and sexually to invite the male at all times during the menstrual cycle. The changes which occur in sexual motivation are, therefore, a change in the degree of active rather than passive receptivity and seem to fall in line with Beach's idea of proceptive behavior (Beach 1976). In this context, both estrogens and

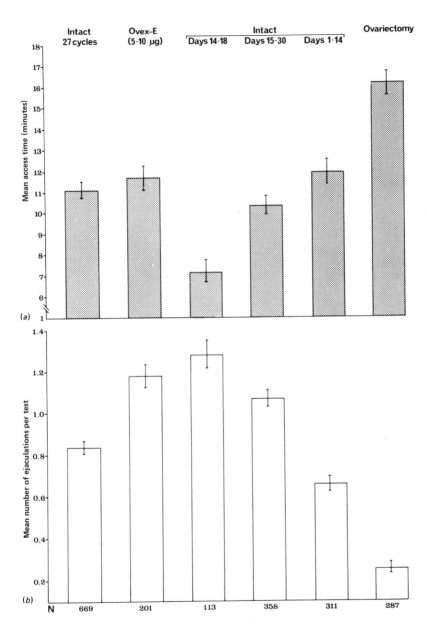

Fig. 3. (a) Operant responding of four female rhesus monkeys and (b) sexual behavior of their two male partners at different stages of the menstrual cycle, following ovariectomy and given estradiol replacement ("Ovex-E"). On estrogen replacement, females achieved access in times comparable to the follicular phase but not so fast as at mid-cycle, although the sexual behavior of their male partners is comparable on estrogen replacement. (N equals number of tests.)

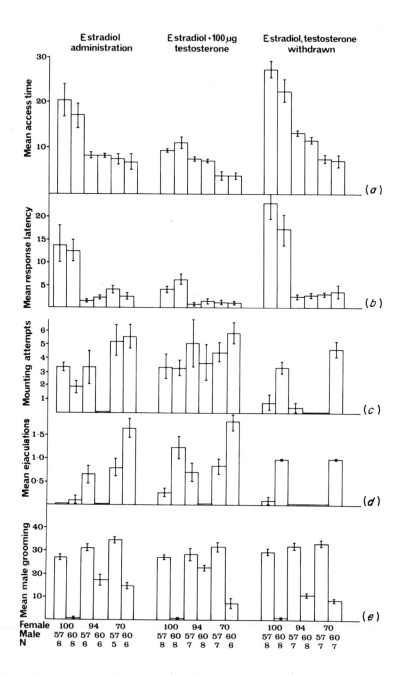

Fig. 4. Improved access time and male sexual behavior with testosterone administered to estrogenized female partners. (*N* equals number of observations.)

androgens seem to be important for the female's initiation of the interaction. Administration of estrogen to the ovariectomized female increases her sexual invitations (Michael and Welegalla, 1968; Michael and Zumpe, 1970a; Trimble & Herbert, 1968) and speeds up her lever pressing for access to the male. It should be remembered, however, that such estrogens are administered on a background of adrenal androgens. At mid-cycle there are rarely behavioral measures of female proceptivity because of the male's immediate interest and high mounting rate, leaving the female neither the time nor necessity to perform sexual invitations before the male ejaculates. Thus it is interesting to find that on estrogen replacement, the female's pressing for access to her male partner does not reach fast rates like those recorded around mid-cycle. Even after low-dosage estrogen priming for several weeks, followed by the high doses of estradiol (5–10 μg daily), females did not show lever pressing rates equivalent to those recorded around mid-cycle. Low doses of testosterone administered together with es-tradiol did, however, result in as rapid female pressing for access to males as at mid-cycle. Moreover, the demonstration of a mid-cycle peak in plasma androgens in the female rhesus monkey, probably of ovarian origin, suggests a physiological role for ovarian androgens in determining mid-cycle proceptivity (Hess and Resko, 1973).

In the luteal phase of the menstrual cycle, progesterone levels are high, and female motivation to press for access to male partners is low. The implication is that progesterone, an ovarian hormone, could influence female receptivity. Certainly, intramuscular administration of progesterone (1 mg daily) to an estrogenized female suppressed her lever pressing for access to the male (Michael et al., 1972); similar doses have also been shown to lower sexual invitations (Zumpe and Michael, 1970). However, there is no indication that during the luteal phase of the menstrual cycle females become actively unreceptive, since refusals of male mounting attempts at this time are rare. Moreover, it is only when nonphysiologically high doses of progesterone are administered (Michael, Saayman, and Zumpe, 1968) that the female actually starts to refuse the male's sexual approaches. Since progesterone is known to suppress androgen secretion in female rhesus monkeys (Hess and Resko, 1973), such high doses of proges-terone might be achieving their effects on unreceptivity by way of lowering plasma androgens. It is equally possible that such pharmacological doses of progesterone are having direct central effects on neural mechanisms mediating unreceptive behavior. Whether it is competing with androgens for receptor sites or enhancing unreceptive behavior by direct action on some other part of the nervous system remains to be determined. Progesterone secretion during the luteal phase of the menstrual cycle does not, however, appear to make the female unreceptive, although it does depress her active solicitations, or procep-tivity.

In summary, ovarian hormones appear to influence female proceptivity and not unreceptiveness, as evidenced by the female's active participation in sexual interactions during the follicular and especially mid-cycle periods. Estrogens on a background of adrenal androgens appear to be involved in this proceptive behavior, whereas the mid-cycle peak of proceptivity requires the estrogen plus androgen surge, both probably of ovarian origin. The decline in female proceptive behavior in the luteal phase of the menstrual cycle is probably due to progesterone secretion. Still to be determined is whether progesterone is influencing neural mechanisms controlling receptive behavior directly or whether it is influencing them indirectly by suppression of adrenal androgens.

C. ANDROGENS AND FEMALE RECEPTIVITY

While the ovarian hormones are primarily involved in the female's proceptive behavior, adrenal androgens are important for female receptive behavior. Ovariectomized females, even when given estradiol, actively refuse their male partners' mounting attempts if adrenal androgens are suppressed by administration of dexamethasone (Everitt and Herbert, 1969, 1971). Receptivity can be restored by giving dexamethasome-treated animals testosterone or androstenediol but not progesterone or cortisol. Subsequent studies have shown that bilateral adrenalectomy itself greatly reduces the sexual receptivity of the estrogenized rhesus monkey (Everitt, Herbert, and Hamer, 1972). Such adrenalectomized females show increases in the number of times they refuse the male's attempts to mount and decreases in their sexual presentations. Females' clasping of the male at ejaculation was not altered, but since males ejaculated infrequently, data for clutching reactions by the female could not be computed. These effects of adrenalectomy could be reversed by giving females an adrenal androgen, androstenedione, but not dehydroepiandrosterone. Not all androgens influence female receptivity; and in the lever-pressing situation, although a rapid onset of fast pressing for males was achieved when the females received low doses of testosterone, androsterone failed to improve receptivity except at very high nonphysiological levels (20 mg daily). Testosterone and androstenedione appear, therefore, to be the most potent androgens regulating female receptivity, and since both these hormones are present at detectable levels in the plasma of nonhuman primates (Hess and Resko, 1973), they clearly play a physiological role.

While estradiol may influence female receptive behavior by peripheral effects in causing lubrication of the vagina of the long-ovariectomized rhesus monkey, thereby making intromission more pleasurable, there is no evidence to date that estrogen alone is acting upon primate brain mechanisms mediating receptive behavior. On the contrary, there is evidence that females given estrogen without a background of adrenal androgens show unreceptive behavior (Everitt and Herbert, 1971). Nevertheless, there is the possibility that estrogens may be acting synergistically with androgens to promote proceptive behavior, since the female initiates more interaction as the follicular phase of her menstrual cycle progresses. During this time estrogen levels are rising while plasma androgens remain at a steady level. Such correlative evidence is indecisive since females are undergoing marked changes in attractiveness at this time, and it is difficult to determine how much the female's behavior alters as a result of changes in the male's behavior toward her. Some weight might be added to the case for estrogens influencing primate receptivity if small estrogen implants could be localized in that area of the hypothalamus mediating sexual receptivity. Estrogen has been applied directly to the rhesus monkey's brain (Michael, 1971), but since these implants were large enough to induce peripheral effects on attractiveness and were, moreover, implanted into the tegmentum and red nucleus of the midbrain, they tell us very little about hypothalamic mechanisms mediating female receptivity. Small amounts of testosterone propionate implanted into the hypothalamus (anterior hypothalamus/preoptic area) have restored receptivity in female monkeys made unreceptive after bilateral adrenalectomy. Control implants in the same area, and testosterone implanted into the posterior hypothalamus/pretectal area, or cerebral cortex, have no consistent effect on behavior (Everitt and Herbert, 1975). Further evidence that diffusion of the hormones outside the area of the implants did not occur was provided by the absence of peripheral effects (e.g., on the clitoris and sex skin).

It has been suggested that androgens induce female receptive behavior as a result of their aromatization to estrogen at centrally active sites, as occurs in the rat brain (MacDonald et al., 1970; Naftolin, Ryan, and Petro, 1971). It seems unlikely that this mechanism applies to rhesus monkeys, since estrogen-treated females still show unreceptive behavior after adrenalectomy. Moreover, the operant studies on the female rhesus monkey show that estradiol alone was ineffective in producing the fastest access times, which were only achieved when additional testosterone was administered in these same females. The effects of testosterone on lever pressing for access are very rapid (1–3 days after subcutaneous administration), compared with some 14 days before changes occur in female proceptivity when estrogen is given. It is unlikely, therefore, that androgens are producing their effects after conversion to estrogen, since this seems to be the slower-acting hormone.

To dissect out a role for each sex hormone in mediating sexual behavior is of some importance in understanding the neuroendocrine control of sexual receptivity. Problems arise from the fact that one hormone may affect more than one element of sexual receptivity, while a second hormone may act synergistically yet appear to be without effects of its own. So far as the female monkey is concerned, androgens are important for the inhibition of unreceptive behavior. Females without their adrenals or ovaries, but maintained on corticosteroids and estrogen, show elements of unreceptive behavior in that they actively refuse the male. Estrogen and progesterone in physiological doses appear to be without effect on these behaviors yet influence proceptivity (solicitations or lever pressing for males), but only on a background of adrenal androgens. All three groups of steroids appear to influence proceptive behavior: estrogen and androgens enhance it, and progesterone suppresses it. It is not yet clear whether the effects of estrogen and progesterone are directly on central nervous system mechanisms mediating sexual receptivity, and are independent of androgens, or whether estrogen acts in synergy with androgens, while progesterone produces its effects by suppressing androgen secretion from the ovary. If progesterone acts by suppression of androgen secretion, then why do progesterone-treated females not show the elements of unreceptive behavior characteristic of dexamethasone-treated or adrenalectomized females? The answer is they do, but only with very high doses of progesterone (Michael, Saayman, and Zumpe, 1968). If, therefore, progesterone has its effects by suppression of androgens in the luteal phase of the menstrual cycle, then it is only suppressing those elements of androgen-induced proceptive behavior.

Females that have been adrenalectomized and ovariectomized show marked increases in unreceptive behavior and decreased proceptive behavior even though they are still receiving estrogen. Since most of these females are, however, still permitting the male to mount (female acceptance ratio is high in most cases), it would be useful to determine if females ever become totally unreceptive when their additional estrogen is withdrawn. Of course, without estrogen females would become unattractive and further precautions would have to be taken to maintain the male's interest (e.g., application of vaginal secretions, or intravaginal estrogen). If females still continue to accept most of the male's mounting attempts, then clearly it could be argued that receptivity in the female rhesus monkey is to a certain extent independent of sex hormones, and these serve simply to regulate the amount of proceptive and unreceptive behaviors. In the meantime, it would appear that the marked dependence of receptivity on adrenal androgens rather than estrogen or progesterone would account for the continuous receptivity of the female primate during her menstrual cycle, whereas changes in ovarian hormone secretion serve the function of modulating proceptive behavior.

VI. PARTNER PREFERENCES AND FEMALE RECEPTIVE BEHAVIOR

Although hormones have been described as of some importance in determining sexual activity between male and female rhesus monkeys, the formation of consort relationships may be governed by factors in addition to the female's endocrine status. The most dominant males in free-living groups of rhesus monkeys prefer some estrous females to others, and the less favored ones pair off with subordinate males (Carpenter, 1942; Altmann, 1962), suggesting that social factors may overide endocrine determinants of sexual behavior. In captive pigtail macaques, the probability that a preovulatory female would show increased sexual activity was in part related to her dominance status, with high levels of sexual behavior in dominant females and no sexual behavior in the lowest-ranking female (Goldfoot, 1971). Endocrine factors increased the probability that insemination occurred at an optimum time for conception, while social factors operated to decrease the likelihood of conception with females of low rank. These observations suggest that receptivity in primates may manifest itself as a complex interaction of social and endocrine factors (cf. Rowell, 1972).

Quantitative laboratory studies on the sexual activity of consort pairs of rhesus monkeys has shown that large variations in sexual behavior may occur between individual females paired with the same male (Michael and Saayman, 1967). In a triadic choice situation, these differences became even more marked, and a male mated with one female to the complete exclusion of the other (Herbert, 1968). Nevertheless, females have also been seen to exert their individuality on the patterns of sexual interaction, refusing the mounting attempts of one male while actively soliciting the mounts of another during the same period (personal observations). In the chacma baboon, females were observed to offer sexual presentations more frequently to some males than to others, the more sexually potent male receiving most of the receptive females' sexual invitations (Saayman, 1971).

The influence of the physical characteristics of the male chimpanzee upon his acceptability to females has also been noted (Yerkes, 1939), and it was observed that females preferred those males showing greater sexual vigor and less aggression. Harlow (1965) demonstrated that female rhesus monkeys would readily open the door of a detained male's cage by pulling a chain. In a dual-choice situation, the females preferentially selected feral males to those which had been reared in social isolation. Socially deprived males exhibited deficits in sexual behavior, and although these animals had experience of each other in previous experiments, specifically what determined the female's preference towards feral males was not discussed.

In the operant situation where females had to lever press for access to male partners, a certain degree of control over the interaction resided with the female partner. Thus, the relative rates of lever pressing for each male might indicate whether one was responded for preferentially. Of the five females involved in this study, only three showed a preference: of these, one preferred the sexually more potent male; two, the less potent. This contrasted with the sexual likes of the two males, both of which showed the same ascending order of females in terms of their ejaculation scores. Looking at the females' preferences more closely, these were always more marked in the luteal half of their menstrual cycle, and no significant changes were seen at mid-cycle around the period of

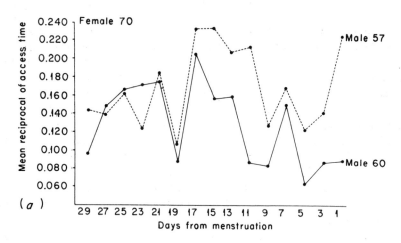

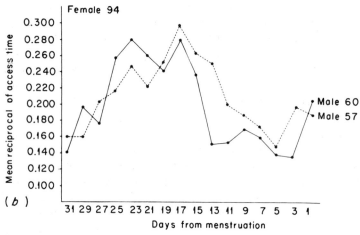

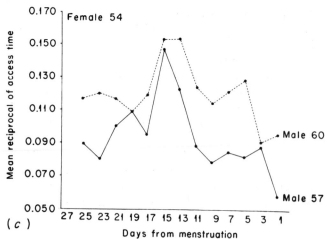

ovulation (Fig. 5). In all cases, the female's expression of preference for a male partner in terms of lever pressing disappeared after ovariectomy and appeared not, therefore, to be irreversibly fixed, but varied according to hormonal conditions. The failure to show a preference both at mid-cycle and following ovariectomy may, however, have reflected the limitation of the testing procedure. Females were pressing for both male partners within 5 minutes at mid-cycle; they did not press for either male in the 30 minutes allowed after ovariectomy. So at both these times, although a marginal preference may have existed, no measure of this could have been obtained.

The females' preference was not established until after a substantial number of tests had been conducted, indicating that a certain amount of learning was involved. What then are the behavioral characteristics of each male which the females learn to distinguish and prefer? Sexual rather than grooming behavior seemed to be operative in determining the preferences of these females, since differences in the grooming behavior of the two males occurred at times during the menstrual cycle and also after ovariectomy, when no partner preferences were shown by the females. But although behaviors can be quantified, their qualitative values cannot be assessed, and therefore all behaviors, including grooming, may have contributed to the preference. From the quantitative aspect, better correlations were obtained with the male's sexual behavior. Behaviorally, the favorite male of females 70 and 94 ejaculated and mounted less in the luteal phase of the menstrual cycle, groomed the females more than the other male, and responded positively to more of their grooming invitations. In turn, these females tended to offer the favorite male more grooming invitations, refused fewer of his mounting attempts and, in the case of female 94, made more sexual invitations to the preferred male. The preference of these females was, therefore, towards the male which synchronized his behavior with their hormonal status, that is, mounted less and groomed more in the luteal phase of her cycle.

Female 54 preferred the sexually more potent male at all times during the menstrual cycle other than mid-cycle, when the incidence of ejaculations was maximal and not significantly different between the two male partners. This female made a large number of sexual invitations to both males (four times as many as females 70 and 94) and never refused any male mounting attempts. It is also interesting that this female ranked high with both males on ejaculatory scores, which were twice as high as with females 70 or 94, while neither male groomed female 54 for long.

It would seem, therefore, that the operant responding of these females for access to males has a dual relationship to their hormonal status. First, there are centrally mediated effects of the hormones on sexual motivation. Second, the

---

Fig. 5. Effects of partner preference on females rates of operant responding (lever pressing) for two male partners. (a) Mean of 8 cycles for female 70; (b) mean of 10 cycles for female 94; (c) mean of 6 cycles for female 54.

peripheral effects of hormones influence female attractiveness, which in turn influences the behavior of male partners in different ways. These differences in the behavior of males feed back to the female and alter her operant responding because of the changed stimulus value of the male; that is, changes in a female's own attractiveness has indirectly modified her operant responding.

A logical tautology can present itself here, and in seeking supportive evidence for the females' lever-pressing preference it would be useful to present differences between female behavior to the two males that confirm the operant preference. Other indices of consort behavior were, however, restricted and the sparse distribution of sexual invitations and refusals of male mounting attempts made statistical analysis difficult. By selection of a menstrual cycle from female 94's data, an example is provided where the lever-pressing partner preference has supportive behavioral evidence (Fig. 6). The lever-pressing preference for male 57 clearly showed up in the luteal phase of the cycle when mounting and ejaculations by this male stopped, and his grooming times were long. Mounting and ejaculatory activity by this male was restricted to days 6–15 of the menstrual cycle and during this period the female made 34 sexual invitations to the preferred male and only 4 invitations to the male 60, which continued to mount and ejaculate for most of the cycle and was refused by the female on one occasion during the luteal phase of the cycle.

While a variety of species form lifetime mating pairs, information about actual preference for mating partners is rare. The work of Beach (Beach and Le Boeuf, 1967; Beach, 1969) with dogs demonstrated preferences that endured throughout years of testing. The present research also shows that the preference of female rhesus monkeys for certain male partners continues through many months and even years of testing, and as in the dog (Beach, 1969) and rat (French et al., 1972) the preference varies with the female's hormonal status. To analyze the behavioral characteristics of the male that determine the female rhesus monkey's preference is not easy. Even with this small number of animals (ten pairs), not all five females showed a preference, and of those that did, not all females favored the same male. Perhaps this is more in line with the human situation where female preferences are dependent on a wide variety of male characteristics. Certainly, as Harlow (1965) has shown, events which occur early in the social development of rhesus monkeys affect their status as preferred cage mates; moreover, there may be behavioral or sensory cues about which the observer is unaware. A more elaborate experimental design with a multiple choice of available partners might provide further information as to these sensory or behavioral determinants of the female's partner preference.

Thus, sexual receptivity in the female rhesus monkey in even the simplest diadic testing situation is not a straightforward correlate of hormonal status. Hormones can act centrally, activating neural mechanisms controlling receptivity, but because males respond differently to the concurrent changes in

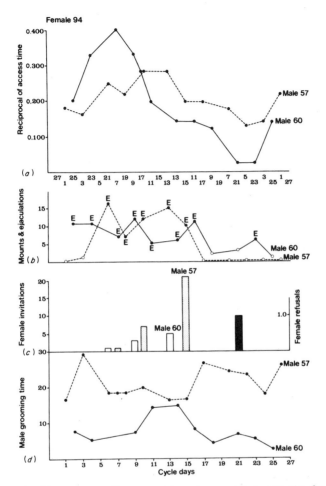

Fig. 6. Female 94 operant performance (*a*), male sexual behavior (*b*), female sexual behavior (*c*), and male grooming behavior (*d*), illustrating preference for male 57 during a menstrual cycle.

attractiveness that hormones induce, the levels of female receptiveness can be modified (see also Herbert, 1970). In the situation described, proceptivity has been shown to be influenced by certain aspects of male sexual behavior, but even with as few as five females there were marked inconsistencies. Perhaps other behavioral or sensory signals such as dominance (Goldfoot, 1971) or odor (Wilson, 1972) can also influence the female's receptive response towards a male and account for why a female might refuse the mounting attempts of one male while actively soliciting another. Diadic tests may tell us something about neuroendocrine mechanisms which control sexual behavior, but how much bearing they have on the way hormones affect sexual behavior in a social group remains an open question. Such studies, while valuable in themselves, are not designed to consider another variable of the greatest importance both to monkeys and human society: the way in which the structure and composition of the group in which an animal lives affects the primary interaction between hormones and behavior.

VII. SEXUAL ATTRACTIVENESS IN THE FEMALE RHESUS MONKEY

The most consistent behavioral changes which occur during the female's menstrual cycle relate to the male and are reflected in his ejaculation and mounting scores. The female will, for the most part, permit the male to mount throughout her menstrual cycle, and changes which occur in male behavior are probably correlates of changes in the stimulus value of the female. What then are the stimuli which make a female attractive and induce the male to mount? Are they principally visual or olfactory? The male receives visual information concerning the sexual status of the female both from the female's behavioral gestures and from color changes in her red perineum. Of the former, sexual invitations, as already detailed in Section VI on receptivity, are not consistent indices of sexual interaction; for example, they are invariably low at mid-cycle when male sexual behavior is high. Conversely it is possible to induce very high levels of sexual invitations in a female without inducing male sexual behavior— for instance, by giving ovariectomized females testosterone (Herbert and Trimble, 1967; Michael and Keverne, 1972). Female rhesus monkeys do not show a sexual skin swelling, but there are changes in coloration during the menstrual cycle, and following ovariectomy the sexual skin fades to a pale pink. In such females, intense redness can be brought about by direct application of estradiol (low doses of 2.5 μg daily) to the sexual skin area. Females treated in this manner become scarlet around the perineum, but this color change is without influence on male interest as assessed by lever pressing for access to the females (Michael and Keverne, 1970) or on male sexual behavior (Herbert, 1966; Michael and Saayman, 1968). Therefore the red color of the sex skin is not an adequate stimulus under these conditions. A number of field and laboratory studies have noted that males sniff the female's genital region prior to copulatory behavior, and perhaps it is this odor which influences her sexual attraction and determines whether or not the male shall mount. Carpenter (1942) first observed that the vaginal overflow of the rhesus monkey possessed a characteristic odor, which he thought might provide additional stimuli attracting males to females. Jay (1965) perceived a strong-smelling vaginal discharge in toque macaques, *Macaca sinica,* and observed males to examine the genitalia of females in the group each day. Bonnet macaques, *Macaca radiata*, have rarely been seen to present for copulation unless solicited by the male (Simonds, 1965). This involved flipping the tail aside, olfactory examination of the genitalia, and on occasions insertion of the finger into the vagina followed by smelling and tasting of the secretion (Rahaman and Partharsarathy, 1969). In the pigtail macaque, *Macaca nemestrina*, the male displayed the Flehmen posture following olfactory inspection of the female's genitalia (van Hooff, 1962). In the stumptail macaque, *Macaca arctoides*, sniffing, fingering, and licking of the perineal region occurs following female presentation (Bertrand, 1969) and prior to copulation (Blurton-Jones and Trollope, 1968). Although olfactory cues from the urine of receptive females are not ruled out, it would appear from these observations that in the macaque, communication of sexual status is by way of vaginal secretions.

   To test the proposition that olfactory cues can be employed to determine the female's sexual status, use has been made of operant conditioning techniques: male rhesus monkeys (four males) were required to press a lever in order to raise a partition which physically separated them from a female partner (six females) but through which they could both see and smell the partner. Males had to work with some dedication, pressing the lever 250 times to gain access to the female. They regularly responded for ovariectomized partners treated with estrogen but rarely performed when faced with untreated ovariectomized females (Michael and Keverne, 1968). Temporarily depriving these males of their sense of smell did not markedly affect either their pressing for or behavior with the estrogen-treated females (see the bottom graph of Fig. 7); these females were presumably remembered as being attractive because of previously rewarding sexual experiences with them. However, the temporarily anosmic male failed to respond to unfamiliar ovariectomized females after these females were administered estrogen and shown to be sexually stimulating to normal males.

   When the olfactorily deprived males had their sense of smell restored, they readily began pressing for access to these females. Thus while anosmia did not impair males' sexual arousal and sexual activity with familiar estrogenized females, anosmic males were not able to detect the onset of attractiveness which estrogen promoted in their unfamiliar partners. In a social group of rhesus monkeys (eight females, two males), olfactorily bulbectomized males were also capable of copulating, but it is interesting that the female partners were extremely active in soliciting male sexual attention (Akers, Conaway, and Kling, 1976). Each time a new male was admitted he was solicited by one of four females as soon as he entered the cage. Females followed and presented constantly, and at no time did males initiate sexual activity with females not already in pursuit. In contrast to field observations, male following was observed infrequently and only after consort relations were established. Since initiative in sexual interactions seemed to reside predominantly with the female in these studies, there is every possibility that her exaggerated behavior resulted from the

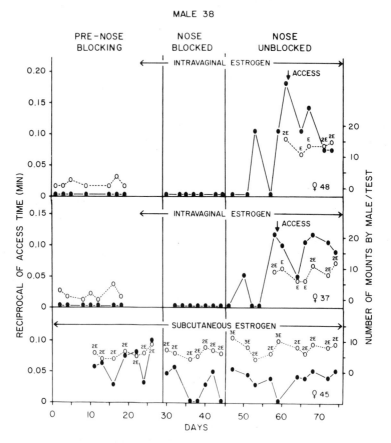

Fig. 7. Effects of reversible anosmia on the sexual behavior of a male rhesus monkey and on the time taken to obtain access to three female partners in a lever-pressing situation. [Lower graph (♀45) represents control female.] When females received intravaginal estrogen, the male only started lever-pressing after olfactory acuity had been restored. Key: o, mounts by male; •, operant performance; E, ejaculations. (From Michael *et al.*, 1972.)

anosmic males' unresponsiveness and female competition. These studies are consistent with the view that odor cues are unnecessary for copulation to occur but assist the male in determining the sexual status of his female partner.

Males sniff the genital region of females, especially of new partners and also following estrogen administration to ovariectomized females. Since giving estrogen to ovariectomized females makes them attractive and stimulates male sexual interest, we studied the effects on male behavior of transferring vaginal secretions from estrogenized "donor" monkeys to ovariectomized, unattractive "recipient" partners.

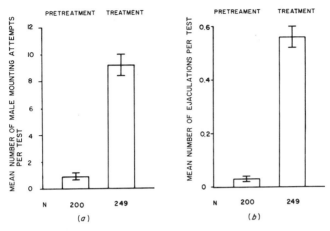

Fig. 8. Effects of applying vaginal secretions from estrogenized "donor" females to the sexual skin area of ovariectomized "recipient" females on the sexual stimulation of males. Data for 11 pairs involving five males, five females, and five donors. (N equals number of observations.)

Application of vaginal secretions to the sexual skin area of recipients, which were themselves quite unreceptive to males, nevertheless resulted in a marked stimulation of the male partner's sexual activity (Michael and Keverne, 1970). Estrogen-primed vaginal secretions have now been applied to the sexual skin area of ovariectomized recipient rhesus monkeys on 249 separate occasions, and a 1-hour behavior test has been observed on each occasion in an acoustically isolated testing booth housed behind a one-way screen. These tests involved 11 pairs of animals (five males and five females), and the secretions significantly increased the male partners' sexual behavior above pretreatment periods when only control substances were applied (Fig. 8). In the pretreatment period eight ejaculations were recorded in 200 tests and these increased to 139 during 249 tests when vaginal secretions were smeared on the sexual skin of unreceptive recipients. Of even greater significance was the increase in male mounting attempts from 174 during the pretreatment period to 2292 during applications to the same female partners. This high number of mounting attempts with few ejaculations was an indication of the unreceptive condition of the ovariectomized recipients and clearly demonstrates the males' increased sexual interest in these females.

VIII.   CHEMICAL ANALYSIS OF VAGINAL SECRETIONS

To determine the chemical nature of the substances in vaginal secretions responsible for these behavioral effects, extraction and fractionation procedures were used in conjunction with behavioral assay methods. The early stages of this procedure involved the use of ether extracts of secretions, collected by lavage with water from estrogen-treated donor females (Keverne and Michael, 1971). Ovariectomized rhesus monkeys were again the recipients for these extracts, and the very low levels of sexual activity during the pretreatment period were in marked contrast to the high levels seen during the applications of ether extracts. A gas chromatographic comparison of ether extracts of the vaginal secretion from ovariectomized untreated females indicated that volatile components were absent or scarce, while estrogen treatment stimulated production of volatile components and improved the sex-attractant properties of vaginal secretions (Michael, Keverne, and Bonsall, 1971). Identification of these volatile components was obtained by preparative gas chromatography and mass spectrometry (Curtis *et al.*, 1971). The resultant mass spectra were compared with authentic samples and established the identification of the first five peaks as acetic,

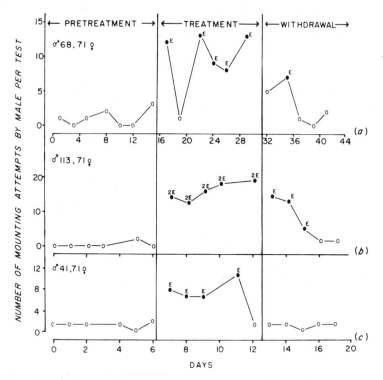

Fig. 9. The sexual stimulation of three male rhesus monkeys by the application of a synthetic mixture of authentic fatty acids to the sexual skin of an ovariectomized "recipient" female: a significant increase in mounting activity and in ejaculations occurred. Key: •E, one ejaculation in the test; •2E, two ejaculations in the test; ○, test without ejaculation. (From Michael *et al.*, 1972.)

propionic, isobutyric, butyric, and isovaleric acids. A mixture of authentic acids was made up to match their concentration in a pool of vaginal washings, and a small sample of this mixture when tested for behavioral activity was demonstrated to possess sex-attractant properties (Fig. 9).

IX. RELATIVE EFFECTIVENESS OF VAGINAL SECRETIONS AND SYNTHETIC PHEROMONE

The effectiveness of such odor cues in stimulating sexual behavior in the rhesus monkey does, however, vary according to social conditions: with some partners and in certain tests no sexual stimulation occurs. Moreover, when the behavioral effects of fresh vaginal secretions and a synthetic mixture of their acid contents were compared in the same nine pairs of animals, vaginal secretions appeared to be more effective in stimulating the male's sexual behavior (Fig. 10). Although both vaginal secretions and the synthetic pheromone complex stimulated male sexual activity at significantly higher levels than in the pretreatment tests, vaginal secretions were effective in 59% of applications compared with only 35% effectiveness of the synthetic acid mixture. Moreover, vaginal secretions stimu-

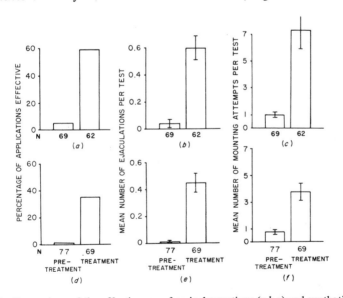

Fig. 10. Comparison of the effectiveness of vaginal secretions (a,b,c) and synthetic pheromones (d,e,f) on the sexual behavior of male rhesus monkeys. Treatment using both methods produced a significant response, but vaginal secretions were more effective than synthetic pheromone. (From Keverne, 1976. *J. Soc. Cosmet. Chem.* 27, 11–23. Reproduced with permission from Blackwell Scientific Publications.)

ERIC B. KEVERNE

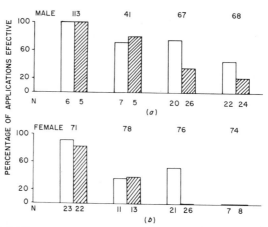

Fig. 11. (a) Variability in the response of different males to vaginal and synthetic pheromones and (b) their relative effectiveness when applied to different female partners. Clear bar: vaginal secretions; cross-hatched bar; synthetic pheromones. (From Keverne, 1976. J. Soc. Cosmet. Chem. 27, 11–23. Reproduced with permission from Blackwell Scientific Publications.)

lated 452 male mounting attempts, compared with only 257 attempts during application of synthetic pheromone to the same female partners.

This lower proportion of effective tests during applications of the synthetic pheromone was due to its failure to stimulate mounting behavior in certain pairs (Fig. 11). The effectiveness of fresh vaginal secretions and the synthetic acid mixture varied with the male partners from 100% in the case of male 113 to 45% success with male 68. With males 113 and 41, synthetic pheromone and vaginal secretions were equally effective, and this was also the case with females 71 and 78, although with female 74 they were equally ineffective (Fig. 11). With males 67 and 68, the synthetic acid mixture was approximately half as effective as the fresh secretion. This was due to these males being paired for some of their tests with female 76, for which—although secretions stimulated sexual activity in 52% of tests—the acid mixture was always ineffective.

Thus it can be seen that the male's response to olfactory attractants varies between individuals and is also, in part, dependent on the female partner with which they are paired. Whereas some females readily evoke a sexual response from the male, others when treated in the same manner fail to do so [see also Goldfoot et al. (1976)]. Hence, the response to odor cues in this infrahuman primate is not stereotyped. Furthermore, it can be seen that, for certain pairs, the synthetic acid mixture is not as effective in stimulating male sexual activity as the original vaginal secretions. This could mean that there is a component in fresh secretions that is lacking in the synthetic mixture.

Phenylpropanoic acid (PPA) and para-hydroxyphenylpropanoic acid (HPPA) are both odorous compounds identified in the rhesus monkey's vaginal secretion but quite ineffective in stimulating male sexual activity when applied alone to the

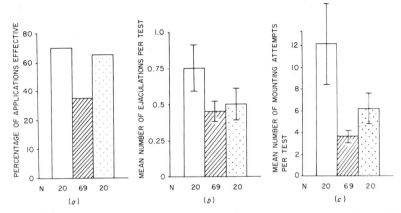

Fig. 12. Improvement in the effectiveness of synthetic pheromones when PPA and HPPA are added. Clear bar: vaginal secretions; cross-hatched bar: synthetic pheromones; dotted bar; synthetic pheromones + PPA and HPPA. (From Keverne, 1976. *J. Soc. Cosmet. Chem.* **27**, 11–23. Reproduced with permission from Blackwell Scientific Publications.)

sexual skin area of an ovariectomized female partner. By addition of PPA and HPPA to the synthetic acid mixture, an enhancement of the effectiveness of synthetic pheromone has been obtained (Fig. 12). Sexual interactions were shown by the male in more tests (65%) than when just a synthetic mixture of acids alone was applied (37%). The mixture containing enhancers was almost as effective as the untreated vaginal secretions (70% of tests), although the amount of sexual behavior stimulated was not so high. Untreated vaginal secretions when applied to the sexual skin of ovariectomized females in this test series stimulated 252 male mounting attempts and 15 ejaculations, compared with 123 mounting attempts and 9 ejaculations during 20 tests when the synthetic mixture plus enhancers was applied.

From these results there is an indication that these phenolic components have an enhancing effect on the sexually stimulating properties of the synthetic pheromones. Nevertheless, it remains true that in some pairs the simple acid mixture appears to be completely effective. It seems likely that the odor of the estrous vaginal secretion is the optimal attractant and that the acid mixture, mimicking the most odorous of the components, can in certain cases act as sufficient stimulus for some males. Others require additional volatile components such as PPA and HPPA, while still others require the whole untreated estrous vaginal secretion. Hence, the odor cue is in itself complex.

Moreover, the odor cue does not appear to be either merely a glandular secretion or an exudate through the vaginal wall but the result of microbial action on the vaginal secretions. Aliphatic acid concentrations increase during incubation of the vaginal lavage, while autoclaving or the addition of penicillin prevents production of these fatty acids (Michael *et al.,* 1972). It seems probable, therefore, that the production of these acidic pheromones depends upon the bacteria of the vagina, and that the ovarian hormones exert their influence on acid production in the intact animal by determining the availability of nutrients in the form of cornified cells and mucus.

X. PLASTICITY IN THE MALE'S RESPONSE TO ODOR CUES

An additional complication is to be found in the plasticity of the male's behavioral response to the odor cue. It has already been shown that this can be modified by a partner preference, but perhaps of even more interest is the different behaviors which these odor cues can stimulate. The variability of the male's behavioral response to the same odor cue with different female partners is shown in Fig. 13. With pairs 67–76, 41–71, and 68–71 estrogen-primed vaginal secretions markedly stimulated male sexual activity. With pairs 67–78, 41–79, and 68–78, an increase was produced in the social responsiveness of the male and he was prepared to groom his female partner longer, although no stimulation of sexual activity occurred. With pairs 67–74, 41–79, and 68–78, no stimulation of sexual activity occurred during the treatment with pheromone, but a marked reduction was observed in each male's aggressive behavior toward his partner. It could be argued that we are dealing with more than one odor cue and that the vaginal secretion contains a grooming stimulant and an aggression-reducing pheromone in addition to the sex attractant. The present author's view is that the coding for the behavioral response is not restricted to the olfactory cue but is integrated in higher areas of the neocortex. This opinion is reinforced by the variability in the male's response both to ether extracts of secretions (in Fig. 13, those pairs marked with an asterisk) and in some cases to the synthetic acid mixture itself, which clearly rules out different odor cues.

It is most important that this lack of a stereotyped response to odor cues should be emphasised, especially if consideration is to be given to the social group or situation in the wild. The term *pheromone* has been used somewhat reluctantly in this instance, since it is perhaps debatable whether such a term, defined in the context of insect behavior, can now be applied to the complex behavior of a higher primate where both the nature of stimulants and type of response produced can be varied. Moreover, sexual interactions in the rhesus monkey do not depend exclusively on one sense, although in these experiments odor cues have been shown to be effective when they were the only ones available. The term pheromone is perhaps too readily associated with the silkworm moth and other insects, where chemical cues attract males from miles around. As we have seen, nothing quite so spectacular or stereotyped occurs in the rhesus monkey, and communication depends upon multiple sensory cues, the functions of each overlapping extensively. What then is the role of odor cues

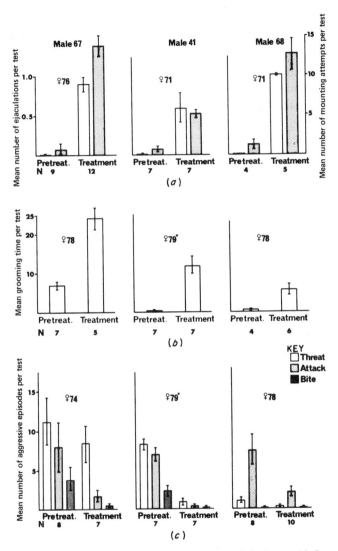

Fig. 13. Increases in (a) sexual behavior or (b) grooming behavior, or (c) the reduction of aggression, by applications of pheromone but depending on the female partner. Those pairs marked with an asterisk had ether extracts of vaginal secretions applied. (From Keverne, 1976. *J. Soc. Cosmet. Chem.* 27, 11–23. Reproduced with permission from Blackwell Scientific Publications.)

on the behavior of the male rhesus monkey? The present writer proposes that odor cues from the female may act on the male in two ways, both of which result in a rhythmical response in the male's behavior in relationship to the female's menstrual cycle. In those males which show an "all-or-none" response to the female and only copulate in the follicular and ovulatory part of the cycle, odor cues appear to be acting on the arousal mechanism. Males which copulate throughout the female's menstrual cycle are permanently aroused in the presence of the female but are also showing relative changes in their behavior as a result of odor cues influencing their sexual performance (see also Bielert and Goy, 1974).

What experimental evidence is there, if any, to support such a hypothesis? The short-chain aliphatic acids responsible for stimulating the sexual behavior of some males have been quantified in the vaginal secretions collected from five intact rhesus monkeys (Michael, Keverne, and Bonsall, unpublished data). In experiments where vaginal secretions were taken from intact females throughout the menstrual cycle and applied to an ovariectomized recipient, there is evidence in some cases that male behavior shows a cyclic response (Fig. 14). Aliphatic acid content varies with the menstrual cycle, and where secretions were used in behavioral testing there was a positive correlation between the short-chain fatty acid content and the number of mounting attempts stimulated (Fig. 15). Changes in the aliphatic acid content of vaginal secretions during 10 menstrual cycles in a total of four female monkeys did, however, show great variability. In at least four of these cycles there was a luteal peak in aliphatic acid content, whereas in four other cycles there was a mid-cycle peak. This again is an example of the variability one might expect to find in the rhesus monkey, just indeed as there is variability in a male's cyclic response in behavior with females. Nevertheless, the sampling technique used only reveals what is present within the vagina at a given time, not what is volatizable and available to the male, which is important for assessing a behavioral response.

It remains possible, therefore, that differences in vaginal secretions during the menstrual cycle might contribute to the rhythmic patterns in the behavior of male partners. Attempts at masking the female's odor have not been very successful, although two males did fail to show rhythmicity in their sexual behavior when paired with an intact female receiving intravaginal penicillin. (Such antibiotics inhibit short-chain fatty acid production.)

XI. PROGESTERONE AND FEMALE ATTRACTIVENESS

So far we have considered how odor cues might act on the male's arousal mechanism, and these appear to have importance during the follicular half of the cycle and especially around ovulation. But how can the marked decline in male sexual behavior during the luteal phase of the female's cycle be accounted for? Clearly the stimulus value of the female is declining during this part of the cycle,

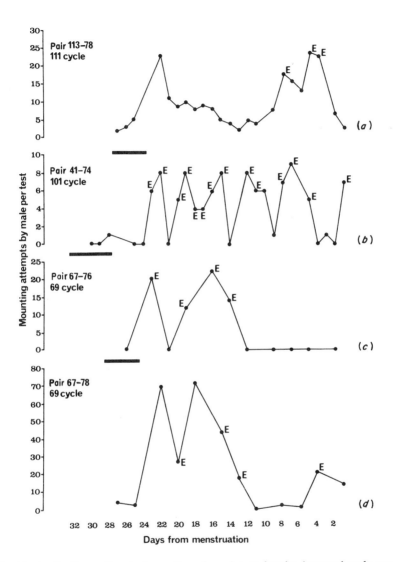

Fig. 14. Applications of vaginal secretions from intact females increased male sexual behavior with ovariectomized females, in some cases in a cyclical manner. In the case of pair 113–78 the pattern of behavior, although not cyclical, bore some resemblance to the aliphatic acid profile (see Fig. 15b). (R. P. Michael, E. B. Keverne, and R. W. Bonsall, unpublished observations.)

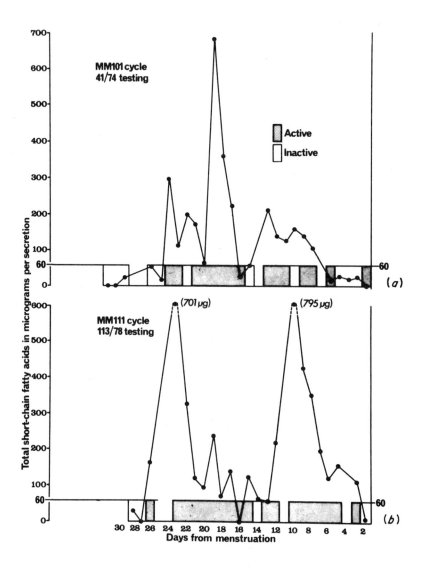

Fig. 15. Correlation between high acid content and sex-attractant activity in vaginal secretions collected from *M. mulatta* during the menstrual cycle. Tests in which the number of mounting attempts exceeded the baseline mean by at least one standard deviation were termed active. Secretions with more than 60 µg short-chain fatty acids were more likely to be active. MM101 = donor female; MM111 = donor female. (R. P. Michael, E. B. Keverne, and R. W. Bonsall, unpublished observations.)

and this is indicated by the loss in effectiveness of her sexual invitations to stimulate the male at this time (Michael, Saayman, and Zumpe, 1967). Since relatively high levels of progesterone are secreted in the luteal phase of the rhesus monkey's cycle, it seems likely that this hormone may be of importance in the loss of female attractiveness. Certain experimental evidence supports this view, and a decline in female attractiveness was one explanation given for the loss of sexual interest which males showed with progesterone-treated partners in both a diadic (Michael, Saayman, and Zumpe, 1968) and triadic testing situation (Everitt and Herbert, 1968). The possible involvement of olfactory cues in the decrease in female attractiveness as a result of progesterone administration has been looked at in the operant situation already described. Four males were studied, and each abruptly stopped lever pressing for access to attractive females (ovariectomized and estrogenized) when they received progesterone but continued to press for the estrogenized control female [Fig. 16 (Michael and Keverne, unpublished observations)]. It seems likely that this decline in male interest was mediated via distance receptors, since behavioral tests were not permitted and no tactile information was available to the male concerning female receptivity. Males pressed for access in all 33 tests before their female partners received progesterone, 23% of 48 tests when females were under the influence of progesterone, and 92% of 39 tests after withdrawal bleeding following progesterone termination. A return of female attractiveness was confirmed by the males' high levels of mounting after they achieved access again and also by the fact that access was not permitted until lever pressing to criterion was performed on three separate occasions with each female.

That this loss of attractiveness was communicated olfactorily was tested in a second experiment adopting a similar procedure, where anosmic males were tested with a progesterone-treated female. Only two of the four males were used, but when anosmic they pressed for access to their progesterone-treated females more than in the previous experiment during the same period. The incidence of responding was variable, but the fact that they continued to respond at all and, moreover, showed high levels of mounting with these progesterone-treated females would strongly indicate that they were not aware of odor cues concerning the hormonal status of their partners. Following reversal of anosmia and a return of olfactory acuity, both males stopped lever pressing for access to these females and in subsequent behavior tests showed no sexual interest in them.

These same males were then paired with an ovariectomized female receiving vaginal secretions from an attractive "donor" female (ovariectomized and estrogenized), and showed sexual interest in their female partners with both mounting and ejaculations. When the donor female was given progesterone, her vaginal secretions lost their stimulating properties, and the males no longer showed any

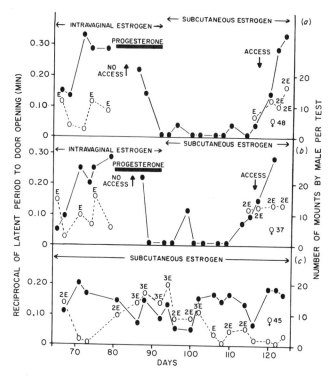

Fig. 16. Effects of progesterone administration to two female rhesus monkeys on a male's operant responding for access to them. A third female (45) received estrogen throughout and served as a control. Key: o, mounts by male; E, ejaculation; •, operant performance.

sexual interest in their "recipient" partners. A return in male sexual interest in the recipient partners did not occur until after the donor female underwent withdrawal bleeding following termination of progesterone treatment. Both males mounted and ejaculated, signaling a return in attractiveness of the donor female's vaginal secretions.

XII. ODOR CUES IN SEXUAL AROUSAL AND PERFORMANCE

It would appear, then, that odor cues from vaginal secretions can both "turn on" and "turn off" the males sexual interest, but whether the latter is due to loss of attractants in the vaginal secretion or presence of some positively aversive odor remains to be determined. This "on-off" effect might account for the behavior of those males which only show sexual interest in their female partners during the follicular part of her cycle, especially at ovulation, and show no sexual behavior during the luteal phase of the cycle. It does not, however, account for the behavior of males which show sexual interest in the female throughout her menstrual cycle but increase their mount frequency and ejaculations at mid-cycle. That is not to say that odor cues play no part in the behavior of such males, but clearly they are not determining whether or not he will be aroused. What then might be the effect, if any, of odor cues in this kind of male? Data have been extracted from a number of experiments (Fig. 17) which might well have some bearing on this kind of situation. Following withdrawal of the sex attractant from the female partner, males usually lose sexual interest in the female and make no further mounts, but occasionally (Fig. 17a,b) males maintain their sexual arousal and, paradoxically, show increased mounting and thrusting prior to a loss of sexual interest. Moreover, if the estrogenized female donor is given progesterone, her vaginal secretions lose their sexually stimulating properties when applied to the recipient. However, prior to the male's loss of sexual interest there is a marked increase in his mounting and thrusting (Fig. 17c). Since the only change in all these experiments is the odor of the female partner, we can interpret this increased mounting behavior as an increase in male sexual performance to compensate for the odor deficit of the female partner, that is, an increase in tactile input compensating for decreases in another sensory cue, namely olfactory. Similarly, following reversal of anosmia there may be an increase in male ejaculations with no marked increase in mounting (Fig. 17d). Here the introduction of the olfactory sense (together with an attractive female) initially improves the sexual performance of the male and briefly increases his ejaculatory score.

These, of course, are data taken from "sensitive responders" which clearly show the "on-off" effect, but it has relevance for males which mount throughout the cycle, because it is indicative of two separate neural pathways for the integration of olfactory cues. It is possible that sexual attraction involving odor cues is brought about by olfactory connections to the pyriform cortex and other cortical regions, via the medialis dorsalis of the thalamus, before a neural connection is obtained with the limbic system and finally the hypothalamus. This neural circuitry may be envisaged as serving a filtering function, with the cortex analogous to a computer incorporating certain "go" and "no go" programs. As mentioned earlier, the rhesus monkey's behavior incorporates a number of "no go" programs, as is seen by the modifying effects of partner preferences, past experiences with certain females, and presence of another male in the social group. This is the neural network whereby the male can be "turned on" if all conditions are appropriate. If on the other hand we consider those males that are permanently turned on, or (perhaps more appropriately) more sensitive to their own endocrine status than to odor cues concerning the female's hormonal status, then the type of response observed is one of changing sexual

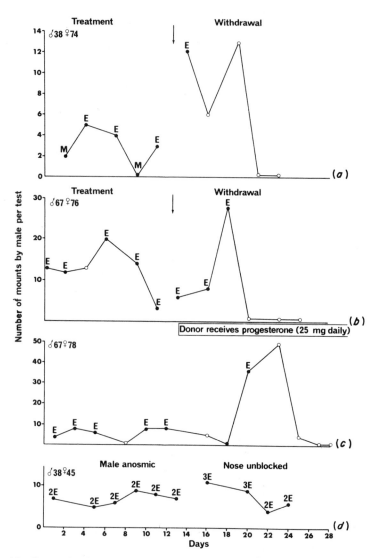

Fig. 17. Changes in the sexual performance (mounting patterns) of male rhesus monkeys following odor changes of their female partners.

performance in relation to the female's menstrual cycle. Considering odor cues and sexual performance (Fig. 17), it is possible that a more direct neural input to the hypothalamus is involved. There is evidence that even in primates the bed nucleus of the stria terminalis, particularly that part which lies in the medial preoptic region, forms a definite part of the olfactory system, the projection originally being thought to travel via the anterior limb of the anterior commissure (Meyer and Allison, 1949). More evidence is now in favor of the connection from the olfactory bulb passing directly to the corticomedial nucleus of the amygdala and from there via the stria terminalis to the preoptic anterior hypothalamic area (Cowan, Raisman, and Powell, 1965). Either way, that area of the hypothalamus known to govern sexual behavior in primates (Everitt and Herbert, 1975) receives a fairly direct olfactory input, and since this is not passing via the cortex, it seems unlikely that any complex neural processing is taking place. This then might be considered a neural pathway whereby olfactory information could modify the rhesus monkey's sexual performance at a level below the threshold of conscious awareness, and this would apply equally to both types of male.

In conclusion, then, olfactory cues have been shown to play an important part in communicating the sexual attractiveness of the female rhesus monkey. It should be remembered that these effects have been demonstrated under conditions which optimize obtaining a response, not only by selection of males which were sensitive to the stages of the female's menstrual cycle, but by arranging a procedure whereby odor cues became the only introduced variable. Even with this bias, the effectiveness of such a procedure was at the most 60%, and marked individual differences were recorded. Nevertheless, as outlined in this section, odor cues alone were sufficient to stimulate strongly the sexual behavior of some males, whereas visual cues, such as increased redness of the sexual skin and increased presentations, were without effect. Perhaps female presentation is an invitation to sniff or mount, and (as outlined earlier) the peripheral vasodilation which produces the intense perineal redness equally serves to lose heat and evaporate any odors in that region. While it is clear that olfactory cues are but one of many stimulus components which influence the probability of copulation, it is nonetheless remarkable that vaginal odors can play an active role in the sexual behavior of a microsmatic higher primate.

While one must exercise some inferential caution on the basis of diadic testing and modest sample size, for which heterogeneity cannot be in any sense guaranteed, the experiments described seem to cast some light on the factors which underlie receptivity and attractiveness in the female rhesus monkey. The estrogens and progesterone, while not without effect on the proceptive components of receptive behavior, mainly exert their influence on the sexual interactions of the pair by changing female attractiveness. Androgens from both the adrenal and the ovary mainly influence receptive behavior. In their absence elements of unreceptive behavior predominate, whereas in their presence unreceptiveness diminishes and elements of proceptive behavior increase with increased androgen titers. That is not to say that all males show no sexual interest in unattractive females, nor do unreceptive females refuse the advances of all males or, for that matter, all the advances of a given male. Indeed, individual differences in the behavior of subjects have to some extent overridden many of the findings reported in this chapter, making generalized statements difficult.

The concepts of attractiveness and receptivity hold good for interpreting the neuroendocrine events which lead to sexual behavior in ovariectomized females administered certain hormone treatments; but when applied to the behavior of normal intact females, to some extent these concepts lose their pertinence. Dichotomizing behavioral interactions in this way during the menstrual cycle is limited by their covariance, and since proceptive behavior presumably adds to a female's attractiveness while unreceptive behavior may reduce her stimulus value, attractiveness and receptivity are not totally inseparable.

Even more problematic is the application of such terms to anything other than the diadic testing situation, since attractiveness and receptivity have no absolute values, even in a given female. Hence, one can find the paradox of a female inviting one male to mount while actively refusing the mounting attempts of another male. These concepts are derived from the nature of the sexual interactions of a male and female, and such interactions in group-living primates are strongly influenced by the social environment as well as past and recent experiences. Somewhere along the line all these variables have to be integrated to determine whether sexual interactions are going to take place and what form they will take. Endocrine status is but one variable in this chain of events, while attractiveness and receptivity are but two components of endocrine status. We are still, therefore, a long way from understanding the way neuroendocrine mechanisms operate in the social group, where structure and organization can modify or impair the effects of a given hormone on behavior and even modify the levels of hormones in individual animals themselves.

Acknowledgments

Most of the original work reported here was conducted at the Institute of Psychiatry, University of London. Many of the ideas stem from discussion with colleagues, in particular Joseph Herbert, Michael Baum, and Barry J. Everitt, and to them I am indebted. My particular thanks go to Professor R. A. Hinde and Dr. Herbert for critical reading and reconstruction of the manuscript.

References

Akers, J., Conaway, C., and Kling, A. 1975. Role of the female (*M. mulatta*) in sexual behaviour. *Folia Primatol.* (in press).

Altmann, S. A. 1962. A field study of the sociobiology of rhesus monkeys. *Ann. N. Y. Acad. Sci.* **102,** 338–435.

Ball, J., and Hartman, C. G. 1935. Sexual excitability as related to the menstrual cycle in the monkey. *Amer. J. Obstet. Gynecol.* **29**, 117–119.

Beach, F. A. 1969. Locks and Beagles. *Amer. Psychol.* **24**, 971–989.

Beach, F. A. 1976. Sexual attractivity, proceptivity, and receptivity in female mammals. *Horm. Behav.* (in press).

Beach, F. A., and Le Boeuf, B. J. 1967. Coital behaviour in dogs: I. Preferential mating in the bitch. *Anim. Behav.* **15**, 546–558.

Bernstein, I. S. 1967. A field study of the pigtail monkey (*Macaca nemestrina*). *Primates* **8**, 217–228.

Bernstein, I. S., Rose, R. M., and Gordon, T. P. 1974. Behavioural and environmental events influencing primate testosterone levels. *J. Human Evol.* **3**, 517–525.

Bertrand, M. 1969. The behavioural repertoire of the stumptail macaque. *Biblio. Primatol.* **11**, 1–265.

Bielert, C. F., and Goy, R. W. 1974. Sexual behavior of male rhesus: Effects of repeated ejaculation and partner's cycle stage. *Horm. Behav.* **4**, 109–122.

Blurton-Jones, N. G., and Trollope, J. 1968. Social behaviour of the stump-tailed macaques in captivity. *Primates* **9**, 365–394.

Bolwig, N. 1959. A study of the behaviour of the chacma baboon, *Papio ursinus. Behaviour* **14**, 136– 63.

Bullock, D. W., Paris, C. A., and Goy, R. W. 1972. Sexual behaviour, swelling of the sex skin, and plasma progesterone in the pigtail macaque. *J. Reprod. Fert.* **31**, 225–236.

Carpenter, C. R. 1942. Sexual behaviour of free-ranging rhesus monkeys (*M. mulatta*). II. Periodicity of estrus, homosexual, autoerotic and non-conformist behavior. *J. Comp. Psychol.* **33**, 143–162.

Chalmers, N. R. 1968. The social behaviour of free-living mangabeys in Uganda. *Folia Primatol.* **8**, 263–281.

Conaway, C. H., and Koford, C. B. 1964. Estrous cycles and mating behaviour in free-ranging bands of rhesus monkeys. *J. Mammal.* **45**, 577–588.

Cowan, W. M., Raisman, G., and Powell, T. P. S. 1965. The connections of the amygdala. *J. Neurol. Neurosurg. Psychiat.* **28**, 137–151.

Curtis, R. F., Ballantine, J. A., Keverne, E. B., Bonsall, R. W., and Michael, R. P. 1971. Identification of primate sex-pheromones and the properties of synthetic attractants. *Nature (London)* **232**, 396–398.

Eckstein, P., and Zuckerman, S. 1956. The oestrus cycle in the mammalia. *In* "Marshall's Physiology of Reproduction" (A. S. Parkes, ed.), pp. 226–396. Longmans, London.

Everitt, B. J., and Herbert, J. 1969. The role of ovarian hormones in the sexual preference of rhesus monkeys. *Anim. Behav.* **17**, 738–746.

Everitt, B. J., and Herbert, J. 1971. The effects of dexamethasone and androgens on sexual receptivity of female rhesus monkeys. *J. Endocrinol.* **51**, 575–588.

Everitt, B. J., and Herbert, J. 1975. The effects of implanting testosterone propionate into the central nervous system on the sexual behaviour of adrenalectomised female rhesus monkeys. *Brain Res.* **86**, 109–120.

Everitt, B. J., Herbert, J., and Hamer, J. D. 1972. Sexual receptivity of bilaterally adrenalectomised female rhesus monkeys. *Physiol. Behav.* **8**, 409–415.

Ford, C. S., and Beach, F. A. 1951. "Patterns of Sexual Behaviour." Eyre and Spottiswood, London.

French, D., Fitzpatrick, D., and Law, T. O. 1972. Operant investigation of mating preference in female rats. *J. Comp. Physiol. Psychol.* **81**, 226–232.

Gartlan, J. S. 1969. Sexual and maternal behaviour of the vervet monkey, *Cercopithecus aethiops. J. Reprod. Fert. Suppl.* **6**, 137–150.

Goldfoot, D. A. 1971. Hormonal and social determinants of sexual behaviour in the pigtail monkey (*Macaca nemestrina*). *In* "Normal and Abnormal Development of Brain and Behaviour" (G. B. Stoelinga and J. J. van der Werff ten Bosch, eds.), pp. 3255–342. Leiden Univ. Press, Leiden.

Goldfoot, D. A., Kravetz, M. A., Goy, R. W., and Freeman, S. K. 1976. Lack of effect of vaginal lavages and aliphatic acids on ejaculatory responses in rhesus monkeys: Behavioural and chemical analyses. *Horm. Behav.* 7, 1–27.

Hall, K. R. L., and DeVore, I. 1965. Baboon social behaviour. *In* "Primate Behaviour" (I. de Vore, ed.) pp. 53–110. Holt, New York.

Harlow, H. E. 1965. Sexual behaviour in the rhesus monkey. *In* "Sex and Behaviour" (F. A. Beach, ed.), pp. 234–265. Wiley, New York.

Hartman, C. G. 1932. Studies in the reproduction of the monkey *Macacus (Pithecus) rhesus*, with special reference to menstruation and pregnancy. *Contrib. Embryol.* 23, 1–161.

Herbert, J. 1966. The effect of oestrogen applied directly to the genitalia upon the sexual attractiveness of the female rhesus monkey. *Excerpta Med. Int. Congr. Ser.* 3, 212.

Herbert, J. 1968. Sexual preference in the rhesus monkey, *Macaca mulatta*, in the laboratory. *Anim. Behav.* 16, 120–128.

Herbert, J. 1970. Hormones and reproductive behaviour in rhesus and Talapoin monkeys. *J. Reprod. Fert. Suppl.* 11, 119–140.

Herbert, J., and Trimble, M. R. 1967. Effect of oestradiol and testosterone on the sexual receptivity and attractiveness of the female rhesus monkey. *Nature (London)* 216, 165–166.

Hess, J. P. 1973. Observations on the sexual behaviour of captive lowland gorillas. *In* "Comparative Ecology and Behaviour of Primates" (R. P. Michael and J. Crook, eds.), pp. 507–581. Academic Press, New York.

Hess, D. L., and Resko, J. A. 1973. The effects of progesterone on the patterns of testosterone and oestradiol concentrations in the systemic plasma of the female rhesus monkey during the inter-menstrual period. *Endocrinology* 92, 446–453.

Jay, P. 1965. Field studies. *In* "Behaviour of Non-human Primates" (A. M. Schrier, H. F. Harlow, and F. Stollnitz, eds.), pp. 525–592. Academic Press, New York.

Josimovich, J. B., and Knobil, E. 1961. Placental transfer of I^{131} insulin in rhesus monkeys. *Amer. J. Physiol.* 200, 471–476.

Kaufmann, J. H. 1965. A three year study of mating behaviour in a free ranging band of monkeys. *Ecology* 46, 500–512.

Kerber, W. T., and Reese, W. H. 1969. Comparison of the menstrual cycle of cynomolgus and rhesus monkeys. *Fertil. Steril.* 20, 975–979.

Keverne, E. B., and Michael, R. P. 1970. Annual changes in the menstruation of rhesus monkeys. *J. Endocrinol.* 48, 669–670.

Keverne, E. B., and Michael, R. P. 1971. Sex-attractant properties of ether extracts of vaginal secretions from rhesus monkeys. *J. Endocrinol.* 51, 313–322.

Kummer, H. 1968. "Social Organization of Hamadryas Baboons." Karger, Basel.

Lindburg, D. G. 1967. A field study of the reproductive behaviour of the rhesus monkey (*Macaca mulatta*). Ph.D. Thesis, Univ. of California, Berkeley.

Loy, J. 1970. Peri-menstrual sexual behaviour among rhesus monkeys. *Folia Primatol.* 13, 286–296.

Loy, J. 1971. Estrous behaviour of free-ranging rhesus monkeys (*Macaca mulatta*). *Primates* 12, 1–31.

Macdonald, P., Beyer, C., Newton, F., Brian, B., Baker, R., Tan, H. S., Sampson, C., Hitching, P., Greenhill, R., and Pritchard, D. 1970. Failure of 5-dihydroxytestosterone to initiate sexual behaviour in the castrated male rat. *Nature (London)* 227, 964–965.

Maslow, A. H. 1936. The role of dominance in the social and sexual behaviour of infra-human primates: III. A theory of sexual behaviour of infra-human primates. *J. Genet. Psychol.* **48**, 310–338.

Meyer, M., and Allison, A. C. 1949. An experimental investigation of the connections of the olfactory tracts in the monkey. *J. Neurol. Neurosurg. Psychiat.* **12**, 274–286.

Michael, R. P. 1971. Neuroendocrine factors regulating primate behaviour. *In* "Frontiers in Neuroendocrinology" (L. Martin and W. F. Ganong, eds.), pp. 359–398. Oxford Univ. Press, London and New York.

Michael, R. P., and Keverne, E. B. 1968. Pheromones: their role in the communication of sexual states in primates. *Nature (London)* **218**, 746–749.

Michael, R. P., and Keverne, E. B. 1970. Primate sex pheromones of vaginal origin. *Nature (London)* **225**, 84–85.

Michael, R. P., and Keverne, E. B. 1972. Differences in the effects of estrogen and androgen on the sexual motivation of female rhesus monkeys. *J. Endocrinol.* **55**, xl–xli.

Michael, R. P., and Saayman, G. S. 1967. Individual differences in sexual behaviour of male rhesus monkeys (*Macaca mulatta*) under laboratory conditions. *Anim. Behav.* **15**, 460–466.

Michael, R. P., and Saayman, G. S. 1968. Differential effects on behaviour of the subcutaneous and intravaginal administration of oestrogen in the rhesus monkey (*Macaca mulatta*). *J. Endocrinol.* **41**, 231–246.

Michael, R. P., and Welegalla, J. 1968. Ovarian hormones and the sexual behaviour of the female rhesus monkey (*Macaca mulatta*) under laboratory conditions. *J. Endocrinol.* **41**, 407–420.

Michael, R. P., and Zumpe, D. 1970a. Sexual initiating behaviour by female rhesus monkeys (*Macaca mulatta*) under laboratory conditions. *Behaviour* **36**, 168–186.

Michael, R. P., and Zumpe, D. 1970b. Rhythmic changes in the copulatory frequencies of rhesus monkeys (*Macaca mulatta*) in relation to the menstrual cycle, and a comparison with the human cycle. *J. Reprod. Fert.* **21**, 199–201.

Michael, R. P., Herbert, J., and Welegalla, J. 1967. Ovarian hormones and the sexual behaviour of the male rhesus monkey (*Macaca mulatta*) under laboratory conditions. *J. Endocrinol.* **39**, 81–98.

Michael, R. P., Keverne, E. B., and Bonsall, R. W. 1971. Pheromones; isolation of male sex-attractants from a female primate. *Science* **172**, 964–966.

Michael, R. P., Saayman, G., and Zumpe, D. 1967. Sexual attractiveness and receptivity in rhesus monkeys. *Nature (London)* **215**, 554–556.

Michael, R. P., Saayman, G., and Zumpe, D. 1968. The suppression of mounting behaviour and ejaculation in male rhesus monkeys (*Macaca mulatta*) by administration of progesterone to their female partners. *J. Endocrinol.* **41**, 421–431.

Michael, R. P., Keverne, E. B., Zumpe, D., and Bonsall, R. W. 1972. Neuroendocrine factors in the control of primate behaviour. *Rec. Progr. Horm. Res.* **28**, 665–706.

Naftolin, F., Ryan, K. J., and Petro, Z. 1971. Aromatisation of androstenedione by the anterior hypothalamus of adult male and female rats. *Endocrinology* **90**, 295–297.

Rahaman, H., and Partharsarathy, M. D. 1969. Studies on the sexual behaviour of bonnet monkeys. *Primates* **10**, 149–162.

Riesen, J. W., Meyer, R. K., and Wolf, R. C. 1971. The effect of season on occurrence of ovulation in the rhesus monkey. *Biol. Reprod.* **5**, 11–114.

Rowell, T. E. 1963. Behaviour and reproductive cycles of female macaques. *J. Reprod. Fert.* **6**, 193–203.

Rowell, T. E. 1967a. Female reproductive cycles and the behaviour of baboons and rhesus macaques. *In* "Social Communication in Primates" (S. Altmann, ed.), pp. 15–32. Univ. Chicago Press, Chicago, Illinois.

Rowell, T. E. 1967b. A quantitative comparison of the behaviour of a wild and caged baboon group. *Anim. Behav.* 15, 499–509.

Rowell, T. E. 1972. Female reproductive cycles and social behaviour in primates. This series. 4, 69–105.

Rowell, T. E., and Chalmers, N. R. 1970. Reproductive cycles of the mangabey, *Cercocebus albigena. Folia Primatol.* 12, 264–272.

Saayman, G. S. 1970. The menstrual cycle and sexual behaviour in a troop of free-ranging chacma baboons, *Papio ursinus. Folia primatol.* 12, 81–110.

Scruton, D., and Herbert, J. 1970. The menstrual cycle and its effects on behaviour in the Talapoin monkey (*Miopithecus talapoin*). *J. Zool.* 162, 419–436.

Simonds, P. E. 1965. The bonnet macaque in South India. *In* "Primate Behaviour" (I. deVore, ed.), pp. 175–196. Holt, New York.

Southwick, C. H., Beg, M. A., and Siddiqi, M. R. 1965. Rhesus monkeys in North India. *In* "Primate Behaviour" (I. deVore, ed.), pp. 111–159. Holt, New York.

Trimble, M. R., and Herbert, J. 1968. The effect of testosterone or oestradiol upon the sexual and associated behaviour of the adult female rhesus monkey. *J. Endocrinol.* 42, 171–185.

van Hooff, J. A. R. A. M. 1962. Facial expressions in higher primates. *Symp. Zool. Soc. London* 8, 97–125.

van Lawick-Goodall, J. 1968. The behaviour of free-living chimpanzees in the Gombe Stream Reserve. *Anim. Behav. Monogr.* 1, 161–311.

van Wagenen, G. 1945. Optimal mating time for pregnancy in the monkey. *Endocrinology* 37, 307–312.

Wilson, M. 1972. Hormonal control of sexual behaviour in the male rhesus monkey (*Macaca mulatta*). Ph.D. Thesis, London University.

Yerkes, R. M. 1939. Sexual behaviour in the chimpanzee. *Human Biol.* 11, 78–111.

Yerkes, R. M., and Elder, J. H. 1936. Oestrus, receptivity and mating in the chimpanzee. *Comp. Psychol. Monogr.* 13, No. 5.

Young, W. C., and Orbison, W. D. 1944. Changes in selected features of behaviour in pairs of oppositely sexed chimpanzees during the sexual cycle and after ovariectomy. *J. Comp. Psychol.* 37, 107–143.

Zuckerman, S. 1932. "The Social Life of Monkeys and Apes." Kegan Paul, London.

Zumpe, D., and Michael, R. P. 1968. The clutching reaction and orgasm in the female rhesus monkey (*Macaca mulatta*). *J. Endocrinol.* 40, 117–123.

Zumpe, D., and Michael, R. P. 1970. Ovarian hormones and female sexual invitations in captive rhesus monkeys (*Macaca mulatta*). *Anim. Behav.* 18, 293–301.

Prenatal Parent–Young Interactions in Birds and Their Long-Term Effects

MONICA IMPEKOVEN

INSTITUTE OF ANIMAL BEHAVIOR
RUTGERS UNIVERSITY
NEWARK, NEW JERSEY

I. INTRODUCTION

The present review is very selective: apart from emphasis on the writer's own work, preference has been given to studies which seem to illustrate particularly well certain aspects of our subject. The study of the development of the mutual relationship between parental care and filial behavior in birds has focused mainly on the postnatal period. Here emphasis will be put on events taking place during the incubation period. The parents' behavior is in part controlled by stimuli arising from the eggs; embryonic growth and responsiveness are, in turn, affected by parental stimuli. Mutual stimulation during incubation may have immediate as well as long-term effects on the onset of chick care in the parent and on hatching and early postnatal responses in chicks. In order to understand better the kinds of stimuli incubating birds provide for their embryos and vice versa, pertinent studies on incubation behavior and embryonic development will be briefly reviewed.

II. ASPECTS OF INCUBATION BEHAVIOR

The incubation behavior of domestic fowl (*Gallus domesticus*) was described and quantified earlier this century (e.g., Eycleshymer, 1907; Chattock, 1925; Olsen, 1930). Since the early 1950s a number of studies has accumulated on detailed qualitative and/or quantitative observations of incubation patterns in wild birds [e.g., Kendeigh (1952) in the House Wren (*Troglodytes aedon*) and some other songbirds; Poulson (1953) in swans, grebes, pigeons, etc.; Skutch (1962) in a variety of songbirds, woodpeckers, hummingbirds, etc.; Beer (1961, 1962, 1966) in the Black-headed Gull (*Larus ridibundus*); Drent (1970), Drent *et al.* (1970), and Baerends *et al.* (1970) in the Herring Gull (*Larus argentatus*); Impekoven (1973a) in the Laughing Gull (*Larus atricilla*); Caldwell and Cornwell (1975) in the Mallard (*Anas platyrhynchos*)].

In some species both male and female take part in incubating the eggs; they change over or relieve each other periodically. In other species one parent (usually the female) incubates alone, although its mate may visit the nest. In general the percentage of time the eggs are covered is greater where both mates share the duty (Skutch, 1962; White and Kinney, 1974). The period between nest reliefs, during which one of the parents tends the eggs [i.e., the sitting bout, according to Beer (1961)], differs greatly between species, extending from minutes in small passerines to hours or even days in larger birds. Similarly the duration of off-periods or recesses may range from minutes to hours (Skutch, 1962). Drent (1972, 1973) has discussed the differential degrees of attentiveness (i.e., time the eggs are covered) in different species as adaptations to different climatic conditions and predators. Periods of continuous incubation by one bird [i.e., sitting spells, according to Beer (1961)] are periodically interrupted by the bird's rising, assuming a stooping posture, and looking down at its eggs. The bird may then turn around in the nest to face a new direction, and it may shift its eggs with its beak before resettling. Chickens, for instance, shift their eggs every 10–50 minutes (Chattock, 1925; Olsen, 1930) or every 30–60 minutes (Kuiper and Ubbels, 1951); Black-headed Gulls, about every 40 minutes (Beer, 1966; Impekoven, 1973a); Herring Gulls, every 2 hours and 20 minutes (Drent, 1970); and Mallards at least every 50 minutes (Caldwell and Cornwell, 1975). Not only the shifting with the beak, but also the trampling and turning of the bird in the nest may change the position of the eggs. Resettling typically consists of a sequence of behavior patterns which Beer (1961) labeled *chest-dropping, waggling*, and *quivering* (a movement by which close contact between the brood patch and the eggs is reestablished). Sometimes waggling is not followed by quivering, in which case the resettling has been referred to as incomplete. On the other hand quivering can occur temporally unassociated with other resettling movements (Beer, 1961; Impekoven, 1973a). During the act of resettling or while looking down at the eggs, before or after shifting them, the bird may utter brief vocalizations [e.g., Tschanz (1968) in the Guillemot, or Common Murre, *Uria aalge*; Baerends *et al.* (1970) in the Herring Gull; Guyomarc'h (1972) in the Domestic Chicken; Impekoven (1973a) in the Laughing Gull]. Calls are also given during nest reliefs or visits by the mate [e.g., Impekoven (1971a) and Herrmann (personal communication) in the Laughing Gull]. Sitting spells can also be interrupted by the approach of a predator in which case the bird may leave the nest and utter characteristic alarm calls [e.g., Kruuk (1964) in the Black-headed Gull; Impekoven (1976) in the Laughing Gull], and by flights away from the nest to defecate (e.g., Beer, 1961) in the Black-headed Gull; Baerends (1959) in the Herring Gull; Miller and Miller (1958) in the Ringed Turtle Dove, *Streptopelia risoria*[1]].

It is well known for a variety of species that birds incubate less constantly before their clutch of eggs is complete (e.g., Beer, 1961; Skutch, 1962; Drent, 1970; Caldwell and Cornwell, 1975). However once incubation behavior has well set in, no significant changes as the incubation period progresses have been observed by Beer (1961), Skutch (1962), or Caldwell and Cornwell (1975), but a gradual increase in the duration of sitting spells and a shortening of breaks (rising-resettling) was clearly established by Drent (1970). During prehatching and hatching marked changes have been noted for many species. The duration of sitting spells becomes shorter and the intervening breaks longer (see Drent, 1970, and references cited therein). Rising-resettling and the proportion of incomplete settling sequences increase in frequency (Beer, 1966; Impekoven, 1973a), and also the rate of egg shifting tends to be enhanced [Tschanz (1968) and Norton-Griffiths (1969) in the Oystercatcher, *Haematopus ostralegus,* and Impekoven (unpublished) in the Laughing Gull]. In species like the above, where both mates take part in incubation, they relieve each other more frequently. In some species it has been noted that incubating birds vocalize more as hatching approaches, often in conjunction with rising-resettling [e.g., Domestic Chicken (Olsen, 1930); Wood Ducks, *Aix sponsa* (Gottlieb, 1963); Mallards (Bjärvall, 1968; Hess, 1973); Guillemots (Tschanz, 1968); Oystercatchers (Norton-Griffiths, 1969); Laughing Gulls (Impekoven, 1973a)]. One of the calls uttered before hatching

---

[1] *Streptopelia risoria* is also sometimes called the Ring Dove or the Ring-neck Dove.

also becomes important after hatching in the context of luring and feeding the chicks.

Around hatching new behavior patterns appear and replace the old ones. For instance, Beer (1966) has observed in gulls how a bird frequently does not rise completely in response to chicks but merely lifts its chest. The chick-brooding posture differs from the typical incubation posture in that the carpal joints are out of their pockets in the body plumage and the wings are slightly extended downwards, i.e., "drooped." Comparable postural changes, using a somewhat different nomenclature, were reported for the Black-tailed Godwit, *Limosa limosa* (Lind, 1961), and for the Oystercatcher (Norton-Griffiths, 1969). In contrast to the eggs, which are incubated ventrally, chicks of these and other semiprecocial and precocial species are brooded between the wing and the side of the body (or sometimes under the tail) (e.g., Beer, 1966; Tinbergen, 1965). In certain altricial birds the brooding posture after hatching does not seem to differ from the incubation posture (e.g., Cheng, personal communication, in Ringed Turtle Doves; Impekoven, unpublished observations, in Reed Warblers, *Acrocephalus scirpaceus,* and Barn Swallows, *Hirundo rustica*). In some semiprecocial species, behavior leading up to and including attempts of parental feeding have been observed to occur for the first time during prehatching stages when the embryos are vocal, although such incidents are not common [Beer (1966), Tschanz (1968), Norton-Griffiths (1969), Emlen and Miller (1969), in the Ring-billed Gull, *Larus delawarensis*].

III. ASPECTS OF EMBRYONIC DEVELOPMENT

A. BEHAVIORAL DEVELOPMENT

Oppenheim (1974) has extensively reviewed the behavioral events during the incubation period. Therefore we shall restrict ourselves here to a brief outline of the most significant aspects. The development of embryonic motility has been studied qualitatively and quantitatively in the Domestic Chicken (Kuo, 1932a; Hamburger, 1963), in the Peking Duck, *Anas platyrhynchos* (Gottlieb and Kuo, 1965; Oppenheim, 1970), and the pigeon, or Rock Dove, *Columba livia* (Harth, 1971). The first movements appear after about the first fifth of the incubation period (i.e., day 3 in the chick embryo; day 5 in the duck). They consist first of stereotyped undulating body movements, later of apparently uncoordinated jerky movements of all parts of the body and the limbs. At the beginning such movements occur at a low rate, but gradually they increase in frequency and duration, reaching a peak around the midpoint of the incubation period, after which time they decrease again. During much of the incubation period, the embryo exhibits bursts of activity, interspersed by periods of inactivity. This motility occurs in the absence of sensory stimulation (e.g., Hamburger, 1963), although such stimulation may temporarily affect the rate and amplitude of movement (e.g., Oppenheim, 1972a; Impekoven and Gold, 1973).

Prehatching and hatching behavior have been described in detail for the Domestic Chicken (Hamburger and Oppenheim, 1967), the Peking Duck (Oppenheim, 1970), and a variety of species including gulls, pigeons, quails, and songbirds (Oppenheim, 1972b, 1973; Vince, 1969, 1974). A few days before hatching a series of new complex and coordinated movements appear which lead to the attainment of the hatching position. During episodes of these prehatching movements, earlier motility patterns are suspended. In order to assume the first prehatching position the embryo lifts its head and beak out of the yolk sac in which they have been buried and tucks them under the right wing. Next it shifts position within the egg so that the beak now pushes against the membranes separating the embryo from the air space, close to the shell. Shortly after this the beak actually penetrates the membranes and extends directly into the air space. Lung ventilation begins around this time. Embryos of precocial and semiprecocial species (chickens, ducks, gulls, etc.) also begin to vocalize at this point, whereas altricial species (songbirds, pigeons) have not been heard to utter sounds before emergence from the shell (Poulson, 1953; Oppenheim, 1972b, 1973; Vince, 1974, and references cited therein). In the former group, vocalizations increase in frequency, intensity, and complexity as hatching approaches. The first crack in the eggshell usually appears on the upper surface of the blunt end of the egg: in many species like chickens and ducks, this occurs after air-space penetration; but in others, like the Black-Tailed Godwit (Lind, 1961), other waders, gulls, terns, and pigeons, it happens during the tucking stage (e.g., Drent, 1970; Oppenheim, 1972b; Impekoven, unpublished observations). The movement involved in cracking the shell and/or making a hole in it are termed *pipping.* They consist of so-called backthrusts with the head and beak against the shell. These movements increase markedly in frequency during the last hours before hatching. In species where the first pip crack, usually below the air space, is seen during tucking, it most likely results from the beak of the embryo striking the shell during a tucking movement. Another movement observed during the prehatching stages, but whose function in the hatching process is unknown, is bill clapping, a rapid opening and closing of the beak. During the last prehatching stages the pipping hole gets enlarged. Then the embryo begins a sequence of movements which rotate it counterclockwise within the shell and at the same time further crack the shell about two-thirds of the way around (although there are species differences in the extent of this rotation). The embryo then pushes the shell cap off and emerges. More detailed descriptions of prehatching and hatching movements have been given by Oppenheim (1970, 1972b, 1973, and references cited therein). Most recently a study has been completed on the hatching movements of chicks placed in transparent glass "eggshells" (Bakhuis, 1974). Oppenheim (1972b) lists the duration of different prehatching stages for various species. For instance, from tucking to hatching takes nearly 2½ days in the Domestic Chicken, close to 3 days in the Peking Duck, and 3½ days in the Laughing Gull. The pip-hatch interval ranges from 20 hours in the Domestic Chicken to 41 hours in the Laughing Gull (in the latter the interval was calculated from the time the first pip crack was made after air-space penetration).

B. THERMOGENESIS AND CHANGES IN WEIGHT AND GRAVITATIONAL PROPERTIES

In close correlation with embryonic growth and weight increase, embryonic heat production increases steadily during incubation. Different methods have been employed to measure this thermogenesis. One such method is the measurement of the temperature gradient between the interface of the parental brood patch/upper egg surface and the lower egg surface/nest floor; the temperature gradient decreases with progressing incubation, as shown for the Herring Gull and reviewed for other species by Drent (1970). Other methods include the measurement of the rapidity and extent of temperature decline during cooling trials of the egg, CO_2 production as measured in a respiration chamber, and evaporative heat loss, measured in terms of weight decrease during incubation. Even though heat generation by the embryo reaches 75% in the total heat requirement for normal incubation on the day before hatching, the embryo is quite incapable of independently maintaining its temperature or of compensating adequately for a fall in ambient temperature. By contrast the newly hatched chick responds to a decline in air temperature by increasing its own heat production and thus regulates its body temperature to some extent. Drent (1970) has illustrated this difference for eggs and chicks of the Herring Gull. Early postnatal development of thermoregulation has also been described for other precocial and altricial species (reviewed by Freeman, 1974; Oppenheim and Levin, 1975). According to King and Farner (1961) and Freeman (1974) some precocial species have good thermoregulation soon after hatching, whereas the young of some passerine species may not develop completely effective thermoregulation until the end of the nestling period.

Although embryonic weight increases, the egg as a whole loses weight during incubation because of water loss, as just stated. The daily loss remains near constant until lung ventilation sets in, at which time evaporation greatly increases (Drent, 1970). The Herring Gull egg reduces its weight by close to 9% between the onset of continuous incubation (after completion of the clutch—see Section II) and pipping. Smaller eggs lose proportionately more weight through evaporation; for example, in the Ringed Turtle Dove it is 15% (Gibson, personal communication).

The gravitational properties of eggs change as incubation progresses. This has been assessed by daily measurements of the position of eggs in the nest (Lind, 1961; Drent, 1970; Caldwell and Cornwell, 1975) and by placing eggs in a dish of water (Drent, 1970; Oppenheim, 1970). During the first third or so of incubation, eggs can lie in any position according to Lind (1961) and Drent (1970); on the other hand, Cornwell and Caldwell (1975) found that egg position was nonrandom. Thereafter the position tends to become increasingly restricted in the nest, and in the water dish a constant position is assumed. This change accompanies the assumption by the embryo of a fixed position within the shell. The restriction of egg position reflects a progressive intensification of weight asymmetry. Particularly during the last third of incubation, this asymmetry can be assessed visually by candling the egg. The air space previously symmetrical around the blunt end of the egg becomes asymmetrical, i.e., extended downward toward the small end of the egg on one side (Oppenheim, 1970). This represents also the site of the future pipping hole, which comes to be situated uppermost [see Drent (1970), Oppenheim (1972b, 1973), and Tolhurst (1974) for illustrations of the embryo's prehatching positions]. Drent (1970), Kovach (1968, 1970), and Oppenheim (1970) have carried out experiments in order to investigate at what time in development the position of the embryo within the shell and the site of the pipping hole—and thus the particular weight asymmetry of the egg—are fixed. The findings of these authors do not fully agree with each other. Oppenheim (1970) concludes that active movements (motility) play a role in bringing the embryo into the position which enables it to pip uppermost. When these movements are absent or at least reduced after tucking (i.e., about 2 days before hatching in the Domestic Chicken) the position within the shell and the site of the pipping hole can no longer be changed. Thus in eggs whose position has been fixed such that the site of the future pipping hole faces down, embryos are incapable of turning around to pip on the upper half of the egg (Oppenheim, 1973). In Kovach's (1968, 1970) experiments, chick embryos in eggs fixed in a "head-down" position were still able to make a certain degree of adjustment on days 19 and 20. Since recordings of motility from eggs in different positions did not differ, Kovach (1970) concluded that active behavioral forces cannot be involved in this turning.

C. SENSORY CAPACITIES

Oppenheim (1974) has extensively reviewed the role of sensory stimulation in the embryogenesis of behavior, discussing primarily the cutaneous, proprioceptive, and vestibular systems. Other reviews (e.g., Gottlieb, 1968; Vince, 1974) have dealt with the onset of functioning of different sensory modalities in their believed chronological order of appearance. Nonvisual photic sensitivity appears first, followed by tactile (or cutaneous), vestibular, proprioceptive, and visual modality, in that order. Shortly after the onset of motility (i.e., before the eyes are functional) the avian embryo apparently reacts nonvisually to light. Bursian (1964) reported that, under unnaturally strong light, embryonic motility of the Domestic Chicken could be affected as early as day 3 of incubation. At first the light increased embryonic motility; on the 8th and 9th day the effect became inhibitory. The structures mediating these effects have not been discovered so far, nor have any independent replications of this finding been published. Recently nonvisual light sensitivity has also been discovered in embryos of the altricial pigeon at a time when the visual system is known not to be functional (Heaton and Harth, 1974a).

Tactile sensitivity is the first one to become functional with respect to sensorimotor reflex activity. Experiments using a loop of baby hair have demonstrated sensitivity in the oral region after the first third of the incubation period in precocial as well as altricial species [reviewed by Gottlieb (1968)]. More recently Oppenheim (1972c) in chickens and Harth (1974) in pigeons have expanded on these earlier findings [reviewed by Vince (1974)]. The onset of behavioral function coincides with the establishment of the cutaneous reflex arc (e.g., Visintini and Levi-Montalcini, 1939).

In order to discover the onset of functioning of the vestibular sense, eggs were rotated on a disk. With this method, head nystagmus was elicited in Domestic Chicken embryos around day 8, which is the time when the appropriate neural structures have been completed (Visintini and Levi-Montalcini, 1939). Oppenheim and Gottlieb (personal communication), in preliminary findings, have been unable to replicate these results, nor have they so far found any evidence of vestibular sensitivity up to at least day 15 with this method. The reports of Decker (1970) and Kovach (1968, 1970) agree with these findings. Oppenheim (1973) expressed the belief, based on these results, that the vestibular sense may not be functional until a few hours before hatching. Further research, using different kinds of vestibular stimulation (e.g., egg turning as provided by an incubating bird), is needed to settle this point.

Proprioception, according to Gottlieb (1968) is a possible form of self-stimulation and may occur during normal development as a natural consequence of the embryo's movements. Provine (1973) carried out a critical experiment to test for the relative importance of such stimulation. His results led to the conclusion that movement-produced stimulation had little if any effect on ongoing motility at the stage (day 15) tested. Experimentally evoked proprioceptive muscle reflexes were observed in chick embryos for the first time on day 10, the time of closure of the monosynaptic reflex circuits (Visintini and Levi-Montalcini, 1939), a finding which has not been challenged since.

Regarding auditory sensitivity, cochlear microphonic effects of stimulation with pure tones of low frequencies have been reported for the chick embryo as early as day 12 of incubation, i.e., after 57–61% of the total incubation period

(Vanzulli and Garcia-Austt, 1963). At the level of the cochlear nuclei the first indication of evoked responses occurred on day 11 of incubation. On subsequent days an improvement was observed in the threshold sensitivity of the response as well as the frequency range over which it could be recorded. Auditory responses from the brainstem present an adultlike pattern, at least at low frequencies, about a day before hatching. The onset of auditory function was found to be clearly related to the histogenesis of the acoustic ganglion and cochlear nuclei between days 11–13 (Saunders et al., 1973; Saunders, 1974). In Peking Duck embryos, single-unit recording from cochlear nuclei revealed that embryos respond to low frequencies (500–600 Hz) on days 19–20, i.e., after about 70% of the 26-day-long incubation period. On the following days more units respond, and the response is to sounds of higher frequencies and lower amplitudes. By day 22 the distribution of characteristic frequencies no longer differs from the adult pattern. Histological examination indicates the presence of all basic adult features of cochlear nuclei as early as day 14 and of the cochlea on days 17–18 (Konishi, 1973). Nothing is known about the prenatal development of auditory sensitivity in altricial birds.

The report by a Russian investigator, Sviderskaya (1967), on effects of sound on embryonic motility in chick embryos prior to day 14 has met with scepticism (e.g., Oppenheim, 1972a), although it is not inconsistent with the findings of Saunders (1974) and Saunders et al. (1973). Since the sound was unduly intense, the possibility cannot be ruled out that vibration was the effective stimulus which might act via the tactile or proprioceptive modality. Gottlieb (1968) has also reviewed several studies using conditioning procedures for the establishment of audition. This author elaborated particularly on one investigation which was not designed to explore the onset of audition per se but rather the prenatal origins of conditioning to sound (e.g., Sedláček, 1964). Chick embryos were trained to a tone of 3 kHz, using local beak and head movements as the conditioned response and electric shock as the unconditioned stimulus. From the results of this experiment Sedláček concluded that there were different stages in the development of the "temporary connection," only the last of which (day 20) involves genuine conditioning. The different stages correspond to different functional conditions of the nervous system. In the first stage the nervous system cannot yet preserve traces of previous excitation. Improvement proceeds over the next stages in terms of the immediate response as well as of setting up trace effects which may last into early postnatal life.

Again Gottlieb (1968) and Vince (1974) have extensively reviewed studies designed to establish the onset of visual function in the avian embryo. Such findings are based on neuroanatomical, biochemical, and electrophysiological evidence. Recently Heaton (1971, 1973) and Heaton and Harth (1974b) have conducted research in which the (neurally mediated) pupillary reflex was taken as an index of visual sensitivity. In the Domestic Chicken this reflex could be elicited on days 16–17, i.e., after about 84% of the total incubation period, according to Heaton's calculations. This finding agrees well with the time of onset of visual function established by means of other techniques. In other precocial species (ducks, quails) the pupillary response could be elicited earlier, i.e., after about 67% of the total incubation period, whereas in the pigeon, the only representative of altricial species tested so far, after 86–88%.

Thermal sensitivity was not covered by Gottlieb or Vince in their reviews; however Oppenheim and Levin (1975) presented evidence of physiological responsiveness (i.e., alterations in heart rate) to temperature changes on day 6 in the chicken embryo, but behavioral responsiveness was not detected until day 15.

IV. EFFECTS OF EMBRYONIC STIMULI ON BEHAVIOR OF THE INCUBATING BIRD AND THE ONSET OF CHICK CARE

Regarding effects of stimuli arising from the eggs on incubation responses, much attention has been devoted to how the number of eggs in a clutch, their size, shape, movability, and visual properties affect the incidence of rising and resettling and the duration of sitting spells (e.g., Beer, 1961; Baerends, 1959; Baerends et al., 1970). Far less attention has been given to stimuli that might result from the growing embryo inside the egg. However the intriguing possibility that the incubating parent may be physiologically and behaviorally responsive to stimuli from growing embryos, even before pipping stages, is presently under investigation at our institute (M. Gibson and R. Silver, in preparation). The results obtained so far show that female Ringed Turtle Doves spend more time on a nest with fertile developing eggs than with infertile eggs. Other observational and experimental work that bears directly or indirectly on this issue will be reviewed here. During pipping, of course, stimulation by the embryo becomes more dramatic, and quantitative observations as well as experimental studies have been devoted to this issue.

A. THERMAL STIMULI

Drent (1970, 1972, 1973, 1975) has extensively reviewed studies on the effects of temperature on the behavior of the incubating bird. Much of this work has been focused on the role of ambient temperature, which of course can affect the temperature of the eggs, particularly during times when they are not covered by the parent. The issue of maintenance of constant incubation temperature, despite fluctuating air temperatures, has been studied in a variety of species, including those which nest under extreme environmental conditions. While most birds in the temperate (and arctic) zones have to keep the eggs warm, some desert species [e.g., the White-winged Dove, *Zenaida asiatica* (Russel, 1969), or the Gray Gull, *Larus modestus* (Howell *et al.*, 1974)] face the problem of keeping their eggs from overheating. Other examples of this sort are cited by Drent (1972, 1973) and Vince (1974). Mechanisms involved in maintaining a uniform temperature consist of changes in the metabolic rate and blood flow through the brood patches, as well as behavioral adaptations such as the duration of sitting spells and various resettling movements like trampling and quivering.

Less attention has been given to the role of the egg or embryonic temperature in controlling parental behavior, irrespective or independent of the environmental temperature. Highly relevant to this question are studies which demonstrate the progressive heat production of the growing embryo. Accordingly, compensatory behavior of the parent is called for to keep the incubation temperature constant. The parent's necessary contribution to the heat requirement for normal development is 100% at the beginning but reduces itself to 25% at the close of incubation, according to Drent's (1970) calculations. This change led White and Kinney (1974) to the assumption that, in species in which only the female attends the nest and her periods of attentiveness have been shown to be temperature dependent, she should be able to take progressively more time off as incubation progresses. No data are presented on this issue, however. A decrease in nest attentiveness may in some species, e.g., gulls, be incompatible with other functions of this behavior, such as protection from predation. Attentiveness in the Herring Gull even increases with progressing incubation. Drent (1970) sees a functional correlate of this trend in the declining resistance of the embryo to deviations from normal incubation temperature (see also Moreng and Shaffner, 1951; Moreng and Bryant, 1956). Drent (1972), in discussing signals arising from the eggs that may affect the thermal aspects of incubation, mentioned also the vocalization of the embryo. During pipping the distress call can be heard when the eggs cool, as may happen when the parent interrupts incubation. Drent suggests that these vocalizations help to control parental attentiveness.

Direct experimental alteration of egg temperature has been performed (e.g., by Franks, 1967) in the Ringed Turtle Dove. The frequency of various behavioral activities such as footwork (presumably equivalent to trampling; see Section II), turning in the nest and egg shifting were influenced by raising or lowering of the egg temperature. In addition gular fluttering (i.e., panting) and preening could be observed in response to an increase of egg temperature; shivering (presumably equivalent to quivering; see Section II) and elevation of feathers (i.e., ruffling), in response to a decrease. Comparable findings were made in the Herring Gull by Drent *et al.* (1970), elaborating on an earlier study by Baerends *et al.* (1960). These authors concluded that only the adjustment of the egg–brood patch contact (i.e., quivering) can be aimed at regulating the egg temperature directly.

Some of the other activities are aimed at safeguarding the body temperature of the sitting bird and, only as a corollary thereof, the egg temperature.

Drent *et al.* (1970), who measured incubation temperatures in their experiments, showed convincingly how the parents are much better equipped to compensate for too low than for too high egg temperatures. This ability clearly relates to the natural situation, where the parents have to provide heat for the essentially poikilothermic embryo while the danger of overheating of eggs is probably small in the Herring Gull. In other studies reviewed by Drent (1972) in which (nest) air temperature was manipulated, the birds' behavior may in fact also have been influenced by direct signals from the eggs.

More recently White and Kinney (1974) performed an experiment on captive Village Weaverbirds (*Ploceus cucullatus*), based on the assumption that the brood patch may contain sensory receptors that provide the parent bird with information on egg temperature. This possibility was investigated by anesthetization of the skin of the brood patch. Such birds showed greater attentiveness to their eggs, and the eggs reached higher incubation temperatures.

While these experimental studies convincingly demonstrate that egg temperature affects incubation behavior and its physiological correlates, the changes were drastic and not aimed at simulating the temperature changes that might occur from the increasing heat generation by the growing embryo. Also, no possible long-term effects have been studied. For instance, Franks (1967) reported experiments in which birds were kept with eggs at 46°C for 13 days. It would have been interesting to investigate whether this experience had any effect on the birds' readiness to accept newly hatched squabs.

Another question which has been little studied is how temperature regulation by the incubating birds is affected by the hatching of their first chick. In many species of birds the young do not all hatch at the same time but over hours or even days. The parents therefore must simultaneously respond appropriately to eggs and chicks. Beer (1966), observing transparent nests from underneath, discovered that Black-headed Gulls sat with their chicks and eggs under wing and tail and often with their brood patches empty. These changes in behavior, so he states, almost certainly mean lowering of the efficiency with which eggs are incubated and may be the reason why some last eggs fail to hatch. Similarly, Drent (1970) reports parental neglect for eggs when the first chicks have hatched. These findings are interesting in view of the fact that heat production, much higher in the newly hatched chicks than in pipping eggs (see Section III,B), apparently can exert an overriding effect on the behavior of the parent.

B. TACTILE STIMULI

Tactile stimuli have been investigated in incubating gulls in terms of number of eggs in a clutch, their size, and their shape. For instance, Beer (1961) found that abnormal egg shapes (cylinders) elicit more rising-resettling than normal eggs. Similarly, departures from the normal clutch size lead to more frequent interruption of continuous incubation (Beer, 1961; Baerends, 1959; Baerends et al., 1970).

Tactile sensitivity of the ventral area (brood patch) increases during the breeding period, as has been experimentally demonstrated in the domesticated Canary, Serinus canarius (Hinde et al., 1963). It is conceivable that this enhances the perception of embryonic movement, even before prehatching stages. Also, during egg-shifting stimulation from movement as well as from progressive weight and gravitational changes may be perceived (see Section III,A and B). So far no research has been carried out to test this possibility.

Direct tactile stimuli from the embryo become of importance when the eggs are pipped. Beer (1966) found that some of the quantitative changes in the incubation pattern observed during pipping were comparable to changes that were produced by introducing sharp-edged eggs into the nest (see above). This author therefore concluded that the movements of the bill and the egg tooth, protruding through the pipping hole, are responsible for these changes in the natural course of events. Norton-Griffiths (1969), from a sequential analysis, concluded that the bill movements of the pipping embryos elicited rising, egg shifting, and shuffling in Oystercatchers.

Some investigators ignored the pipping egg stages. However, their experiments in which the effect of tactile stimulation by newly hatched chicks on the parent were examined may be relevant in the present context. For example, Maier (1963) discovered that physical contact between a Domestic Chicken and her day-old chicks was important for the development of broodiness. Buntin (1974) found that tactile stimulation from Ringed Turtle Dove squabs in the nest influences nest attachment and the development of the crop sac (a measure of the readiness to feed the squabs). Males depended on this tactile stimulation more than females.

C. AUDITORY STIMULI

Before the beak penetrates into the air space and the embryo begins to breathe and vocalize, auditory stimuli resulting from its movements are faint (e.g., Vince, 1969). Vocalization begins one to three days before hatching in precocial and semiprecocial species but probably not before emergence in altricial species (see Section III,B). Embryonic vocalizations play an important part in the establishment of parent-offspring relations. For example, Tschanz (1968), Norton-Griffiths (1969), Impekoven (1973a), and Hess (1973) found a strong temporal correlation between embryonic vocalizations and certain parental activities like rising, egg shifting, and calling, at least during advanced pipping stages (Fig.1). Corresponding to the increasing number and intensity of embryonic vocaliza-

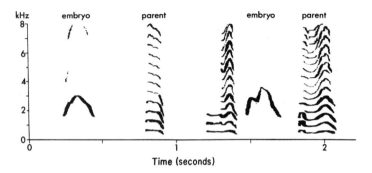

Fig. 1. Vocal interactions between an incubating Laughing Gull and its pipping "egg" several hours before hatching. The recording was made with a Uher-4200-Stereo tape recorder and a microphone placed underneath the nest cup. The figure was drawn after a sonagram made on a Kay Electric Company sonagraph with a narrow-band filter.

tions, parental activities were found to increase, especially the rate of parental calling. Hess (1973) and Tschanz (1968) recorded peaks of parental and filial calling during emergence from the shell.

In an experimental investigation, Impekoven played taped calls of a hatching chick to Laughing Gulls during the last week of their incubation period via small loudspeakers placed underneath their nest cups. Comparing 20 minutes of sound with 20 minutes of no sound, the author noted various changes in the quantitative features of the incubation pattern typical for pipping stages. The frequency of rising-resettling, egg shifting, and parental calls, both in association with rising-resettling and during a sitting spell, were increased in response to this stimulation (Table I). Responsiveness to these calls seems to be stimulus specific, as calls played at half speed, which changes pitch and temporal pattern, evoked little response (Impekoven, 1973a). In comparable experiments, Hess (1973) was able to elicit maternal calls in Mallard hens by playing embryonic vocalizations to them. In the Turkey, *Meleagris gallopavo,* vocalizations of newly hatched poults appear to be an essential stimulus factor in the control of maternal behavior (Schleidt *et al.,* 1961). "Clicking," another auditory stimulus produced in conjunction with breathing, has been shown to play an important role in the interactions between the embryos (e.g., Vince, 1969, 1973, 1974), but its possible effect on the incubating parent has not been investigated.

D. VISUAL STIMULI

Poulson (1953), Baerends (1959), Tschanz (1959), and Baerends *et al.* (1970) have investigated the influence of changing visual aspects of eggs on incubation responses. Such changes made the birds more hesitant in approaching and/or

TABLE I

Responses of Incubating Laughing Gulls to Calls of a Hatching Chick[a]

Behavior	Control periods	Test periods	Difference	Number of birds	P
Rising-resettling	0.9 (0–2)	5.0 (2–10)	4.1	14	<0.001[b]
Percentage of rises accompanied by egg shifts	0.3 (0–66)	55.0 (11–100)	54.7	10	<0.05
Total number of parental calls	1.0 (0–11)	38.5 (1–202)	37.5	14	<0.001
Parental calls per rise	1.4 (0–22)	3.1 (1–102)	1.7	11	<0.001
Parental calls while sitting	0 (0–1)	11.5 (0–194)	11.5	14	<0.001

[a]Values refer to median numbers or percentages (and ranges) during 20-minutes periods of no sound (control periods) and sound (test periods).

[b]Statistical test: Wilcoxon matched pair signed ranks test, two-tailed.

resettling on their nests, which implies that they had a disturbing effect on them. Holcomb (1969) and Gibb (1970) found that the sight of conspicuous markings on eggs of certain passerine species led to an increase of egg shifting resulting in "removal" of the markings. Stimuli from the embryo become visible when the eggs are pipped. Tschanz (1968), in an attempt to separate auditory from visual effects of pipping eggs, presented incubating Guillemots with choice tests. Eggs without a pip hole painted on them were preferred to eggs with a pip hole: he concluded that in the natural situation the sight of the pip hole is disturbing to the birds. However eggs with a pip hole plus auditory stimuli emanating from them were preferred to silent unpipped eggs, even if the birds' own eggs had not yet pipped. Thus auditory stimuli seem to override the disturbing effect that visual stimuli have. This author attributed the occurrence of certain "displacement" activities such as head shaking and preening to the conflict that arises when certain embryonic activities, e.g., vocalizations, activate parental responses and the progressive visual changes inhibit parental activities. Earlier Goethe (1953) described a comparable conflict situation for the Herring Gull. The experiments of Schleidt et al. (1961) indicate that the visual aspects of newly hatched chicks elicit aggressive responses unless the parent can hear them call. In the present writer's own experiments, it was noted that the sudden sight of a newly hatched chick (or a stuffed specimen) placed into the nest of a Laughing Gull around the potential hatching time of its own eggs sometimes elicited aggressive responses (see Sections IV,E and V,B—Table II).

E. LONG-TERM EFFECTS OF EMBRYONIC STIMULATION

Of importance are the questions of whether and how the perception of stimuli from growing embryos contributes to the subsequent onset of chick care by the parents. Gibson and Silver's (in preparation) work in the Ringed Turtle Dove is aimed at establishing whether stimuli from developing embryos (before pipping) influence the prolactin level in the blood and the development of the crop sac, a measurement of the readiness to feed the newly hatched squabs. So far the results are inconclusive.

How does the perception of stimuli emanating from pipping eggs affect the onset of chick care? A somewhat comparable question was asked by Noirot (1972) with regard to small mammals. In order to test the idea that prior exposure to pup stimuli might "prime" or sensitize maternal responsiveness, she enclosed a live mouse pup in a perforated metal box. Adult female mice were presented with these stimulus objects for a brief period, and then their behavior toward pups was compared with that of untreated control animals. Animals without pretreatment showed exploratory and avoidance behavior at first. Primed animals responded maternally immediately. In birds, in contrast to mammals, nature provides, in effect, the "perforated box experiment," when a pip hole appears in the shell. Beer (1966) has some anecdotal evidence that parent Black-headed Gulls which have been sitting on pipped eggs switch more readily to chick care than gulls that were given unpipped eggs.

In a recent study designed to investigate various environmental factors involved in the onset of chick care in the Laughing Gull, the present writer collected further data on this issue. One group of birds was kept sitting on eggs, at least one of which had been in an advanced pipping stage and thus vocal for about 1 day; the other group was kept on unpipped eggs or on eggs in early pipping stages (see Section III,A–last paragraph) and thus not yet vocal. In some cases the birds' own eggs had been exchanged for less developed eggs during early pipping. A newly hatched chick was introduced (and the most advanced egg removed) around the potential hatching time (±4 days). Observations were carried out immediately upon the introduction of the chick. In this way it was discovered that of 31 birds which had been sitting on a pipping, vocal egg, all accepted a chick immediately, whereas 15 out of 26 birds which had not gone through this experience at first aggressively pecked at the chick ($P < 0.001$, chi-square, two-tailed), although subsequently they showed parental responses. Prior breeding experience was unknown for these individuals.

At this point it is not known with certainty to what extent these priming effects are due to embryonic vocalizations rather than other types of auditory stimuli (e.g., clicks) or tactile stimuli from the pipping eggs. Perhaps experiments in which taped embryonic vocalizations were played to incubating birds for several hours, and at rates comparable to embryonic vocalizations, might help to answer this question.

V. EFFECTS OF PARENTAL STIMULI DURING INCUBATION ON SURVIVAL AND BEHAVIOR OF THE EMBRYO AND NEWLY HATCHED CHICK

Research carried out in various disciplines bears on the problem of how parental stimuli during incubation affect the embryo:

1. Poultry scientists have aimed at empirically establishing optimal conditions of artificial incubation for maximal survival and hatchability. However, much of this research has not been based on an attempt to duplicate the behavior of a setting hen [reviewed by Landauer (1961) and Lundy (1969)].

2. Sensory physiologists and embryologists have been interested in the embryo's responsiveness to different types of sensory stimulation—in part with the aim of determining the onset of functioning of different sensory systems (as described in Section III,C), in part in an attempt to discover to what extent

embryonic motility is dependent on or independent of sensory input (as reviewed by Oppenheim (1972a, 1974). Again, in many of these experiments the kind and pattern of stimulation were not directly based on stimulation naturally encountered during incubation.

3. Developmental psychobiologists have concerned themselves with the developmental origins of postnatal behavior. For example, there has been interest in the prenatal origins of learning (Sedláček, 1964; see Section III,C), filial attachment (Schneirla, 1965; Grier et al., 1967; Dimond, 1970), motor patterns (Kuo, 1932b; Kovach, 1970; Oppenheim, 1972b), feeding preferences (Oppenheim, 1968a), or species recognition (e.g., Gottlieb, 1971).

4. Students of animal behavior with a primarily functional approach, observing the natural pattern of incubation by incubating birds, have been wondering how this behavior affects the embryo and the newly hatched chick (e.g., Drent, 1970, 1972, 1973, 1975). Accordingly, questions about causal aspects of development have been derived from questions about the suspected effects of the adults' behavior in the belief that animals are best adapted to respond preferentially to certain types of naturally occurring stimulation [e.g., Impekoven and Gold (1973) and references cited therein].

Stimuli provided for embryos by incubating birds consists of: (a) temperature changes, due to their periodic rising and resettling on the nest, or in species where only the female attends the nest, also during her feeding trips; (b) movement and changes of position, when the adult bird every now and then shifts the eggs or resettles on them; (c) sound, when the incubating bird or its mate vocalize; and (d) light, occurring during brief rises or prolonged departures from the nest. Virtually nothing is known about parental control of relative humidity and the gaseous environment, and thus these factors, although investigated under conditions of artificial incubation, will not be considered here.

The following discussion will concentrate on experimental studies in which stimulus factors that might result from parental activities were manipulated, including those where such manipulations were not directly based on naturalistic observations. Effects on survival and hatchability will be briefly mentioned first. More emphasis will be placed on immediate effects of such stimulation on the behavior of the embryo and the long-term effects on the behavior of the newly hatched chick. Studies that have been concerned with effects of mutual stimulation between clutch mates (e.g., Vince, 1969, 1973, 1974) or self-stimulation (Gottlieb, 1971, 1975a,b,c; Oppenheim, 1972c) will not be reviewed here, although they will be cited where differences in effects of parental, sibling, or self-stimulation are at issue.

Past and ongoing research will be presented in terms of stimulation provided by the parent, that is, temperature (and its changes), egg turning, calls, and light. The interaction of different types of stimulation will also be discussed.

A. INCUBATION TEMPERATURE

Eggs are warmed by contact with the ventral surface of the parent(s) except in Megapodiidae (e.g., Baltin, 1969) and Sulidae (Nelson, 1966, 1969). Accordingly the upper surface of the eggs is maintained at a higher temperature than the lower surface. At one time it was erroneously assumed, by analogy with conditions of natural incubation, that good results of artificial incubation depended on the existence of such a temperature gradient from the upper to lower surface of the eggs, and early still-air incubators were designed accordingly (Landauer, 1961). Modern force-draft incubators do not produce this gradient, and yet hatchability in domestic fowl is equal or often superior to that in still-air incubators. It is possible to hatch some eggs if they are maintained at a temperature within the range of 35–40.5°C. However the temperature that yields the greatest hatching success has been established to be somewhere between 37–38°C for force-draft incubators and about 1°C higher for still-air incubators (e.g., Lundy, 1969). This empirically established optimal temperature yields embryonic temperatures identical to those which were measured under natural conditions of incubation (Drent, 1970, 1972, 1973). Other wild species (reviewed by Drent, 1970, 1972, 1973, 1975) have incubation temperatures between 34–39°C, as measured during undisturbed incubation by telemetry. White and Kinney (1974), who give further references on this issue, stress the similarity in thermal requirements for a wide range of species.

Incubation temperatures in the wild tend to be less constant than in incubators (see Section II); nonetheless, hatching success is usually high [reviewed by Vince (1974)]. However it has been shown experimentally for domestic fowl that relatively minor long-term deviations from incubation temperatures optimal for survival can result in great changes of hatchability (Landauer, 1961; Lundy, 1969; Drent, 1973). Regarding temporary changes, embryos are more resistant to cooling than to overheating. Chicken embryos were shown to becomes increasingly susceptible to chilling after day 4 of incubation but somewhat more resistant to overheating around the same time (e.g., Moreng and Shaffner, 1951; Moreng and Bryant, 1956; and other references cited by Lundy, 1969). Comparable findings for chilling exist in Mallard embryos (Batt and Cornwell, 1972). In this study the oldest embryos tested (about 2 days before hatching) were the least tolerant of the cold (0°, 4°, or 8°C) for 10 hours, approximating the maximum length of time the parent would be away from the nest when foraging. These results were discussed in light of the natural situation of incubation, where it was found that hatching success can be severely reduced by abnormally cold spring weather during late stages of incubation.

Some poultry researchers believe in cooling eggs for a few hours every day. Several Russian studies [critically reviewed by Kosin (1964) and Lundy (1969)] have actually demonstrated beneficial effects of such cooling on hatchability. This can be interpreted to mean that embryos may be optimally adapted to near-natural conditions of incubation where the hen leaves the nest uncovered for a certain period of time every day. Batt and Cornwell's study (1972) indicates an increase in hatchability as a result of exposure to cold (0–8°C) in early incubation (day 3) or before the start of incubation.

It has been found that repeated egg cooling delays hatching, most probably as a result of slowed down physical development of the embryos. For instance, Hess (1973) found seasonal differences in the duration of the incubation period in wild Mallards due to differences in the ambient temperature which have an effect during times when the hen leaves the nest (as just discussed). In addition, this author presents experimental data according to which daily chilling to 7°C for 2 hours delays hatching as compared to eggs cooled to 27°. More surprisingly, this chilling also contributes to hatching synchrony. Hess does not offer any comment as to how this effect may be achieved. Andrews (1976) in the marsh-breeding Clapper Rail, *Rallus longirostris*, found a strong correlation between the number of hours the eggs were flooded by high tides (and thus were not incubated) and the duration of the incubation period.

In an attempt to investigate possible effects of an increase in incubation temperature, Oppenheim and Levin (1975) found that a 1-hour exposure to 44°C during pipping did not affect the time of hatching. In contrast to these results, earlier findings by Romanoff (1936) indicated that raising the incubation temperature by up to 1.5°C during the last 4 days of incubation (or longer) advances hatching but reduces hatching success.

Concerning behavioral effects, Oppenheim and Levin (1975) cited various contradictory studies dealing with the influence of temperature changes on embryonic motility in the Domestic Chicken. In their own experiments they raised the temperature up to 44°C or lowered it to 30.5°C for periods of 0.5 to 2 hours, which would be comparable to the period an incubating hen might be absent from the nest. In earlier stages of embryonic development such changes altered the heart rate and amniotic contractions significantly, but embryonic movement remained unaffected. The impression that the vigor or velocity of the movements was less at lower than normal temperature and greater at higher than normal temperatures has not been supported by quantitative data. Late in incubation (beginning on day 15; see Section III,C) the rate of movements was affected, and during prehatching stages the rates of vocalization, bill clapping, and breathing were also changed in response to these treatments. During pipping Collias (1952) in the Domestic Chicken, Lind (1961) in the Black-tailed Godwit, Tschanz (1968) in the Guillemot, and Ingold (1973) in the Razorbill, *Alca torda*, noted distress vocalizations in response to cooling of the eggs, as may happen when the parent interrupts incubation. Warming them, on the other hand, led to rapid cessation of such vocalizations.

Long-term behavioral effects of temporary or prolonged temperature changes during incubation have not been studied so far. For example, it would be interesting to see whether neonates from shorter or longer incubation periods, resulting from different amounts of egg cooling, differ in any way (e.g., in general activity, locomotor ability, or imprintability). Following Gottlieb's (1961) findings one would predict that birds hatched after shorter incubation periods should follow and imprint at a correspondingly later postnatal age than those hatched after longer incubation periods. However, Hess (1973) concludes from his results that postnatal age is a more important indicator of imprintability than developmental age.

B. EGG TURNING AND EGG POSITIONING

The function of egg turning, as summarized by New (1957), Robertson (1961), and Drent (1970, 1973), is seen in preventing adhesion between the embryo (or extraembryonic membranes) and the shell, promotion of gaseous exchange with the environment, correct orientation of the embryo, and even distribution of temperature among eggs in large clutches.

Poultry scientists empirically established the minimal and optimal rate of egg turning for the survival of embryos and their hatchability. For instance, replicating and expanding on earlier findings by Olsen and Byerly (1936), Robertson (1961) found that turning eggs artificially 48 or 96 times a day yielded a greater hatching success than lower or higher turning rates. However the largest difference in mortality occurred between no turning at all and twice a day during the first 10 days of incubation and no turning and once every 2 days after the 10th day. These findings were not discussed with regard to the natural situation. It should be pointed out that the rate of turning by an incubating hen falls well within the range for best survival (see Section II). In contrast Kuiper and Ubbels (1951) based their experiments on naturalistic observations: a turning frequency comparable to that of their incubating hens (24 times per day) was found to yield better hatches than a much lower frequency (3 times). These results again call attention to the possibility that the embryo is best adapted to near natural rates of turning (or vice versa). Comparing commercial with natural incubation, Olsen (1930) was able to show that turning as provided by an incubating hen, i.e., of an irregular nature and around different axes, promotes the survival of the embryos better than the smooth turning of commercial incubators. Similarly Funk and Forward (1952) have established that turning in more than one plane enhances survival. Further experiments dealing with the frequency and angle of turning, axes of setting and rotation, and number of planes of rotation have been reviewed by Lundy (1969).

Egg turning (unlike rotation on a disk, see Section III,C) may provide vestibular stimulation to the embryo, and Olsen (1930) argued that the egg-turning pattern by a broody hen involves acceleration sufficient to stimulate the vestibular sense but that the slow even turning of commercial incubators may not. Egg turning may also provide tactile and proprioceptive stimulation to the embryo.

Studies on possible effects of naturalistic types of egg turning on the embryo's movements have not been published to date. Gottlieb (1968) assumed that behavioral responses are elicited by this type of stimulation, at least during the last few days before hatching.

Recently the present author carried out observations on Domestic Chicken embryos on the last day of incubation in a plexiglass box kept at about 33°C. One egg at the time was placed there on a small automatic turning tray [designed similarly to a frankfurter roller and to a turning device used by Olsen and Byerly (1936)] which could turn the horizontally positioned egg 90° around its longitudinal axis (during which the pip hole was moved in an arc from 45° to the right to 45° to the left, as seen from the blunt end). With this method the writer discovered that the rate of backthrusts, a characteristic prehatching movement (see Section III,A) was significantly increased during a 5-minute period following turning as compared to a similar period preceding it (Table II). The rate of bill clapping, another movement that was quantified during these observations was not significantly changed by this stimulation. Some of the backthrusts (not shown in the table) occurred during the turning motion and thus may represent an immediate response to it. The movements that followed after the end of the turning motion (shown in the table) may represent either a long-term response to the rotation itself or to the changed position of the egg.

New (1957) concluded from his study that egg turning in the chicken was most crucial for survival during days 4–7 of incubation. Experiments by Kaltofen (1960) led to the conclusion that frequent turning is most important during the second week of incubation. Robertson's (1961) work suggests that after the midpoint of incubation egg turning becomes of little importance for

TABLE II

Backthrusts and Bill Clapping in Domestic Chick Embryos on the
Last Day of Incubation Before and After Egg Turning[a]

Number of embryos	Backthrusts			Bill clapping		
	Before	After	P	Before	After	P
18	2.5 (0–5)	5 (0–11)	<0.001[b]	85.5 (29–141)	61 (19–202)	NS[c]

[a]Values refer to the median number of movements (and ranges) during 5-minute observation periods.
[b]Wilcoxon matched pair signed ranks, two-tailed.
[c]NS, statistically not significant.

survival. Drent (1970) stated that "studies of artificial incubation have not yet clarified the biological function of turning in the latter half of incubation." During the second half of incubation the eggs tend to assume and maintain a stable position (see Section III,B) despite parental egg shifting (Lind, 1961; Drent, 1970). By observing transparent Herring Gull nests from underneath them, Drent found that if the eggs were not already in this equilibrium position, the egg-shifting movement would return them to that position. The observation that when the pipping hole appears it is nearly always situated uppermost led to the erroneous assumption that egg shifting by the parent ceases at this time (e.g., Tinbergen, 1953); however, according to more recent observations on other species, egg shifting even tends to occur more often (see Sections II and IV,C). Würdinger [(1970) and as cited by Drent (1973, 1975)] found in *Anser indicus* that turning eggs with their pipping holes facing down elicits distress calls in the embryos. These calls stimulate the parent to shift its eggs which presumably leads to their positions being readjusted such that the pip hole comes to be situated uppermost.

Lind (1961) and Drent (1973) suggest that parental egg shifting may be important for keeping the embryo in an optimal position for assuming the prehatching position and for hatching. However, according to Tschanz (1968), artificially incubated Guillemot eggs hatched out normally if fixed in a position with the pipping hole facing down.

In an experiment designed to discover whether and how egg position in Domestic Chickens affects the time of hatching, the present author incubated two groups of eggs, in one of which the site of the future pipping hole was pointed straight up, and in the other it was facing 90° to the left (as seen from the blunt pole). The eggs remained fixed in these positions (on the turning tray described above) for the last 1–2 days of incubation. No clear differences in hatching time were discovered. In a subsequent experiment eggs fixed with their pip hole facing down surprisingly hatched even earlier than eggs with their pip hole facing up. These findings suggest that deviations from the equilibrium position during the last 1–2 days of incubation do not tend to slow down or delay hatching, but further research on this issue would be desirable. In the natural situation it may still be crucial that the pip hole faces up as otherwise the embryo may suffocate (see Tschanz, 1968) or the egg shell may get crushed (Drent, 1975).

The foregoing observations on behavioral responsiveness to egg turning on the last day of incubation suggest that turning may affect the time of hatching by increasing the frequency of prehatching movements. In order to test this possibility, the present writer used an automatic turning tray (with a capacity for 36 chicken eggs, similar to the one described on p. 222) which turned the eggs at regular intervals about 90° in one direction and later in the reverse direction. The rate of turning could be set independently for the two halves of the tray.

The position of the eggs was fixed, i.e., they could not roll about freely, but when the pipping hole appeared their position was readjusted if necessary so that the hole was always on the upper half of the egg.

The effect of two turning rates (4 and 30 times daily) which fell within the range for good survival (discussed earlier) was compared. Hatching success was close to 100% in these experiments. The writer found that the higher rate of turning advanced hatching by about 3 hours (Table III). This effect was similar in a batch of eggs given the differential treatment during the last 6–7 days and a later batch which experienced differential turning for the last 1–2 days only. In experiments (not shown on the table) in which eggs turned 30 times for either the last 6–7 days or the last 1–2 days were incubated together, no significant differences were found between their hatching times. This means that egg turning affects the time of hatching only within (but not before) the last 2 days before hatching.

In detailed observations it was discovered that the interval between the first pip crack in the eggshell and hatching was reduced by more frequent turning, but accelerating effects took place also prior to pipping. These findings are comparable to those of Vince (reviewed 1969, 1973, 1974), who discovered that factors (clicking) advancing the time of hatching in quails (*Coturnix* spp.) produced their effect during prehatching stages.

In some of these experiments the present writer tested the chicks after hatching in an approach situation. Assuming with Gottlieb (1968) that egg turning increases embryonic movement (in addition to the prehatching movements described, possibly also leg movements), the writer speculated that by some yet to be discovered mechanism this would contribute to improving postnatal locomotor ability. An opposite prediction would follow from an experiment by Vince and Chinn (1971, 1972): they showed that quails or domestic fowl in which hatching had been advanced by stimulation with the click rate of more advanced embryos were less developed in their standing and locomotor ability at a comparable postnatal age. In the present experiments locomotor ability was assessed in terms of latency and speed of approach to a speaker emitting the maternal clucking of a broody hen. As has been established by Collias (1952), parentally naive chicks readily approach such a stimulus. The chicks were tested 5–6 hours after hatching, i.e., at a stage when their legs were still wobbly and their locomotion slow. The two groups, differing in their rate of egg turning, did not differ in their locomotor ability, measured in this way. However, since the group with the higher turning rate had hatched earlier, these chicks were developmentally younger—if age is assessed from the beginning of incubation—than the group with the lower turning rate. As mentioned in Section V,A, the question of whether total development or posthatching age is the more crucial indicator of the stage in development is a controversial issue (e.g., Gottlieb, 1961; Hess, 1973).

TABLE III

Incubation Periods of Eggs Turned 4 Times and 30 Times Daily during the Last 1–2 or 6–7 Days of Incubation[a]

Number of birds in each group	Beginning of treatment	Duration of treatment	Incubation period (groups combined)	Incubation period of groups turned		Difference	P
				4 times	30 times		
16	14 days + 2½ hours	6 days + 16½ hours	20 days + 19 hours	20 days + 20 hours	20 days + 17½ hours	3 hours (1–6)	<0.001[b]
17	19 days + 5 hours	1 day + 16 hours	20 days + 21 hours	20 days + 22 hours	20 days + 21 hours	3 hours (1–6)	<0.001

[a]Values refer to median numbers of days and hours (and range). The time of the beginning of treatment and its duration are based on the median incubation periods of the two groups combined. The difference between the groups is based on intervals between matched pairs of chicks, based on their order of hatching. Replications of these experiments yielded similar results.
[b]Wilcoxon matched pair signed ranks, two-tailed.

The results of these experiments indicate that parental egg shifting may serve an additional function besides bringing the embryo into an optimal hatching position.

C. PARENTAL CALLS

No work has been done to test for effects of parental calls on hatchability and survival of the neonate, since it is generally assumed that no such effects exist. However Hess's (1973) demonstration that naturally occurring parental calls synchronize the hatching of Mallard eggs suggests that, in the absence of such calls, late hatchers might be left behind in the nest and thus not survive.

Konishi's (1973) study (see Section III,C) had been initiated by Gottlieb's (1971) findings on behavioral responsiveness of embryos to recordings of the conspecific maternal call. The characteristic frequency responses of cochlear nuclei correspond well to the harmonics of the Mallard's broody calls, which she utters with increasing frequency just before and during hatching (Hess (1973). Similarly, Saunders (1974) and Saunders et al. (1974) who tested evoked responses of the brainstem of 24-hour-old chicks and ducklings, found that frequency regions of peak sensitivity were related to the frequencies of peak energy output of the maternal calls of their species. Gottlieb (1971) in Peking Ducks and Heaton (1972) in Wood Ducks showed that playbacks of the maternal call selectively affected the rate of ducklings' bill-clapping movements (and leg movements in the case of the former). In the Peking Duck embryo responses could be elicited for the first time on day 22, i.e., 4–5 days before hatching.

Dr. P. S. Gold and the present writer observed embryonic motility (in particular leg and wing movements) in Laughing Gull embryos in response to recordings of the conspecific attraction call *crooning*, the alarm call *kow*, and a call referred to as *long call* [such parental calls will be discussed shortly; see also Impekoven and Gold (1973)]. Eggs were collected in the breeding colony shortly after laying and were incubated in an incubator. For observation, windows were made over the air space and the underlying membrane was made transparent with petroleum jelly (Kuo, 1932a). The embryos were observed one at a time in a sound-attenuated box with a transparent top, kept at approximately incubation temperature. A sequence of the three calls was presented twice to each embryo. Sound periods of 30 seconds were compared with a 1-minute period preceding and a 1-minute period following such test periods. The frequency values of the pre- and posttest periods were combined and averaged. Accordingly the frequency of motor patterns has been presented as per minute of exposure to either sound or no sound [for further details on methods see Impekoven and Gold (1973)]. It was found that the parental attraction call crooning enhanced motility as early as 8–9 days before hatching, that is, by day 15. The rate of movement remained unchanged in the presence of the other calls (except for kow calls on day 15). Similar effects of crooning were found on day 17, 19, and 21 (Table IV).

Day 15 in gulls corresponds roughly to day 13 in chicken embryos and day 17–18 in ducks. Whether this early onset of behavioral responsiveness in the Laughing Gull is due to methodological or spcies differences is not known at present. In Gottlieb's tests the embryo's head was pulled out of the shell, whereas in the experiment with gulls the embryos were left in their natural position surrounded by embryonic fluid. Saunders and Gottlieb (personal communication) have suggested that certain frequencies of parental calls will penetrate the shell of Domestic Chicken and Peking Duck eggs very well. Also, transmission seems to be greater if the shell is filled with egg fluid or water than if it is empty.

During early pipping, i.e., days 21–22, Impekoven and Gold (unpublished) recorded bill clapping and leg movements in incubator reared gull embryos to the same calls, using a somewhat different schedule of presentation. In these experiments the rate of movement was again selectively enhanced in response to crooning but did not change in response to the other two calls.

Attention has also been given to embryonic vocalizations and their control by parental calls. According to Tschanz (1968), Norton-Griffiths (1969), and Hess (1973) the first vocalizations, which in the species studied by these authors are given about 2 days before hatching, tend to occur spontaneously, i.e., not in close temporal association with parental activities. As hatching approaches they become more frequent and increasingly occur in response to parental activities. In experimental work, Tschanz (1968) in Guillemot embryos and Impekoven (unpublished) in Laughing Gull embryos could elicit vocalizations at first only by moving the egg from side to side, or by turning it. At a later stage the embryos could be made to utter a variety of vocalizations in response to taped recordings of parental calls. Gottlieb (1965a, 1971) found that vocalizations of Peking Duck embryos, a domesticated form of the Mallard, were selectively elicited by Mallard maternal calls and their siblings' calls on the day before hatching. Earlier work on this issue in a variety of species has been reviewed by Tschanz (1968) and Vince (1969, 1974). According to Baeumer (1955) in Domestic Chickens alarm calls given by the parent cause the embryo to cease vocalizing and moving. However these findings are based merely on qualitative observations.

Tschanz (1968) has experimentally demonstrated that parental luring calls stimulate prehatching and hatching movements in Guillemots. Hess (1973) conducted some elegant experiments which showed that the increased rate of vocalization in the Mallard hen during late prehatching stages speeds up and synchronizes the hatching of the brood. This effect appears to rest on a mutual feedback mechanism of vocal interactions between the parent and the embryos.

TABLE IV

Effects of Conspecific Calls on Embryonic Motility in the Laughing Gull[a]

Stage of incubation	15 days + 1 hour		16 days + 22 hours		18 days + 20 hours		20 days + 19 hours	
Number of embryos tested	12		12		10		10	
Test condition	No sound	Sound	No sound	Sound	No sound	Sound	No sound	Sound
Crooning	34.2	47.6	27.7	49.4	26.5	49.2	20.8	30.8
	(7.9)	(16.5)	(5.6)	(20.5)	(6.3)	(17.8)	(7.2)	(11.9)
P		<0.05[b]		<0.02		<0.01		<0.02
Kow	36.5	29.2	30.9	32.2	29.1	28.4	19.9	15.7
	(9.1)	(12.8)	(6.3)	(11.7)	(7.9)	(10.6)	(9.1)	(9.2)
P		<0.05		NS		NS		NS
Long	33.5	34.4	24.6	33.8	28.7	31.3	23.2	19.7
	(11.7)	(13.5)	(3.9)	(13.0)	(8.7)	(7.6)	(7.9)	(8.4)
P		NS[c]		NS		NS		NS

[a]Values refer to mean number of movements per minute (and standard deviation) during no sound and sound conditions at different stages.

[b]Wilcoxon matched pair signed ranks, two-tailed.

[c]NS, statistically not significant.

Using tape recordings of maternal exodus calls, the present writer investigated experimentally whether the fact that parental vocalizations are often contingent on embryonic activity had any effect on subsequent activity in the Peking Duck embryo (Impekoven, 1973b). Embryos were tested in pairs several hours before hatching in a transparent incubator kept at normal incubation temperature. The rate of embryonic movement was recorded during a 16-minute silent control period and a 40- or 80-minute test period during which calls were presented for 5 seconds each time one of the embryos, the experimental one, moved its foot (or rather its toes as visible through the enlarged pipping hole). The other embryo, the yoked control, was exposed to the same number of calls. In this way the author discovered that the number of foot movements and prehatching movements (backthrusts) was increased as a function of the contingency as compared to yoked controls. This effect was achieved only with the Mallard but not with the Domestic Chicken exodus call (Table V). However, embryonic calls should have been used in this experiment rather than movements, because in the natural setting the hen most clearly responds to these. Nevertheless, in conjunction with Hess's (1973) study, Impekoven's experiment indicates how response-contingent interactions between the mother and her young might lead to speeding up and synchronizing the hatching of the brood. The experiment does not necessarily prove the effect of contingency; it could show merely that the maternal call is most effective in certain states of arousal.

Tschanz (1968) was the first to show the role of prenatal experience of parental calls on early postnatal responsiveness. Increased rates of parental calling in the Guillemot during the pipping stages of the eggs permits selective learning of the parental luring call [see reviews by Impekoven and Gold (1973) and Vince (1973)]. In comparing and contrasting Guillemots to Razorbills, a closely related species, Tschanz and Hirsbrunner-Scharf (1975) exposed embryos during pipping repeatedly to recordings of a conspecific parental luring (i.e., acceptance) call. After hatching the chicks were presented with a choice between a familiar and an unfamiliar call in an approach situation. All Guillemot chicks were highly responsive to these calls and most of them approached the familiar call. Similarly trained Razorbills made more "mistakes," and many of them did not approach at all. Guillemots breed in dense colonies on cliff ledges without a defined nest area. Thus it is probably adaptive for the chicks to respond selectively to their own parents' calls immediately upon hatching. By contrast Razorbills live spatially isolated in crevices and caves, and thus there appears to be less of a pressure to develop strong responsiveness to and recognition of parental calls at such an early age. In Laughing Gulls repeated prenatal exposure to individually different calls did not lead to statistically significant preferences for these calls in the newly hatched chicks as measured by rate of vocalization and orientation in a choice situation between the familiar and an unfamiliar call. Many chicks showed no sign of approach (Impekoven and Gold, 1973). Simi-

TABLE V

Frequency of Movement in Peking Duck Embryos Exposed to the Mallard or Chicken Maternal Call[a,b]

Call	Test condition	Foot movements				Backthrusts			
		Number of embryos	Control period (no sound)	Test period (sound)	P	Number of embryos	Control period (no sound)	Test period (sound)	P
Mallard	Experimental (E)	23	1.73 (1.06)	2.40 (0.94)	<0.001[c]	16	0.23 (0.27)	0.87 (0.51)	<0.001
	Yoked (Y) control	23	1.86 (1.13)	2.00 (0.70)	NS[d]	16	0.20 (0.20)	0.39 (0.32)	<0.05
	P (E vs. Y)		NS	<0.05			NS	<0.01	
Chicken	Experimental	22	1.75 (0.98)	1.88 (0.55)	NS	19	0.34 (0.39)	0.49 (0.43)	NS
	Yoked control	22	1.80 (1.38)	1.76 (0.86)	NS	19	0.26 (0.39)	0.46 (0.30)	<0.01
	P (E vs. Y)		NS	NS			NS	NS	

[a]From Impekoven (1973b).
[b]Values refer to mean number of foot movements and backthrusts (and standard deviation) per minute.
[c]Wilcoxon matched pair signed ranks, two-tailed.
[d]NS, statistically not significant.

larly to Razorbills, there seems to be no "need" for Laughing Gulls to respond efficiently and selectively to individual characteristics of their own parents' calls immediately after hatching, since they live in well-defined nest areas without any danger of meeting a stranger until at least a few days after hatching. By this time individual recognition of certain parental calls is well developed (Beer, 1973). Prenatal experience of parental calls can, however, play a role in species recognition, as demonstrated by Evans (1973) for the Herring Gull (as we shall see).

Other studies relevant to this issue concern prenatal auditory imprinting, although they have no clear reference to the natural situation. For instance, Grier *et al.* (1967) exposed Domestic Chicken embryos to artificial low-frequency sounds (200 Hz) in a 1-second-on/1-second-off pattern between days 12 and 18 of incubation. This experience increased the postnatal attractiveness of the familiar sound over a novel (2000 Hz) sound, as measured in an approach and a following test. Rajecki (1974), giving the same prenatal experience to his chicks between days 13 and 18, was unable to show any effects on their approach tendencies. However this author found that the chicks uttered fewer distress calls in the presence of the prenatally experienced sound than in the presence of a novel sound. Whether these effects had been established during the whole exposure period or only its latter part is unknown.

Based on naturalistic observations in a breeding colony of Laughing Gulls, the present author studied the effects of late prenatal experience of certain parental calls on newly hatched chicks' vocalizations and behavior. Laughing Gulls utter various kinds of calls during incubation of their eggs and in the presence of their chicks (see also Section II and Impekoven, 1973a, 1976). During nest reliefs the oncoming mate "croons." Newly hatched chicks approach their parents and peck at their bill tip for food in response to this call. Another call, "uhr," different in its temporal characteristics but similar in pitch, is given by the incubating bird (and sometimes by a brooding bird) during rising and resettling but does not evoke distinct responses in newly hatched chicks. Alarm calls, "kow," are uttered during disturbances of the breeding colony both during incubation and after hatching of the brood. In the presence of these calls chicks often crouch.

In earlier experiments the writer had established that prenatal exposure to taped recordings of crooning affects pecking in the presence of this call (Impekoven, 1971a). In a recent study (Impekoven, 1976) different groups of embryos were exposed during pipping (last 2½ to 3 days) to crooning, uhr calls, kow calls, or no calls at all, 12–15 times daily for 2 minutes each time, in order to discover to what extent and with what degree of selectivity such exposures would affect early postnatal responsiveness to crooning and kow calls. The chicks were kept together in the incubator and were tested 5–6 hours postnatally in a runway. The numbers of their vocalizations, their postures, the amount of their movement, and the distance approached toward a speaker emitting these calls were compared between the different treatment groups. With regard to posture, "up" refers to sitting with the body lifted from the ground or to standing up; "down" refers to lying on the belly with the head sometimes touching the ground (this posture has also been described as "crouching," as mentioned earlier). Unstimulated chicks frequently sat and looked around, i.e., they turned their head from side to side. During sound stimulation these movements either stopped or continued. Additional movements could be observed: in particular, foot movements which could result in approach. In each test a 2-minute period during which parental calls were played was compared to a 1-minute period of no sound preceding and following the sound period (Figs. 2 and 3).

The results of this experiment show that prenatal exposure to crooning led to enhancement of vocalization and movement in the presence of such calls, although approach scores were not significantly affected. Effects of uhr calls point in the same direction. The prenatal experience of kow calls did not contribute to early postnatal responsiveness to crooning. Posthatching movements and vocalizations of chicks without any prenatal exposure to calls of adults were not enhanced by crooning but in some cases were suppressed by it. In response to kow calls vocalizations and movements were strikingly reduced, and most of the chicks assumed the "down" (or crouching) posture. Responsiveness to kow calls was selectively affected by prenatal exposure to these calls. In contrast to crooning, prenatal exposure to kow calls did not lead to an increase in vocalization and movement postnatally but merely reduced the extent of their activity-suppressing effects (Fig. 3).

Prenatal sound stimulation can have two kinds of effects: on the one hand, it may influence the ability to discriminate between different calls; on the other, it may affect the type of response given to one type of call, i.e., it may determine whether embryos or chicks are activated or inhibited by this call, or it may determine the frequency, duration, and intensity of response. Most previous research emphasized effects of sound stimulation on the neonate's ability to discriminate between different calls, although some of the findings at the same time revealed something about the activating or inhibiting properties of these calls. For instance, Tschanz (1968), while concentrating on individual recognition of parental calls in the Guillemot, also discovered that chicks which had been exposed to any parental calls during the prehatching period were more likely to approach a speaker emitting such calls than chicks without this experience. Similarly, Evans (1973) found that in the Herring Gull the number of approaches and vocalizations to parental "mew" calls (homologous to crooning) were increased after prenatal experience with such calls.

Several studies have been concerned with the extent of the importance of prior exposure to parental calls for subsequent responsiveness to those calls. In many precocial species it was discovered that the hearing of parental calls is unimportant for their later attractiveness. For instance, Gottlieb (1965b) discovered that

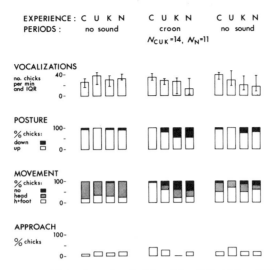

Fig. 2. Crooning tests with incubator-hatched Laughing Gull chicks which prenatally were exposed to either crooning (C), uhr calls (U), kow calls (K), or no calls (N). In each test the 2-minute sound period was preceded and followed by 1 minute of no sound. For statistical tests used and p values see Impekoven (1976). (N, number of chicks tested; IQR, interquartile range.)

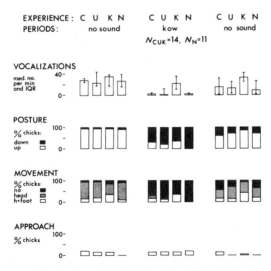

Fig. 3. Kow tests with incubator-hatched Laughing Gull chicks which prenatally were exposed to either crooning (C), uhr calls (U), kow calls (K), or no calls (N). In each test the 2-minute sound period was preceded and followed by 1 minute of no sound. For statistical tests used and p values see Impekoven (1976). (N, number of chicks tested; IQR, interquartile range.)

in the Peking Duck the hearing of the maternal exodus call is not a necessary prerequisite for its attractiveness after hatching, although it could be shown that prenatal exposure (Impekoven, 1973b) or early postnatal exposure to such calls (Gottlieb, 1965b) increased the extent of their subsequent attractiveness. Similarly, Evans (1973) showed that parentally naive Ring-billed Gull chicks selectively approached and vocalized to the conspecific mew call. In contrast to this finding, parentally naive Herring Gull chicks avoided the conspecific luring call as indicated by turning away from the stimulus and crouching in silence, implying that in this species prior experience with conspecific calls is required. Heaton (1972) found in Wood Ducks that incubator-hatched ducklings were "fearful" when confronted with recordings of maternal calls. However a more recent investigation by Gottlieb (1974) indicates that a larger number of brood mates present and vocalizing can provide sufficient auditory stimulation, and the newly hatched ducklings then approach the maternal call without fear. In the Laughing Gull it was shown that crooning is not attractive to neonates unless they had some prior experience with such calls, or with similar calls. The experiments described here indicate that the vocalizations of brood mates to which all experimental groups had ample exposure cannot compensate for the lack of prenatal experience with calls of adults [for further discussion of this issue, see Evans (1973) and Impekoven (1976)].

   Gottlieb (1973) distinguished between two different kinds of developmental effects that prenatal auditory (or other types of) stimulation may have—one contributing to the maturation and functioning of the auditory system, and the other merely maintaining and stabilizing its functioning. In later papers Gottlieb (1975c, 1976) distinguishes between three different effects of experience: (a) channeling or determining development; (b) facilitating development; and (c) maintaining development. A candidate for the first possibility, although not experimentally proven, may be the experience of sibling vocalizations for the discrimination of the conspecific maternal call in the Wood Duck (Gottlieb, 1974). Providing evidence for the second in studies of Peking Ducks, Gottlieb (1975a, b, c) showed that ducklings prevented from hearing their siblings' or even their own voices (surgically devocalized) before hatching were retarded in their perception of high frequencies. Although the maternal call is predominantly composed of low frequencies, it contains a harmonic at the frequency range of certain embryonic vocalizations which may be an important characteristic for its identification. Concerning the maintenance function, Heaton (1972) postulated that pre- or perinatal exposure to the maternal call in the Wood Duck would serve to maintain and stabilize responsiveness in the neonate which prenatally develops even in the absence of maternal care. Graves (1973) demonstrated in the Domestic Chicken postnatally that periodic input of maternal clucking is required in order to maintain its attractiveness. Additional examples are given by Gottlieb (1976). In Laughing Gulls parentally naive embryos selectively responded to crooning by increasing their activity (over-all motility, bill clapping, and leg movements; see our comments earlier in this section and Table IV). Repeated prenatal exposure to crooning, or related calls, seems to function in maintaining and consolidating responsiveness to this call. In chicks lacking prenatal stimulation by calls of adults, crooning loses its activity-enhancing effects shortly after hatching and increasingly elicits alarm or avoidance responses (Impekoven, 1976). In contrast, kow calls prenatally neither enhance nor suppress embryonic movements (cf. Table IV). Repeated exposure to this alarm call does not maintain the prenatally observed indifference to this call but merely reduces the extent to which it acquires activity-suppressing effects.

Further research involving simultaneous discrimination tests between the conspecific attraction call (crooning) and a call deficient in certain species-specific characteristics is required in order to determine whether prenatal experience with the attraction call serves only to maintain responsiveness or whether it also contributes to the sharpening of auditory perception. Also, what has been described as maintenance of responsiveness may reflect a process not on the receptor level, as implied by Gottlieb (1973, 1976), but on the motivational level; that is, the absence of certain types of auditory input may not lead to a deterioration of the auditory system but may merely effect the readiness to respond in a certain way.

D. LIGHT STIMULATION

Several poultry-research studies have experimentally demonstrated effects of illumination on embryonic development and survival. More recently Walter and Voitle (1972), in line with earlier findings by Lauber and Shutze (1964) and Siegel et al. (1969), found that embryos grow faster when incubated in light. At hatching, dark- and light-reared chicks did not differ in weight (a measure of their physical development), although their incubation period differenced by several hours or as much as a day according to Lauber and Shutze (1964). Cooper (1972) discovered that in Turkeys incubation in the dark and hatching in the light improved hatchability, whereas continuous light during the 24 days of incubation reduced hatchability. Lauber and Shutze (1964), Siegel et al. (1969), and Walter and Voitle (1972), on the other hand, found no deleterious effects of incubating eggs in the light for part or all of the incubation period.

We must here distinguish between light stimulation before and after maturation of the visual modality. Thus the experiments of Lauber and Shutze (1964) and Siegel et al. (1969), which showed that eggs illuminated only during the first week of incubation (or a fraction thereof) grow faster than nonilluminated controls (and eggs illuminated during the second and third week), indicate nonvisual sensitivity to photic stimulation. As more extensively reviewed by Gottlieb (1968), it is not known whether exposure to light causes the visual system to function sooner than usual, although anatomical development is speeded up.

Gold (1971) pointed out that the relation of these experimental results to the natural incubation pattern of the hen awaits systematic investigation. The extremely low light intensities which entrain circadian rhythms in the House Sparrow (*Passer domesticus*) (Menaker, 1968) indicate a strong possibility that shaded daylight affects embryonic development.

Unlike most other investigators of the onset of visual function in the avian embryo, Heaton (1971, 1973) and Heaton and Harth (1974b) related their findings to the natural situation (see Section III,C). According to detailed measurements, light intensities which during the last few days reach the embryo's eyes through the shell are sufficient to elicit the pupillary reflex in quails and ducks. As a consequence, a strong possibility exists for environmental interaction mediated by this system prior to hatching. This, according to Heaton (1971, 1973), may be particularly so in open nesters like the Bobwhite Quail, *Coturnix coturnix,* in which the hen leaves the nest for up to 7 hours daily (Stoddard, 1931). It would be interesting to carry out a more systematic comparative study on the visual effects of natural intensities of light penetrating the eggshell in open- and hole-nesting precocial birds. Similar quantities of light might enter the eggshell despite different lighting conditions, because eggs of open nesters are often pigmented whereas eggs of hole nesters are not. Lauber and Schutze (1964) found, using the same light intensities, that although embryonic development was speeded up in brown chicken eggs, the effect was less than in white ones.

In the altricial pigeon, natural light intensities penetrating the egg shell are insufficient to elicit a pupillary response, although they may be sufficient to elicit a nonvisual response (Heaton and Harth, 1974a,b). However if the nest is constructed in a dark location, as is often the case in pigeons, the light reaching the embryo may be insufficient for a response to occur.

The behavioral effects of light during embryogeny have been studied but using strong artificial light and temporal patterns of stimulation not resembling those which occur under more natural conditions of incubation (Bursian, 1964; see Section III,C). From 12 to 40 hours before hatching, Oppenheim (1968b) could increase the rate of bill clapping of (Domestic) chicks and (Peking) ducklings by 1-minute exposures to a heat-filtered microscope light. Other prehatching and hatching movements were not observed in these experiments.

As mentioned earlier, continuous egg lighting during the whole or one part of the incubation period speeds up development and thereby advances the time of hatching. The effect is strongest with light during the first week of incubation but also occurs in response to light during the second or the last week of incubation, after the development of visual function (see Section III,C; also Lauber and Shutze, 1964; Siegel *et al.,* 1969; Walter and Voitle, 1972; Gold, 1971).

Effects of intermittent light stimulation on the time of hatching in Domestic Chickens were investigated by Adam and Dimond (1971a). Illumination was given for 5-minute periods every hour over a 12-hour day. It was found that this type of stimulation promotes early hatching when provided around or after the onset of visual function, which occurs on days 16–17 (see Section III,C). The authors suggest that the effective stimulus for accelerated hatching may have been the change in illumination rather than illumination itself. It is not known whether the stimulation provided in this experiment affected the time of hatching by accelerating growth or by increasing the rate of prehatching movements, or both.

Dimond (1970) reviewed some of his own earlier research on Domestic Chickens dealing with effects of egg lighting on filial attachments and fear responses after hatching. Chicks that had been illuminated throughout incubation approached the imprinting stimulus less than chicks raised in the dark. In a subsequent experiment Dimond discovered that it is only light during the last week of incubation that produces this effect. In accord with these findings (although not stated explicitly) are the observations that light-reared chicks tended to "freeze" more in the presence of a moving object. Gold (1971) found that, while approach and following scores were not significantly affected, the number of loud vocalizations or distress calls was markedly increased in a group that received light stimulation between days 13 and 19.

More recently Adam and Dimond (1971b) investigated the differential effects of light stimulation within the last 6 days of incubation, again using 5 minutes of light every hour. Chicks that had received illumination after the functional development of vision appeared less fearful in an imprinting situation (involving a rotating disk) than those which had received it before or at the time of functional development: the former took less time to approach an imprinting stimulus and uttered distress vocalizations of lower intensity than the latter. Dimond and Adam (1972) established that prenatal exposure to visual flicker of 20 c/sec facilitated later approach behavior. Exposure to slower or faster rates of flicker did not have this effect. There is no mention anywhere of how all these findings may relate to a more naturalistic setting. Rajecki (1974) showed that intermittent light (1 second on/1 second off) given between days 13 and 18, while not affecting approach latencies to a similar imprinting stimulus or a moving three-dimensional object, reduced the number of distress vocalizations. Effects of prenatal visual stimulation of this kind were found to be far less striking than those of auditory stimulation on subsequent responsiveness to sound. Again, no clear connection has been made between the experimental procedures and the natural situation of incubation.

Rajecki (1974) distinguishes between nonspecific effects of prenatal light exposure on postnatal responsiveness to imprinting stimuli and the specific effects demonstrated when prenatal experience of a stimulus (e.g., flicker) enhances responsiveness to that same stimulus. Gottlieb (1976) lists the effect of prior light experience on subsequent responsiveness to an imprinting stimulus as a facilitative effect (see also Section V,C).

Bateson and Wainwright (1972) demonstrated that early postnatal exposure to constant light not only enhances the initial approach of an imprinting stimulus but also facilitates the visual imprinting process. Whether late prenatal light exposure would accelerate imprinting remains to be investigated.

The findings discussed here apply to nidifugous species like chickens, ducks, and geese that have been used in classical imprinting experiments in which the parent is approached and followed. In birds like gulls that do not follow, filial responses have been assessed in terms of begging for food, and emphasis has been placed on natural rather than imprinted preferences. In this way strong preferences for the color, brightness, thickness, orientation, and movement of the parental beak have been found (e.g., Hailman, 1967, 1971). Even in species that feed independently distinct pecking preferences have been discovered. Here the possibility exists that prior visual stimulation may sharpen such natural preferences (see also Gottlieb, 1976). This idea was tested by Oppenheim (1968a), but he was unsuccessful in showing any effect of late prenatal exposure to colored light on postnatal pecking preferences for different colors in the Peking Duck. However this author mentions the possibility that earlier and prolonged exposure to differently colored light might show that light experience during incubation is involved in shaping color preferences. Dawkins (1968) showed that the shading cue preferences in Domestic Chickens remained unaffected by early postnatal rearing conditions with light coming from either above or below. This result leaves open the possibility that the direction of prenatal light exposure might have some effect. Further research on effects of prenatal light exposure on early postnatal preferences would be desirable.

As described in Section II, the amount and temporal patterning of light exposure during natural incubation differs widely among species. Some experience only brief exposures to light when the parent rises and resettles. Others are exposed to light during prolonged periods while the parent forages. Accordingly, under natural conditions visual experience may play a different role for different species. It would be interesting to investigate more closely the long-term effects of species-typical patterns of light exposure.

The differing importance of visual stimulation for different species was pointed out earlier, on the basis of observations and experiments of early postnatal filial responses. For instance, Lorenz (1970) distinguished between the Mallard, which is not clearly imprintable to visual stimuli alone, and the Greylag Goose, *Anser anser*. Gottlieb (1963) distinguished between the hole-nesting Wood Duck, which relies exclusively on auditory stimulation, and the Mallard, which is more responsive when there are both visual and auditory stimuli in the imprinting situation. Graves (1970) has demonstrated even more clearly the relationship between the ecological setting of different species and the relative importance of visual and auditory stimuli in eliciting and directing filial responses. This may in turn be related to differences in the importance of prenatal visual and auditory stimulation in influencing filial responses.

E. INTERACTION OF DIFFERENT PARENTAL STIMULI

As stated previously (Impekoven and Gold, 1973), under natural conditions of incubation different stimulus modalities interact. For instance, when an incubating bird rises it exposes the eggs simultaneously to a change in temperature and light. When the bird shifts its eggs it adds to these stimuli vestibular and possibly tactile and proprioceptive stimulation. Again, when it resettles it combines tactile stimulation with a change in photic and thermal stimulation. As mentioned in Section II, rising, resettling, and egg shifting are often accompanied by vocalizations. In other words, under natural conditions of incubation one type of stimulation rarely occurs by itself, yet in all of the experimental studies reviewed so far only one type of stimulus was systematically manipulated at a time.

Possibly the effectiveness of different stimulus modalities summates as has been shown for the responsiveness of adult animals in various behavioral contexts [reviewed by Hinde (1970)]. Schneirla (1965) in his theory of approach and withdrawal processes, concerned himself with the interaction of different sensory modalities in the developing organism. Under the heading *stimulus equivalence* he suggested that stimuli may be fed into a common "pool," where—irrespective of their differing qualities—they come to elicit differential responses on the basis of their quantity. Alternatively, or in addition, Schneirla proposed a pattern of "conditioning," whereby stimuli of a later maturing sensory system become effective, or more effective, by temporal association with stimuli pertaining to a sensory system previously matured. For instance, visual and auditory stimuli may become more effective by association with tactile, thermal, or vestibular stimuli.

Oppenheim and Levin (1975) suggested that such stimulus interactions may become of increased importance during the last quarter of the incubation period, when the embryos show overt behavioral responses to most kinds of sensory stimulation.

For the experimenter, a particularly attractive because easily testable combination of stimuli is provided by those arising from egg shifting and parental calls. Parental calls may become more effective in eliciting approach reactions (Schneirla, 1965) by temporal association with egg shifting. Approach reactions in the newly hatched precocial chick consist of orientation (and locomotion) toward a sound source emitting maternal or parental calls, for example, as well as of the utterance of pleasure notes or twitters (and the absence of distress calls or peeps) in the vicinity of the parental stimulus. Withdrawal reactions consist of withdrawal from the sound source and predominance of distress vocalizations. A distinction between pleasure notes and distress calls has been made in domestic fowl (e.g., Collias, 1952; Guyomarc'h, 1972), ducks (e.g., Gottlieb, 1971), and other precocial species (e.g., Guyomarc'h, 1971). Andrew (1969) emphasized that these two calls represent merely extremes of a continuum of vocalizations all typical for shifts of attention. The situation is more complex in the case of Gulls (e.g., Impekoven, 1971b), Guillemots (Tschanz, 1968), Razorbills (Ingold, 1973), and other semiprecocial species which depend on their parents for shelter and food.

In an experiment by the present author using Domestic Chickens, two groups of eggs were incubated in the same (still-air) incubator. In one group, egg turning (of the type described in Section V,B) once every 48 minutes was followed by recorded clucks of a hen [as previously used by Gottlieb (1971)] for 15 seconds; the other group experienced the same rate of turning at different times, i.e., temporally unassociated with the playback. This treatment was provided during the last 3½–6 days of incubation. The chicks were tested 5–6 hours after hatching.

The following preliminary results emerged: no clear-cut effects were found with regard to latency and speed of approach towards a speaker emitting the maternal clucks; however the proportion of the 5-minute test period during which the chicks gave pleasure notes rather than distress calls was significantly higher in those which had experienced the calls contingent on turning, indicating that the maternal call was more attractive to them (Table VI).

This result may not represent a case of prenatal classical conditioning as described by Sedláček (1964), (see Section III,C) since maternal clucking is attractive even to naive chicks (Collias, 1952) and therefore is not a conditioned stimulus. However, Guyomarc'h (1972) hypothesized that the chick inside the

TABLE VI

Pleasure Notes versus Distress Calls (P/D) in Newly Hatched Chicks
Which Experienced Maternal Clucking Either Temporally Associated or
Unassociated with Egg Turning[a]

Number of chicks	Test conditions	P/D	P
24	Temporally associated	18.26 (61.17)	$<0.03^b$
24	Unassociated	1.99 (3.37)	

[a]Values refer to mean number of P/D (and standard deviation) during 5-minute approach tests.
[b]Wilcoxon matched pair signed ranks, two-tailed.

egg perceiving its own twitters in association with embryonic approach activities (such as head or beak movements) may, by conditioning, develop a preference for maternal clucking the frequency modulation of which is similar to that of the twitter. Such vocalizations also occur in response to egg turning, as noted in the foregoing experiments and earlier described by Collias (1952) and Guyomarc'h (1972). In order to test this hypothesis, the maternal cluck would have to be associated with stimulation which elicits distress calls so that the influence of this on filial vocalizations in the presence of maternal stimuli could be assessed postnatally.

Another, somewhat simpler interpretation is that egg turning preceding sound may affect the embryo's state of arousal to the extent that the embryo becomes more alert or attentive to the maternal call. A pilot study with Guillemots supports this notion. Embryos were exposed to artificial sounds preceding or following egg turning. After hatching, the chicks in the latter group were more responsive to the sound in an approach situation than the former (J. Lien and M. Clemens, in preparation). The possibility of such an arousing effect had earlier been pointed out for this species by Tschanz (1968) based on his observations that parental luring calls often follow rising and shifting of the eggs. In subsequent experiments designed to teach pipping embryos certain parental calls, the eggs were moved from side to side in order to make sure that the embryo would attend to the playbacks. In this way, Tschanz concluded, the embryos learn the calls of their own parents rather than those of a neighbor, which are not temporally associated with other types of stimulation. A systematic investigation of the role of egg shifting (and/or other types of stimulation) in conjunction with the parental luring call would be an interesting research project.

Another pilot study was carried out which indicates that the association of the supposedly unpleasant experience of chilling prenatally with parental alarm calls (uttered during disturbances of the breeding colony) makes these calls more effective in eliciting avoidance responses (crouching) in the newly hatched Herring Gull chick (Nyström, personal communication). Again, this seems a promising contingency of stimuli to follow up.

VI. SUMMARY AND CONCLUSIONS

Studies on qualitative and quantitative aspects of the incubation behavior of a variety of species have been described (Section II). Certain aspects of embryonic development, in particular those which are considered of potential significance in the mutual responsiveness between the parent(s) and the embryos, have been discussed (Section III). It has been suggested that an incubating bird may be affected by the growing embryos inside its eggs even before the prehatching stages (Section IV). The effects may result from embryonic movements as well as progressive thermogenesis, changes in weight, and gravitational properties. Preliminary data have become available which show that the degree of attentiveness (time spent covering the eggs) can be affected by whether birds (Ringed Turtle Doves) are sitting on fertile developing or infertile eggs. More detailed observations would be desirable on the degree of attentiveness in correlation with incubation temperature, as well as on the frequency of rising, egg shifting, and parental vocalization, both in birds sitting on developing and nondeveloping eggs.

Studies in which egg temperature was manipulated showed that various aspects of the incubation pattern were influenced by raising or lowering the egg temperature. However, these experiments were not aimed at simulating the progressive heat production of the embryo. Therefore, in future experiments, birds sitting on artificial eggs that are increasingly warmed during incubation (and thus would progressively reduce the heat requirement from the parent) might be compared to birds whose eggs remain cold; or birds sitting on eggs of different weights might be compared. Immediate effects of such changes on the incubation pattern might be studied, as well as long-term changes becoming effective at the onset of chick care.

Under normal conditions of incubation the behavior of the incubating birds undergoes significant changes, starting in some cases about 2 days before the hatching of their young. In particular, the birds rise more frequently and utter more calls, some of which become important in early postnatal parent-young interactions. These parental changes are correlated with changes in the eggs. Some of the precocial and semiprecocial species begin to vocalize 1–3 days before hatching and thus provide auditory stimulation to their parents. The pipping of the egg (as well as the egg tooth protruding through the pip hole) provides tactile stimulation, and the progressive enlargement of the pipping hole introduces visual changes. Some of the changes in the incubation patterns shown during the pipping stages were found to be comparable to those produced by experimental manipulations of the tactile and visual characteristics of the clutch in earlier stages of incubation.

Embryonic vocalizations are probably most important for the switch from incubation behavior to chick care. Observation in several species revealed progressively stronger correlations between these calls and certain parental activities as hatching approached. Experiments demonstrated: (a) the selective responsiveness of parents to such calls; (b) their role in overriding the disturbing effects that the progressive visual changes produce. The results of one experiment suggest that vocal stimuli perceived by the parent (Laughing Gull) while sitting on pipping eggs may be important for the smooth onset of chick care in that they "prime" parental responses and suppress aggressive responses. Further research is needed to show whether this effect is in fact due to auditory stimulation alone and in what way it depends on previous breeding experience.

Visual aspects deserve some further attention too. In particular, do the slow progressive changes from pipping through hatching contribute to the smooth onset of chick care? How would birds which had the opportunity to experience their chicks' hatching compare with those which did not?

In contrast to precocial and semiprecocial avian species, the stimulus factors involved in the transition from incubation behavior to chick care in altricial species have so far been little studied.

Factors involved in the onset of maternal care has received much attention in mammals (e.g., Noirot, 1972; Rosenblatt, 1970), but the role of the growing embryo or fetus in affecting the parent's physiological condition and behavior has been largely ignored. Birds, due to the physical separateness between parent and embryo, lend themselves better to such investigations, which might provide new insights into the control of maternal behavior.

In Section V different kinds of issues have been raised. An attempt has been made to bring together research from different disciplines in which stimulation of the embryo that might result from parental activities was experimentally manipulated. Such stimulation consists of temperature and light changes when the incubating bird rises from its nest, movement and changes of position when it shifts the eggs and resettles on them, and sound when it (or its mate) vocalizes. Parental stimuli become effective via the tactile, proprioceptive, vestibular, auditory, and visual modalities as these modalities mature. In some cases, however, it is not certain which modalities are involved, as in the case of egg turning. In other instances, where it has been shown that stimulation affects development prior to the onset of the sensory function of that modality (as in the case of light), responsible structures mediating such effects need yet to be discovered.

Studies in the field of poultry research have been largely concerned with ways to improve incubation in commercial incubators. Therefore in most of these studies various stimulus factors affecting the survival and the hatchability of chicken eggs were manipulated, without reference to any behavioral aspects. Through such work much was learnt about the range, the limits, and developmental changes of tolerance for short- and long-term temperature alterations, and the rate and other aspects of egg turning and light regimes. At the same time some of the results revealed that embryos appear to have certain adaptive preferences, i.e., that their hatchability, growth rate, etc., are optimal under near-natural conditions of incubation provided by an incubating bird.

Other studies were carried out to investigate possible influences of parental stimulation on embryonic motility. This type of work is related to research, not reviewed here, in which other than parental sources of stimulation [amniotic contractions, stimulation from touching self, etc., as reviewed by Oppenheim (1972a)] were experimentally examined in order to explore to what extent embryonic movement is influenced by such naturally occurring stimulation. This question has sometimes merged with the question of whether embryonic movement and development are or are not dependent on sensory stimulation, as studied in "sensory deprivation" experiments [reviewed by Oppenheim (1974)]. As pointed out earlier (Impekoven and Gold, 1973; Vince, 1973), results from such investigations merely concern the question of whether movement and further development can or cannot occur in the absence of certain modalities of stimulation; they do not touch the question of whether naturally occurring stimulation, for instance, as provided by rising-resettling of the incubating bird, affects the embryo in any way. Temporal changes of the rate of embryonic motility have been reported in response to sound, light, and temperature changes. Still to be investigated are the questions of whether such stimulation also influences other aspects of embryonic motility and development and whether such temporary changes lead to long-term effects.

In late stages of incubation, stimulation was shown to affect prehatching movements, bill clapping, and embryonic vocalizations. In some of these studies both immediate effects of stimulation on embryonic activity and long-term effects could be shown. Only in the case of egg turning has a direct relationship between the increased rate of prehatching movements and advanced hatching been established. In the case of other types of stimulation (light, or parental calls) the evidence for behavioral effects on hatching is more indirect. Effects of sound and egg lighting on early postnatal filial responses were described. Prenatal exposure to certain parental calls can affect the ability to discriminate between these calls and a different call, or it can affect responsiveness to one type of call. Although these effects usually go hand in hand, they can be studied separately. An example of the first-mentioned effect is the late prenatal development of individual recognition in the Guillemot, as described by Tschanz (1968). An example of the second effect is provided by the Laughing Gull, where it was shown that parental attraction calls which prenatally elicit certain types of responses lose their effectiveness unless embryos (or hatchlings) are repeatedly exposed to them (Impekoven, 1976). This means that exposure to parental calls as it occurs under natural conditions of incubation may maintain and consolidate responsiveness to such calls, which initially can develop even in the absence of the parent. This finding is contrasted with the effect of the conspecific alarm call, which prenatally does not evoke any response but soon after hatching elicits crouching and suppresses movements and calls. Repeated exposure to such calls in the late prenatal stage reduces merely the extent to which they acquire activity-suppressing effects.

In studies of light stimulation the relationship between experimental manipulation and the naturalistic situation again becomes more obscure. Even if the investigators reviewed had had the natural incubation pattern in mind, it would have been difficult to assess the effect of species-typical patterns of egg lighting on prenatal and early postnatal responsiveness to visual stimuli. Related to this issue is the problem that the "imprinting" situation is often quite unnatural, either because of the artificiality of the testing situation or because visual imprinting to a parent has often been viewed without consideration of the role of parental calls. As has been pointed out, future studies might be aimed at investigating effects of species-typical intensities and patterns of light stimulation, taking into account the differential importance of visual stimulation versus sound in the parent–young interactions of different species in adaptation to their ecological setting.

Finally, Section V,E has been devoted to the interaction of stimuli of different sensory modalities. Although under natural conditions of incubation modalities always interact, very little research has been done on the effect of such interactions. Suggestions for several promising contingencies are made.

To close this chapter, a few sentences must be devoted to the relationship between the parent(s) and their embryo(s). In Section IV we dealt primarily with how the parent responds to stimuli arising from the embryo; in Section V, on how the embryo responds to (would be) parental stimuli. In other words, prenatal parent–young "interactions" have been primarily viewed as a stimulus-response or cause-effect relationship in which research has been focused on either the parent or the embryo as the stimulus object. Little attention has been given to the dynamics of interactions between the parent bird and the embryo with respect to establishment of, developmental changes in, and long-term effects of mutual responsiveness and interdependence. In earlier stages of development the parent is the sole initiator or rather controller of the situation in the sense that it will make all the necessary adjustments in terms of temperature and gravitational changes. During late prenatal stages, when the embryo begins to vocalize and perform prehatching movements, it begins to assume a more active role. Some findings (e.g., Tschanz, 1968; Norton-Griffith, 1969; Hess, 1973) indicate that these prenatal interactions go through several developmental stages. Activities can be initiated by the parent or the embryo, but they tend to be little synchronized at first (as measured by small-scale temporal or sequential correlations). As time goes on, mutual responsiveness between parent and embryo becomes intensified. Early postnatal interactions (as observed, for example, in the Laughing Gull) suggest that the degree of mutual synchronization may depend on what happens before and around hatching. Observations at nests where a chick had been introduced by the experimenter showed that (due to the parent, or the chick, or both) interactions were often at first little synchronized. For instance, either the parent or the chick were active when the other was in a state of rest, or the parent would "misinterpret" the chick's behavior by performing incubation responses when the chick uttered the feeding call, or the parent would present food and croon when the chick was looking the other way. A fine-grain temporal and sequential analysis of observations like these in comparison with the normal uninterrupted situation may yield information on the role of prenatal interactions in the synchronization and mergence of individual idiosyncrasies and temperaments. This type of approach has been used more extensively in mammals for the study of developmental changes of interrelationships between mothers and their young (e.g., Hinde, 1974, and references cited therein), but the possible role of prenatal or perinatal influences on such interactions is as yet unknown.

Acknowledgments

This is Publication No. 232 of the Institute of Animal Behavior, Rutgers University. The author's own research reported here was supported by Public Health Service Grants MH-08604, GM 16727, and MH 23350-01, Rutgers University Research Council Grants, and a grant from the Alfred P. Sloan Foundation.

Drs. M. Numan, R. W. Oppenheim, and M. A. Vince made several valuable comments on an earlier draft of the manuscript.

The cooperation and hospitality of the Brigantine National Wildlife Refuge are greatly acknowledged.

References

Adam, J., and Dimond, S. J. 1971a. Influence of light on the time of hatching in the domestic chick. *Anim. Behav.* 19, 226–229.
Adam, J., and Dimond, S. J. 1971b. The effect of visual stimulation at different stages of embryonic development on approach behavior. *Anim. Behav.* 19, 51–54.
Andrew, R. J. 1969. The effects of testosterone on avian vocalizations. *In* "Bird Vocalizations" (R. A. Hinde, ed.), pp. 97–130. Cambridge Univ. Press, London and New York.
Andrews, H. F. 1976. Behavioral ecology of the Clapper Rail (*Rallus longirostris*). Unpublished Ph.D. Thesis, Rutgers University.
Baerends, G. P. 1959. The ethological analysis of incubation behavior. *Ibis* 101, 357–368.
Baerends, G. P., Postuma, K. H., and Joustra, T. 1960. Die Reaktion der brütenden Silbermöwe auf die Temperatur des Eies. *Arch. Néerl. Zool.* 13, 586–588.
Baerends, G. P., Drent, R. H., Glas, P., and Groenewold, H. 1970. An ethological analysis of incubation behavior in the Herring Gull. *Behaviour Suppl.* 17, 135–235.
Baeumer, E. 1955. Lebensart des Haushuhnes. *Z. Tierpsychol.* 12, 386–401.
Bakhuis, W. L. 1974. Observations on hatching movements in the chick. *J. Comp. Physiol. Psychol.* 87, 997–1003.
Baltin, S. 1969. Zur Biologic und Ethologie des Telegalla Huhns (*Alectura latham:* Gray) unter besonderer Berücksichtigung des Verhaltens während der Brutperiode. *Z. Tierpsychol.* 6, 524–572.
Bateson, P. P. G., and Wainwright, A. A. P. 1972. The effects of prior exposure to light on the imprinting process in domestic chicks. *Behaviour* 42, 279–290.
Batt, P. D. J., and Cornwell, G. W. 1972. The effect of cold on Mallard embryos. *J. Wild. Mgmt.* 36, 745–751.
Beer, C. G. 1961. Incubation and nest-building behaviour of Black-headed Gulls. I. Incubation-behaviour in the incubation period. *Behaviour* 18, 62–106.

Beer, C. G. 1962. Incubation and nest-building behaviour of Black-headed Gulls. II. Incubation behaviour in the laying period. *Behaviour* 19, 283–304.

Beer, C. G. 1966. Incubation and nest-building behaviour of Black-headed Gulls. V. The post-hatching period. *Behaviour* 26, 190–214.

Beer, C. G. 1970. On the responses of Laughing Gull chicks to the calls of adults. I. Recognition of the voices of the parents. *Anim. Behav.* 18, 652–660.

Beer, C. G. 1973. A view of birds. *Minn. Symp. Child Psychology.* 7, 47–86.

Bjärvall, A. 1968. The hatching and nest-exodus behaviour of Mallard. *Wildfowl* 19, 70–80.

Buntin, J. D. 1974. Stimulus factors involved in squab-induced crop-sac growth and parental responsiveness in the Ring Dove (*Streptopelia risoria*). Unpublished Ph.D. Thesis, Rutgers University.

Bursian, A. V. 1964. The influence of light on the spontaneous movements of chick embryos. *Bull. Exp. Biol. Med. (USSR)* 58, 7–11.

Caldwell, P. J., and Cornwall, G. W. 1975. Incubation behavior and temperatures of the Mallard Duck. *Auk* 92, 706–731.

Chattock, A. P. 1925. On the physics of incubation. *Phil. Trans. Roy. Soc. (London) Ser. B.* 213, 397–450.

Collias, N. E. 1952. The development of social behavior in birds. *Auk* 69, 127–159.

Cooper, J. B. 1972. Effect of light during incubation on hatchability of Turkey eggs. *Poult. Sci.* 51, 1105–1108.

Dawkins, C. R. 1968. The ontogeny of a pecking preference in domestic chicks. *Z. Tierpsychol.* 25, 170–186.

Decker, J. D. 1970. The influence of early extirpation of the otocysts on development of behaviour in the chick. *J. Exp. Zool.* 174, 349–364.

Dimond, S. J. 1970. Visual experience and early social behaviour. *In* "Social Behaviour in Birds and Mammals" (J. H. Crook, ed.), pp. 441–466. Academic Press, New York.

Dimond, S. J., and Adam, J. H. 1972. Approach behaviour and embryonic visual experience in chicks: Studies of the effect of rate of visual flicker. *Anim. Behav.* 20, 413–420.

Drent, R. H. 1970. Functional aspects of incubation in the Herring Gull (*Larus argentatus*). *Behaviour Suppl.* 17, 1–132.

Drent, R. H. 1972. Adaptive aspects of the physiology of incubation. *Proc. Int. Ornithol. Congr., 15th* pp. 255–280.

Drent, R. H. 1973. The natural history of incubation. *In* "Breeding Biology of Birds" (D. S. Farner, ed.), pp. 262–311. Nat. Acad. Sci., Washington, D.C.

Drent, R. H. 1975. Incubation. *In* "Avian Biology" (D. S. Farner, J. R. King, and K. C. Parkes, eds.), Vol. V, pp. 333–420. Academic Press, New York.

Drent, R. H., Postuma, K., and Joustra, T. 1970. The effect of egg-temperature on incubation behaviour an the Herring Gull. *Behaviour Suppl.* 17, 239–258.

Emlen, J. T., and Miller, P. E. 1969. Pace-setting mechanisms of the nesting cycle in the Ring-billed Gull. *Behaviour* 33, 237–261.

Evans, R. M. 1973. Differential responsiveness of young Ring-billed Gulls and Herring Gulls to adult vocalizations of their own and other species. *Can. J. Zool.* 51, 759–770.

Eycleshymer, A. C. 1907. Some observations and experiments on the natural and artificial incubation on hatchability. *Res. Bull. Agr. Exp. Sta. Mo.* 502, pp. 3–12.

Franks, E. C. 1967. The response of incubating Ringed Turtle Doves (*Streptopelia risoria*) to manipulated egg-temperatures. *Condor* 69, 268–276.

Freeman, B. M. 1974. Development of the avian embryo. Part 2: Physiology. *In* "Development of the Avian Embryo" (B. M. Freeman and Vince, M. A., eds.), pp. 119–265. Chapman & Hall, London.

Funk, E. M., and Forward, J. F. 1952. Effect of multiple plane turning of eggs during incubation on hatchability. *Res. Bull. Agr. Exp. Sta. Mo.* **502**, pp. 3–12.

Gibb, J. A. 1970. The turning down of marked eggs by Great Tits. *Bird-Banding* **41**, 40–41.

Goethe, F. 1953. Experimentelle Brutbeendigung und andere brutethologische Beobachtungen bei Silbermöwen (*Larus argentatus*). *J. Ornithol.* **94**, 160–174.

Gold, P. S. 1971. The effects of sensory stimulation during embryogeny on growth, hatching and imprinting in the domestic chick. Unpublished Ph.D. Thesis. New York University.

Gottlieb, G. 1961. Developmental age as a baseline for determination of the critical period in imprinting. *J. Comp. Physiol. Psychol.* **54**, 422–427.

Gottlieb, G. 1963. Imprinting in nature. *Science* **139**, 497–498.

Gottlieb, G. 1965a. Prenatal auditory sensitivity in chickens and ducks. *Science* **147**, 1596–1598.

Gottlieb, G. 1965b. Imprinting in relation to parental and species identification by avian neonates. *J. Comp. Physiol. Psychol.* **59**, 345–356.

Gottlieb, G. 1968. Prenatal behavior in birds. *Quart. Rev. Biol.* **43**, 148–174.

Gottlieb, G. 1971. "Development of Species Identification of Birds: An Inquiry into the Prenatal Determinants of Perception." Univ. of Chicago Press, Chicago, Illinois.

Gottlieb, G. 1973. Introduction of behavioral embryology. *In* "Studies on the Development of Behavior and the Nervous System (G. Gottlieb, ed.), Vol. 1 Behavioral Embryology, pp. 1–48. Academic Press, New York.

Gottlieb, G. 1974. On the acoustic basis of species identification in Wood-ducklings (*Aix sponsa*). *J. Comp. Physiol. Psychol.* **87**, 1038–1048.

Gottlieb, G. 1975a. Development of species identification in ducklings. I. Nature of perceptual deficit caused by embryonic auditory deprivation. *J. Comp. Physiol. Psychol.* **89**, 387–399.

Gottlieb, G. 1975b. Development of species identification in ducklings. II. Experiential prevention of perceptual deficit caused by embryonic auditory deprivation. *J. Comp. Physiol. Psychol.* **89**, 675–684.

Gottlieb, G. 1975c. Development of species identification in ducklings. III. Maturational rectification on perceptual deficit caused by auditory deprivation. *J. Comp. Physiol. Psychol.* **89**, 899–912.

Gottlieb, G. 1976. The roles of experience in the development of behavior and the nervous system. *In* "Studies on the Development of Behavior and the Nervous System" (G. Gottlieb, ed.), Vol. 3: Neural and Behavioral Specificity, pp. 25–54. Academic Press, New York.

Gottlieb, G., and Kuo, Z. Y. 1965. Development of behavior in the duck-embryo. *J. Comp. Physiol. Psychol.* **59**, 183–188.

Graves, H. B. 1970. Comparative ethology of imprinting: Field and laboratory studies of wild Turkeys, Jungle Fowl and Domestic Fowl. *Amer. Zool.* **10**, 483. (Abstr.)

Graves, H. B. 1973. Early social responses in *Gallus:* A functional analysis. *Science* **182**, 937–938.

Grier, J. B., Counter, S. A., and Shearer, W. M. 1967. Prenatal auditory imprinting in chickens. *Science* **155**, 1692–1693.

Guyomarc'h, J. C. 1971. Les cris maternels chez les Gallinacés et leur ontogenèse. *J. Psychol. Norm. Pathol.* **34**, 381–400.

Guyomarc'h, J. C. 1972. Les bases ontogénétiques de l'attractivité du gloussement maternel chez la poule domestique. *Rev. Comp. Anim.* **6**, 79–94.

Hailman, J. P. 1967. The ontogeny of an instinct. The pecking response in chicks of the Laughing Gull and related species. *Behaviour Suppl.* 15, 1–159.

Hailman, J. P. 1971. The role of stimulus-orientation in eliciting the begging response from newly hatched chicks of the Laughing Gull (*Larus atricilla*). *Anim. Behav.* 19, 328–335.

Hamburger, V. 1963. Some aspects of the embryology of behavior. *Quart. Rev. Biol.* 138, 342–365.

Hamburger, V., and Oppenheim, R. W. 1967. Prehatching motility and hatching behavior in the chick. *J. Exp. Zool.* 166, 171–204.

Harth, M. S. 1971. Behavioral embryology of Pigeons. Paper read at Symposium on Prenatal Ontogeny of Behavior and the Nervous System. AAAS meeting.

Harth, M. S. 1974. The ontogeny of tactile sensitivity in the pigeon embryo (*Columba livia*). *In* "Ontogenesis of the Brain" (L. Jilek and S. Trogan, eds.), Vol. 2, pp. 57–65. Universitas Carolina Pragensis, Praha CSSR.

Heaton, M. B. 1971. Ontogeny of vision in the Peking Duck (*Anas platyrhynchos*): The pupillary light reflex as means for investigating visual onset and development in avian embryos. *Develop. Psychobiol.* 4, 313–332.

Heaton, M. B. 1972. Prenatal auditory discrimination in the Wood Duck (*Aix sponsa*). *Anim. Behav.* 20, 421–424.

Heaton, M. B. 1973. Early visual function in Bobwhite and Japanese Quail embryos as reflected by the pupillary reflex. *J. Comp. Physiol. Psychol.* 84, 134–139.

Heaton, M. B., and Harth, M. S. 1974a. Non-visual light responsiveness in the Pigeon: developmental and comparative considerations. *J. Exp. Zool.* 188, 251–264.

Heaton, M. B., and Harth, M. S. 1974b. Developing visual function in the Pigeon embryo with comparative reference to other avian species. *J. Comp. Physiol. Psychol.* 86, 151.

Hess, E. H. 1973. "Imprinting: Early Experience and the Developmental Psychobiology of Attachment." Van Nostrand, New York.

Hinde, R. A. 1970. "Animal Behavior: A Synthesis of Ethology and Comparative Psychology," 2nd ed. McGraw-Hill, New York.

Hinde, R. A. 1974. "Biological Basis of Human Social Behavior." McGraw-Hill, New York.

Hinde, R. A., Bell, R. Q., and Steel, E. 1963. Changes in sensitivity of the Canary brood patch during the natural breeding season. *Anim. Behav.* 11, 553–560.

Holcomb, L. C. 1969. Egg turning behavior of birds in response to color-marked eggs. *Bird-Banding* 40, 105–113.

Howell, T. R., Araya, B., and Millie, W. R. 1974. Breeding biology of the Gray Gull (*Larus modestus*). *Univ. Calif. Publ. Zool.* 104, 57 pp.

Impekoven, M. 1971a. Prenatal experience of parental calls and pecking in the Laughing Gull chick (*Larus atricilla*). *Anim. Behav.* 19, 441–476.

Impekoven, M. 1971b. Calls of very young Black-headed Gull chicks under different motivational states. *Ibis* 113, 91–96.

Impekoven, M. 1973a. The response of incubating Laughing Gulls (*Larus atricilla*) to calls of hatching chicks. *Behaviour* 46, 94–113.

Impekoven, M. 1973b. Response contingent prenatal experience of maternal calls in the Peking Duck (*Anas platyrhynchos*). *Anim. Behav.* 21, 164–168.

Impekoven, M. 1976. Responses of Laughing Gull chicks (*Larus atricilla*) to parental attraction and alarm calls, and effects of prenatal auditory experience on the response to such calls. *Behaviour* 56, 3–4, 250–278.

Impekoven, M. and Gold, P. S. 1973. Prenatal origins of parent—young interactions in birds: a naturalistic approach. *In* "Studies on the Development of Behavior and the Nervous

System" (G. Gottlieb, ed.), Vol. 1: Behavioral Embryology, pp. 325–356. Academic Press, New York.

Ingold, P. 1973. Zur lautlichen Beziehung des Elters zu seinem Küken bei Tordalken (*Alca torda*). *Behaviour* 45, 155–190.

Kaltofen, R. S. 1960. De invloed van de keepfrequentie op de embryonensterfte in vershillende fasen van het broed process. III. Veeteelt-en Zuivelberichten 3, 96–102. *Anim. Breed. Abstn.* 30, 112 [as cited by Lundy (1969)].

Kendeigh, S. C. 1952. Parental care and its evolution in birds. *Ill. Biol. Monogr.* 22, 1–358.

King, J. R., and Farner, D. S. 1961. Energy metabolism, thermoregulation and body temperature. *In* "Biology and Comparative Physiology of Birds" (A. J. Marshall, ed.), Vol. II, pp. 215–288. Academic Press, New York.

Konishi, M. 1973. Development of auditory neuronal responses in avian embryos. *Proc. Nat. Acad. Sci. U.S.* 70, 1795–1798.

Kosin, I. L. 1964. Recent research trends in hatchability related problems in the domestic fowl. *World's Poult. Sci. J.* 20, 254–268.

Kovach, J. K. 1968. Spatial orientation of the chick embryo during the last five days of incubation. *J. Comp. Physiol. Psychol.* 66, 283–288.

Kovach, J. K. 1970. Development and mechanisms of behavior in the chick embryo during the last five days of incubation. *J. Comp. Physiol. Psychol.* 73, 392–406.

Kruuk, H. 1964. Predators and anti-predator behavior of the Black-headed Gull (*Larus ridibundus*). *Behaviour Suppl.* 11, 1–139.

Kuiper, J. W., and Ubbels, P. 1951. A biological study of natural incubation and its application to artificial incubation. *Rap. Off. Congr. Mond. Avicult.*, 9th Vol. I, pp. 52–58.

Kuo, Z. Y. 1932a. Ontogeny of embryonic behavior in aves. I. Chronology and general nature of behavior of chick embryos. *J. Exp. Zool.* 61, 395–430.

Kuo, Z. Y. 1932b. Ontogeny of embryonic behavior in Aves. IV. The influence of embryonic movements upon the behavior after hatching. *J. Comp. Psychol.* 14, 109–122.

Landauer, W. 1961. The hatchability of chicken eggs as influenced by environment and heredity. *Storrs Agr. Exp. Sta. Monogr.* 1, pp. 1–278.

Lauber, J. K., and Shutze, J. V. 1964. Accelerated growth of embryo chicks under the influence of light. *Growth* 28, 179–190.

Lind, H. 1961. Studies on the behavior of the Black-tailed Godwit (*Limosa limosa*). *Medd. Naturfredningsrådets Reservatudvalg (Copenhagen)* 66, 1–157.

Lorenz, K. 1970. "Studies of Animal and Human Behaviour," Vol. I. Harvard Univ. Press, Cambridge, Massachusetts.

Lundy, H. 1969. A review of the effects of temperature, humidity, turning and gaseous environment in the incubator on the hatchability of the hen's egg. *In* "The Fertility and Hatchability of the Hen's Egg" (T. C. Carter and B. M. Freeman, eds.), pp. 143–179. Oliver & Boyd, Edinburgh.

Maier, R. A. 1963. Maternal behavior in the domestic hen: the role of physical contact. *J. Comp. Physiol. Psychol.* 56, 357–361.

Menaker, M. 1968. Extra retinal light perception in the sparrow. I. Entrainment of the biological clock. *Proc. Nat. Acad. Sci. U.S.* 59, 414–421.

Miller, W. J., and Miller, L. S. 1958. Synopsis of behaviour traits of the Ring-neck Dove. *Anim. Behav.* 6, 3–8.

Moreng, R. E., and Bryant, R. L. 1956. The resistance of the chicken embryo to low temperature exposure. *Poult. Sci.* 35, 753–757.

Moreng, R. E., and Shaffner, C. S. 1951. Lethal internal temperature for the chicken from fertile egg to mature bird. *Poult. Sci.* 30, 255–268.

Nelson, J. B. 1966. The breeding biology of the Gannet, *Sula bassana* on the Bass Rock, Scotland. *Ibis* 108, 584–626.

Nelson, J. B. 1969. The breeding ecology of the Red-footed Booby in the Galapagos. *J. Anim. Ecol.* 38, 181–198.

Noirot, E. 1972. The onset of maternal behavior in rats, hamsters, and mice: A selective review. This series. 4, 107–145.

Norton-Griffiths, M. 1969. The organisation, control and development of parental feeding in the Oystercatcher (*Haematopus ostralegus*). *Behaviour* 34, 55–114.

New, D. A. T. 1957. A critical period for the turning of hen's eggs. *J. Embryol. Exp. Morphol.* 5, 293–299.

Olsen, M. W. 1930. Influence of turning and other factors on the hatching power of hen's eggs. Unpublished Masters Thesis, Iowa State College

Olsen, M. W., and Byerly, T. C. 1936. Multiple turning and orienting eggs during incubation as they affect hatchability. *Poult. Sci.* 15, 88–95.

Oppenheim, R. W. 1968a. Color preferences in the pecking response of newly hatched ducks (*Anas platyrhynchos*). *J. Comp. Physiol. Psychol. Monogr. Suppl.* 66, 1–17.

Oppenheim, R. W. 1968b. Light responsivity in chick and duck embryos just prior to hatching. *Anim. Behav.* 16, 276–280.

Oppenheim, R. W. 1970. Some aspects of embryonic behavior in the duck (*Anas platyrhynchos*). *Anim. Behav.* 18, 335–352.

Oppenheim, R. W. 1972a. The embryology of behavior in birds: A critical review of the role of sensory stimulation in embryonic movement. *Proc. Int. Ornithol. Congr., 15th* pp. 283–302.

Oppenheim, 1972b. Prehatching and hatching behavior in birds: A comparative study of altricial and precocial species. *Anim. Behav.* 20, 644–655.

Oppenheim, R. W. 1972c. An experimental investigation of the possible role of tactile and proprioceptive stimulation in certain aspects of embryonic behavior in the chick. *Dev. Psychobiol.* 5, 71–91.

Oppenheim, R. W. 1973. Prehatching and hatching behavior: Comparative and physiological consideration. *In* "Behavioral Embryology: Studies on the Development of Behavior and the Nervous System" (G. Gottlieb, ed.), Vol. 1: Behavioral Embryology, pp. 164–244. Academic Press, New York.

Oppenheim, R. W. 1974. The ontogeny of behavior in the chick embryo. This series. 5, 133–172.

Oppenheim, R. W., and Levin, H. L. 1975. Short-term changes in incubation temperature: Behavioral and physiological effects in the chick-embryo from 6 to 20 days. *Dev. Psychobiol.* 8, 103–115.

Poulson, H. 1953. A study of incubation responses and some other behavior patterns in birds. *Vidensk. Medd. Dan. Naturhist. Foren.* 115, 1–131.

Provine, R. R. 1973. Neurophysiological aspects of behavioral development in the chick embryo. *In* "Studies on the Development of Behavior and the Nervous System" (G. Gottlieb, ed.), Vol. 1: Behavioral Embryology, pp. 77–102. Academic Press, New York.

Rajecki, D. W. 1974. Effects of prenatal exposure to auditory or visual stimulation on postnatal distress vocalizations in chicks. *Behav. Biol.* 11, 525–536.

Robertson, I. S. 1961. The influence of turning on the hatchability of hens' eggs. I. The effect of turning on hatchability. *J. Agr. Sci.* 36, 49–57.

Romannoff, A. L. 1936. Effects of different temperatures on the prenatal and postnatal development of the chick. *Poult. Sci.* 15, 311–315.

Rosenblatt, J. S. 1970. Views on the onset and maintenance of maternal behavior in the rat. *In* "Development and Evolution of Behavior: Essays in Memory of T. C. Schneirla" (L.

R. Aronson, E. Tobach, D. S. Lehrman, and J. S. Rosenblatt, eds.), pp. 489–515. Freeman, San Francisco.

Russel, S. M. 1969. Regulation of egg-temperatures by incubating White-winged Doves. *In* "Physiological Systems in Semi-arid Environments" (C. C. Hoff and M. L. Riedesel, eds.), pp. 107–112. Univ. of New Mexico Press, Albuquerque.

Saunders, J. C. 1974. The development of auditory evoked responses in the chick embryo. *Minerva Otorinolaringol.* 24, 221–229.

Saunders, J. C., Coles, R. B., and Gates, G. R. 1973. The development of auditory evoked responses in the cochlea and cochlea nuclei of the chick. *Brain Res.* 63, 59–74.

Saunders, J. C., Gates, G. R., and Coles, R. B. 1974. Brain-stem evoked responses as an index of hearing thresholds in one-day old chicks and ducklings. *J. Comp. Physiol. Psychol.* 86, 426–431.

Schleidt, W. M., Schleidt, M., and Magg, M. 1961. Störung der Mutter-Kind-Beziehung bei Truthühnern durch Gehörverlust. *Behaviour* 16, 254–260.

Schneirla, T. C. 1965. Aspects of stimulation and organization in approach/withdrawal processes underlying vertebrate behavioral development. This series. 1, 1–74.

Sedláček, K. J. 1964. Further findings on the conditions of formation of the temporary connection in chick embryos. *Physiol. Bohemoslov.* 13, 411–420.

Siegel, P. B., Isakson, S. T., Coleman, S. N., and Huffman, B. J. 1969. Photoacceleration of development in chick embryos. *Comp. Biochem. Physiol.* 28, 753–758.

Skutch, A. V. F. 1962. The constancy of incubation. *Wilson Bull.* 74, 115–152.

Stoddard, H. L. 1931. "The Bobwhite Quail." Scribners, New York [as cited by Heaton (1973)].

Sviderskaya, G. E. 1967. Effect of sound on the motor activity of chick embryos. *Bull. Exp. Biol. Med. (USSR)* 63, 24–28.

Tinbergen, N. 1953. "The Herring Gull's World." Collins, London.

Tinbergen, N. 1965. "Animal Behavior," Life Nature Library. Time Inc., New York.

Tolhurst, B. E. 1974. Development of the chick embryo in relation to the shell, yolk, albumen and extra-embryonic membranes. *In* "Development of the Avian Embryo, a Behavioural and Physiological Study" (B. M. Freeman and M. A. Vince, eds.), pp. 277–291. Chapman & Hall, London.

Tschanz, B. 1959. Zur Brutbiologie der Trottellumme (*Uria aalge*). *Behaviour* 14, 2–100.

Tschanz, B. 1968. Trottellummen: Die Entstehung der persönlichen Beziehung zwischen Jungvogel und Eltern. *Z. Tierpsychol. Suppl.* 4, 1–103.

Tschanz, B., and Hirsbrunner-Scharf, M. 1975. Adaptations to colony life on cliff-ledges: A comparative study of Guillemot and Razorbill chicks. *In* "Evolution in Behavior" (G. P. Baerends, C. G. Beer, and A. Manning, eds.), pp. 149–156. Oxford Univ. Press (Clarendon), London and New York.

Vanzulli, A., and Garcia-Austt, E. 1963. Development of cochlear microphonic potentials in the chick embryo. *Acta Neurol. Latinoamer.* 9, 19–23.

Vince, M. A. 1969. Embryonic communication, respiration and the synchronization of hatching. *In* "Bird Vocalizations" (R. A. Hinde, ed.), pp. 233–260. Cambridge. Univ. Press, London and New York.

Vince, M. A. 1973. Some environmental effects on the activity and development of the avian embryo. *In* "Studies on the Development of Behavior and the Nervous System (G. Gottlieb, ed.), Vol. 1: Behavioral Embryology, pp. 286–325. Academic Press, New York.

Vince, M. A. 1974. Development of the avian embryo. Part 1: Behaviour. *In* "Development of the Avian Embryo, a Behavioural and Physiological Study" (B. M. Freeman and M. A. Vince, eds.), pp. 3–116. Chapman & Hall, London.

Vince, M. A., and Chinn, J. S. 1971. Effect of accelerated hatching on the initiation of standing and walking in the Japanese Quail. *Anim. Behav.* **19**, 62–66.

Vince, M. A., and Chinn, J. S. 1972. Effects of external stimulation on the domestic chick's capacity to stand and walk. *Brit. J. Psychol.* **63**, 89–99.

Visintini, F., and Levi-Montalcini, R. 1939. Relazione tra differenciazione strutturale dei centri delle vie nervose nell'embryone di pollo. *Schweiz. Arch. Neurol. Psychiat.* **43**, 1–45 [as cited by Gottlieb (1968)].

Walter, J. H., and Voitle, R. A. 1972. Effects of photoperiod during incubation on embryonic and post-embryonic development of broilers. *Poult. Sci.* **51**, 1122–1126.

White, F. N., and Kinney, J. L. 1974. Avian incubation. *Science* **186**, 107–115.

Würdinger, I. 1970. Erzeugung, Ontogenie und Funktion der Lautäusserungen bei vier Gänsearten (*Anser indicus, Anser caeruleus, Anser albifrons* und *Branta canadensis*). *Z. Tierpsychol.* **27**, 257–302.

Life History of Male Japanese Monkeys

YUKIMARU SUGIYAMA

PRIMATE RESEARCH INSTITUTE, KYOTO UNIVERSITY
INUYAMA, JAPAN

I. INTRODUCTION: THE SOCIAL STRUCTURE OF JAPANESE MONKEYS

It has long been well known that Japanese monkeys (*Macaca fuscata*) form large, well-organized troops and that the older males are occasionally seen alone in the hill forest. But details of the social structure of Japanese monkeys were revealed only after the studies of Itani (1954), Mizuhara (1957), Itani and Tokuda (1958), and others, which were based mainly on the observations of baited troops. According to Itani (1954), the multimale and multifemale troop of Japanese monkeys at Takasakiyama was controlled by a group of leader males. Females and infants occupied the central part of the troop under the protection of leader males. Females were likely to stay there throughout their long life. On the other hand as male juveniles develop they go out to the peripheral part of the troop, where they move and play with age mates and elder males. Mature males gradually try to return to the central part of the troop to take over the leadership, but young and inexperienced males are chased off by the central females as well as by the dominant males. Mizuhara (1957) studied intensively the relationships among adult males and found that their ranking relationships were maintained for long periods. Moreover, physically developed and experienced males at Takasakiyama, who were excluded from achieving higher social status by the many leader and subleader males, deserted the natal troop to become solitary. Following Mizuhara's study, Sugiyama (1960) found that three active and virile males who had taken over leadership of the peripheral part of the troop established social bonds with females who moved out to the periphery as the population grew, budded out with those females and young males, and formed a troop as an independent reproductive unit.

During these studies, some solitary males aggressively approached the troop, fought with troop males and were chased off by them, but other solitary males approached only submissively and joined it with a low rank. These observations indicated that solitary males are "outlaws" who cannot carry on troop life or who fail to climb up the ranking hierarchy.

On the other hand, all females must live their whole life in their natal troop, as a solitary female was seldom found near the troop and few desertion of the troop by a female was recognized. Koyama (1967) found that females, like males, had ranking status in the troop, and that this depends strictly on their family's rank. It was thus recognized that all Japanese monkeys, except those males who leave the troop, were members of a strict ranking hierarchy.

From the expectation that leadership of such a highly organized troop could be carried out only by a few selected animals, Imanishi (1957) suggested that some offspring of higher-ranking females, i.e., those males who were brought up in the center of the troop and could thus observe the leader's behavior at close quarters, become able to identify and comprehend the leader's status personality. Even though they spend their youth at the periphery of the troop, only such males can succeed in returning to the central part to take over complete leadership when they mature. Other males fail to take the leadership and stay in a low-ranking status or leave the troop.

Subsequent long-term studies recorded many males living away from any troop, either by themselves or in all-male parties, and in many cases no clear reason for the desertion of the troop could be recognized. Our view of these isolated males gradually changed so that we came to see them not always as unsocial animals and recognized that solitary as well as troop life is normal for male Japanese monkeys (Nishida, 1966).

Although most troops which have been intensively studied are artificially baited, they are part of a natural population. Although the monkey's habitat has been subdivided by human activity, Japanese monkeys can move freely throughout their distribution range, except where water barriers or big towns obstruct their movement. Although there are some phenomena, such as a considerable increase in population, which may have been caused by the artificial baiting, the basic life history of Japanese monkeys observed in their present habitat can be considered the same as of those in the natural condition, which is not that of a closed island colony.

The main research areas discussed in this article are shown in Fig. 1. Four troops budded out from the Takasakiyama troop in 1959 (Sugiyama, 1960), 1962–1963 (Kano, 1964), 1966–1967 (Nishimura, 1973), and 1973. Though the last two of these troops were captured, the main troop (Troop A) and the two troops that budded off first [Troops B and C (or Y)] feed and rest at an artificial feeding ground alternatively, having overlapping moving ranges in the hill forest of Takasakiyama. Though the Arashiyama troop divided into two in 1966 (Koyama, 1970), both troops (Troops A and B) had extremely small moving ranges and stayed in or near the feeding ground throughout each day, in

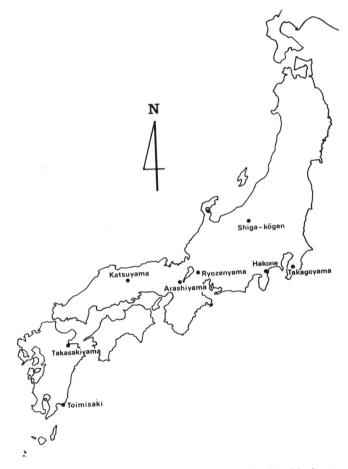

Fig. 1. Distribution of the research areas in Japan considered in this chapter.

TABLE I

Social Composition of Japanese Monkey Troops[a]

Troop locality

Age class (years)	Toi		Takasakiyama A		B		C		Katsu-yama		Arashiyama B		Arashiyama A		Ryozen A		Shiga A		Hakone T		Total (mean)	
	M	F	M	F	M	F	M	F	M	F	M	F	M	F	M	F	M	F	M	F	M	F
Infant and juvenile (0, 1, 2)	21	28	247	292	85	84	61	55	47	59	35	28	29	37	13	16	18	15	17	17	573	631
M/F ratio	(0.75)		(0.85)		(1.01)		(1.11)		(0.80)		(1.25)		(0.78)		(0.81)		(1.20)		(1.00)		(0.91)	
Adolescent (3, 4)	12	6	45	137	28	30	24	34	17	23	11	10	9	17	7	9	6	6	12	12	171	284
M/F ratio	(2.00)		(0.33)		(0.93)		(0.71)		(0.74)		(1.10)		(0.53)		(0.78)		(1.00)		(1.00)		(0.60)	
Young adult (5, 6, 7)			14	89	3	25	6	23			8	13	10	19	1	6	4	10	4	14		
Fully adult (8+)	9	23	30	244	15	71	13	59	20	67	11	27	11	26	4	13	2	17	4	32	169	778
M/F ratio	(0.39)		(0.13)		(0.19)		(0.23)		(0.30)		(0.48)		(0.47)		(0.26)		(0.22)		(0.17)		(0.22)	
Total	42	57	336	762	131	210	104	171	84	149	65	78	59	99	25	44	30	48	37	75	913	1693
Time of observation	1960–1967		Sept. 1975						Oct. 1972		Feb. 1972				March 1973		March 1973		July 1972			
Investigator	Azuma (1974)		Sugiyama, Ohsawa, Nishimura and Masui (1976)						Itoigawa (1974, 1975)		Koyama, Mano, and Norikoshi (1975)				Sugiyama and Ohsawa (1974a,b; 1975)		Tokita and Wada (1974)		Fukuda, Muramatsu, and Tanaka (1974)			

[a] A, B, C, and T are troop names; M, male; F, female.

contact with each other. [Troop A was captured in 1972 and was sent to an enclosure in the United States (Texas).] In Arashiyama, as well as in Takasaki-yama, before troop division there was only one troop (with no adjacent troop within 15 km), and the intertroop relations of both areas after the division have been far more intense because of the artificial feeding than they were in the natural condition.

Though other research areas which appear in this article are artificially baited, there are wild adjacent troops whose moving ranges overlap with those of the baited troops or lie nearby, within the contiguous forest. The Troop A (Kaminyu Troop) of Ryozen (Ryozenyama) was baited, between 1966 and August, 1973, for about 9 months each year, but the study is being continued in the wild condition.

Most of the ages of animals which appear in this article were measured from known birth dates or were estimated when the animals were quite young, but the ages of males who came from outside the troops and of some others were roughly estimated from their appearance and behavior.

II. RENUNCIATION OF THE NATAL TROOP

A. SOCIAL COMPOSITION OF THE TROOP

The social composition of troops discussed in this article are shown in Table I. Although the sex ratio (male/female) of infants at the time of birth is slightly different from year to year, it is always close to 1. However, the sex ratio of the juveniles and adolescents of less than 5 years old falls down to 0.60. That of young adults and full adults decreases to 0.22. Table I shows that the decrease in the number of males with age is much more rapid than that of females.

Japanese monkeys have few enemies except for domestic and feral dogs. As there can be little sex difference in mortality if monkeys are living in the same troop, the reason for the rapid decrease in the sex ratio in the troop must lie not in the death of males but in renunciation of the troop by many of them. Thus the males must desert their own troop and either change to another or become *hanarezaru*, that is, isolated monkeys who live alone or in all-male parties separate from or near the bisexual troop. Even though the exact reason for the disappearance of many males is not confirmed, the present author assumes that many of the males which disappeared deserted the troop by themselves.

B. AGE OF DISAPPEARANCE FROM THE NATAL TROOP

In the Ryozen A Troop, at least 36 males were born between 1965 and 1973, but at least 23 males (that is, 63.9%) disappeared from the natal troop before

February 1975. [Although some females with their offspring budded out from the troop in February 1974, forming a new troop, Troop As, near the main troop, Troop Ap, males who lived with their mother are treated here as being in the natal troop (Table II).] No males born before 1970 can now be seen in the natal troop, most of them having disappeared when 4 or 5 years old. At present there is no male more than 4 years old in the natal troop. Although most males who disappeared when less than 2 years old are presumed to be dead, there was evidence that two male infants deserted the troop with their mothers (Sugiyama and Ohsawa, 1974a, b).

In Toi (Toimisaki) Troop, 36 males were born between 1955 and 1959. Up to 1965, 25 males (69.4%) had disappeared from the natal troop. All of them went when between 3 and 7 years old (Table III). Although there were still some males in the natal troop at that time, all males who were born before 1955 had disappeared from the troop before they were 10 years of age (Azuma, 1974).

In Shiga (Shiga-kogen) A Troop, 27 males were born between 1961 and 1970, and 16 males, or 64% (excluding two males who were captured), disappeared before November 1973 (Table IV). Two males died within a year of their birth; all others disappeared when between 3 and 8 years of age. Most males that disappeared from time to time moved separately from the troop and then rejoined it before they disappeared finally. Three males, out of nine who are still in the natal troop, are less than 5 years old, and three 5-year-old males often leave the troop intermittently as the others did before they disappeared (Tokitε and Wada, 1974).

Eighty-one males out of 162 who were born between 1961 and 1972 in Katsuyama Troop, or 50%, had disappeared before October 1972. Neglecting juveniles and infants less than 4 years old, 67 males (73.6%) had disappeared · (Table V; see also Itoigawa, 1974). Thirty-seven males out of 39 who were born between 1964 and 1969 in Hakone (Yugawara) T Troop, or 94.9%, had disappeared by June 1973 (Table VI; see also Fukuda et al., 1974).

In Arashiyama troops, also, most males disappeared from the natal troop before they were 10 years old (Norikoshi and Koyama, 1975). As the original authors unfortunately abandoned the data from males who disappeared at or before 2 years of age, presuming them to be "dead" without confirmation, the age distribution of males who disappeared before they reached 2 years cannot be shown here (Table VII).

Recently, we (Ohsawa et al., 1976) traced 316 sample animals (174 males and 142 females) at Takasakiyama by artificial marking and plotted the decrease in the number of animals with age (Fig. 2). This figure shows the total number of animals who remain in all the three troops of Takasakiyama. As the sample of infants less than 1 year old is unfortunately small, the number remaining at 1 year of age is estimated from other data, and the sex difference can not be

TABLE II

Age of Disappearance of Males Who Were Born in Ryozen A
Troop between 1965 and 1973[a]

Birth year	Present age	No. of births	Age of disappearance (years)						In natal troop
			0	1	2	3	4	5	
1965	9	2[b]	–	–	–	–	2	–	0
1966	8	2[b]	–	–	–	–	2	–	0
1967	7	4[b]	–	–	–	–	2	2	0
1968	6	3[b]	–	–	–	–	–	3	0
1969	5	5	1	–	–	–	–	4	0
1970	4	4	–	–	–	1	–		3
1971	3	5	–	–	–	1			4
1972	2	4	–	1	1				2
1973	1	7	3	–					4
Total		36	4	1	1	2	6	9	23 \ 13

[a] As of February 1975.
[b] Probably more males were born, but they disappeared before the
intensive study began in 1969.

TABLE III

Age of Disappearance of Males Who Were Born in Toi Troop between 1955 and 1959[a]

Birth year	Present age	No. of births	Age of disappearance (years)										In natal troop
			0	1	2	3	4	5	6	7	8	9	
1955	10	5	–	–	–	–	3	1	–	1	–	–	0
1956	9	3	–	–	–	2	–	–	–	–	–		1
1957	8	12	–	–	–	–	–	–	6	–			6
1958	7	8	–	–	–	–	–	6	–				2
1959	6	8	–	–	–	–	3[b]	3[b]					2
Total		36	–	–	–	2	6	10	6	1	–	–	25 \ 11

[a] As of 1965. [Table adapted from Azuma (1974).]
[b] These six males disappeared at 4 or 5 years of age.

TABLE IV

Age of Disappearance of Males Who Were Born in Shiga A Troop between 1961 and 1970[a]

Birth year	Present age	No. of births	Age of disappearance (years)									Captured	In natal troop
			−1	1	2	3	4	5	6	7	8		
1961	12	1?	—	—	—	—	(1)	—	1	—	—	—	0
1962	11	1?	—	—	—	1(1)	—	—	—	—	—	—	0
1963	10	3	—	—	—	—	(1)	(1)	—	1	1	—	1
1964	9	1	—	—	—	—	1(1)	—	—	—	—	—	0
1965	8	6	—	—	—	—	2(4)	2	—	—	1(1)	—	1
1966	7	0	—	—	—	—	—	—	—	—	—	—	0
1967	6	2	—	—	—	(1)	1(1)	—	1	—	—	—	0
1968	5	6	—	—	—	(1)	2(1)	(3)	—	—	—	—	1–4[c]
1969	4	2	—	—	—	—	—	—	—	—	—	—	2
1970	3	5	2[b]	—	—	—	—	—	—	—	—	2	1
Total		27	2	0	0	1(3)	6(9)	2(4)	2	1	2(1)	2	18
													6–9

[a] As of November 1973. [Adapted from Tokita and Wada (1974); rearranged according to the first author's suggestion.] Numbers in parentheses represent males who began temporary leaving their natal troop.

[b] Died.

[c] Three males repeatedly deserted the troop and returned.

TABLE V

State of Males Which Were Born in Katsuyama Troop[a]

Birth year	Present age	No. of births	Disappeared	Remaining
1961	11	9	9	0
1962	10	8	7	1
1963	9	12	10	2
1964	8	13	11	2
1965	7	11	7	4
1966	6	12	9	3
1967	5	13	8	5
1968	4	13	6	7
1969	3	18	8	10
1970	2	23	4	19
1971	1	15	2	13
1972	0	15	0	15
Total		162	81	81

[a]As of October 1972. [From Itoigawa (1974).]

shown for that age. Since few females leave their troops, the decreasing curve for females must approximately show the survival curve. If the mortality is the same for both sexes while they are living in the same troop, the figure shows that some males deserted the troop soon after reaching the age of 1 year. Although it is difficult to trace animals after they have left the troop, a few males are known to have changed their troop within Takasakiyama when 1 year old. Of the marked samples at Takasakiyama, almost all males disappeared from their natal

TABLE VI

Location of Males Who Disappeared from the Hakone T Natal Troop[a]

Birth year	No. of births	Died before 1 year old	Disappeared	Found in other troops after disappearing						Stayed in natal troop
				P	H	S	I	Hagachi	Not found	
1964	5	–	5	1	–	–	–	–	4	0
1965	9	–	9	3	2	–	–	2	2	0
1966	5	–	4	–	–	1	–	–	3	1
1967	6	1	5	5	–	–	–	–	–	0
1968	8	1	6	2	–	–	3	–	1	1
1969	6	–	6	–	–	–	5	–	1	0
Total	39	2	35	11	2	1	8	2	11	2

[a]As of June 1973. [Adapted from Fukuda et al. (1974).]

TABLE VII

Age of Disappearance of Males Who Were Born in Arashiyama Troop[a]

Age of disappearance	Before troop division (1954–1966)	After troop division (1967–1972)		
		Shifted to adjacent troop	Disappeared from natal troop	Disappeared from adjacent troop
0	–	–	–	–
1	–	–	–	–
2	–	1	–	–
3	–	2	1	–
4	4	25	3	–
5	9	3	3	1
6	5	3	2	2
7	5	1	1	3
8	6	–	–	3
9	6	–	–	3
10	–	–	–	–
11	–	–	3	1
12	–	–	–	–
13	1	–	–	1
Total	36	35	13	14

[a]From Norikoshi (1975).

troop before 11 or 12 years old, though a few exceptions have been recorded by the other studies. Figure 2 also includes some sample animals who may have joined from outside of Takasakiyama (compared with Fig. 5 in Section II,E).

At Ryozen A Troop there were two exceptional cases in which infants of less than one year old deserted their natal troop with their mothers, but males do not usually leave the natal troop until after they are 1 year old. Many or most of the males disappear from their natal troop when between the ages of 3 and 8 years, and only a few remain in the natal troop more than 10 years in any research area where Japanese monkeys have been studied.

C. SEASON OF DISAPPEARANCE FROM THE NATAL TROOP

Seasons when males disappeared from the natal troop are shown in Fig. 3. Some males whose exact month of disappearance was not recorded are distributed between the possible months in the graph for Ryozen (Sugiyama and Ohsawa, 1974b). The first occurrence of movement separate from the natal troop is also shown by the broken-line curve in the graph for Shiga (Tokita and

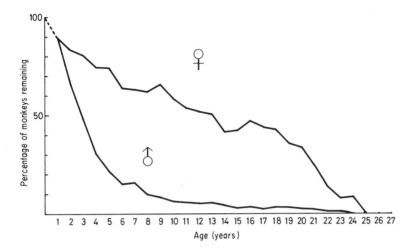

Fig. 2. Proportion of Japanese monkeys remaining in the Takasakiyama Troop, estimated from records of marked samples. (From Ohsawa *et al.*, 1976). The broken line signifies information substituted from other sources, as first-hand data were insufficient. The starting year of the tracing study and the starting age differs among animals.

Wada, 1974). In the graph for Arashiyama, the shift to the adjacent troop is shown separately from the number of disappearances, and the latter is divided into two periods, before and after the troop division (Norikoshi, 1975).

From the troops at Ryozen, 15 males out of 18, or 88.9%, disappeared between August and December. From Shiga A too, 9 males out of 14, or 64.3%, disappeared between August and December. The first attempt to move separately from the natal troop of Shiga A is more confined, 82.4% occurring between September and December. But at Arashiyama no clear seasonality in disappearance of the natal troop can be seen, though 74.3% of the shift to the adjacent troop occurred between October and January. Although the exact data were not presented, Azuma (1974) suggested that many males disappeared between April and August in Toi Troop, and Fukuda *et al.* (1974) believed that many males disappeared between May and June.

Mating behavior in Japanese monkeys usually lasts from October to December, though it begins in early September in a few areas and lasts until late March in a few others (Kawai *et al.*, 1967). In the premating season the preliminary phenomena of sexual behavior can be seen in the Ryozen troops, for example, the facial skin of subadults and young adults becomes scarlet, young couples occasionally stay together as if in consort, and adult males frequently attack

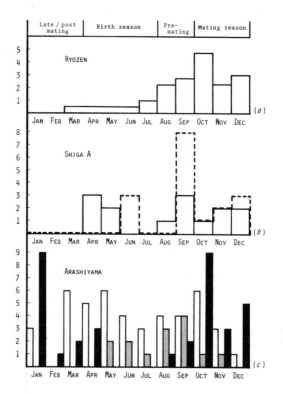

Fig. 3. Monthly distribution of male disappearances from the natal troop (more than 2 years old). (*a*) Ryozen (adapted from Sugiyama and Ohsawa, 1974b, adding new data): Some males whose exact month of disapparance was not recorded are distributed between possible months. (*b*) Shiga A (adapted from Tokita and Wada, 1974): Broken line signifies the first temporary movement away from the troop for each animal. (*c*) Arashiyama (adapted from Norikoshi, 1975): Only animals whom Norikoshi expected would become solitary are represented by the white columns (before the troop division) and shaded columns (after the division). Animals shifting to the adjacent troop are represented by black columns.

females for attracting their attention. Thus, disappearances of males from the natal troop at Ryozen and Shiga, and even shifts from the natal troop to the adjacent one at Arashiyama, coincide with the beginning and the peak of mating activity. Although the reason for leaving the natal troop by male Japanese monkeys is not yet clear, it is possible that they are stimulated by the sexual drive. It is also possible that the forest throughout Japan can supply more food in these months, and monkeys can easily get food even outside their accustomed range.

D. THE PROCESS AND CAUSE OF RENUNCIATION OF THE
   NATAL TROOP

Since the first stage of the study of Japanese monkeys at Takasakiyama, it has been well established that juvenile males 2 or 3 years of age sometimes move out to the peripheral part of the troop away from their mothers and play with age mates and elder males (Itani, 1954). Juvenile males frequently come back to their mothers in the central part, but subadults and young adults rarely do so, staying in the periphery of the troop away from their mothers all the time. The *peripheralization* of juvenile males is commonly seen not only in Takasakiyama but also in Arashiyama (Norikoshi and Koyama, 1975), in Ryozen (Sugiyama and Ohsawa, 1974b), and in all the other research areas. The term *peripheral part* will be used for convenience here in discussions of the spatial distribution of members of a troop; it contrasts with the *central part* occupied by dominant males and females. Spatial distance from the center of the troop is believed also to indicate the psychological and sociological distance from it.

From observations at Arashiyama, Norikoshi (1974) suggested that males usually left the natal troop because they were overcome by lower-ranking or younger males. However, Koyama (1967) found in the same study area that the ranks of troop members are strictly fixed by the ranks of their families. The son of a high-ranking female is thus unlikely to be overcome by lower-ranking or younger males. Nevertheless, in many troops sons of high-ranking females as well as those of low-ranking females desert the troop.

In fact, Sugiyama and Ohsawa (1974b) found that all males of Ryozen A Troop disappeared from their natal troop before the age of 6 years. (One male who deserted the troop at about 11 years of age was believed to have been born in this troop, but this was not certain as he was already about 7 years old when intensive study of the troop began.) In Ryozen A Troop, no decline in rank before a male disappeared was detected, and in many episodes high- and low-ranking subadult and young adult males deserted or disappeared at about the same time. Furthermore, a 2-year-old and a 3-year-old male who disappeared were the sons of the highest-ranking female of Ryozen Ap Troop. From these observations, it can be said both that males were not driven out by a decline in rank and that the sons of higher-ranking females do not stay longer in the natal troop than those of lower-ranking females.

The males who disappeared from Ryozen A Troop when 4 or 5 years old spent much of the daytime in the most peripheral part of the troop and actively traveled a long distance from the central part of the troop when it was resting or feeding (at the feeding ground). Occasionally these males could not be found in or near the troop for from a day to more than a month (Table VIII). For example, the male we called *Niban* was frequently out of the troop and did not return between early July and mid-August 1973. After repeatedly leaving the

TABLE VIII

Behavior of Males of Ryozen A Troop after June 1973[a]

Name of monkey	Birth year	Mother's rank	1973									1974			
			June		July			August			Nov.	Jan.	Feb.	July	Nov.
			m.	l.	e.	m.	l.	e.	m.	l.	l.				
Pyon	1968	High	+	+	+	+	—	+	+	+	—	—	—	—	D
Tonz	1968	Middle	+	+	+	+	+	+	+	+	—	—	—	—	D
Small	1968	Low	+	+	±	—	+	±	±	±	+	+	—	—	D
Niban	1969	(High)	±	±	—	—	+	±	±	±	—	—	—	—	D
Cup	1969	Middle	+	+	+	+	+	+	+	+	—	—	—	—	D
Ion	1969	Middle	+	+	±	+	—	±	±	+	—	—	—	—	D
Rabbit	1969	Low	+	±	+	+	+	+	+	+	—	—	—	—	D
Pigeon	1970	High	+	+	+	+	+	+	±	+	+	+	+	Ap	Ap[b]
Nosuri	1970	High	+	+	+	+	±	+	+	+	—	—	+	Ap	Ap
Flam	1970	Middle	+	+	±	+	+	±	±	—	+	+	+	—	D
Myna	1970	Low	+	+	+	+	±	±	—	+	+	+	—	As	As[b]
Dark	1962+	?	+	+	+	+	—	—	—	—	—	—	—	—	D

[a]Some of the data were obtained from H. Ohsawa and J. Kurland. Key: e., early; m., mid; l., late; +, found with the troop; ±, sometimes found with the troop; —, not found with the troop; D, disappeared. (Between September and mid-November there was no observation.)

[b]A part of Troop A budded out from the main troop (Ap) and formed a new troop (As).

troop and returning to it, he finally disappeared between September and November. Most other males also disappeared from Ryozen A Troop after a similar repetition of leaving and returning.

Most males who disappeared from Shiga A Troop also repeatedly left and returned to the natal troop before they finally disappeared (see Table IV; also Tokita and Wada, 1974).

During temporary absences from the troop, two or more males usually traveled together. Moreover, two or more males were frequently recorded as disappearing at the same time, and as it is difficult to believe that they died on the same day, they must have deserted the troop together. When *Dark*, the highest-ranking male of Ryozen A Troop, moved away from most of the troop members in July 1973, three young males, an old female, and a juvenile female followed him but except for a juvenile female, they came back to the troop one by one (see Table VIII). They all finally disappeared after a month or so. The rank of the male's mother was related neither to his separate movement from the natal troop nor to his leaving.

Itoigawa (1974, 1975) tried to analyze what drives males out of the natal troop at Katsuyama. Although a few more males that are more than 3 years old of the higher-ranking family stay in the natal troop than do those of lower-ranking families, no clear trend could be found. Itoigawa also analyzed the relation between the age of disappearance of a male and the maternal care he received when young, but the relationship with the mother as measured by the distance between them was not clearly related to the time the son spent in the natal troop. On the other hand, Itoigawa observed a few instances of playmates who had spent much time together deserting the natal troop as one group. In one of these cases five 5-year-old playmates, with an elder male (8 years old) who had occasionally left the troop, deserted the natal troop together, but only the elder male returned to it.

Norikoshi (1974) also observed at Arashiyama that when a male shifted to the adjacent troop, his friends in the natal troop or young males of his family might easily also shift to the adjacent troop, thereby maintaining their social bond.

From these observations we can picture the developmental process in young male Japanese monkeys as follows. After weaning, male juveniles range more widely than when they are always with their mothers and frequently visit the elder males in the peripheral part of the troop. With the elder males these juveniles then actively move longer distances and range more widely than the central males and females do. Usually after he is 3 or 4 years old, a subadult male temporarily leaves the natal troop either by himself or with playmates or an elder male, sometimes for less than a day but at other times for more than a week. Through such temporary absences from the troop, male juveniles become accustomed to a wider range than that in which the troop usually moves, and psychologically they become more independent than before. Hence, the final renunciation of the natal troop by young males is preceded by changes when they are juveniles. A decline in rank, the attractiveness of an elder male who was intimate in the natal troop but is now in the adjacent troop, sexual drive to search for new females, sufficient food throughout the forest, and other factors all may accelerate the renunciation of the troop by a young male; and a strong bond with the mother, high rank of the family, and other factors may retard it. But these are only subsidiary elements in the renunciation and are not common to most instances.

Because most males deserted their mother's troop at Arashiyama, Koyama (1974) suggests that they did so to avoid incest. However, incest avoidance can not be a factor which drives males out from the natal troop; it is only a result, not a cause, so far as the data now available indicate.

Drickamer and Vessey (1973) found that male rhesus monkeys of the Puerto Rican island colony desert the natal troop and that many of them join other troops where many females can be found. This fact suggests that males desert the troop and join another troop to get females. In Japanese monkeys, however, most young males do not immediately join another troop but stay away from any troop for a few years, as will be shown later. Moreover, our data for the Ryozen troops show that, even when there are many females and there is no adult male, young males continue to try to desert the natal troop.

E. LOCATION OF MALES AFTER RENUNCIATION OF THE
NATAL TROOP

It is extremely difficult to follow males who disappear from the troop in a natural population of Japanese monkeys. At Arashiyama, although it was a semiexperimental situation in which two divided troops persisted in or near the feeding ground for a year, Norikoshi and Koyama (1975) found that more than half of the males who had disappeared from the natal troop joined the adjacent one.

At Takasakiyama, we traced some 132 sample males who were marked artificially when 4 years old or younger (Ohsawa et al., 1976). It is believed that all these males were marked in their natal troop. Some males were marked in 1962 and have been traced since that time by Nishimura, but others were marked after that. Figure 4 has been prepared in a preliminary way as an approach to the male life table. Unfortunately, as sample numbers for animals less than 1 year old are not sufficient, data for 1-year-old animals are substituted by the census record (Masui et al., 1973). Curve 1 shows the number of males still in the natal troop. All marked males disappeared from the natal troop before reaching 12 years of age. Some males (between Curves 1 and 2) could be found both in the natal troop and in an adjacent troop, or by themselves in Takasakiyama. As the three troops of Takasakiyama come to a common feeding

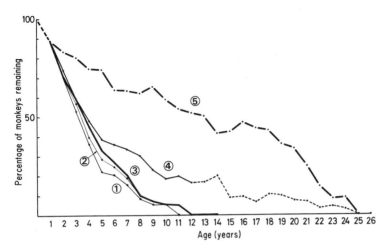

Fig. 4. Disappearance of males from the natal troop of Takasakiyama, estimated from records of marked samples. The broken line signifies information substituted from other sources, as there were insufficient first-hand data. The starting year of our tracing study differs among animals, but the marking was done at or before the age of 4 years. (From Ohsawa et al., 1976). Key: 1, remained in the natal troop; 2, sometimes left the natal troop and followed an adjacent troop; 3, disappeared temporarily; 4, shifted to an adjacent troop; 5, female-survival curve, for comparison.

ground, though the main parts of their ranges are separate from each other, it is possible for a male to follow two troops alternately before he deserts one of them. Other males (between Curves 2 and 3) temporarily left the natal troop and could not be found during the checking time (but returned to it later). Still other males (between Curves 3 and 4) shifted to the adjacent troop of Takasakiyama. Curve 5 is the expected survival rate of females redrawn from Fig. 2. Males between Curves 4 and 5 must be living outside Takasakiyama, if the mortalities of both sexes are the same.

The renunciation of the natal troop by males, which begins when they are 1–2 years old, is quite frequent until they are 7–8 years old. Before leaving finally, some males leave the natal troop temporarily and stay away from the troop, sometimes following an adjacent troop, but within a few years they disappear completely from the natal troop. Some males who shift to the adjacent troop also desert the new troop within a few years and spread over a wide area, though a few males stay in the new troop for more then 4 years (see Section III,B). A few monkeys of Takasakiyama are known to have travelled as far as 20–25 km after deserting the troop, K. Nozawa and T. Shotake (personal communication) found, from a genetic study of polymorphism of blood proteins, that the monkeys of Takasakiyama are genetically related to those of Kawaradake, which lies about 80 km northwest of that area; this finding does not necessarily indicate, of course, that a particular male traveled 80 km.

Fukuda et al. (1974) followed up the males who deserted the Hakone T Troop. Out of 39 males who were born between 1964 and 1969, 2 died when they were infants and 37 deserted the troop or disappeared. Out of the 37, 8 budded out from the natal troop and formed a new troop (Troop I); 14 were found in nearby troops; and 2 were found in a troop at Hagachi, more than 60 km from their natal troop (see Table VI). This is the longest distance which Japanese monkeys have been known to travel an their own habitat.

According to E. Tokita (personal communication) 17 males disappeared from or deserted the natal troop of Shiga A, and most of them were found later in nearby troops (Table IX).

On the other hand, no male who disappeared from Ryozen A Troop has been found in the Ryozen B (Kuregahata) Troop, although the latter is the only troop overlapping its range with that of Ryozen A (as well as Ap and As) Troop(s). This is the more surprising since 21 males who have disappeared from Ryozen A Troop have natural or artificial markings (Sugiyama and Ohsawa, 1974b), although 6 of them were found as part of all-male parties in the ranges of Ryozen A and B Troops (see Section III,D).

Let us now summarize these observations: many males who desert the natal troop join nearby troops for a few years or longer if such troops are available, but others move alone or in all-male parties, or move far away, occasionally more, then 20 km.

III. APPROACH TO AND JOINING
OF THE TROOP BY *HANAREZARU*

A. AGE AND SEASONAL DISTRIBUTION OF THE *HANAREZARU'S* APPROACH

1. Age of Hanarezaru

Though age estimates of *hanarezaru* are inevitably rather rough as they are shy, 88.0% of 50 strange males who were confirmed in or near Ryozen A (as well as Ap and As) Troop(s) were neither subadult nor young adult, nor senile, but fully adult males between 7 and 14 years old (see Table X; also Sugiyama and Ohsawa, 1975). Tokita and Wada (1974) also found a similar age distribution in the strange males who were observed near Shiga A Troop, though these may be slightly older than those of Ryozen.

The important implication is that, although many subadult and young adult

TABLE IX
Location of Males Who Disappeared from the Shiga A Natal Troop[a]

	Reappeared in adjacent troops			Returned	Did not reappear	Total
Troop name	B$_1$	B$_2$	C	A		
No. of animals	1	5	8	1[b]	4	17[c]

[a]As of 1973. (Unpublished data of E. Tokita.)

[b]After coming back to the natal troop with a serious wound, this male died.

[c]After leaving the natal troop one male joined Troop C, then shifted to Troop B$_2$. Another male joined Troop B$_2$, then disappeared. They are counted in both columns.

males that are 3–7 years old disappear from the natal troop, they seldom join any other troop immediately.

2. Seasons when Strange Males Approach

Most strange males reached Ryozen A (as well as Ap and As) Troop(s) in the premating, mating, and late mating seasons (see Table XI; also Sugiyama and Ohsawa, 1975). Since observation during mating season is somewhat difficult at Ryozen, some males must have arrived during the mating season that were not

TABLE X
Age Distribution of Strange Males Who Approached the Ryozen and Shiga A Troops

	Estimated age[a]									
	4	5	6	7	8	9	10–14	15–19	20–25	Total
No. of animals										
Ryozen A, Ap, As[b]	0	3	1	7	7	6	24	2	0	50
Shiga A[c]	1	1	0.5[d]	3	1.5	1	5	4	2	19

[a]Only animals whose ages were estimated even roughly are presented here.

[b]From Sugiyama and Ohsawa (1975).

[c]From Tokita and Wada (1974).

[d]Animals whose age estimation extends over two age classes are divided into both classes.

TABLE XI

Seasonal Distribution of Strange Males Who Approached the Ryozen and Shiga A Troops

	Jan.	Feb.	Mar.	Apr.	May	June	July	Aug.	Sep.	Oct.	Nov.	Dec.	Total
Ryozen A, Ap, As[a]		10			1			17			22		50
Shiga A[b]	1	0	0	0	1	2	6	3	7	5	12	1	38

[a]From Sugiyama and Ohsawa (1975).
[b]From Tokita and Wada (1974).

recorded by the observer: thus most males who were first found in the late mating season may have arrived during the mating season and stayed through the late mating season. The same seasonal distribution is also seen in Shiga A Troop (see Table XI; also Tokita and Wada, 1974). Norikoshi (1974) also recorded that 80% of the intertroop shifts between the two troops at Arashiyama were seen in the mating season.

During the mating season, every troop of Japanese monkeys is surrounded by many male *hanarezaru,* though it is difficult to record each strange male as he moves quickly and is shy of observers. Hence, the seasonal bias in the approach of the *hanarezaru* to the troop must be even clearer than Table XI shows. Such males frequently show courtship behavior to females of the troop to attract their attention and then mate with them. Undoubtedly the sex drive is the main reason why *hanarezaru* that have been living away from any troop approach a bisexual troop.

A genetic study of Shotake and Nozawa (1974) suggests that the mating activity of male *hanarezaru* is higher than purely behavioral observations indicate. Variants in the blood proteins of seven infants who were born in 1972, as well as of most of the members of Ryozen A Troop, were examined electrophoretically. From two infants out of seven (28.6%), a strange type of MDH (malate dehydrogenase isozyme) was found. This type was found neither in their mothers nor in any of the troop males, including a few males who stayed with the troop even after the mating season. Therefore, the fathers of these infants must have been among a group of the *hanarezaru* who approached the troop in the mating season of 1971, mated with its females, and left the troop within a few months without being captured for our examination. From this kind of genetic examination, it cannot be concluded that the other five infants had fathers in the troop, although the genetic types of their blood proteins were common to those of one of the troop males. Strange males who came to the troop only during a mating season probably fathered more than 28.6% of the infants.

3. Behavior of the Hanarezaru

Some *hanarezaru* who penetrate directly to the central part of the troop are expelled by the dominant males of the troop, aided by subordinate males and females, but some others who remain in its peripheral part can occasionally form intimate relations with younger males there and gradually reach the central part after spending many months with the troop. Many *hanarezaru* who reach the troop during the mating season try to mate with troop females, but dominant males of the troop attack and threaten them, and may expel them. But the dominant males are too busy to expel them all, and some male *hanarezaru* succeed in decoying females out of the central part of the troop and mating with them.

Between March 1970 and March 1973, Ryozen A Troop had 45–69 members, including 3–5 full adult males more than 7 years old (Sugiyama and Ohsawa, 1974a). On the other hand, during the mating seasons, more than 10 strange males were occasionally found at the same time near the troop. Some of them established intimate relations with juvenile and subadult males in the peripheral part of the troop and were seen to mate with females. Many *hanarezaru* left the troop after the mating season, but a few were allowed to stay in the central part of the troop with females as well as with the dominant males and became members of the troop. Some males who reached the troop came there every mating season continuously for a few years, and it was difficult to judge when they became members of the troop.

Five males out of 10 who joined Shiga A Troop between 1965 and 1973 were not accepted peacefully into the troop by all its members for more than 1 year after they first appeared near it (Tokita and Wada, 1974).

B. IMMIGRATION AND EMIGRATION

Immigrant males of Ryozen A Troop were always the lowest-ranking among the fully adult males when they first joined the troop. Although the ranking relation among males changed little, they climbed quickly up the rank order as the dominant males disappeared one by one from the troop, and all immigrants disappeared from the troop within 2 years (Fig. 5). The rank of an adult male in Ryozen A Troop depends little on his age, body size (weight), or other individual characteristics, but only on his length of time in the troop as an adult. This also suggests that his family's rank in his natal troop rarely influences his ranking in his new troop.

Tokita and Wada (1974) confirmed that all "immigrant" males who joined Shiga A Troop before 1969 disappeared from it before November 1973, and other males who joined after 1969 are disappearing one by one (Table XII). Although immigrants stay longer in Shiga A Troop than in Ryozen A Troop, all immigrants of both troops disappear within several years.

Fukuda *et al.* (1974) confirmed that 15 males out of 16 who were in Hakone T Troop at the time of the start of the intensive study disappeared before June 1973. One died, and 10 were found again in the nearby troops (Table VI). Norikoshi and Koyama (1975) showed that the rank order of adult males of two troops of Arashiyama almost coincides with the length of time which they have spent in the troop and that the immigrants usually disappear from the troop within 5–6 years. Ohsawa, Sugiyama, Nishimura, and Masui (1976) also found at Takasakiyama that immigrant males who came from the other troops of Takasakiyama usually disappear within 3 years (about 87.5% by a preliminary calculation), though a few males stay there more than 4 years (Ohsawa *et al.* 1976). Fukuda *et al.* (1974) traced the movement of 6 males of the Hakone area

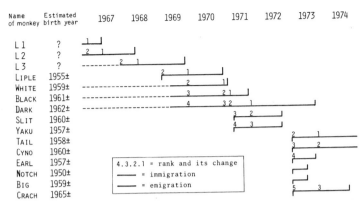

Fig. 5. Status change of fully adult males in Ryozen A Troop. Presumably, the males we called *White, Black,* and *Dark* were born in this troop, but this could not be confirmed as they were already about 7 or 8 years old when the intensive study began. (From Sugiyama and Ohsawa, 1975.)

for 10 years and found that they changed their troop and life-style in a bewildering fashion (Fig. 6). Some males changed the troop every 2 or 3 years. These studies reveal that male Japanese monkeys are usually too "nomadic" to stay in a troop throughout their long life, though a few do stay in a troop more than 10 years. Even when they are members of a troop, they may be psychologically and physically prepared to desert it without any precipitating factor, such as a decline in rank, or social or sexual dissatisfaction, and to live by themselves. *Toku,* the first-ranking male of Takasakiyama A Troop between January 1970 and January 1973, was an exceptional case who stayed in the natal troop for 21 years.

Enomoto (1974) found from observations of the sexual behavior at Shiga A Troop that a male forms an intimate social bond with a female through

TABLE XII
State of Males Who Joined Shiga A Troop[a]

	Year of joining troop									
	1965	1966	1967	1968	1969	1970	1971	1972	1973	Total
No. of animals	1	1	0	1	3	1	2	0	1	10
Again disappeared	1	1	0	1	1	0	0	0	0	4
Still in troop	0	0	0	0	2	1	2	0	1	6

[a]As of November 1973. [From Tokita and Wada (1974).]

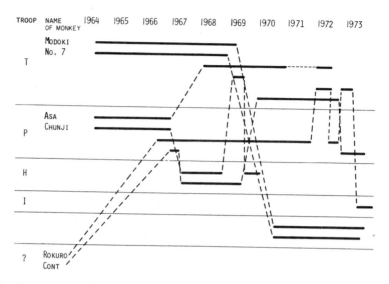

Fig. 6. Males wandering from troop to troop. The broken line shows the estimated route. (From Fukuda *et al.*, 1974.)

a family connection or the mating of previous years, but once he has formed such an intimate social bond with her he rarely mates with her any more. Norikoshi (1975) also found the same trend in the male-female relationships at Arashiyama and hypothesized that all immigrants desert the troop within several years as they have no more new females with which to mate. But his hypothesis cannot explain why all immigrants of Ryozen A Troop deserted it within 2 years though most of them had mated only with several females. Sexual dissatisfaction cannot be common factor driving males out of troops, though it may be a subsidiary factor in some cases.

C. LIFE OF THE *HANAREZARU*

Although most males disappeared within a few years both from their natal troop and from any troop which they later joined, there are not sufficient data to show where they went after they disappeared. Some may have died, some immediately joined an adjacent troop, but many others must have spent their time as *hanarezaru*. Occasionally a *hanarezaru* is found in the forest within the range of a particular troop. Much information about full adult male *hanarezaru* can be obtained from villagers, who say that during the fruiting season they are found not only inside the forest but also near cultivated fields. Even in villages and in the forest where troops are never seen, many sightings of *hanarezaru* are made, and the term *hanarezaru* is common throughout the countryside of Japan.

Many full adult males are found alone, but others, together with subadult males, live in male parties of two or more animals. At times, large male parties have been found near the troops at Arashiyama (Norikoshi and Koyama, 1975), Hakone (Fukuda et al., 1974), Takasakiyama (Masui et al., 1973), and Ryozen.

Twelve young or full adult females, out of 30 that were more than 5 years old which were recorded as members of Ryozen A (as well as Ap and As) Troops(s) between 1969–1974, are known (or probably known) to have deserted the troop alone or with their families (Sugiyama and Ohsawa, 1974a,b, and Sugiyama, 1976). Seven females out of 12 deserted the troop with their children by twos and threes and then joined together to form a new troop, As, near the range of the main troop, Ap. After repetition of temporary leaving and returning, an old mother, Gold, together with her daughter, Gray, and a grandchild finally deserted the troop. Three females, Zust, Dibo, and Hachi, came back to the troop nearly 1 year after they had deserted it, but two of them disappeared again within a few days. On the other hand, three strange females have been seen in the forest in the range of Ryozen A Troop between 1969 and 1973. One of them, New, stayed in the troop for more than a month with her newborn baby, and another was found in the forest with a strange male.

Female hanarezaru have also been recorded at Takasakiyama (Sugiyama, 1976), Katsuyama and Takagoyama (Nishida et al., 1972). Although the number of female hanarezaru is far lower than that of males, there must be a small number of females who desert the troop, although it is usually assumed that females which disappear are dead.

These observations suggest that most mating, delivery, and infant rearing are carried out in the troop, but it is possible that they sometimes occur outside of a troop, the mothers spending their time under the protection of a nearby troop only for a few months after delivery. Although most males must come to a troop to mate with females, approach to the troop is not essential for realizing their sexual desires.

D. RETURN TO THE TROOP

As we have noted, while most males do desert the natal troop sooner or later, a few male hanarezaru return to it. After desertion of the troop for 110 days between July 20 and November 7, 1956, Bacchus, the fifth-ranking male of Takasakiyama Troop, returned to it. Monk, the fourth-ranking male of the same troop, did the same after an absence of 200 days between July 28, 1956, and February 1, 1957, but disappeared again after 3 months (Mizuhara, 1957). There are a few other examples of such returns to Takasakiyama, but fewer than the number of disappearances.

Twenty-one males out of 30, former members of Ryozen A (as well as As and Ap) Troop(s) that disappeared from it after they were 2 years old, can be identified by their natural or artificial markings. *Elgo,* who deserted the troop in October–December 1970, when 4 years of age, came near to As Troop on March 26, 1974, for only a single day with three more males that were also believed to have deserted Ryozen A Troop with him. *Pyon, Tonz, Flam,* and *Nilga,* who deserted Ryozen A (and Ap) Troop(s) in 1973, 1973, 1974, and 1974, when they were 5, 5, 4, and 3 years old, respectively, were found as a male party with 5–6 more strange males in the range of Ryozen B Troop in June 1975. A full adult male, *Sango,* who came from outside, joined Ryozen As Troop in February 1974 and left it after 1 month, shifting to Ryozen Ap Troop. Although a few more deserters have been found since that time in or near the Ryozen A troop, none of them returned to it.

No male who deserted Shiga A Troop returned to it, except one who was injured and returned after an absence of 8 days and soon died (Tokita and Wada, 1974).

In summary it can be said that most males who desert their natal troop move away from its range and do not come back to it.

IV. LONGEVITY AND MORTALITY

During the early stages of field study of Japanese monkeys, some dominant males were believed to be more than 30 years old when they died (Itani *et al.,* 1963). But recent studies on the population dynamics at Takasakiyama have revealed that only a few animals survive more than 25 years. According to the records of 61 identified females, only one lived more than 24 years, and the maximum longevity ever confirmed at Takasakiyama was 27 years old. Nearly half the mature animals die when between 15 and 21 years of age (Masui *et al.,* 1974). The records of marked animals also supports this result (see Fig. 2). The same trend is also confirmed at Arashiyama (Koyama *et al.,* 1975).

As females do not usually desert the natal troop, these data must show the approximate survival rate of females, but all animals of both areas are artificially provisioned. The mortality in the natural condition must be higher than that shown in these data. If the mortality is the same for both sexes, a great number of males in between Curves 4 and 5 of Fig. 5 must be living outside as *hanarezaru.* But if the mortality of animals outside the troop is higher than that in the troop, which is communally protected from enemies and other dangers, the number of *hanarezaru* is smaller than indicated by the above studies.

Anyway, more exact records of males after they desert their natal troop, as well as better understanding of their population dynamics under natural conditions, are strongly needed at present for a comprehensive discussion of the life history of Japanese monkeys.

V. DISCUSSION AND CONCLUSION

Drickamer and Vessey (1973) and Drickamer (1974) confirmed from an intensive study of the population dynamics of a rhesus monkey colony introduced at Paraguera and Guayacan islands, Puerto Rico, that all males desert their natal troop when between 3 and 7 years of age. Although much of the habitat of Japanese monkeys has been destroyed by urbanization and industrialization, intermittent forests still exist for wild life in the mountains, and most male Japanese monkeys also desert their natal troops and spend much of their long life as wanderers. This characteristic life style of the male Japanese monkeys has been confirmed not only at Takasakiyama and Arashiyama, where the forest habitat is isolated from other wooded areas by bushland, cultivated fields, and towns, and where two or more troops have especially close relations because of provisioning (as with the rhesus monkey troops of the Puerto Rican islands), but also in rather more natural habitats where dense forests cover a large area.

Although some male Japanese monkeys which disappear must die, comparisons with the survival curves of females and some individually known cases indicate that many others which leave the troop survive. Unfortunately, it is quite difficult to follow up all the *hanarezaru* that leave the troop throughout their long life in the natural or seminatural habitat, since they may wander throughout Japan unless a water barrier or large town prevents their passage. Modern biotelemetric techniques can be used only for a few weeks and for animals whose range is limited to within a few square kilometers and is already roughly known. Our present studies can not present complete statistical data on the male life history but can present only some examples which we were fortunately able to record. Although Norikoshi (1974, 1975) and Norikoshi and Koyama (1975) believed that animals were dead if they disappeared before they were 2 years old and that others became solitary if they disappeared after 2 years of age, these assumptions are clearly incorrect.

According to Drickamer (1974), the mortality of male rhesus monkeys on the Puerto Rican islands is higher than that of females, especially after they are 4 years old, and the difference in mortality between the sexes coincides with the males' renunciation of the natal troop. Although it is uncertain whether many males died in or out of the troop, and the critical reason for the difference between the mortalities of the sexes is not known, it is likely that the *hanarezaru* are less able to find food and encounter many more dangers.

Whereas 60% of the females of the Japanese monkeys of the birth stock at Takasakiyama survive until they are 8 years old, only 10% of the male stock remain in the Takasakiyama troops until that age, so that 50% of the males would be expected to be living outside of the troop if the mortality of both sexes is same (Fig. 2). If the mortality of the male rhesus monkeys of Puerto

Rican islands applies to the male Japanese monkeys at Takasakiyama, as the survival of Drickamer's female rhesus monkeys virtually coincides with that of the female Japanese monkeys at Takasakiyama, only 16% of the male birth stock can be expected to spread into the wide areas surrounding Takasakiyama at the age of 8 years.

Many males who desert the natal troop may join nearby troops. But since the data show that the age distribution of strange males who approach the troop is higher than that of the males leaving the natal troop, most males must spend at least a few years away from any troop alone or in a male party after leaving the natal troop. However, in the particular situation at Arashiyama, and also at Takasakiyama, males can easily change from one troop to an adjacent one, as these troops occasionally are in proximity to each other.

That all or most males desert the natal troop when 3–7 years old, that most of the *hanarezaru* leave the troop after they satisfy their sexual desires, and that most males who join a troop desert again within a few years all suggest that they are not much attached to troop life—indeed, that most of them spend a large part of their life outside any troop. But, at present, we have little data on how far a male moves and travels, and how many troops a male may reach or join in his life. To discover the complete life history of male Japanese monkeys, study of an isolated colony on a small islet can contribute little, and study in the natural or seminatural habitat which is open to an adjacent forest area is essential.

Although there are some subsidiary factors which drive males out from the troop, such as a decline in rank, the example of a playmate or an elder experienced male, a weak bond with the mother, sexual dissatisfaction, or rich food distribution outside the troop's range, we have to recognize that a wandering propensity which increases with psychological development is common to all males. Observing the life history of Japanese monkeys from the long-range viewpoint, the rank order, the social role, and social hierarchy regulate social friction among spontaneously coexisting animals but have little effect on the free behavior of subordinate animals, and leadership is not restricted to a few elite males since any healthy male can become a troop leader. The social structure of Japanese monkeys is thus more fluent and their group more open than was indicated by previous studies.

Acknowledgment

During preparation of this chapter in English, Professor R. A. Hinde of Cambridge University repeatedly encouraged me and kindly revised the manuscript. E. Tokita of the Jigokudani Monkey Park (Shiga-Kogen) kindly gave me unpublished information. I have cited unpublished data which were collected jointly with my colleagues, A. Nishimura, H. Ohsawa, and K. Masui. I would like to express my heartfelt appreciation to them all.

References[1]

Azuma, S. 1974. Peripheralization and solitarization in Toi-Misaki Troop. *AFSJM* **I**, 12–21. (J)

Drickamer, L. C. 1974. A ten-year summary of reproductive data for free-ranging *Macaca mulatta. Folia Primatol.* **31**, 61–80.

Drickamer, L. C., and Vessey, S. H. 1973. Group changing in free-ranging male rhesus monkeys. *Primates* **14**, 359–368.

Enomoto, T. 1974. The sexual behavior of Japanese monkeys. *J. Hum. Evol.* **3**, 351–372.

Fukuda, F., Muramatsu, M., and Tanaka, S. 1974. Leaving and joining among troops by males of Yugawara-T Troop. *AFSJM* **I**, 41–46. (J)

Imanishi, K. 1957. Identification: a process of enculturation in subhuman society of *Macaca fuscata. Primates* **1**(1), 1–29. (J)

Itani, J. 1954. "Japanese Monkeys of Taksakiyama." Kobunsha, Tokyo. (J)

Itani, J. and Tokuda, K. 1958. "Japanese Monkeys of Koshima Islet." Kobunsha, Tokyo. (J)

Itani, J., Tokuda, K., Furuya, Y., Kano, K., and Shin, Y. 1963. The social construction of natural troops of Japanese monkeys in Takasakiyama. *Primates* **4**(3), 1–42.

Itoigawa, N. 1974. Factors influencing leaving of males from group in Katsuyama. *AFSJM* **I**, 22–27. (J)

Itoigawa, N. 1975. Variables in male leaving a group of Japanese macaques. *Proc. Symp. Congr. Int. Primatol. Soc., 5th.* pp. 233–245.

Kano, K. 1964. On the second division of the natural troop of Japanese monkeys in Takasakiyama. *In* "Wild Japanese Monkeys in Takasakiyama" (J. Itani, J. Ikeda, and T. Tanaka, eds.), pp. 42–73. Keiso-Shobo, Tokyo. (J)

Kawai, M., Azuma, S., and Yoshiba, K. 1967. Ecological studies of reproduction in Japanese monkeys *(Macaca fuscata).* 1. Problems of the birth season. *Primates* **8**, 35–73.

Koyama, N. 1967. On dominance rank and kinship of a wild Japanese monkey troop in Arashiyama. *Primates* **8**, 189–216.

Koyama, N. 1970. Changes in dominance rank and division of a wild Japanese monkey troop in Arashiyama. *Primates* **11**, 335–390.

Koyama, N. 1974. Division of Arashiyama troop—its mechanism and blood relationship. *Anima* **11**, 31–36. (J)

Koyama, N., Norikoshi, K., and Mano, T. 1975. Population dynamics of Japanese monkeys at Arashiyama. *In* "Contemporary Primatology" (S. Kondo, A. Ehara, and M. Kawai, eds.), pp. 411–417. Karger, Basel.

Masui, K., Ohsawa, H., Nishimura, A., and Sugiyama, Y. 1973. Population study of Japanese monkeys at Takasakiyama. I. *J. Anthropol. Soc. Nippon* **81**, 236–248.

Masui, K., Sugiyama, Y., Nishimura, A., and Ohsawa, H. 1974. Life table of Japanese monkeys at Takasakiyama (Preliminary). *AFSJM* **I**, 47–54. (J)

Mizuhara, H. 1957. "The Japanese Monkeys." Sanichi-Shobo, Tokyo. (J)

Nishida, T. 1966. A sociological study of solitary male monkeys. *Primates* **7**, 141–204.

Nishida, T., Sugiyama, Y., and Itoigawa, N. 1972. The female *hanarezaru. Monkey* **16**(3), 36. (J)

Nishimura, A. 1973. The third fission of a Japanese monkey group at Takasakiyama. *In* "Behavioral Regulators of Behavior in Primates" (C. R. Carpenter, ed.), pp. 115–123. Bucknell Univ. Press, Lewisburg.

[1] Abbreviations: *AFSJM*, "Life History of Male Japanese Monkeys—Advances in the Field Studies of Japanese Monkeys" (K. Wada, S. Azuma, and Y. Sugiyama, eds.), Vol. I. Kyoto Univ. Primate Research Inst., Inuyama, Japan. Also, (J) means *written in Japanese.*

Norikoshi, K. 1974. Changes in troop membership of Japanese monkey males and the social structure of wild monkey troops in Arashiyama. *AFSJM* I, 35–40. (J)

Norikoshi, K. 1975. The *hanarezaru*–social structure of Japanese monkeys. *Shizen* 30(5), 35–45. (J)

Norikoshi, K., and Koyama, N. 1975. Group shifting and social organization among Japanese monkeys. *Proc. Symp. Congr. Int. Primatol. Soc., 5th*. pp. 43–61.

Ohsawa, H., Sugiyama, Y., Nishimura, A. and Masui, K. 1976. Population study of Japanese monkeys at Takasakiyama by marking trace. *In* "Population Dynamics of Japanese Monkeys at Takasakiyama." Oita City Municipal Office, Oita (in press). (J)

Shotake, T., and Nozawa, K. 1974. Genetic polymorphisms in blood proteins in the troops of Japanese macaques, *Macaca fuscata*, I. Cytoplasmic malate dehydrogenase polymorphism in *Macaca fuscata* and other non-human primates. *Primates* 15, 219–226.

Sugiyama, Y. 1960. On the division of a natural troop of Japanese monkeys at Takasakiyama. *Primates* 2(2), 109–148.

Sugiyama, Y. 1976. Life history of Japanese monkeys, *In* "Animal Behavior," Kyoritsu-Shuppan, Tokyo (in press). (J)

Sugiyama, Y., and Ohsawa, H. 1974a. Population dynamics of Japanese macaques at Ryozenyama, Suzuka Mts. I. General view. *Jap. J. Ecol.* 24, 50–59. (J)

Sugiyama, Y., and Ohsawa, H. 1974b. Population dynamics of Japanese macaques at Ryozenyama. II. Life history of males. *FASJM* I, 55–62. (J)

Sugiyama, Y., and Ohsawa, H. 1975. Life history of male Japanese macaques at Ryozenyama. *In* "Contemporary Primatology" (S. Kondo, A. Ehara, and M. Kawai, eds.), pp. 407–410. Karger, Basel.

Sugiyama, Y., Ohsawa, H., Nishimura, A. and Masui, K. 1976. Population study of Japanese monkeys at Takasakiyama by periodical censuses. *In* "Population Dynamics of Japanese Monkeys at Takasakiyama," Oita City Municipal Office, Oita (in press).

Tokita, E., and Wada, K. 1974. Some characters of leaving and joining by males among A-Troop and its neighbouring troops at Shiga Height. *AFSJM* I, 28–34. (J)

Feeding Behavior of the Pigeon[1]

H. Philip Zeigler

DEPARTMENT OF PSYCHOLOGY, HUNTER COLLEGE
CITY UNIVERSITY OF NEW YORK
AND
DEPARTMENT OF ANIMAL BEHAVIOR,
AMERICAN MUSEUM OF NATURAL HISTORY, NEW YORK, NEW YORK

[1] This work is dedicated to the memory of Daniel S. Lehrman (1919–1972), first editor of this series.

I. INTRODUCTION

The comparative study of behavior involves the analysis of similarities and differences in the behavior of animals, both within and between major taxonomic divisions. Such analyses require comparisons among a variety of species whose morphology, behavior, and ecology are sufficiently diverse to reflect the range of solutions which have evolved to meet the adaptive requirements of the environment.

From the standpoint of a comparative analysis of feeding behavior, the study of feeding in birds would be expected to yield impressive dividends. The class Aves exhibits an enormous variety of morphological and behavioral specializations for feeding which are reflected most strikingly in the relation between bill structure and food source. The role of such specializations in the adaptive radiation of birds is well documented (Lack, 1947; Storer, 1971) and in recent years there has also been a growing interest in the ecological significance of various aspects of their feeding behavior (Orians, 1971). What have been noticeably lacking, however, are studies of the relation between the neural and behavioral mechanisms mediating food intake in birds.

The paucity of such studies is all the more surprising because it is now more than 150 years since Flourens (1824) published his classic observations on the feeding behavior of the decerebrate pigeon. Although research on feeding behavior has flourished within psychology and physiology (Code, 1967), it has focused largely on a few mammalian species—most notably the rat—and provided little or no systematic data on feeding behavior mechanisms in other vertebrate classes. The neglect of avian neurobehavioral mechanisms was due in part to the widely held assumption that the brains of birds and mammals represent entirely different directions of vertebrate evolution. Within the past decade research by Karten and his associates (Karten, 1969; Karten and Hodos, 1967; Cohen and Karten, 1974) has challenged this assumption and has provided an anatomical foundation for the systematic study of avian brain mechanisms (see also Pearson, 1972; Goodman and Schein, 1974; Wright et al., 1975). Much of this research has been carried out with the pigeon, and many investigators have come to view this species both as an extremely useful preparation for neurobehavioral studies and as an excellent "representative" of the class Aves.

While acknowledging that no single avian species can possibly be "representative" of the entire class (Schleidt, 1974a; Zeigler, 1973c), it must also be acknowledged that the pigeon does have many characteristics which make it an excellent subject for the experimental study of avian feeding behavior mechanisms. By contrast with some other avian groups (e.g., hummingbirds, pelicans, ducks, or parrots) the pigeon's feeding apparatus is relatively unspecialized structurally. However, like other birds its alimentary and digestive systems differ in many respects from those of mammals and include a number of distinctive avian features, such as the absence of teeth and the subdivision of its gastric apparatus into a glandular and a muscular stomach. The pigeon is also one of a number of birds possessing a crop sufficiently well developed to serve as a storage organ (Zisweiler and Farner, 1972).

In addition to these general characteristics, certain specific attributes of its feeding behavior make the pigeon a highly suitable "model system" (Cohen, 1975; Kandel, 1974) for the study of vertebrate feeding behavior mechanisms: (1) The behavioral response is species typical and consists of a sequence of movement patterns which possess relatively limited intra- and intersubject variability. The spatiotemporal organization of these movement patterns involves a time scale (milliseconds) comparable with that used by the neurophysiologist. The pigeon's feeding behavior is thus amenable to precise spatiotemporal description and to the quantitative specification of its response dynamics in a manner compatible with neurophysiological analysis. (2) As a gramnivorous bird, the pigeon's feeding behavior involves a "quantal" response (pecking) which is easily "digitized" for recording purposes. It does not present the problem of defining a "natural" feeding response that arises in the study of most laboratory mammals. (3) Unlike the rat, the movement patterns constituting eating and drinking in the pigeon are distinctive. The differences in response topography are evident not only in responses to water and food but also in the case of operant key-pecking responses in a hungry and thirsty pigeons (Wolin, 1968; Smith, 1967; Jenkins and Moore, 1973). This is a distinct advantage in studies designed to dissociate neural mechanisms underlying hunger and thirst. (4) The morphology and sensory innervation of the pigeon's oral region are such as to make it a useful preparation for deafferentation studies on the role of orosensory mechanisms in the control of feeding behavior (Zeigler, 1973a). (5) A growing body of anatomical, electrophysiological, and neurobehavioral data suggests that studies of the neural control of feeding in the pigeon are likely to contribute significantly to our understanding of mammalian feeding behavior mechanisms. These data indicate that, despite marked differences in morphology and gross location, many nuclear groupings in the avian forebrain have connections and functional associations comparable with those of regions of the mammalian thalamus and neocortex (Karten, 1969). The distribution of avian retinal projections is similar in birds and mammals (Cohen and Karten, 1974), and there are marked similarities between the avian and mammalian trigeminal systems (Zeigler and Witkovsky, 1968) and in the functional organization of certain efferent pathways in birds and mammals (Zeier and Karten, 1971; Towe, 1973). Finally, recent studies from our laboratory have extended our findings on the trigeminal control of feeding from the pigeon to the rat (Zeigler and Karten, 1974).

The control of feeding behavior in any vertebrate species is likely to involve several sensory systems (both interoceptive and exteroceptive), as well as a variety of nuclei and pathways at several levels of the brain. Analysis of the neural mechanisms involved is obviously a task of daunting complexity. In organizing a program of research on avian feeding mechanisms we have therefore made two simplifying procedural assumptions. First, that the behavioral events constituting feeding should be specified with precision and dissected into the smallest *behaviorally meaningful* units (Barlow, 1968) in such a way as to make possible the eventual correlation of behavioral and neural events. Second, that the analysis of neural mechanisms can most fruitfully begin peripherally (i.e., with peripheral afferent and efferent structures), moving eventually towards an analysis of central mechanisms.

Since the neural "control" of any behavior is mediated by a moment-to-moment flow of behavioral sequences with respect to a specific environment ("niche-transactions"; Welker, 1976), the analysis of such transactions is a prerequisite for the study of neural mechanisms (e.g., Pfaff *et al.*, 1974). For this reason the first part of this review is devoted to an analysis of behavioral mechanisms involved in the food intake of the pigeon.

II. CONTROL OF FOOD AND WATER INTAKE
AND THE REGULATION OF BODY WEIGHT

In view of the paucity of information on avian feeding behavior one of our first tasks was the acquisition of a body of systematic data on food and water intake and body weight in pigeons maintained under ad lib conditions for prolonged periods. In addition to its comparative interest, the acquisition of such data is a first step in the study of regulatory processes in any species.

The data in Fig. 1 and Tables I and II illustrate several characteristics of the ingestive behavior of pigeons maintained under ad lib conditions: (*a*) Daily intake fluctuates about a mean which is typical for a given bird, but these variations may be considerable, with coefficients of variation ranging from 0.16 to 0.47 (Table I). (*b*) By contrast with the variability of daily intake the *rate* of

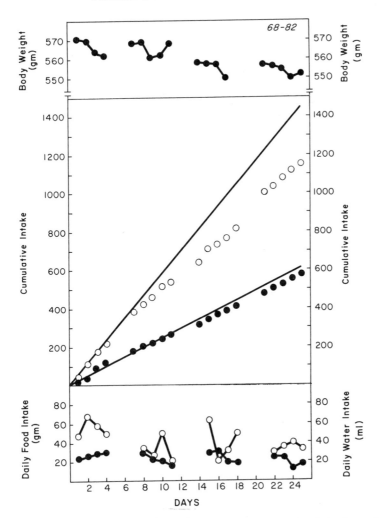

Fig. 1. Food (●——●, in grams) and water (○——○, in milliliters) intake and body weight regulation in the pigeon. Data are for a single representative bird over four successive weeks. Weekend data, excluded from the bottom portion of the figure, are included in calculating the rate of intake plotted in the middle portion. The top portion indicates variability in body weight over the 4-week period. (From Zeigler et al., 1972.)

eating and drinking tends to remain relatively constant over extended periods (Fig. 1). (c) Food and water intake are correlated and directly proportional to body weight (Table II). (d) Despite marked fluctuations in intake the pigeon's body weight tends to be relatively stable with coefficients of variation ranging from 0.008 to 0.020 (Table I). These data suggest, first, that the processes controlling eating and drinking are interrelated in the pigeon and, second, that the control of food and water intake is critically involved in the regulation of body weight.

A. INTERACTION OF EATING AND DRINKING

Under ad lib conditions the average daily water intake of pigeons is about 150% of their food intake. While there are no available data on the temporal association of eating and drinking behavior in the pigeon, McFarland (1964, 1967; McFarland and Lloyd, 1973) has shown that in the Barbary Dove, a closely related species, eating and drinking vary in phase with each other under both ad lib and deprivation conditions. A close temporal association between food and water intake has also been demonstrated in the Japanese Quail (Van Hemel and Meyer, 1969) and the chicken (Lepkovsky et al., 1960). This temporal association probably reflects the fact that eating and drinking behavior in these species is interdependent, and this interdependence is most evident during periods of food and water deprivation. Total water deprivation is followed by a drastic reduction in food intake, and food deprivation produces an equally significant reduction in water intake (Fig. 2). Partial food deprivation produces a reduction in water intake that is directly proportional to the size of the available food ration (Zeigler, 1974, Fig. 5b).

The interdependence of eating and drinking in the pigeon is similar to that seen in a variety of mammalian species (e.g., Bolles, 1961; Strominger, 1947; Cizek, 1959; Kutscher, 1969). Moreover, our data on the relation between the two behaviors have proved to be of considerable value in interpreting the deficits seen after lesions of brain structures mediating ingestive behavior in the pigeon (see Section VII).

B. REGULATION OF BODY WEIGHT

Following Brobeck, Stevenson (1969) has made a useful distinction between the concepts of *regulation* and *control.* It is an essential part of the distinction that regulation implies "the preservation of a relatively constant value" of some parameter, whereas control refers to the mechanisms by which such regulation is achieved. This distinction provides a useful framework for our discussion of the relation between feeding behavior and weight regulation in the pigeon.

Adult pigeons given unrestricted access to food and water characteristically maintain relatively stable body weights in the face of significant variations in their daily intake. Similar data have been reported for a number of mammalian species, suggesting the operation of mechanisms controlling intake over extended periods and regulating body weight within fairly narrow limits. The most striking evidence for the existence of such regulatory processes in the pigeon comes from

TABLE I

Variability in Daily Food and Water Intake and Body Weight
in Pigeons Maintained under Free-Feeding Conditions[a]

Bird number	Food intake			Water intake			Body weight (gm)		
	Mean	SD	V	Mean	SD	V	Mean	SD	V
68–79	20.8	6.4	0.31	38.4	6.9	0.18	503	4.2	0.008
68–80	19.9	6.6	0.33	33.5	8.2	0.24	533	4.7	0.009
68–82	23.6	5.1	0.22	41.3	13.9	0.34	500	7.4	0.013
68–83	25.3	4.8	0.19	49.0	12.4	0.25	616	10.2	0.017
68–84	20.0	9.2	0.46	19.6	6.2	0.31	506	4.7	0.009
68–85	38.0	8.5	0.22	75.0	12.4	0.16	530	7.3	0.011
68–86	35.8	6.9	0.19	87.6	41.0	0.47	542	5.6	0.010
68–87	32.4	7.2	0.22	41.5	5.0	0.12	595	11.9	0.020
68–88	20.5	7.9	0.39	25.8	7.3	0.28	494	6.4	0.013
68–89	25.4	7.2	0.28	32.8	12.7	0.39	517	11.4	0.022
68–90	24.5	6.6	0.27	43.9	12.6	0.28	523	9.9	0.018
68–91	33.2	6.7	0.20	42.6	10.8	0.25	583	11.6	0.019

[a]SD, standard deviation; V, coefficient of variation.

TABLE II

Relation between Food and Water Intake and Body Weight
in Pigeons Maintained under Free-Feeding Conditions[a]

Bird number	Ratio: water/food		Correlation: water and food		Ratio: food/weight (mean)	Ratio: water/weight (mean)
	Mean	SD	r	p		
68–79	1.84	0.65	+0.06	NS	0.041	0.075
68–80	1.68	0.30	+0.76	0.01	0.037	0.061
68–82	1.75	0.29	+0.73	0.01	0.042	0.073
68–82	1.93	0.05	+0.95	0.01	0.040	0.079
68–83	0.98	0.20	+0.78	0.01	0.039	0.039
68–85	1.97	0.30	+0.80	0.01	0.070	0.17
68–86	2.44	1.10	+0.42	0.10	0.064	0.14
68–87	1.28	0.27	+0.55	0.10	0.053	0.069
68–88	1.25	0.24	+0.47	0.10	0.041	0.052
68–89	1.29	0.27	+0.70	0.01	0.048	0.064
68–90	1.79	0.32	+0.63	0.01	0.046	0.083
68–91	1.28	0.12	+0.45	0.10	0.056	0.073

[a]SD, standard deviation; r, Spearman rank-order correlation coefficient; p,
probability.

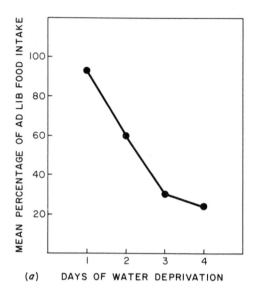

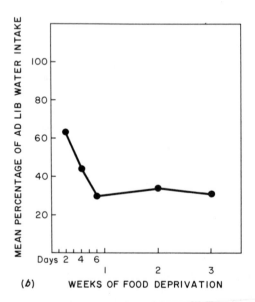

Fig. 2. The interaction of eating and drinking in the pigeon: (*a*) Effects of total water deprivation upon food intake. (*b*) Effects of total food deprivation upon water intake. (From Zeigler *et al.*, 1972.)

analyses of the relation between food intake and body weight (Zeigler *et al.,* 1972).

These studies indicate that there is a linear relation between the log food intake and the log body weight. The relation holds not only under ad lib conditions but also under food deprivation. Thus, during a period of total food deprivation the log body weight declines linearly with time, whereas under partial food deprivation (Fig. 3) the log body weight declines to an asymptotic value which is a linear function of food intake. Furthermore, the linear relation between log intake and log body weight is also present during recovery from food deprivation, since log body weight *gain* is a linear function of log food intake. As the pigeon approaches its ad lib weight, an increasing proportion of its food intake is needed merely to maintain its current body weight, while a decreasing proportion of its intake is available for conversion into additional body weight.

The similarity of our findings on the regulation of body weight in the pigeon to those reported for mammals (Collier, 1969) is of considerable interest in view of the many differences between the alimentary apparatus and digestive systems of birds and mammals (Zisweiler and Farner, 1972). Moreover a series of studies to be reviewed below has demonstrated that in both the rat and the pigeon body weight, rather than food deprivation, is the operative variable producing changes in the animal's "motivational" state.

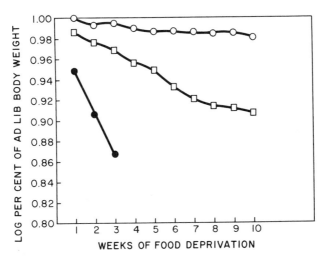

Fig. 3. Relation between food deprivation and body weight loss. Effects of total and partial food deprivation. (●——●), 0% Ration; (□——□), 50% ration; (○——○), 80% ration. (From Zeigler *et al.,* 1972.)

III. HUNGER IN THE PIGEON:
BEHAVIORAL RESPONSES TO FOOD DEPRIVATION

Like most animals, the pigeon does not eat constantly even when the stimulus which presumably elicits eating (i.e., food) is present. Moreover, under conditions of food deprivation pigeons typically show an increased responsiveness to food. Such variation in responsiveness to a constant stimulus is one of the hallmarks of "motivated" behavior (Lashley, 1938) and, in the case of feeding, is usually described by the term "hunger." Because hunger is a behavioral construct, inferred from behavioral observations, the problem of measurement is a critical one (Hinde, 1970; Bolles, 1967).

Increased responsiveness to food may be reflected in some parameter of feeding behavior itself (e.g., latency, rate) or in the probability that an animal will engage in previously learned instrumental behaviors reinforced with food. The observed relations between food deprivation and its behavioral consequences are assumed to reflect the operation of "motivational" processes underlying hunger. Because these measures of hunger are not always highly correlated, some investigators distinguish between "consummatory" and "motivational" measures (Miller, 1967) or between "reflexive" and "motivated" behavior (Teitelbaum, 1967). Indeed, Teitelbaum has argued that the operation of motivational processes may be inferred unambiguously only in situations involving the performance of reinforced operant responses. The theoretical merits

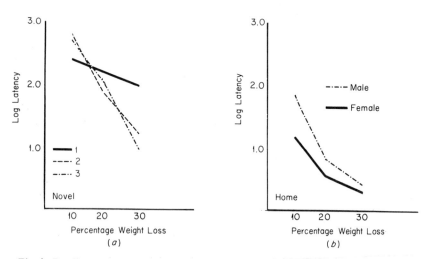

Fig. 4. Readiness to eat as a function of body weight loss in the pigeon. The data are for birds tested both in the home cage and in a novel environment. The parameter in the "novel" graph (a) is replications while that in the "home" graph (b) is sex. (From Megibow and Zeigler, 1968.)

of this distinction are arguable (Campbell and Misanin, 1969), and our own results (cf. Section VIII) suggest that such distinctions may be irrelevant to the causal analysis of feeding behavior mechanisms. Moreover, it is becoming increasingly clear that hunger is not a unitary process and that systematic comparisons among several measures of feeding behavior can help to dissociate the component mechanisms involved. Considerations such as these have prompted us to examine the effect of food deprivation upon a variety of different behavioral

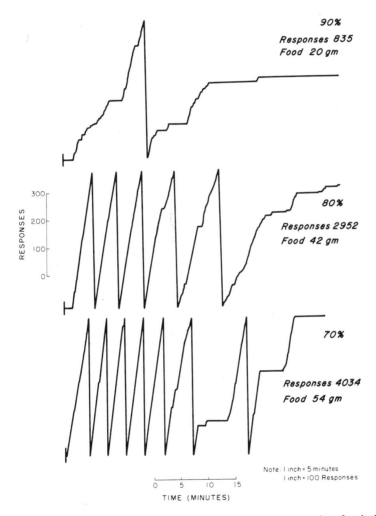

Fig. 5. Cumulative feeding responses and food intake in 1-hour test sessions for single bird tested at 90, 80, and 70% of its free-feeding weight. (From Zeigler and Feldstein, 1971. Copyright 1971 by the Society for the Experimental Analysis of Behavior, Inc.)

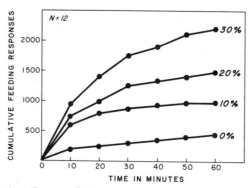

Fig. 6. Effects of body weight loss upon the frequency of feeding responses and the time course of satiation during a 1-hour test period. (From Zeigler *et al.*, 1971. *J. Comp. Physiol. Psychol.* **76**, 468–477. Copyright 1971 by The American Psychological Association. Reprinted by permission.)

measures. In all these studies the independent variable is percentage of body weight loss rather than hours of deprivation.

Figures 4, 5, and 6 present functions relating body weight loss to the latency, rate, and persistence of the pigeon's feeding behavior. The latency data represent perhaps the simplest measure of a behavioral response to food deprivation and have the additional advantage of being unconfounded by oropharyngeal and postingestional consequences of eating. Readiness to eat in the pigeon, as in the rat (Bolles, 1965) varies directly with body weight loss in both a home cage and novel test situation. As the latency of its feeding behavior decreases the amount of food consumed in the test increases, and there is a significant correlation between these two measures of hunger.

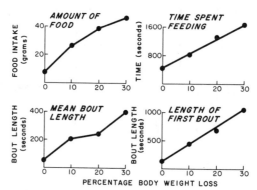

Fig. 7. Functions relating body weight loss and several measures of the consummatory response during a 1-hour test period. (From Zeigler *et al.*, 1971. *J. Comp. Physiol. Psychol.* **76**, 468–477. Copyright 1971 by The American Psychological Association. Reprinted by permission.)

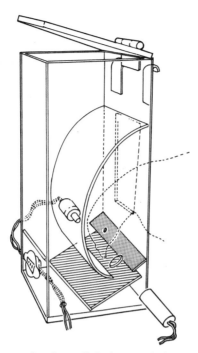

Fig. 8. Schematic diagram of a photocell feedometer designed for automatic monitoring of feeding in the pigeon. (From Zeigler and Feldstein, 1971. Copyright 1971 by the Society for the Experimental Analysis of Behavior, Inc.)

The data of Figs. 5, 6, and 7 were obtained in a 1-hour test situation during which feeding behavior was automatically monitored by a photocell feedometer designed for use with the pigeon (Fig. 8). Both the rate and persistence of this short-term feeding behavior are directly proportional to body weight loss. Since the correlation between feedometer responses and food intake is about +0.93, it is not surprising to find that food intake is proportional to body weight loss over a wide range of deprivation conditions. As Fig. 7 indicates, this increase in food intake is the result of increases in the initial rate of feeding, the length of the first feeding bout, and the duration of subsequent bouts but does not involve an increase in the number of bouts. Similar findings have been reported for the licking responses of rats in studies of short-term drinking behavior following periods of water deprivation (e.g., Stellar and Hill, 1952).

Figure 9 illustrates the long-term effects upon the pigeon's food intake of varying degrees of body weight loss. Following a prolonged period of food deprivation the pigeon exhibits a compensatory increase in food intake that is approximately proportional to the body weight loss during deprivation. This compensatory overeating continues until the original body weight is recovered.

Finally, instrumental responses such as key pecking in the pigeon or bar

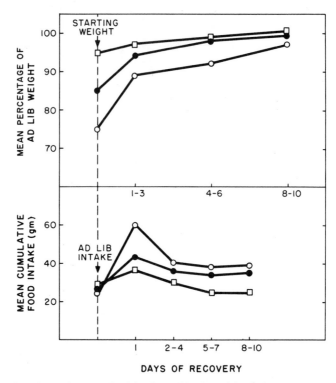

Fig. 9. The relation between food intake and body weight during recovery from varying degrees of weight loss in the pigeon. Following a period of food deprivation sufficient to produce a weight loss of 5 (□), 15 (●), or 25 (○)%, birds were given unlimited access to food. Intake over the next 10 days was proportional to body weight loss and compensatory overeating was evident in all groups. (From Zeigler and Karten, 1973a.)

pressing in rats may be used as a measure of hunger. Previous studies of food deprivation and responsiveness in pigeons (Ferster and Skinner, 1957; Reese and Hogenson, 1962) and chickens (Collier, 1969) suggest that food-reinforced instrumental responding will also vary directly with body weight loss.

Thus weight loss is an excellent predictor of responsiveness to food in the pigeon whether we use consummatory or operant measures. In fact, the various measures which have been used are correlated in the pigeon to a far greater extent than has yet been shown for the rat. This difference between the two species probably reflects the presence, in the pigeon, of a crop sufficiently well developed to serve as a storage organ. In any case the pigeon's behavioral responses to food deprivation indicate that it can detect the extent of its body weight loss and respond to it by means of both short-term and long-term adjustments in its food intake.

IV. THE "CONSUMMATORY RESPONSE" OF
EATING IN THE PIGEON

The food intake of any animal is mediated by feeding response sequences (feeding bouts) whose frequency, duration, and temporal distribution exhibit periodicities (feeding patterns) characteristic of both the individual and the species. These feeding bouts in turn are themselves composed of relatively stereotyped movement patterns (e.g., pecking, chewing, licking, striking, swallowing), which are also species typical (e.g., see Hutchinson and Taylor, 1962; Dawkins and Dawkins, 1973). Such movement patterns ("fixed action patterns" (FAPs); "modal action patterns") have received considerable attention from students of animal behavior. Because of their stereotypy and relative simplicity such patterns have often been studied by ethologists and psychologists as particulate elements of more complex behaviors (Barlow, 1968; Schleidt, 1974b). For the neurophysiologist they offer possible paradigms for analysis of the neural control of behavior patterning (Bullock, 1961; Hinde, 1970).

The movement patterns which constitute eating in the pigeon are of interest in both these respects. Because the temporal organization of the patterns involves a time scale (milliseconds) comparable to that of neural activity, they may be useful neurobehavioral "units" which can serve as end points for the analysis of feeding behavior mechanisms. Moreover, any variable affecting food intake (e.g., deprivation, drugs, lesions, stimulation) must do so via its effect upon one or more parameters of the consummatory response. We have therefore devoted considerable effort to the study of such movement patterns, particularly their behavioral morphology, sensory integration, and motivational control.

A. SPATIOTEMPORAL ORGANIZATION

Examination of film records taken at speeds from 64 to 500 frames/second indicates that the "consummatory" behavior of eating in the pigeon involves the spatial and temporal integration of at least four distinct movement patterns—pecking, grasping, mandibulation, and swallowing. The sequential performance of these four patterns constitutes a *feeding response,* and a *feeding bout* consists of a series of such feeding responses. The spatiotemporal organization of the pigeon's feeding response is illustrated diagrammatically in Fig. 10.

Pecking, with which the response cycle begins, consists of a downward movement of the head with the mouth initially closed and eye fully open. As the head approaches the grain the eyelid and nictitating membrane gradually close and the mouth gradually opens so that the eye is shut and the mouth fully open just prior to contact of the beak with the grain. Contact with the grain terminates the downward head movement and is followed by closing of the beak around the grain, i.e., *grasping.* This is followed by *mandibulation,* the process by which

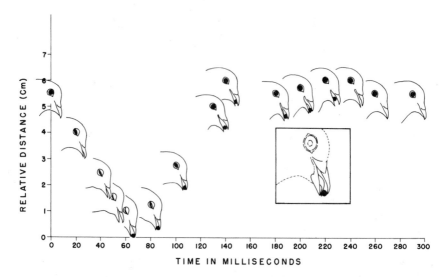

Fig. 10. Feeding behavior movement patterns in the pigeon: the spatial and temporal organization of the response sequences that constitute feeding. The inset diagrams the relation of the tongue to the grain during mandibulation. Drawings are based upon individual motion picture frames taken at speeds between 64 and 500 frames/second.

grain is moved from the beak tip to the back of the mouth. Mandibulation involves a decelerating movement of head withdrawal, punctuated at its start by one or more sharp jerks or shakes of the head which serve to toss the grain from the beak tip into the buccal cavity. Toward the end of mandibulation, while the head is still moving upward, the mouth closes completely and a movement of *swallowing* terminates the response cycle.

Several qualitative features of the pigeon's eating behavior merit further comment. First, the extent of beak opening varies with the size of the grain presented, and this adjustment is made *prior* to tactual contact of the beak with the grain. Second, in addition to the head movements involved in mandibulation, the process also involves a sequence of quasi-peristaltic tongue movements which make an important contribution to mandibulation. Not only do these tongue movements help pass the grain to the back of the mouth, but, by pressing the grain against the palate, they provide a continuous flow of tactile information about its position within the oral cavity. Third, although the pigeon picks up only one grain with each pecking response, a swallowing response does not invariably occur for every pecking response. In some response cycles two and sometimes three grains may be visible in the buccal cavity, one of which has been retained at the back of the mouth from a previous peck. The rearmost grain on the tongue is then brought forward, remandibulated, and swallowed while the newly pecked grain remains at the back of the throat (see also White, 1969).

TABLE III
Temporal Organization of the Components of the Consummatory Response (Duration in Milliseconds)[a]

Bird number	Observation number	Peck			Mandibulation			Swallow			Total
		Mean	SD	V	Mean	SD	V	Mean	SD	V	
118	18	66	13	0.20	178	33	0.19	74	19	0.26	318
337	21	60	9	0.15	149	31	0.21	69	15	0.22	278
535	24	66	7	0.11	147	21	0.14	72	28	0.39	285
509	12	68	8	0.12	206	28	0.14	64	20	0.31	338
380	12	68	20	0.29	128	16	0.13	82	31	0.38	230
372	14	76	18	0.24	131	11	0.08	113	25	0.22	262

[a]SD, standard deviation; V, coefficient of variation.

The quantitative data presented in Table III and Fig. 10 indicate the brevity and relative stereotypy of the movement patterns constituting eating. The entire response cycle takes between 250 and 350 msec, the temporal relationships among its components are quite constant for a given bird and differences among birds are minimal. Schleidt (1974b) has suggested that a useful measure of stereotypy in species-typical movement patterns is the coefficient of variation ($V = s/\bar{x}$), where s is the standard deviation and $\bar{x}$ is the mean. The statistic V may be used to specify the degree of stereotypy along a dimension ranging from randomness ($V = 1$) to relative fixity ($V \leqslant 0.1$). The statistic has been calculated for the data in Table III and indicates that the stereotypy of the movement patterns of eating in the pigeon is comparable to that of other species-typical action patterns (Schleidt, 1974b).

B. EFFECTS OF DEPRIVATION

Food deprivation in the pigeon is followed by an increase in short-term feeding behavior which is approximately proportional to body weight loss. Such increased intake within a fixed time period may be accomplished by shortening one of the component movement patterns of the feeding response, by reducing the interval between successive responses, or by some combination of these strategies. In order to distinguish among these alternatives we carried out a computer analysis of interresponse intervals in six birds whose feeding behavior was monitored at several different body weight levels. In three of the birds the movement patterns were also photographed to provide data on the effects of deprivation upon the spatiotemporal organization of the feeding response.

Figure 11 shows a series of histograms illustrating the effects of weight loss upon the distribution of intervals between successive feeding responses. With increasing body weight loss an increasing proportion of intervals falls within the

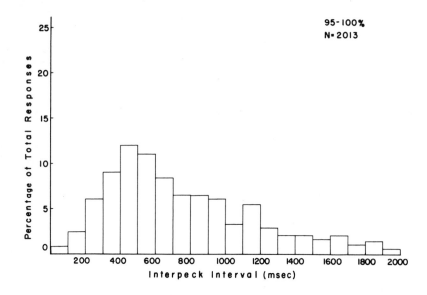

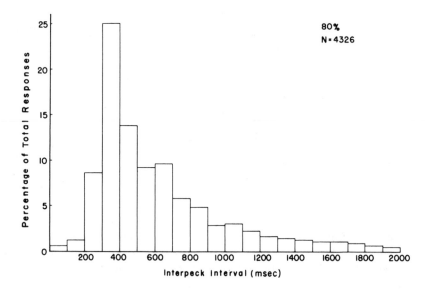

Fig. 11. Effects of food deprivation upon the interpeck interval. The histograms are based upon a computer analysis of pecking at food monitored automatically with a feedometer. Data are taken from the first 10 minutes of a 30-minute feeding test given at each of the four weight levels.

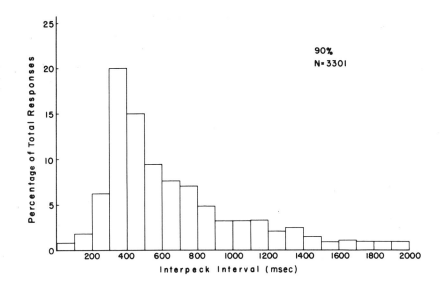

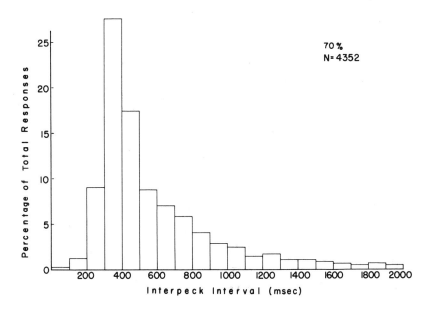

Fig. 11. See facing page for legend.

range 300–400 msec. Analysis of the photographic data failed to reveal any effect of deprivation upon the form or duration of any of the component patterns of the feeding response. The increased food intake of the hungry pigeon is due solely to a reduction in the interval between successive feeding responses.

C. SENSORY CONTROL

As mentioned earlier, the pigeon's feeding behavior involves the coordination of a number of movement patterns—pecking, grasping, mandibulation, swallowing—each of which, in turn, must reflect the operation of distinctive sensorimotor mechanisms. Some data are available on the sensory control of each of the movement patterns.

1. Pecking

Although pecking is undoubtedly elicited by the visual characteristics of the grain, two observations suggest that, once initiated, it may no longer be under environmental control. The first is the extreme brevity of the pecking response, which is comparable in duration with the strike of the praying mantis [48–75 msec, according to Roeder (1959)]. The second is the fact that the pigeon's eye begins to close about 30 msec before contact with the grain and is closed at the moment of contact. In the absence of experimental evidence to the contrary, it is likely that pecking is a ballistic response whose orientation involves an "open" control system, i.e., one in which orientation is completed in the absence of feedback from the orienting stimulus (Mittelstaedt, 1962). The functional significance of the eye closure during the peck remains obscure. Friedman (1975) has noted that actively foraging doves seldom blink or use their nictitating membranes while their heads are stabilized but tend to do so during periods of rapid head motion. Eye closing may simply be a reflex response to the rapidly enlarging image of the grain produced by the downward movement of the head, since it does not occur during the topographically similar but far less rapid response of drinking (Schiff, 1965; Jenkins and Moore, 1973).

2. Grasping and Mandibulation

Both these movement patterns seem to be elicited and guided by somatosensory inputs from the oral region. Electrophysiological studies (see Section VII) indicate that the pigeon's beak and oral cavity are richly supplied with mechanoreceptors innervated by sensory branches of the trigeminal nerve. The functional significance of these trigeminal inputs was explored by examining the effects of trigeminal nerve section upon the movement patterns involved in eating (see Section VIII). Trigeminal deafferentation produces a striking impairment in grasping and mandibulation that is approximately proportional to the number of nerves sectioned bilaterally. In the most successful cases birds were observed to make large numbers of successive pecks without obtaining a single kernel of grain. In most of these cases the peck ends with the opened beak centered around the grain, but the grain either slips out during beak closing or is dropped after grasping. In such cases mandibulation either does not occur at all or is aborted shortly after its initiation.

It is clear from such experiments that the trigeminal system plays a crucial role in the neurosensory control of the pigeon's consummatory behavior. Analogous studies indicate a similar role for the trigeminal system of the duck (Zweers and Wouterlood, 1973).

3. Swallowing

Unfortunately, we do not have a body of data for birds comparable to the exhaustive analysis of mammalian deglutition carried out by Doty and his associates (e.g., Doty and Bosma, 1956). However, incidental observations suggest that swallowing may be reliably elicited from a "trigger zone" located in the roof of the mouth and innervated by fibers of the glossopharyngeal and vagus nerves (Karten, 1975). This zone may also play a role in mediating the swallowing response of fledglings to parental beak stimulation.

4. Integration of the Feeding Response

The various components of the feeding response differ in the extent and nature of their peripheral control. Pecking and swallowing, although elicited by environmental stimuli, seem to be relatively independent of these stimuli once initiated. The occurrence of mouth opening during the peck seems to be a joint function of the pigeon's internal state and the nature of the target stimulus, since a presumably "neutral" response key elicits either a "closed mouth" or an "open mouth" peck, depending upon whether the bird is food or water deprived (Jenkins and Moore, 1973). Moreover, neither swallowing nor any of the components of pecking (eye closing, mouth opening, head descent) are disrupted by trigeminal deafferentation (Zeigler et al., 1975).

Mandibulation, on the other hand, depends on stimuli from the grain for its elicitation, orientation, and persistence. Experimental evidence on this point comes from the analysis of populations of pecks which are not followed by successful grasps or in which, after grasping, the grain drops out of the beak. Such pecks may be observed to occur naturally in a small percentage of the pecks made by normal pigeons. They may be seen in very substantial numbers in trigeminally deafferented birds or produced systematically in normal birds by presenting them with grains glued to the surface of the feeding dish.

Out of 250 such pecks made by normal pigeons, only 8% exhibited mandibulation following a failure to grasp the grain or a dropping of the grain. In these few cases observations suggested that mandibulation was elicited by the presence of a previously unswallowed grain still in the mouth. Similar data have been obtained from deafferented pigeons (see Section VIII), and normal pigeons tested with glued grains fail to show any of the head toss and tongue movement components characteristic of mandibulation. Furthermore, normal birds in danger of losing the grain are frequently seen to vary the mandibulation pattern, thereby preventing the grain from dropping out of the mouth. Such observations indicate that mandibulation does not "run itself off" in the absence of feedback from the eliciting stimulus.

Analyses such as these illustrate the role of peripheral inputs in coordinating individual movement patterns into feeding response sequences. Thus pecking is presumably elicited by visual stimuli from the grain, whereas grasping, mandibulation, and swallowing are elicited by contact of the grain with the beak tip and with various loci within the buccal cavity. The fact that each segment of the response sequence produces eliciting stimuli for the next segment contributes to the spatiotemporal integration of the separate movement patterns into an adaptive behavior for the efficient ingestion of food.

V. FEEDING BEHAVIOR PATTERNS

A. BOUT CHARACTERISTICS AND THE PATTERNING OF FOOD INTAKE

Whatever the mechanisms by which individual feeding responses are integrated into bouts of feeding, there is no doubt that the bout itself is a basic unit for the analysis of feeding behavior. Animals given continuous access to food rarely make individual pecks, nor do they eat continuously, but engage in discrete episodes of feeding (bouts, meals), interspersed with periods of other activity. Studies of feeding bout characteristics thus represent a necessary intermediate step between the microanalysis of movement patterns and the more molar analysis of the feeding behavior patterns themselves.

Such studies confirm the impression, gained from informal observation, that the bulk of the pigeon's daily food intake is consumed in distinct bouts of relatively fast pecking (about 0.6 to 1.2 responses/second; Fig. 12). Analysis of the distribution of pecking responses *within* individual feeding bouts (Table IV) indicates that for most bouts the initial rate of pecking is close to the mean response rate for that bout and that there is a significant ($p < 0.01$) decline in the response rate towards the end of the bout. By comparison with the rat, the number of these feeding bouts per day is relatively large and their duration relatively brief (Zeigler et al., 1971). Comparable data have been reported for the Japanese Quail (Van Hemel and Meyer, 1969) and the domestic fowl (Duncan et al., 1970). Analysis of the frequency distribution of bout sizes for a

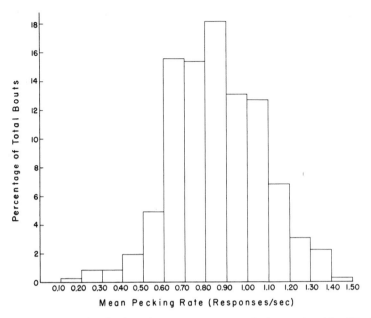

Fig. 12. Frequency distribution of mean response rates for bouts of pecking (N = 417) at food in pigeons (N = 6) maintained under free-feeding conditions.

TABLE IV

Intrabout Distribution of Feeding Response Rates[a]

Bird number	Bouts (N)	Feeding responses per second					
		First 10 seconds		Mean bout rates		Last 10 seconds	
		Mean	SE	Mean	SE	Mean	SE
339	74	0.83	0.067	0.85	0.038	0.43	0.068
350	64	0.89	0.066	0.86	0.168	0.38	0.045
373	76	1.00	0.091	1.05	0.043	0.54	0.077
378	77	1.00	0.088	0.99	0.050	0.45	0.255
502	69	0.90	0.060	0.75	0.027	0.43	0.059
504	59	1.07	0.084	0.76	0.043	0.47	0.056

[a]SE, standard error.

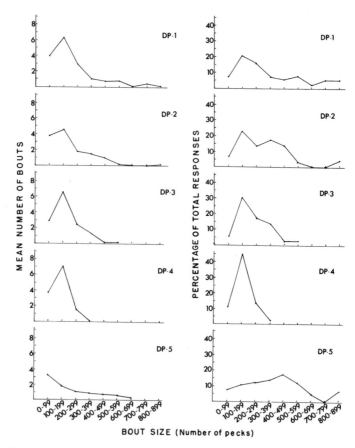

Fig. 13. Frequency distribution of bout size categories characteristic of pigeons maintained under free-feeding conditions. Left: Data plotted in absolute frequencies. Right: Data plotted as a percentage of the total daily feeding activity to indicate the relative contribution of the different bout size categories.

group of 10 birds indicates that the bulk of the pigeon's ad lib food intake is consumed in bouts of 500 responses or fewer (2 to 5 gm). Bouts containing more than 500 responses are rarely if ever seen in nondeprived birds (Fig. 13). While the number and size of individual bouts may vary somewhat from bird to bird, they tend to be stable over time and quite characteristic for an individual bird (Miller, 1974; Zeigler et al., 1971).

It has often been pointed out that for any individual animal the total daily food intake is simply the product of three parameters: number of feeding bouts, size of feeding bouts, and rate of feeding. While this is undoubtedly true, equal daily food intakes may be achieved by different combinations of these parameters. As Collier has noted (Collier et al., 1972) the flexibility of feeding

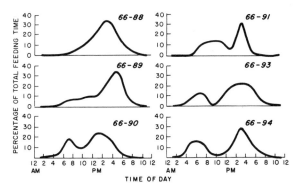

Fig. 14. Individual differences in the temporal distribution of feeding bouts over 24-hour periods under free-feeding conditions for a group of six pigeons. Data are summed across four successive weeks. (From Zeigler *et al.,* 1971. *J. Comp. Physiol. Psychol.* 76, 468–477. Copyright 1971 by The American Psychological Association. Reprinted by permission.)

behavior patterns plays an important role in the animal's adaptation to metabolic and environmental demands. It is not surprising therefore that the feeding behavior of a given species tends to exhibit periodicities whose patterns are quite characteristic of the species. Such periodicities were readily apparent in our first study of the pigeon's feeding behavior patterns (Zeigler *et al.,* 1971). The birds were maintained on a 12-hour light/dark cycle (6 AM to 6 PM) with a 1-hour maintenance period at noon. For most of the light period the birds were exposed to stimuli which accompany the normal daily laboratory routine. Under laboratory conditions, as in the field, pigeons are diurnal feeders, and there was no evidence of eating during the dark portion of the cycle. Moreover the distribution throughout the day tends to be bimodal (Fig. 14), with a small peak in the morning and a larger one in the afternoon. The laboratory data are in reasonable agreement with Murton's field observations on the feeding behavior of the Wood Pigeon and with data obtained by analysis of the crop contents of pigeons (Murton, 1965) and doves (Schmid, 1965).

B. FOOD DEPRIVATION AND LONG-TERM FEEDING PATTERNS

In a recent study from our laboratory, Miller (1974) has analysed the behavioral mechanisms mediating the pigeon's response to body weight loss. It will be recalled that after a period of deprivation the pigeon exhibits a compensatory increase in food intake which continues until the lost body weight is regained (Section III, Fig. 9). The feeding behavior patterns involved are illustrated in Fig. 15 for a bird reduced to 90% of its ad lib weight and then given unrestricted access to food. Under ad lib conditions food intake tends to be highest at the start of the feeding period, gradually tapering off over the next few hours. Body weight loss has its most dramatic effects upon the initial bout of feeding

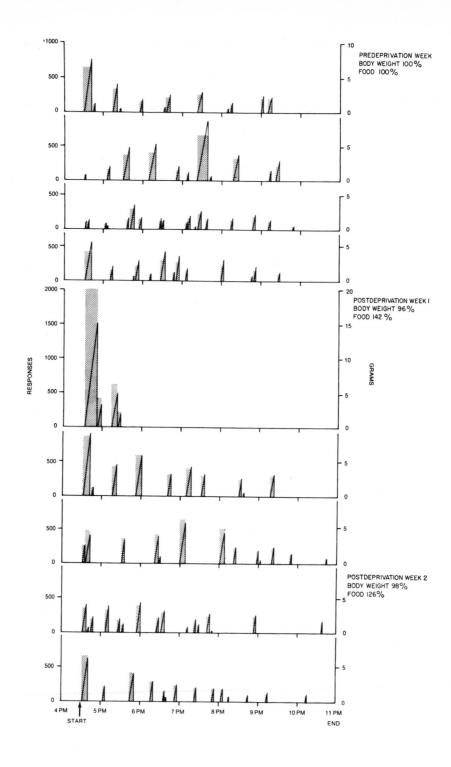

following a period of restriction. Under these conditions the size of the initial feeding bout is proportional to the extent of body weight loss (Fig. 7), and birds may consume up to 75% of their daily food intake in this one initial oversized bout. Not surprisingly this oversized initial bout is accompanied by a marked reduction in the number of subsequent bouts during the remainder of the feeding period.

The reduction in the number of individual bouts seen on the first day of free feeding becomes less marked over the next few days. Throughout this period, birds compensate for the reduction in bout frequency by increases in mean bout size. During the first week of free feeding, for example, mean bout sizes range from 150 to 175% of their predeprivation levels. The change in bout size reflects a reduction in the proportion of small bouts (200 responses or less) and an increase in the proportion of the daily food intake which is consumed in large and oversized bouts (500 or more). As a result of the compensatory increase in bout size, the reduction in bout frequency has no significant effect upon food intake. Thus the rate at which food intake attenuates during the remainder of the main feeding period differs very little from the attentuation rate in the nondeprived condition. Finally, as body weight regains its predeprivation level, the parameters determining the feeding pattern gradually resume their predeprivation values (Fig. 16).

Miller's (1974) analysis has clarified the behavioral mechanisms mediating the compensatory overeating of the food-deprived pigeon. Body weight loss is followed by an increase in the rate and persistence of eating at the start of each feeding period, resulting in increased initial food intake. Under ad lib conditions the ingestion of such large amounts of food leads to a decline or total cessation of feeding during the subsequent portion of the feeding period (see Section IV). However, except for the first day of free feeding, this decline is absent or considerably reduced so long as there is any significant degree of body weight loss. The feeding behavior of the deprived pigeon is thus characterized by increased intakes during the initial portion of the feeding period and normal levels of intake during the remainder of the period. The inevitable result of these two processes is a net increase in daily food intake and a rapid recovery of body weight.

Fig. 15. Deprivation effects upon patterns of feeding behavior in the pigeon. The bird is on a 15-hour light/9-hour dark cycle. Four days of free feeding are followed by a period of deprivation sufficient to reduce body weight to 90% of its free-feeding value. Effects of body weight loss upon the subsequent patterning of food intake are evident in the size of the initial bout and the number of subsequent bouts each day.

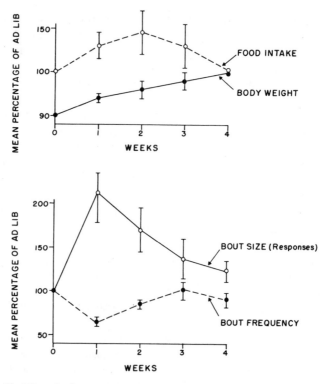

Fig. 16. Variations in the parameters controlling food intake during recovery from a 10% body weight loss ($N = 5$). Bars indicate standard errors.

VI. OROPHARYNGEAL AND POSTINGESTIONAL CONTROL OF EATING

A. THE ALIMENTARY CANAL AND DIGESTIVE SYSTEM

The ingestion of food is accompanied by stimulation of a variety of receptors in the oral region and buccal cavity, as well as by the gradual accumulation of nutrients within the alimentary canal and digestive system. Investigations of these oropharyngeal and postingestional factors in mammals have shown that they influence the animal's subsequent food intake by contributing differentially to the satiating and rewarding consequences of eating (Epstein, 1967; Janowitz, 1967; Mook, 1963).

The pigeon's alimentary and digestive systems differ in a number of ways from those of the most commonly used laboratory mammals. The major differences, of course, are the presence of a beak and crop, the absence of teeth, and the division of the gastric apparatus into a glandular stomach (proventriculus) and a muscular stomach (gizzard). A number of early studies involving X-ray observations of pigeons and fowl eating barium sulfate meals give the following general picture of the events which follow food intake (von Ihnen, 1928; Henry *et al.*, 1933; Vonk and Postma, 1949).

In previously fasted birds with an initially empty crop the first few boluses of food pass across the mouth of the crop and are swept directly into the gizzard, while the remainder of the meal lodges in the crop. If the bird has previously been fed and there is food in the gizzard and lower tract, no food passes out of the crop during eating. However, at varying intervals following ingestion of a meal the crop contracts on its contents forming a bolus of food, which is then pinched off by a constriction of the esophagus at the base of the crop and pushed onward to the proventriculus and gizzard by peristalsis. Although the crop's obvious function is storage, there is evidence that it has some digestive capacity (Bolton, 1965). The proventriculus appears to be primarily involved in chemical digestion, whereas mechanical digestion takes place in the gizzard assisted by well-defined rhythmic contractions of that organ and the presence of small bits of stone (Zisweiler and Farner, 1972).

Finally, two observations on the relation between the crop and the remainder of the digestive system are of interest with respect to the operation of postingestional processes. First, several studies (von Ihnen, 1928; Richardson, 1972) suggest that fullness of the lower portions of the digestive tract inhibits expulsion of food from the crop. Second, observations on fowl maintained on a 2 hours/day feeding schedule indicate that while the amount of food remaining in the crop declines after feeding, the amounts of food remaining in other portions of the digestive tract stay fairly constant (Shannon and McNab, cited in Richardson, 1970).

B. POSTINGESTIONAL FACTORS

The fact that the crop of fowl and pigeons is sufficiently developed to serve as a storage organ has made this structure a focus for the few investigations concerned with the origin of "satiety" signals in birds. Researchers have employed the same techniques which have proved informative in analogous experiments on the mammalian stomach: excision, artificial distention, preloading, and a combination of intragastric fistula-feeding and operant-conditioning procedures.

Cropectomy does not appear to affect the survival or growth of domestic chicks if food is continually available, nor does it interrupt their over-all pattern of feeding behavior (von Ihnen, 1928; Fisher and Weiss, 1956; Richardson, 1970). However, the behavioral measures employed in these studies were relatively crude, and recent X-ray observations of feeding in cropectomized birds suggest that the remaining portion of the upper esophagus retains some storage capacity. In any case, such experiments can tell us only that the crop is inessential, without clarifying its normal contribution to the control of feeding.

More direct evidence is provided by experiments manipulating crop contents either by artificial distention or by preloading with food. Artificial distention via an implanted balloon produced a significant reduction in food intake in a short-term (15-minute) feeding test. The reduction was roughly proportional to the extent of the distention and could be counteracted somewhat by an increased period of deprivation prior to testing (Richardson, 1970). Experiments employing preloading procedures have provided data on the long-term consequences of food in the crop. Cardini (1971) has shown that pigeons preloaded daily with 13–51% of their regular food ration maintained an essentially normal intake by reducing the amount taken orally. When preloaded with 60–85%, however, oral intake decreases were inadequate and the pigeons overate.

C. OROPHARYNGEAL FACTORS

A large body of data attests to the importance of oropharyngeal factors in the control of mammalian feeding. As Epstein (1967) points out, inputs from the oral region provide feedback which is demonstrably involved in the initiation, persistence, and possibly the termination of eating, as well as in dietary selection. Our knowledge of the role of oral inputs is derived from experiments with mammals in which such inputs have either been abolished or severely reduced, varied quantitatively or qualitatively, or dissociated from their normal relation to postingestional factors. Little or no comparable data exists for birds (but see Sterrit and Smith, 1965; McFarland, 1969).

Most work with mammals has concentrated on the role of olfaction and taste, which are clearly important modalities in the control of mammalian feeding (but see Section X). While there is no longer any doubt that birds have a well-developed olfactory system (Wenzel, 1971), there is no evidence that olfaction makes any significant contribution to the feeding behavior of the pigeon. Similarly, chickens can make discriminations based on taste under laboratory conditions, and Gentle (1971, 1975) has reported that lingual nerve sections reduce food intake. However, under natural conditions neither the chicken nor the pigeon takes its food in aqueous solution, and it is likely that gustatory stimuli play only a minor role in their feeding behavior. It might be predicted therefore that the sole remaining oral sense, the trigeminal system, would make a major contribution to the oropharyngeal control of feeding in the pigeon.

This expectation is borne out by the disruptive effects upon eating which follow trigeminal deafferentation in this species (Zeigler, 1973, 1975a; Section VIII). The reduction in the pigeon's responsiveness to food is even more severe than that seen in "functionally deafferented" rats feeding themselves intragastrically through a nasopharyngeal catheter (Epstein and Teitelbaum, 1962; Snowdon, 1969). In birds, as in mammals, orosensory inputs seem to function as positive feedback signals sustaining ingestive behavior (McFarland, 1969).

D. FEEDING BEHAVIOR MECHANISMS IN THE PIGEON

We are now in a position to provide a descriptive account of some of the processes controlling the pigeon's feeding behavior. Pecking in gramnivorous birds appears to be a response with a very high probability and is probably the most frequently occurring response in the pigeon's repertoire. Murton (1965), for example, has reported that pigeons feeding under natural conditions may make up to 35,000 pecking responses per day, and this figure includes only food-directed pecking. Pecking is elicited by visual stimuli, and its direction is controlled by such characteristics as texture, shape, and color (Fantz, 1957; Dawkins, 1968).

Feeding in the pigeon is not continuous but intermittent, occurring in bouts interrupted by other activities. For any given bout of feeding, pecking is initiated at a rate very close to its maximum, but there is a gradual decline in pecking rate within the bout. Once initiated, pecking is usually followed by mandibulation, which provides orosensory inputs sustaining pecking in the face of competing stimuli for other behaviors. Not all pecking is followed by mandibulation, nor is mandibulation inevitably followed by swallowing. While the primary control of food selection is likely to be visual, monitoring can take place in the oral region under the control of both trigeminal and gustatory afferents (Moon, 1975; Gentle, 1975). The continued ingestion of food leads to both short-term and long-term reductions in the probability of pecking that may involve both orosensory adaptation and inhibitory inputs from the alimentary system.

This account of feeding in the pigeon is similar to that proposed for both the blowfly and the rat, two species whose feeding has been analyzed in great detail. In attempting to account for the control of feeding in the blowfly, Dethier and Gelperin (1967; Dethier, 1969) have proposed a model formulated primarily in terms of peripheral sensory mechanisms. In their model, variations in the moment-to-moment probability of feeding (feeding threshold) result from the continuing interplay between excitatory and inhibitory inputs acting upon feeding response mechanisms (e.g., proboscis extension; sucking). The inhibitory inputs arise mainly from the action of postingestional processes related to the rate of crop emptying, which is controlled, in turn, by the solute concentration of the blood. Excitatory inputs originate exclusively from peripheral chemosensory receptors, and sensory adaptation of these receptors plays a role in short-term termination of feeding in the fly. It should be noted that the blowfly model does not require a *direct* causal link between the fly's feeding mechanisms and its metabolic needs. It is the degree of stimulation provided by various solutions, rather than their nutrient value, that determines their effectiveness in driving feeding. Similarly, the crop and its contents is not *directly* concerned with the regulation of feeding thresholds but is linked indirectly to both nutrient levels and behavior via its rate of emptying.

The model presented by Dethier and Gelperin does account persuasively for the initiation, persistence, and termination of feeding in the blowfly, and Snowdon (1970) suggests that there are striking similarities in the peripheral mechanisms controlling these aspects of feeding in the rat. However, he argues that the manner in which the rat responds to dilution and food deprivation (i.e., by increases in the size of a few meals) requires the additional postulation of central regulatory mechanisms:

> These (two) facts suggest that a central monitor of nutrient levels operates to change the range within which meal sizes vary in response to deficits or surfeits accumulated over the course of a few hours. This change may be made with reference to a central set-point for nutrient stores or body weight. (Snowdon, 1970, p. 74)

Whatever the validity of Snowdon's objections with respect to the rat (see, e.g., Davis and Campbell, 1973; Panksepp, 1973), the peripheral model does seem to account for the initiation, persistence, and termination of feeding in the pigeon if we substitute visual, trigeminal, and visceral afferents as the source of excitatory and inhibitory influences upon the "pecking response mechanisms." It may also account for many aspects of the pigeon's response to food deprivation more parsimoniously than models incorporating "set-point" mechanisms.

Food deprivation has both short-term and long-term effects upon the pigeon's feeding behavior. Short-term effects include a reduction in latency and increases in the rate and persistence of eating, resulting in increased food intake, particularly of the initial meal. The pigeon's long-term compensatory overeating is mediated primarily by an increase in the number of large-size meals (including the initial meal) and a decrease in the attentuation of eating that normally accompanies such massive food intakes.

While set-point mechanisms might be postulated to account for such effects, certain characteristics of the pigeon's alimentary processes suggest an alternative hypothesis. It will be recalled (cf. Section VI,A) that the rate of crop emptying is related to the degree of fullness of the lower portions of the digestive tract. In the deprived bird the initial portion of a meal bypasses the crop and continues toward the gizzard. If, as is likely, the crop is a major source of inhibitory inputs, such inputs would be minimized in a food-deprived bird and the initial meal should be considerably prolonged.

Furthermore, it is well known that pigeons, unlike rats, can tolerate periods of food deprivation lasting for several weeks, during which time they can lose 25 to

30% of their ad lib body weight without apparent ill effects. Birds recovering from such prolonged periods of food deprivation appear to process very large quantities of food each day (Zeigler et al., 1972, Fig. 7). Under these conditions calls on the crop are likely to be far more frequent, with a consequent increase in the rate of crop emptying and a decrease in the level of visceral inhibition. In birds which have sustained such weight losses, ingestion of a unit quantity of food should produce significantly less attentuation of subsequent feeding than the ingestion of an equivalent amount of food by free-feeding pigeons.

Finally, it is a fact that in the free-feeding situation neither the pigeon's crop nor its digestive tract are likely to be empty, so that there will always be some level of inhibition present. Visual stimuli from the food will also be present, but so will other stimuli which may elicit a variety of pecking behaviors other than eating, as well as a host of competing stimuli for other behaviors. Under these conditions the value of the excitatory and inhibitory inputs playing upon the pecking response mechanism may be expected to oscillate about some mean in the manner suggested by the Dethier and Gelperin model (Dethier, 1969, Fig. 54), and feeding would take place in intermittent bouts.

Collier (see Collier et al., 1972, 1975) has questioned the utility of "homeostatic" or "depletion-repletion" models for the study of feeding behavior patterns. He argues that under natural conditions animals are rarely "metabolically hungry" and that feeding patterns, rather than being a response to depletion, reflect the animal's anticipation of its needs and its adjustment to the ecological constraints imposed by its environment. Fitzsimmons (1971) has advanced a similar argument with respect to drinking. He notes that the rat modulates its water intake in such a fashion that it anticipates its future requirements for water by drinking the appropriate amount with its meals.

As we have noted, there is evidence that in the chicken the amount of food remaining in the crop after feeding declines while the amounts in other portions of the digestive tract stay fairly constant. This would indeed suggest, as Richardson points out, that "the chicken is never metabolically hungry and may regulate its daily intake in nonmetabolically related ways." He goes on to speculate that the crop may have evolved solely in response to variations in the availability and nutritive density of the food supply, "acting as a buffer against short-term changes in food availability" (Richardson, 1970, p. 637). In fact many of the differences in the deprivation-intake functions of the rat and the pigeon may be attributable to the greater storage capacity provided by the pigeon's crop. A similar explanation has been advanced to account for the differences in deprivation-intake functions of several species of fish whose digestive systems differ in an analogous manner (Rozin and Mayer, 1964). Comparative analyses of such functions in the many avian species which do not possess well-developed crops would help to clarify the relation between ecology, structure, and feeding behavior in birds (Zeigler, 1973c).

The peripheral control model discussed above has the obvious utility of organizing a large body of data on the control of food intake in the pigeon. It also enables us to specify the afferent systems controlling feeding, a prerequisite for the analysis of physiological mechanisms. Moreover, like the blowfly model, it will generate adaptive behavior in animals living under natural conditions without postulating direct causal links between the pigeon's feeding mechanisms and its adaptive requirements.

These similarities between the blowfly and pigeon models should not, however, be allowed to obscure the fact that the mechanisms mediating feeding in these two species will be of very different orders of complexity. As Dethier points out: "The adult blowfly, *Phormia regina,* is an animal that requires for its maintenance only water, carbohydrate and oxygen. All other necessary materials are bequeathed by the larval stage . . . . In the case of the blowfly feeding is thus reduced to its lowest common denominator. . . ." (Dethier, 1969, p. 112). By comparison, feeding in the pigeon, as in many vertebrate species, plays a role in its maintenance, its growth, and its reproduction. It has a complex developmental history, is influenced by social factors, and plays a central role in the organization of reproductive behaviors (e.g., "courtship" feeding; "parental" feeding). It is hoped that the continued analysis of mechanisms controlling its food intake will provide a foundation for future studies of the more complex aspects of feeding behavior in the pigeon.

VII. BRAIN MECHANISMS AND FEEDING BEHAVIOR IN THE PIGEON

A. ANATOMICAL FOUNDATIONS

It has long been known that bilateral removal of the pigeon's cerebral hemispheres produces an apparently permanent aphagia. The decerebrate pigeon walks, grooms, and swallows food placed in its mouth but does not eat (Flourens, 1824; Äkerman *et al.,* 1962). Moreover, although electrical stimulation of hypothalamic regions is reported to elicit feeding in the intact pigeon, such stimulation does not have such an effect in the decerebrate preparation (Äkerman *et al.,* 1960, 1962). While massive ablations of dorsal endbrain regions do not produce feeding behavior deficits in the pigeon (Zeigler, 1963), aphagia has been reported after lesions of the basal telencephalon of the pigeon (Rogers, 1922) and of the diencephalon of doves (Wright, 1968) and chickens (Feldman *et al.,* 1957). Furthermore, electrical stimulation of basal forebrain regions elicits a variety of "feeding movements" in chickens (Putkonen, 1967; Phillips and Youngren, 1971; Tweeton *et al.,* 1973), ducks (Phillips, 1964), pigeons (Äkerman *et al.,* 1960), doves (Harwood and Vowles, 1966), and gulls (Delius, 1971).

Such observations indicate that forebrain structures are involved in the neural control of feeding, but until recently the precise location of these structures had remained uncertain.

Within the past few years our collaborative studies with Karten have made possible a more precise delimitation, within the avian telencephalon, of the regions whose destruction is responsible for the aphagia of the decerebrate pigeon (Zeigler et al., 1969a,b; Zeigler and Karten, 1973a,b). Furthermore, analysis of the afferent and efferent connections of these regions indicates that they are part of a network of structures at several levels of the avian brain, and lesion studies have implicated all of them in the neural control of feeding (Zeigler, 1974). It may be expected that future research will clarify their relation to other structures (e.g., the visual system; the vagal system) which are also likely to be relevant to feeding behavior.

The *afferent* limb of this network includes three central components of the avian trigeminal system (Fig. 17). The Principal Sensory Trigeminal Nucleus (PrV) receives a topographically organized projection from the Gasserian ganglion and is the origin of an ascending projection to the endbrain, the quinto-frontal tract (QFT). Arising from both dorsal and ventral subdivisions of PrV, the QFT undergoes partial decussation and projects bilaterally and monosynaptically to the basal portions of the hemisphere (Wallenberg, 1903; Woodburne, 1936; Cohen and Karten, 1974); the QFT enters the telencephalon with the lateral forebrain bundle, passes through the paleostriatum primitivum and augmentatum to terminate in the nucleus basalis (NB) in the basolateral portion of the anterior telencephalon. On the basis of comparative anatomical data from a number of avian species, Stingelin (1961) has noted that the relative size of NB is directly proportional to the magnitude of PrV, which, in turn, reflects the relative extent of beak development in the species.

The nucleus basalis is the source of an efferent projection, the fronto-archistriate tract (FAT), which terminates in a region of the caudal neostriatum overlying the dorsolateral nucleus of the archistriatum (Zeier and Karten, 1971). Until recently, the avian archistriatum had been homologized, in its entirety, with the mammalian amygdala. However, on the basis of its afferent and efferent connections Karten has suggested that the archistriatum consists of two major functional subdivisions—a "limbic" and a "somatosensorimotor" division. The limbic division, which includes the medial and posterior nuclear groups, gives rise to a descending diencephalic pathway (HOM) which terminates in the hypothalamus. The somatosensorimotor division, which includes the anterior and intermediate nuclear groups, is the origin of a second major descending pathway, the occipitomesencephalic tract (OMT), which has been traced down to the level of the pons and cervical spinal cord but which has no hypothalamic terminations. On the basis of comparative anatomical data Karten (see Cohen and Karten, 1974) and Towe (1973) have suggested that OMT is analogous to the

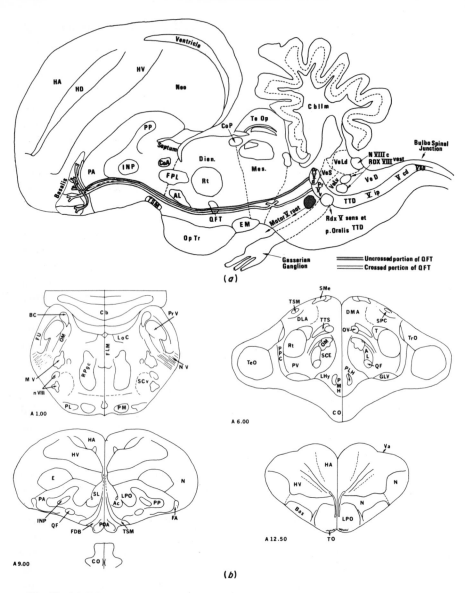

Fig. 17. (a) Schematic diagram of the trigeminal system in the pigeon. The origin and distribution of the quintofrontal tract (QFT) are indicated with its ipsilateral projection shaded. (b) Four frontal sections through the brain of the pigeon, illustrating the location of PrV, QFT, NB, and OMT at several levels and their relation to adjacent structures. Numbers at the left of each section correspond to section levels, in millimeters from the stereotaxic zero plane, according to the Karten and Hodos (1967) atlas. (From Zeigler and Karten, 1973a.)

bundle of Bagley of ungulates (Haartsen and Verhaart, 1967) which is a component of the mammalian pyramidal system. The anatomical and neurobehavioral data on OMT (see Section VII,C,3) suggest that it is involved in the *efferent* control of the pigeon's feeding behavior.

Having delimited a group of brain structures which on both anatomical and functional grounds may be considered as components of a feeding behavior "system," our ultimate goal is to determine the specific contribution of each of these structures to the neural control of feeding. We have therefore attempted to relate the anatomical connections and physiological characteristics of each of these structures to the nature of the deficits produced by lesions of that structure. In our initial studies this combined approach has helped to clarify the role of trigeminal structures in the neural control of feeding.

B. ELECTROPHYSIOLOGICAL STUDIES OF THE AVIAN TRIGEMINAL SYSTEM

The trigeminal nerve is, after the optic tract, the largest of the avian cranial nerves, and it is richly endowed with a variety of specialized mechanoreceptors (Andersen and Nafstad, 1968; Gottschaldt and Lausmann, 1974). Its mor-

---

Abbreviations:

AL, Ansa lenticularis
Ac, nucleus accumbens
Bas, nucleus basalis
Co, optic chiasm
CoA,P, anterior, posterior commissure
DLA, DMA, nuclei dorsolaterialis, dorsomedialis thalami
E, ectostriatum
EM, nucleus ectomammilaris
FA, fronto-archistriate tract
FDB, diagonal band of Broca
FLM, fasciculus longitudinalis medialis
FPL, fasciculus prosencephali lateralis
FU, fasciculus uncinatus
GLv, nucleus geniculatus lateralis
HA, HD, HV, hyperstriatum accessorium, dorsale, ventrale
INP, nucleus intrapeduncularis
LHy, nucleus lateralis hypothalami
LoC, locus ceruleus
LPO, lobus parolfactorius
MV, nucleus motoris nervi trigemini
N, neostriatum
OM, tractus occipitomesencephalicus
Ov, nucleus ovoidalis
PA, paleostriatum augmentatum

POA, nucleus preopticus anterior
PL, nucleus pontis lateralis
PLH, nucleus lateralis hypothalami posterioris
PMH, nucleus medialis hypothalami
PM, nucleus pontis medialis
PP, paleostriatum primitivum
PPC, nucleus principalis precommisuralis
PrVd, v, nucleus sensorius principalis trigemini, pars dorsalis, ventralis
PV, nucleus posteroventralis thalami
QFT, tractus quintofrontalis
Rt, nucleus rotundus
SCE, stratum cellulare externum
SMe, stria medullaris
SCv, nucleus subceruleus ventralis
SL, nucleus septalis lateralis
SPC, nucleus superficialis parvocellularis
Te Op, tectum opticum
TSM, tractus septomesencephalicus
TTD, nucleus et tractus descendens nervi trigemini
TTS, tractus thalamostriaticus
Ve, vestibular nuclear complex
V,ip,cd,sp, pars interpolaris, caudalis, spinalis of TTD

phology and peripheral distribution have been described in detail for a number of species (Barnikol, 1953; Cords, 1904; Zeigler and Witkovsky, 1968; Watanabe and Yasuda, 1970), and the innervation of the beak has been shown to vary considerably in different species.

Gross dissection of the trigeminal nerve in the pigeon [Fig. 18; see also Fig. 2 in Zeigler and Witkovsky (1968)] indicates that it innervates the jaw, the orbit, the beak, and the oral cavity (exclusive of the tongue). By contrast with its distribution in many mammalian forms there is a more limited innervation of the orbital regions, with both the ophthalmic and maxillary divisions distributing primarily to the upper beak, while the mandibular sensory branch innervates the lower beak, extending through its entire length. Recent work by Tucker (1971) has also defined a nonolfactory trigeminal contribution to the nasal cavity in pigeons. However, our primary concern in this review is with the trigeminal innervation of the oral region.

1. Trigeminal (Gasserian) Ganglion

In birds, as in mammals, trigeminal afferents terminate in the head and mouth region, with their cell bodies in the Gasserian ganglion. The response properties of first-order trigeminal neurons may be studied either by recording from individual nerve fibers (Kitchell *et al.*, 1959; Gregory, 1973) or from ganglion cells (Necker, 1972; Zeigler *et al.*, 1975). In our study almost all units encountered in the ganglion were responsive to light tactile stimulation of the beak, the

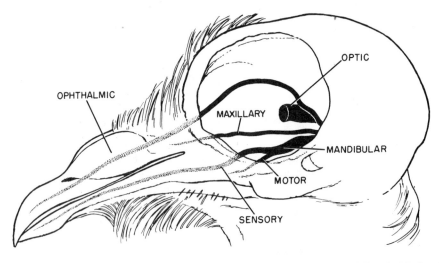

Fig. 18. A gross dissection of the trigeminal nerve in the pigeon, showing the ophthalmic, maxillary, and mandibular branches entering the orbit and beak regions. The eye has been removed to expose the location and course of nerve branches within the orbit. (From Zeigler *et al.*, 1975. *J. Comp. Physiol. Psychol.* **89**, 845–858. Copyright 1975 by The American Psychological Association. Reprinted by permission.)

oral cavity, or the orbital region. Some representative receptive fields of such units are illustrated in Fig. 19. Receptive field sizes ranged from less than 2 mm^2 to more than 100 mm^2 and were continuously distributed in shape from almost perfectly circular to roughly elliptical. On the beak and in the oral cavity most of the receptive areas were located either on the soft palate tissue or along the narrow hard rim of the beak. The shape of palatal fields was often elliptical, with the long axis of the field lying in parallel with the long axis of the beak.

The representation of the orbital region and of the soft tissue of the oral cavity was about equally divided between slow- and fast-adapting units. However, all units responsive to stimulation of the hard external beak surface were fast adapting. Similar findings have been reported for the bill of the duck (Gregory, 1973).

2. The Main Sensory and Spinal Trigeminal Nuclei

On the basis of Fink-Heimer studies the central projections of the Gasserian ganglion have been described for both the pigeon (Cohen and Karten, 1974) and the Mallard (Dubbeldam and Menken, 1973). In both species, trigeminal fibers terminate in the main sensory nucleus (PrV) and the spinal trigeminal nuclei (TTD). A microelectrode analysis of TTD indicates that its cells may be divided into two categories: *tactile* units are driven by stimulation of the beak and the

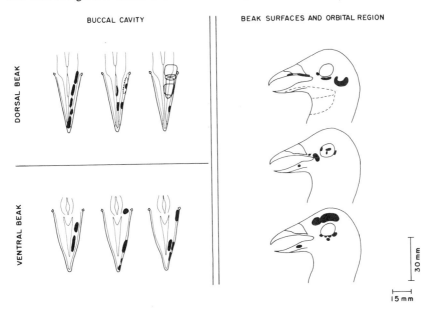

Fig. 19. Several views of the head and buccal cavity of the pigeon to illustrate the relative sizes and locations of the receptive fields of units recorded in the trigeminal ganglion. (From Zeigler *et al.*, 1975. *J. Comp. Physiol. Psychol.* **89**, 845–858. Copyright 1975 by The American Psychological Association. Reprinted by permission.)

oral cavity; *joint* units respond to the opening and closing of the mouth by displacement of the lower beak from its resting position (Silver and Witkovsky, 1973). One type of joint unit relays continuous information about the degree to which the mouth is open, while the other type appears specialized to convey information about changes in the degree of mouth opening. Most tactile units also fall into two subgroups, one of which has receptive fields on the soft palate tissue inside the upper and lower beaks, whereas the other fires on mechanical stimulation of the inner rim or the external horny surface of the beak. The receptive fields of tactile units displayed a number of characteristics which might be relevant to the sensory control of eating in the pigeon. First, cells with receptive fields in the palate region tended to have smaller receptive fields than those encountered on the hard beak surface, and the smallest fields in either subgroup tended to be located near the beak tip or along the inner beak rim. Second, a substantial number of tactile units had discrete, noncontiguous receptive fields located in corresponding palatal area of the upper and lower beaks. Finally, a small group of "complex" cells had inhomogeneous receptive areas, in that different patterns of firing were elicited when different regions of the receptive field were stimulated. Figure 20 illustrates some functional characteristics of TTD units.

Neurons of PrV, like those of the spinal trigeminal complex, process inputs from tactile and joint units with receptive fields in the beak, mouth, and head region. The response properties of the two classes of units (joint and tactile) are roughly similar in the two nuclei, with the bulk of the tactile units having relatively small receptive fields. However, tactile units in PrV do not exhibit the "spontaneous" activity seen in TTD neurons, nor are their receptive fields of comparable complexity (Zeigler and Witkovsky, 1968).

3. The Nucleus Basalis

This nucleus is located in the basal portion of the anterior telencephalon (Fig. 17) and receives a direct projection from the PrV, via the quinto-frontal tract. No other inputs to the nucleus are currently known. Almost all basalis neurons encountered in our microelectrode studies had a characteristic pattern of spontaneous firing in which intermittent bursts of activity appeared every few seconds. All basalis units responded to light mechanical stimulation of either the horny outer beak surfaces, the beak rims, or the soft palate tissues. No cells were driven by tactile stimulation of the tongue, nor were any joint units found.

The receptive field characteristics and response properties of basalis neurons differed in a number of respects from those of PrV and TTD. First, although units with both large and small receptive fields were seen, almost 60% of the basalis units had large fields, extending over one-third or more of the total surface area of one beak. Second, the bulk of the basalis neurons were "phasic" units, exhibiting a relatively fast rate of adaptation to a maintained tactile

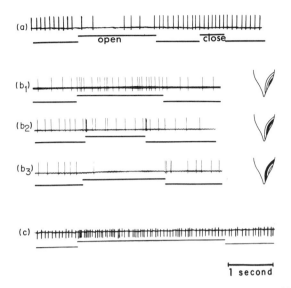

Fig. 20. Response characteristics of units recorded in the pigeon TTD: (*a*) Response of a joint unit to opening and closing the mouth. (*b*) Tactile unit of the external ventral beak, that responded differentially when adjacent areas were touched. The figurine indicates the three receptive field zones, the black area being the stimulated one. (*c*) A slowly adapting tactile unit with a receptive area on the ventral beak palate. (From Silver and Witkovsky, 1973.)

stimulus. Finally, as would be expected from the topography of the PrV projection, the nucleus basalis contains cells with bilateral receptive fields as well as those with exclusively contralateral or ipsilateral fields (Witkovsky *et al.,* 1973). Figure 21 illustrates the receptive field characteristics and response properties of some representative nucleus basalis units. (It is important to note that no units responsive to tongue stimulation have ever been encountered in any of the pigeon's trigeminal nuclei.)

5. Comparison of the Avian and Mammalian Trigeminal Systems

It is clear that at their more caudal levels the avian and mammalian trigeminal sensory systems share a similar functional organization. In both, afferent fibers terminate in the head and mouth region. Their cell bodies lie in the Gasserian ganglion, and most of the centrally directed axons branch, sending one axon each to the PrV and the TTD (Woodburne, 1936). The dorsal to ventral sequence from mandibular-maxillary to ophthalmic divisions is true for both classes. Moreover, in addition to many similarities in their secondary connections, the neuronal populations of TTD and PrV exhibit similar receptive field

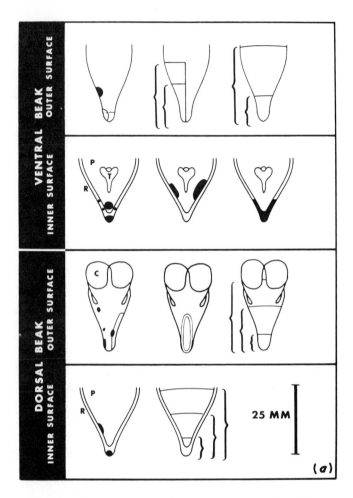

Fig. 21. Receptive fields and response characteristics of units recorded in the nucleus basalis. (*a*) Receptive field sizes and locations (*abbreviations:* C, cere; T, tongue; P, palate; R, beak rim). (*b*) Response properties of an NB unit with a small receptive field located inside the mouth: (1) spontaneous firing; (2) brief, repeated contacts with the sensitive region; (3) a prolonged contact; (4) the probe is moved through the receptive area in one direction only; (5) the probe is moved back and forth through the receptive area. Time marker: 50 msec. (From Witkovsky *et al.,* 1973.)

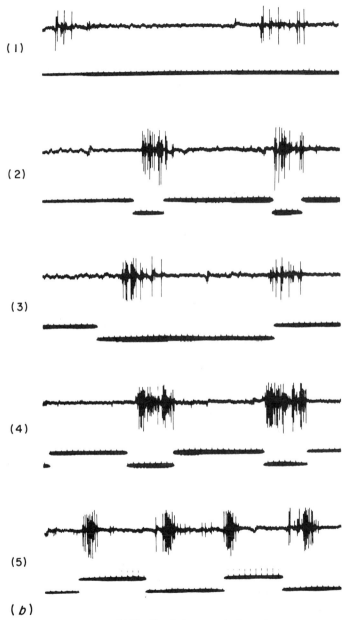

Fig. 21(b). See facing page for legend.

characteristics and response properties in birds and mammals when allowance is made for differences in the morphology of the head region. Furthermore, in both avian and mammalian forms the jaw muscle spindle afferents have their cells of origin in the trigeminal mesencephalic nucleus, forming a monosynaptic reflex arc ("masticatory reflex") terminating on neurons of the motor nucleus of the trigeminal (e.g., Szentagothai, 1948; Jerge, 1963; Manni *et al.,* 1965).

However, at more rostral levels there are some obvious differences between the two classes with respect to the location and gross morphology of central trigeminal structures. In the avian brain PrV projections terminate in nucleus basalis of the telencephalon without an intervening thalamic relay. There are some electrophysiological data suggesting a somatosensory projection to the thalamus, particularly the dorsolateral posterior nucleus (DLP) (Delius and Bennetto, 1972; Witkovsky *et al.,* 1973), but it is not clear whether trigeminal afferents are involved. In any case the origin of these somatosensory inputs to the thalamus is unknown, since there is no evidence for a thalamic projection from either TTD or PrV. By contrast, the ventrobasal complex of the mammalian thalamus is the recipient of a massive projection of somesthetic afferents from the head region projecting to the thalamus via both of these components of the sensory trigeminal complex (Welker, 1973) and is, in turn, the source of a projection to the somatosensory region of the cortex.

These differences may simply be related to the obvious morphological differences between the structure of the forebrain in birds and mammals. However, Karten (1969; also Cohen and Karten, 1974) has presented a considerable body of evidence indicating that despite marked differences in morphology and gross location many nuclear groupings in the avian forebrain have connections and functional associations comparable to those of regions of the mammalian thalamus and neocortex. On the basis of a variety of structural considerations Karten (personal communication, 1972) has suggested that the avian quinto-frontal tract corresponds to the trigeminal lemniscus of mammals and that, accordingly, the nucleus basalis, despite its location in the avian telencephalon, may be the counterpart of the face portion (VPM) of the ventrobasal complex of the mammalian thalamus. Neurobehavioral evidence bearing on this proposition will be presented below.

6.   What the Pigeon's Mouth Tells the Pigeon's Brain: Implications for the Neurosensory Control of Eating

In recent years it has become increasingly apparent that the sensory systems of organisms are specialized for the detection of those stimulus properties which are of adaptive significance for a particular species (e.g., Dethier, 1969; Ewert, 1974; Welker, 1973). Our electrophysiological studies indicate that neurons of the pigeon's trigeminal system display a number of characteristics which are obviously relevant to the sensory control of eating.

The size and shape of receptive fields of many tactile units (see Figs. 19 and 20), as well as their adaptation rates, suggest that they would be particularly responsive to the stimulus properties of individual kernels of grain during eating. Moreover, their location at the beak tip, along the beak rim, and within the mouth would insure continuous tactile stimulation which could guide the movement patterns of grasping and mandibulation. The presence of TTD units with complex receptive fields and fields on corresponding dorsal and ventral palate sites are additional examples of adaptive specializations. Similarly, inputs from joint and muscle spindle afferents could provide important information about the rate and angle of mouth opening during eating. At the level of the nucleus basalis, most units are fast adapting and have large receptive fields, so that they would be driven most effectively by stimuli moving within the buccal cavity.

Thus the properties of neurons in the pigeon's trigeminal system are such that they could detect the presence of a kernel of grain at the beak tip, provide complimentary information about both its static position and movement, and signal opening and closing of the mouth. Such neurons may well act as "grain detectors" for the pigeon, functioning within the avian trigeminal system in a manner analogous to that of the "bug detectors" described for the visual system of the frog (Lettvin *et al.*, 1959).

C. NEUROBEHAVIORAL ANALYSES

The primary aim of our neurobehavioral studies is to clarify the contribution of identified structures at various levels of the avian brain to the neural control of feeding. Now the control of feeding (and the regulation of body weight) must involve the integration of a number of behavioral and physiological processes, each with its own neural mechanisms, as well as linkages between related mechanisms (e.g., food and water intake). Moreover, the deficits in feeding behavior seen after brain lesions must reflect the disruption of one or more of the processes which control feeding in the normal animal. For these reasons, the neurobehavioral analysis of feeding involves two discrete tasks: first, a careful teasing apart of the behavioral subsystems involved in feeding; and, second, a comparison of the effects upon these subsystems of lesions at various levels of the nervous system. Progress on the first of these tasks has been described in Sections II to VI of this chapter. The remainder of the present section reviews the effects of brain lesions upon the feeding behavior of the pigeon.

1. Quinto-frontal Structures

Of the five major nuclear groupings which make up the pigeon's trigeminal system (TTD; Mes V; motor V; Pr V. NB), systematic neurobehavioral studies have been carried out only on PrV and NB. Because these nuclei are linked by the quinto-frontal tract, we have grouped them under the rubric of "quinto-frontal" (QF) structures (Zeigler and Karten, 1973a,b) and treated them as a functional unit for purposes of analysis.

    a. Effects upon Food and Water Intake. Electrolytic lesions of QF structures produce a disruption of feeding behavior whose persistence and severity vary directly with the bilateral extent of the lesions. Even in cases with minimal damage, QF lesions are followed by a transient period of aphagia (2 to 3 days), and in birds with more extensive lesions, maintained by intubation of a liquid diet, this aphagic period persists from several weeks to several months (Zeigler *et al.*, 1969a).

    The postoperative aphagia of QF birds always produces a significant degree of body weight loss. However, the resumption of feeding is usually accompanied by a period of hypophagia which varies in duration from a few days to several months. Thus the compensatory overeating characteristic of normal birds, food deprived to produce equivalent weight loss, may be absent or considerably delayed in QF birds, and their weight may therefore be maintained at a reduced level for prolonged periods (Fig. 22).

    Despite their drastic effects upon eating, QF lesions do not appear to disrupt drinking. While many lesioned birds show a reduction in water intake, prolonged periods of adipsia and hypodipsia are never seen in the absence of a deficit in feeding behavior, and the resumption of drinking invariably precedes or occurs simultaneously with the resumption of eating. Moreover, in birds with four or more days of aphagia the reduction in water intake is comparable to that produced by equivalent periods of total food deprivation in normal birds. Finally, the correlation between food and water intake characteristic of normal pigeons is also seen in QF birds, and their water intake remains a relatively constant fraction of their body weight (cf. Zeigler and Karten, 1973a, Table 5). Taken together, these several lines of evidence suggest that the postoperative reduction of water intake seen after QF lesions is not directly attributable to lesion effects but is an indirect effect of the decreased food consumption characteristic of the lesioned birds. Such a conclusion is certainly compatible with the interdependance of eating and drinking that has been demonstrated for many species of birds and mammals (see Section II).

    b. Effects upon Body Weight Regulation. Following the resumption of eating in QF birds, the recovery of body weight lost during the period of aphagia is significantly retarded in comparison with birds that have been deprived of food for equivalent periods. Several types of observations suggest that this retardation does not reflect lesion effects upon digestive or metabolic processes. First, aphagic birds lose weight at a rate comparable to food-deprived normal birds. Second, aphagic birds may be maintained satisfactorily over long periods by intubation of a liquid diet or by force-feeding of grain. Under these conditions, lesioned birds show weight gains which are proportional to the size of the daily

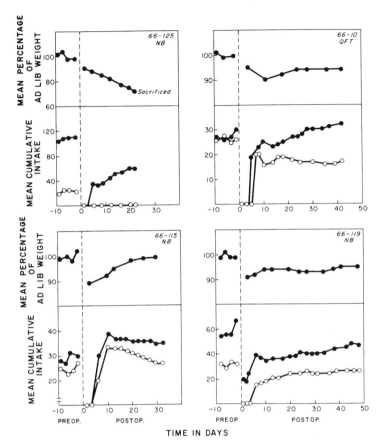

Fig. 22. Effects of lesions of QF structures upon food and water intake and body weight in the pigeon. (o———o), Food, in grams; (•———•), water, in milliliters. (From Zeigler and Karten, 1973a.)

ration. Finally, in lesioned birds which have resumed eating but remain hypophagic, the relation between food intake and body weight is similar to that of normal birds maintained on a reduced food ration (Zeigler *et al.*, 1969a, 1972).

These observations indicate that lesioned birds are utilizing their available food and regulating their body weight as efficiently as normal birds. The prolonged reduction in their body weight would therefore seem to be a direct consequence of their reduced intake (hypophagia) rather than an effect of QF lesions upon the regulation of body weight.

   c. Effects upon the Consummatory Response. In addition to effects upon food intake, lesions of QF structures also disrupt the pigeon's eating behavior in a manner which suggests interference with the sensory control of mandibulation—the process by which grain is moved from the beak tip to the back of the mouth prior to swallowing. Birds with such deficits can peck normally and will swallow food placed manually at the back of the mouth. However, they often fail to grasp the grain properly, or having grasped it, are unable to retain it in the mouth during mandibulation. As a result, the efficiency of their eating behavior may be severely impaired. A simple measure of the reduction in their feeding efficiency can be derived by calculating the number of pecks made to obtain a unit quantity of food. Long-term observations involve the automatic monitoring of pecking behavior at food in the home cage. Alternatively, short-term data may be obtained in simple "pick-up" tests carried out in an observation chamber with birds tested at a standard level of body weight loss to insure a constant level of responsiveness to food. The ratios obtained in these pick-up tests are quite stable over prolonged periods and characteristic of individual birds.

As the data in Table V indicate, normal pigeons consume about 95% of the available grains, and the ratio of feeding responses to grains consumed is about 1.5. Quintofrontal lesions produce significant reductions in the efficiency of feeding, which are approximately proportional to the extent of the lesions. The identification of such disruptions as sensory rather than motor is in accord with the electrophysiological data (presented in Section VII,B) and with the finding that a similar deficit is produced by section of the trigeminal sensory nerves (see Section VIII). By contrast, damage to the trigeminal motor nucleus produces a characteristic flaccidity of the lower beak which interferes with both eating and drinking (Zeigler, unpublished observations).

d. Effects upon Responsiveness to Food.   In view of the marked impairment of feeding efficiency seen after QF lesions, the reduced food intake of lesioned birds may simply reflect a reduction in their ability to carry out the consummatory response. Alternatively, the aphagia and hypophagia of QF birds may be due to lesion effects upon neural mechanisms underlying responsiveness to food. Fortunately, it is possible to dissociate these two effects experimentally by using a feedometer to monitor pecking in the bird's home cage. By examining the relation between food intake and feedometer responses we can determine whether the decreased food intake seen postoperatively is due to a reduction in the efficiency of the feeding response or to a reduction in the pigeon's responsiveness to food. In the former case, we would expect many feedometer responses but little or no ingestion of food during the immediate postoperative period. In the latter case, absence or reduction of food intake would be paralleled by the abolition or reduction of pecking responses.

As the examples in Fig. 23 illustrate, lesions of QF structures produce both "consummatory" and "responsiveness" deficits. While pecking responses are either abolished or dramatically reduced during the aphagic period, birds who later begin ingesting measurable amounts of food usually also show a reduction in their feeding efficiency. However, the relation between responsiveness to food, feeding efficiency, and food intake is not a simple one. In birds which have

TABLE V
Effects of QF Lesions upon the Efficiency of Feeding Behavior[a]

| | Preoperative | | | | Postoperative | | | |
Bird number	No. of observations	No. of pecking responses	Grains obtained (%)	Ratio: pecks/ grain	No. of observations	No. of pecking responses	Grains obtained (%)	Ratio: pecks/ grain
PrV group:								
77	5	130	100	1.3	4	1241	57	36.5
149	4	105	100	1.7	4	909	90	12.6
332	5	144	94	1.5	5	268	3	89.3
338	5	162	95	1.6	5	1517	69	21.9
NB group:								
43	5	255	100	1.7	5	304	85	2.4
47	5	201	95	1.3	5	524	76	4.6
53	5	218	95	1.5	5	473	55	4.7
68–71	5	165	95	1.6	6	498	98	4.2
Control group:								
55	5	102	92	1.3	5	123	89	1.3
90	5	141	100	1.4	5	150	97	1.5

[a]Modified from Zeigler and Karten (1973b, Table 2).

sustained some degree of body weight loss the presence of a marked reduction in feeding efficiency is not incompatible with a high level of responsiveness to food. (Indeed, it is this fact which underlies the use of deprivation procedures in our "pick-up" tests of feeding efficiency.) Using the present procedures, then, an accurate determination of the postoperative time course of responsiveness is confounded by the facilitatory effects of reduced body weight in aphagic and hypophagic birds. Experiments currently in progress in our laboratory will provide such data by monitoring feeding responses in QF birds maintained at 95% of their ad lib weight by daily hand feeding.

    e. Effects upon Food-Reinforced Operant Responses. Because of the widespread use of operant paradigms as measures of "hunger" in studies of mammalian brain mechanisms, it seems appropriate to examine the effects of QF lesions upon key-pecking responses reinforced either with food or water. Our test situation permits the independant measurement of the number of key-pecking responses, the number of reinforcements delivered, the number of feeding (or drinking) responses, and the amount of food (or water) consumed. By calculating the ratio of pecks made into the food hopper to grams of food consumed, a simple measure of feeding efficiency in the operant situation is obtained.

    Although lesions of QF structures do not disrupt the performance of a

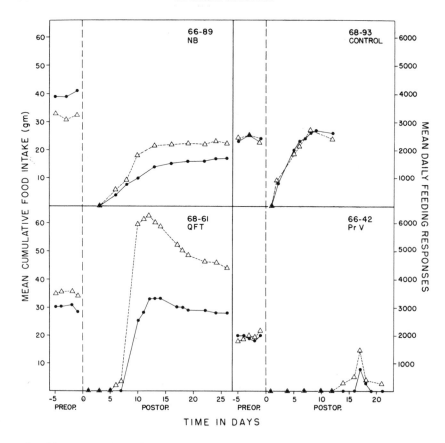

Fig. 23. The relation between food intake (●———●) and feeding responses in pigeons with lesions of QF structures. Feeding behavior is monitored automatically in individual birds: a feedometer (△———△) is used which detects pecks into the food box and provides a measure of the number of feeding responses made each day. By relating intake to number of feeding responses, lesion effects upon both feeding efficiency and responsiveness to food may be measured. (From Zeigler and Karten, 1973b.)

key-pecking response reinforced with water (Fig. 24), they abolish food-reinforced responses for periods ranging from a few days to several weeks postoperatively. Once again, the persistence of the deficit is proportional to the bilateral extent of the lesion. Not only is key pecking abolished during this period, but the birds do not make pecking responses into the food magazine on probe trials during which the magazine is presented automatically for the standard 6-second reinforcement interval. In all cases, the reappearance of key pecking and magazine responses to preoperative levels takes place simultaneously and fairly abruptly (Fig. 25). However, many of the birds showed a significant

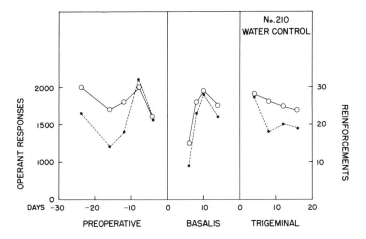

Fig. 24. Effects of an NB lesion and of trigeminal nerve section upon an operant key-pecking response (●) reinforced with water (○). (From Zeigler and Karten, 1973b.)

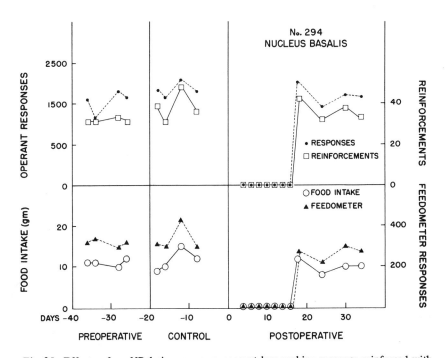

Fig. 25. Effects of an NB lesion upon an operant key-pecking response reinforced with food. Key pecking is abolished for seven sessions and then returns abruptly to its preoperative level. (From Zeigler and Karten, 1973b.)

increase in the ratio of feeding responses to food intake, indicating a reduction in feeding efficiency. The presence of high levels of food-reinforced key pecking in birds showing clear-cut impairments of the consummatory response was not unusual and an instructive example is shown in Fig. 26. Except for a transient decrease following a bilateral PrV lesion, key pecking remains at normal levels, as do feeding responses. However, because of the neurosensory deficit, food intake is substantially reduced. The addition of what proved to be an essentially unilateral NB lesion increased the neurosensory deficit to the point where little or no food was being obtained from a magazine. Nevertheless, the reduction in food-reinforced key pecking is minimal by comparison with the effects of bilateral NB lesions. Moreover, many of the birds which did not peck either at the key or into the food magazine would eat a supplementary food ration presented in a dish offered either in the Skinner box or in the home cage.

As we have noted above, the relationship between "consummatory" and "responsiveness" measures of hunger is not a simple one, and it was data such as these which first suggested to us the possibility of experimentally dissociating the neural mechanisms controlling operant and consummatory responses (see Section VIII). In any case, it is clear from our studies that lesions of QF

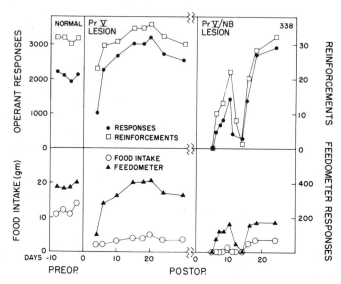

Fig. 26. Effects of several consecutive procedures upon performance of an operant key-pecking response reinforced with food. *Left:* Preoperative data. *Middle:* Following a bilateral lesion of PrV, Case 338 continues to show a high level of key pecking despite a neurosensory deficit which results in reduced food intake. *Right:* The addition of a large unilateral NB lesion increases this deficit to the point where little or no food is being obtained, but key pecking is maintained although reduced in rate. (From Zeigler and Karten, 1973b.)

structures disrupt *both* the neurosensory and the motivational control of feeding in the pigeon.

2. Archistriatum

Anatomical data (Zeier and Karten, 1971) indicate that this area receives a variety of afferent projections from other forebrain regions, including a major projection from nucleus basalis via the fronto-archistriate tract, and is the origin of several efferent systems. Furthermore, the archistriatum is a morphologically heterogeneous structure divisible into at least four major nuclear regions. According to Zeier and Karten two of these regions—the posterior and medial archistriatum—should be considered analogous to mammalian "limbic" structures, while the anterior and intermediate archistriatum may be functionally equivalent to the somatosensorimotor cortex in mammals.

The location of the archistriatum at a junction pioint for several afferent and efferent systems related to feeding suggests that the structure might play a major role in the neural control of ingestive behavior. However, neurobehavioral analyses are complicated both by this structure's histological complexity and by the fact that many of its neurons are the cell bodies of descending fiber systems. Placement of discrete lesions confined to a histologically homogeneous region will be difficult, as will be the interpretation of their effects, since they could be due either to nuclear damage or to interruption of efferent pathways (or both). Considerations of this sort make it exceedingly difficult to evaluate the few available reports of deficits seen after archistriate lesions in pigeons.

Preliminary studies from our laboratory have shown that such lesions are followed by a disruption of food intake whose extent and persistence are similar to that seen after QF lesions (Zeigler et al., 1969b). Studies of the eating behavior of such birds suggest a "sensorimotor" disruption in their consummatory response with a consequent reduction in the efficiency of feeding. Zeier (1974) has observed comparable deficits after archistriate lesions. However, as with QF lesions it is possible to dissociate sensorimotor and responsiveness deficits using the feedometer (Fig. 27). The results of such analyses suggest that the decreased food intake seen after archistriate lesions reflects primarily a reduced responsiveness to food.

Zeier (1971) has examined the effects of relatively discrete archistriate lesions upon food-reinforced operant key pecking under either VI (60 seconds) or DRL (10 seconds) reinforcement schedules.[2] He suggests that optimal performance on such schedules involves some degree of response inhibition, but of different types. Lesions of somatosensorimotor regions produced increased responding on the VI schedule but decreased responding (and increased reinforcement) on the DRL schedule. Converse effects were seen after lesions of limbic regions. Zeier

[2] VI: Variable interval schedule; DRL: differential reinforcement of low rate.

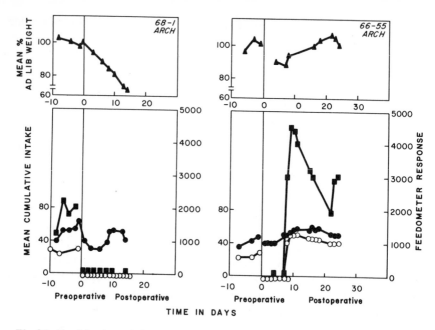

Fig. 27. Food intake and feedometer responses in two birds with archistriate lesions. ■, Feedometer; ○, food (in grams); ●, water (in milliliters), ▲, weight.

interprets these results in terms of an interaction between limbic "gate-setting" mechanisms and motor effector systems.

Zeier's observation that some types of archistriate lesions increase responding on a VI schedule is not easy to reconcile with our finding that both nucleus basalis and OMT lesions (see the next subsection) markedly reduce food-reinforced key pecking on a VI (60-second) schedule, particularly in view of the close anatomical relationships among basalis, archistriatum, and OMT. However, resolution of this problem must await completion of a systematic neurobehavioral analysis of archistriate deficits similar to that carried out for QF structures. In the interim it seems appropriate merely to include the archistriatum as part of a network of structures involved in the neural control of feeding.

3. The Occipitomesencephalic Tract (OMT)

Arising from neurons in the archistriatum, this tract has two major subdivisions which may be differentiated on the basis of both their origins and terminations. One pathway (HOM) terminates upon hypothalamic regions, whereas the other (OMT) projects to diencephalic, mesencephalic, pontine, and spinal levels. Its distribution within these levels is quite extensive and includes terminations in both the visual and trigeminal systems (Zeier and Karten, 1971; Cohen and Karten, 1974). This pattern of projections suggests that, like the archistriatum, it should play an important role in the control of ingestive behavior.

Given so extensive and varied a pattern of termination, the first step in a neurobehavioral analysis of OMT would be its decomposition into a set of functionally distinct subsystems related to specific components of ingestive behavior. Such an analysis would involve a combination of stimulation procedures, section of the tract at different levels, and placement of lesions within its major nuclear terminations. Only the barest start has been made at such an analysis in a series of studies (Levine, 1976) of the deficits in ingestive behavior that follow lesions of OMT at the mesencephalic level [A 4.00 in the Karten and Hodos (1967) atlas].

It is clear from Table VI that such lesions are followed by a significant reduction in intake and that there is little or no responding during the period of aphagia. Differential effects upon various components of the consummatory response are reflected in the data of Table VII, which were obtained from food-deprived birds tested at 80% of ad lib weight. While OMT lesions do not impair swallowing, they dramatically reduce the efficiency of eating. Superficially, the consummatory response deficits seen after OMT lesions resemble those seen after damage to trigeminal structures in that both increase the ratio of pecks made to grains consumed in the drop test. However, cinematographic analysis of eating behavior indicates that the reduction in eating efficiency reflects different types of deficit in the two groups.

TABLE VI

Effects on OMT Lesions upon Food Intake and Feeding Responses

Bird number	Preoperative (feeding) 7 days		Postoperative (aphagic)			Postoperative (feeding) 7 days	
	Total food intake	Total pecking responses	Days of aphagia	Total pecking response	Percent weight loss	Total food intake	Total pecking responses
524	242	13,656	2	2	10	85	3,885
541	145	15,420	13	428	20	144	52,755
543	187	10,437	2	3	8	99	3,831
545	178	17,065	0	–	–	81	4,272
547	218	27,185	36[a]	0	35	–	–
555	216	8,106	40[a]	0	30	–	–
559	235	19,689	0	–	–	88	5,778
562	219	15,599	4	0	11	167	9,383
565	212	34,667	4	86	7	164	18,851
568	138	9,405	11	0	23	161	8,822

[a]Sacrificed prior to resumption of feeding.

TABLE VII

Effects of OMT Lesions upon the "Consummatory Response" of Eating

	Preoperative						Postoperative					
		Pecking		Mandibulation		Swallowing		Pecking		Mandibulation		Swallowing
Bird number	No. of observations	No. of pecking responses	Rate of pecks/second	Grains obtained (%)	Ratio of pecks/grain	Grains swallowed (%)	No. of observations	No. of pecking responses	Rate of pecks/second	Grains obtained (%)	Ratio of pecks/grain	Grains swallowed (%)
188	9	1583	3.6	99	1.8	100	9	7411	2.0	45	18.2	100
321	8	1162	2.9	99	1.5	100	6	4701	2.9	97	8.1	100
337	6	763	3.9	100	1.3	100	5	3463	2.3	51	13.6	100
436	9	1084	2.7	80	1.5	100	7	2731	1.8	52	7.5	99
535	7	932	2.8	99	1.3	100	6	3035	2.8	99	5.1	100

In normal birds the extent of beak opening during pecking is proportional to the size of the grain, and this adjustment is made prior to tactual contact with the grain. After damage to the trigeminal structures the mouth opens normally during the peck, which ends with the open beak centered over the grain. By contrast the eating behavior of OMT birds is characterized either by a complete failure to open the mouth during the peck or by an incomplete degree of opening. On tests involving both large (peas) and small (milo) grains, the deficit is evident with both but is greatest with the large grains (Fig. 28). These observations suggest that, by contrast with the disruption of neurosensory processes seen after trigeminal damage, the consummatory response deficits of OMT birds reflect a disruption of the neuromotor control of eating behavior.

Furthermore, OMT lesions disrupt several aspects of performance in an operant conditioning situation involving food reinforcement on a VI 60-second schedule. The effects are similar to those seen after nucleus basalis lesions in that key pecking is abolished for prolonged periods. During this period birds did not make any feeding responses during probe trials on which the food magazine was presented for an 8-second reinforcement interval. In those cases where key

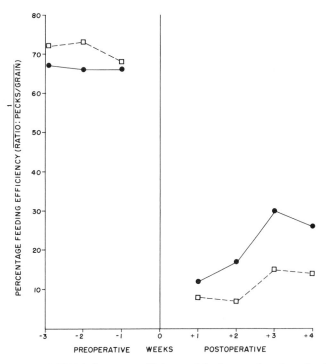

Fig. 28. Effects of OMT lesions upon efficiency of feeding as a function of grain size. (□), Peas; (●), milo. $N = 5$.

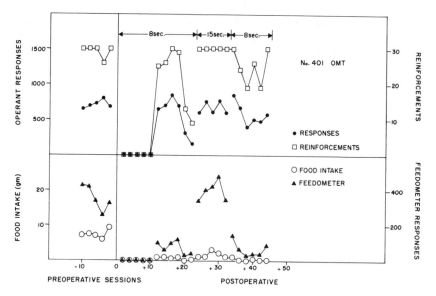

Fig. 29. Effects of OMT lesions upon food-reinforced operant key pecking in the pigeon, showing the effects of manipulating the reinforcement interval.

pecking returns, it is accompanied by a reduction in responses to food during the reinforcement interval and by a decrease in the efficiency of eating. This combination of deficits often leads to extinction of the recovered key-pecking response. However, increasing the reinforcement interval from 8 to 15 seconds leads to an increase in the number of feeding responses and a reinstatement of key pecking. As the data in Fig. 29 indicate, key pecking may remain at high levels even during periods of reduced responsiveness to food and relatively trivial food intake, suggesting that the brain mechanisms controlling key pecking, responsiveness to food, and feeding efficiency are potentially separable.

Our findings on the effects of OMT lesions are not incompatible with the anatomical data and do indeed suggest that OMT is an efferent component of the pigeon's putative "feeding system." However, in the absence of more systematic analyses of both archistriatum and OMT, we must aknowledge that their functional contribution to that system is unknown.

D. BRAIN STIMULATION: STIMULUS-BOUND FEEDING AND
SELF-STIMULATION

The development of techniques for intracranial stimulation through chronically implanted electrodes has undoubtedly facilitated the identification of loci in the mammalian brain as components of the "feeding systems" of various species. These techniques have also been used to demonstrate the phenomenon of intracranial reinforcement by self-stimulation in mammalian species from rat to man. Studies of the relation between self-stimulation and stimulus-bound feeding in mammals have suggested that the circuits for feeding and self-stimulation either share common anatomical substrates or overlap to a considerable extent. Comparable studies might be expected to prove similarly informative with respect to the brain mechanisms underlying each of these behaviors in the pigeon.

Such studies are relatively rare, however, largely due to the fact that there have been few convincing demonstrations of either stimulus-bound feeding or intracranial self-stimulation in birds. Although Äckerman et al. (1960) reported stimulus bound feeding in the pigeon, attempts to replicate his findings on the pigeon (Goodman and Brown, 1966) or with the chicken (Phillips and Youngren, 1971) or duck (Maley, 1969) have proved largely unsuccessful. An equal lack of success has characterized most attempts to demonstrate the potency of intracranial stimulation as a reinforcer of operant behavior in birds (MacPhail, 1966, 1967; Harwood and Vowles, 1966); for a review of the literature on electrical stimulation of the brain in birds, see Wright (1975).

Three alternatives suggest themselves as explanations of these failures: first, that intracranial stimulation functions in a qualitatively different manner within the avian and mammalian brain; second, that completely different brain structures mediate these same phenomena in the two classes (birds and mammals); and third, that the behaviors involve homologous neural structures at different loci in the avian and mammalian brains. In view of the many similarities in the functional organization of the brain in birds and mammals (Cohen and Karten, 1974; Nauta and Karten, 1970), the first alternative seems unlikely. Some recent findings suggest that a combination of both the remaining alternatives may be operative.

In 1970, Webster and Beale reported an unequivocal demonstration of intracranial self-stimulation in the pigeon. A key-pecking response was shaped and maintained with intracranial stimulation as the sole reinforcer, and response rates of from 500 to 1000 per hour were reported. Because the electrode placements in these birds were ostensibly in the neostriatum, an area presumably not homologous with sites from which self-stimulation can be elicited in mammals, a subsequent study was carried out to demonstrate that lateral hypothalamic stimulation could also be positively reinforcing in the pigeon (Davis et al., 1972). A reexamination of the histological material suggests that the telencephalic placements were actually in the ectostriatum, whereas the diencephalic placements seem to coincide with the location of the QFT at the level of the lateral hypothalamus.

In order to clarify the problem of intracranial self-stimulation in the pigeon we have recently initiated a series of collaborative studies with Webster and his colleagues (Zeigler et al., 1976). Preliminary data indicate that intracranial stimulation at both ectostriatum and nucleus basalis will reinforce operant key pecking in the pigeon. The response topography (i.e., duration; interresponse time) of the key pecks reinforced by brain stimulation is similar to that of key pecks reinforced with food and is uninfluenced by water deprivation. Furthermore, trigeminal deafferentation abolishes intracranial self-stimulation in the pigeon while resection of the olfactory nerve has no apparent effect. Studies currently in progress are designed to examine the effects of food deprivation upon self-stimulation elicited from the two sites and to explore the possibility that they will also support stimulus-bound feeding.

The mere demonstration of self-stimulation in yet another species is of little intrinsic significance. However, it is of interest that the regions involved are telencephalic relay nuclei of the two exteroceptive sensory systems most directly involved in the pigeon's feeding behavior—the visual and trigeminal systems. For each of these systems there is a considerable body of data on its anatomical organization, its electrophysiological characteristics, and the degree to which it is functionally equivalent to its mammalian counterpart (Cohen and Karten, 1974). It would therefore be feasible to carry out a program of stimulation, lesion, and recording experiments to identify the neural circuits mediating self-stimulation in the pigeon far more readily than has hitherto been the case with the rat (Valenstein, 1968).

E. LEVELS OF BRAIN ORGANIZATION AND THE NEURAL CONTROL OF FEEDING

Lesions of a number of different structures at several levels of the avian brain disrupt the consummatory response of eating, reduce responsiveness to food, and impair performance of food-reinforced operant responses. Although the different types of deficit may be experimentally dissociated, they appear to be mediated by common neural substrates. Moreover, the syndromes of deficits produced by lesions of the different structures appear, at least superficially, to be quite similar, so that it is not easy to differentially characterize the OMT and QFT syndromes.

Such similarities in the deficits produced by lesions of different structures may be accounted for by the fact that all these structures are anatomically and functionally connected. The deficits seen after a lesion of one of the structures may reflect both direct damage to that structure and indirect effects (e.g., deafferentation) upon other structures in the pigeon's putative "feeding system." On the other hand, the fact that at least a tentative distinction between "neurosensory" and "neuromotor" deficits has been possible with respect to the consummatory response suggests that the observed similarities are indeed superficial and that our techniques of behavioral analysis have been insufficiently discriminating.

It is interesting to note that perhaps the most useful information has been provided by detailed analyses of feeding behavior (see Section VIII) patterns and of the spatiotemporal organization of the consummatory response. However tedious and time consuming such analyses may be, they do increase the "resolution" of our behavioral observations. It is likely that only such a "microanalysis" of behavior will enable us to determine the unique contribution of specific brain structures to the neural control of feeding.

VIII. TRIGEMINAL DEAFFERENTATION AND FEEDING BEHAVIOR

In our thinking about the neural control of behavior the conceptual distinction between "sensorimotor" and "motivational" mechanisms (Lashley, 1938) has always seemed a reasonable one. The distinction has certainly provided a useful framework for categorizing the types of deficits seen after lesions of central components of the pigeon's feeding behavior system. Such lesions do, indeed, produce deficits which may be characterized as either sensorimotor or motivational. However, implicit in the conceptual distinction has been the assumption that the two types of mechanisms would prove to be embodied in distinctly different neural structures. As the evidence reviewed in Section VII indicates, this has not proved to be the case with respect to the neural control of feeding in the pigeon. While the effects of brain lesions may be dichotomized into either sensorimotor or motivational deficits by means of behavioral techniques, a given lesion invariably produces *both* types of deficit.

There are at least two possible explanations for this finding. First, it is possible that the conceptual dichotomy between sensorimotor and motivational mechanisms does not reflect a corresponding dichotomy in the actual organization of neural mechanisms underlying feeding behavior. Second, the failure to achieve a neural dissociation of the two types of deficits may reflect the fact that all these brain structures have a variety of inputs and outputs. Thus the deficits observed after a brain lesion will reflect not only direct damage to that structure but deafferentation effects upon other structures.

In a somewhat naive, but ultimately rewarding, attempt to dissociate sensory and motivational control mechanisms we reasoned that section of the peripheral sensory branches of the trigeminal nerve—presumably a purely "sensory" intervention—should produce only neurosensory deficits in the control of feeding. This hypothesis was consistent with a substantial body of data indicating that, in the rat, oropharyngeal sensations are not essential either for the arousal of hunger and thirst or for the regulation of body weight (Epstein, 1967). However, this generalization was derived from experiments involving the combination of intragastric feeding techniques and operant conditioning procedures (Epstein and Teitelbaum, 1962) rather than from studies of feeding behavior in surgically deafferented animals. The pigeon has proved to be a superb preparation for deafferentation studies for two reasons. First, because taste and smell play so minimal a role in the sensory control of its feeding. Second, because the location and distribution of the sole remaining oropharyngeal sensory pathway, i.e., the trigeminal nerve, permits deafferentation of the oral region without disruption of either motor or proprioceptive functions. The results of our first study (Zeigler, 1973a) rapidly disabused us of the notion that deafferentation would produce only "sensory" deficits and prompted a detailed analysis of feeding behavior in the deafferented pigeon.

A. EFFECTS UPON INTAKE AND BODY WEIGHT REGULATION

Trigeminal deafferentation, although it has no effect upon drinking, is followed by a disruption of feeding behavior as severe and persistent as any we have encountered after lesions of central trigeminal structures (Zeigler et al., 1975; Zeigler, 1975a). Bilateral section of all three sensory branches has produced periods of aphagia ranging from 1 to 8 weeks and followed by equally prolonged periods of hypophagia. As the data in Fig. 30 (b) indicate, the magnitude of these deficits is proportional to the number of nerve branches sectioned bilaterally. From experiments in which sections are carried out in several stages (Fig. 31) it is clear that the magnitude of the deficit does not vary with the specific branch sectioned. Moreover, the effects of sectioning any single trigeminal branch are increased when the denervation is superimposed upon a previous section, even if the bird has already recovered from the first procedure. Thus the impairments produced by successive nerve sections appear to be cumulative.

The rate of weight loss during the period of aphagia in deafferented birds is comparable to that of normal pigeons food deprived for equivalent periods, and there is no evidence for an impairment in metabolic or digestive processes. However, even after their food intake has returned to its preoperative level, deafferented birds typically fail to show the degree of compensatory overeating appropriate to their state of body-weight loss. As Fig. 30 (a) indicates, the body weights of such birds remain below preoperative levels for prolonged periods. A similar deficit is evident in the data for birds subjected to two-stage sections. Although intake may gradually approach its preoperative level, the recovery of lost body weight is severely retarded because of the absence of compensatory overeating. Thus while the deafferentation does not impair the pigeon's capacity for weight regulation, their reduced intake produces a prolonged reduction in body weight to levels below those of normal birds.

B. EFFECTS UPON THE CONSUMMATORY RESPONSE

Although it does not effect either the rate or the efficiency of drinking (Zeigler et al., 1975, Table 3), trigeminal deafferentation is followed by a striking reduction in the efficiency of eating. The magnitude of the deficit is

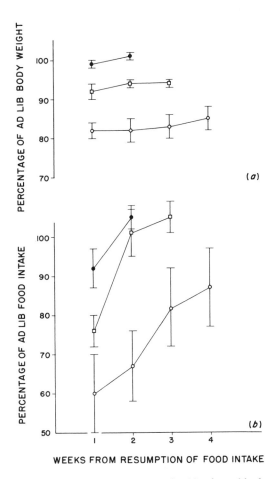

Fig. 30. Effects of trigeminal deafferentation on food intake and body weight. Postoperative body weight (*a*) and food intake (*b*) as a percentage of their free-feeding values. Data for each bird were calculated from the resumption of feeding and standard error is indicated by vertical bars. For each group $N = 8$. (●———●) Control; (□———□), 2 branch; (○———○), 3 branch. (From Zeigler, 1975a. *J. Comp. Physiol. Psychol.* **89**, 827–844. Copyright 1975 by The American Psychological Association. Reprinted by permission.)

approximately proportional to the number of nerve branches sectioned bilaterally. In some cases with three branch sections, birds frequently made more than one hundred successive responses without obtaining a single kernel of grain. The severity and persistence of these deficits is illustrated in Fig. 32, which presents data gathered in "pick-up" tests of feeding efficiency.

A combination of behavioral tests and cinematographic analyses has enabled us to determine which specific components of the feeding behavior sequence are disrupted by trigeminal sensory nerve section. Deafferentation does not impair

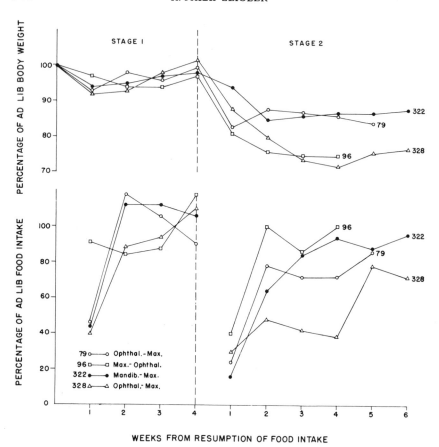

Fig. 31. Effects of bilateral trigeminal deafferentation carried out in two stages. (From Zeigler, 1975a. *J. Comp. Physiol. Psychol.* **89**, 827–844. Copyright 1975 by The American Psychological Association. Reprinted by permission.)

the ability to swallow kernels of grain placed manually at the back of the mouth, nor does it reduce the *frequency* of pecking in pick-up tests. Thus the reduction in feeding efficiency must be due to an impairment of either pecking accuracy or of the grasp and mandibulation components of eating. The data presented in Table VIII indicates that deafferentation affects both pecking and grasping. Out of a total of 209 pecks initiated by unoperated birds, 99% terminate in contact with the grain while the mean percentage of contacts in deafferented birds is about 87% (if the analysis is based only upon three-branch data, the figure is 73%). The reduction in the probability of contact does not involve any disorganization of the temporal patterning of pecking but reflects a slight (though noticeable) displacement of the beak to the side of the grain. Although the effect on pecking is rather subtle, the impairment of grasping is quite obvious.

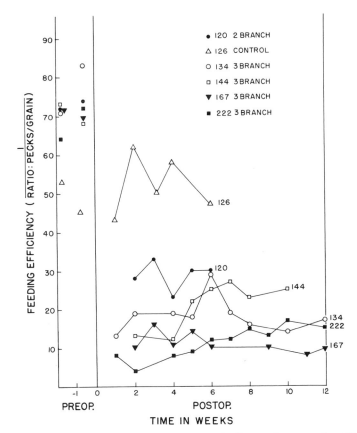

Fig. 32. Effects of varying degrees of trigeminal deafferentation upon the efficiency of eating in the pigeon. Birds are tested at 80% of their free-feeding weight, and the efficiency measure used is the reciprocal of the ratio of pecks made to grains consumed in a 10-minute pick-up test. (From Zeigler *et al.*, 1975. *J. Comp. Physiol. Psychol.* **89**, 845–858. Copyright 1975 by The American Psychological Association. Reprinted by permission.)

By comparison with a 96% rate of successful grasps preoperatively, three-branch birds succeed in grasping only about 30% of the grains with which they make tactile contact. In most of these cases the peck ends normally with the open beak centered around the grain, but the grain either slips out during the beak closing or is dropped after grasping.

The impairment in accuracy of pecking, which has been observed in many deafferented birds, is difficult to explain. The possibility that it reflects damage to eye muscles during section of the infraorbital branch of the ophthalmic nerve is unlikely because of the extreme care taken to avoid such damage. Moreover, the data of two birds in Table IX were obtained using a three-stage resection procedure, and the deficit in pecking accuracy did not appear until the third

TABLE VIII
Trigeminal Deafferentation and the Consummatory Response:
Cinematographic Analysis

Bird number	Treatment	No. of pecks	Contacts (%)	Grasps (%)	Ratio: pecks/grain
433	Preoperative	55	96	81	1.3
	1-branch	44	98	88	1.2
	2-branch	96	91	23	6.8
	3-branch	61	80	14	8.7
434	Preoperative	40	100	98	1.0
	1-branch	53	100	92	1.2
	2-branch	52	100	65	5.1
	3-branch	42	64	22	8.4
167	3-branch	120	75	51	3.4
Control group:					
424	Normal	37	97	94	1.1
426	Normal	39	100	100	1.1
430	Normal	38	100	94	1.2

stage, which in both cases was a maxillary section. It is possible that tactile input from an initial beak contact is used to correct the placement of subsequent contacts and that the persistent displacement seen after deafferentation reflects the absence of such feedback. In any case, the problem of how disruption of somatosensory input can produce an impairment in what appears to be a visually elicited ballistic response is an intriguing one.

The impairments in grasping and mandibulation are consistent with the electrophysiological data discussed in Section VII. Deafferentation effects upon the efficiency of feeding in the pigeon undoubtedly reflect a disruption of phasic sensory inputs involved in the somatosensory control of these two movement patterns. On the basis of analogous experiments employing electromyographic (EMG) and cinematographic techniques, Zweers and Wouterlood (1973; Zweers, 1974) have suggested a comparable role for the trigeminal system in the neurosensory control of feeding behavior in the duck.

C. EFFECTS UPON RESPONSIVENESS TO FOOD

Although we had tentatively hypothesised that trigeminal deafferentation would produce purely "sensory" deficits, the monitoring of feeding responses in the home cage under ad lib conditions provided clear evidence of an effect upon responsiveness to food. During the period of postoperative aphagia the number

TABLE IX

Effects of Trigeminal Deafferentation upon Food Intake and Feeding Efficiency in the Pigeon

Bird number	Preoperative (feeding) for 7 days			Postoperative (aphagic)		Postoperative (feeding) for 7 days		
	Total food intake (gm)	Total pecking responses	Ratio of responses per gram	Days of aphagia	Total pecking responses	Total food intake (gm)	Total pecking responses	Ratio of responses per gram
61	179	27,089	151	40	5,242	66	76,310	1,156
63	139	14,203	102	13	1,320	64	8,964	140
71	109	21,123	193	5	1,687	60	15,771	263
107	211	26,361	125	7	1,055	214	17,930	83
109	223	19,852	89	7	933	131	18,893	144
130	107	18,502	173	5	840	107	13,232	123
132	215	14,962	69	7	973	138	15,710	113
140	161	13,348	82	5	572	99	8,996	91

of daily pecking responses at food was drastically reduced (Table IX). As the birds began to ingest measureable amounts of food a reduction in feeding efficiency also was apparent. However, although efficiency gradually improved, food intake remained insufficient to permit recovery of body weight at normal rates. The severity of these deficits in the most successful cases is illustrated by the data presented in Fig. 33.

Body Weight Loss and Responsiveness to Food after Trigeminal Deafferentation

In the normal pigeon, reductions in body weight produced by food deprivation are followed by increases in responsiveness to food which are proportional to the extent of the weight loss. This increased responsiveness is evident in both

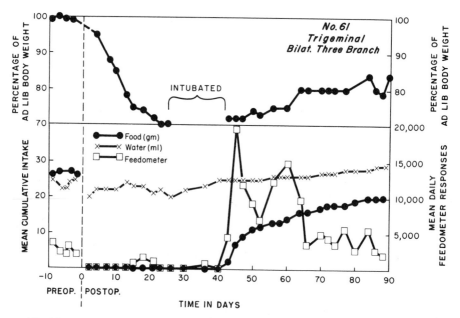

Fig. 33. Effects of three-branch trigeminal deafferentation on intake and responsiveness to food in a case typical of those showing prolonged disruption of food intake. In the week before surgery, Case 61 made a total of 27,089 pecking responses for 179 gm of food (ratio 151) and drank 170 ml of water. During the first postoperative week, the bird made only 445 feeding responses, obtained no food, but drank 150 ml of water. In the next 5 weeks, 4797 pecking responses were recorded with no measurable food intake. For a portion of this period the bird was maintained by intubation of a liquid diet. During the seventh postoperative week, the bird made 76,310 pecking responses and obtained 66 gm of food (ratio 1156). Although feeding efficiency improved gradually over the following weeks, there was no compensatory overeating and body weight stabilized at about 80% of its free-feeding value. (From Zeigler, 1973a. Copyright 1973 by The American Association for the Advancement of Science.)

short-term and long-term measures of hunger. The short-term effects are manifested in a decreased latency to eat and an increased food intake in a 1-hour test. Long-term effects are reflected in a period of compensatory overeating which varies in magnitude with the extent of the weight loss and which persists until the weight is recovered (see Sections III and V).

The data of the "pick-up" tests indicates that deafferented pigeons can show a high level of responsiveness to food under conditions of food deprivation. This suggests that in deafferented pigeons, as in normal ones, body weight loss has facilitatory effects upon responsiveness to food. Systematic data on the relationship between weight loss and responsiveness were therefore gathered under both short-term and long-term conditions.

Figure 34 indicates that with increasing weight loss latency to eat decreases and intake in a 1-hour test increases in both normal and deafferented birds. For the less extreme weight loss levels (10%, 20%) deafferented birds are less responsive to food, but under conditions of extreme deprivation (30%) both intake and latency values are comparable in the two groups.

However, body weight loss in deafferented pigeons does not produce the long-term facilitation of responsiveness seen in normal birds. Figure 35 illustrates the effects upon responsiveness, food intake, and body weight of trigeminal deafferentation performed in four birds who had previously been reduced to 80% of their free-feeding weight. For three of the birds deafferentation was

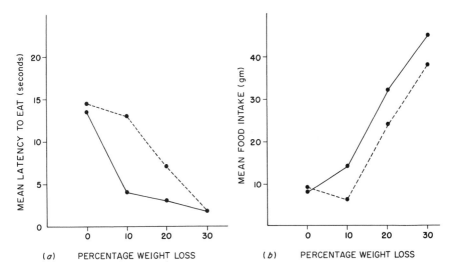

Fig. 34. Effects of varying degrees of body weight loss upon (a) latency to eat and (b) short-term food intake in normal and deafferented pigeons. (●——●), Control (N = 4); (●– – –●), deafferented (N = 8). (From Zeigler, 1975a. *J. Comp. Physiol. Psychol.* **89,** 827–844. Copyright 1975 by The American Psychological Association. Reprinted by permission.)

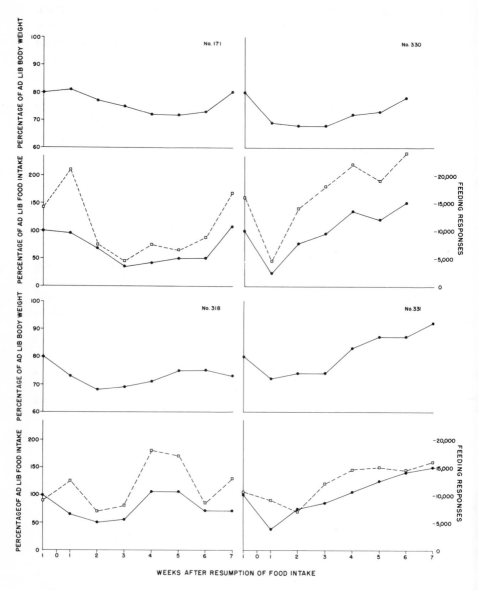

Fig. 35. Effects of trigeminal deafferentation carried out on food-deprived birds. Body weight, food intake (●), and feedometer responses (□) in four pigeons reduced to 80% of their free-feeding weight prior to deafferentation. (From Zeigler, 1975a. *J. Comp. Physiol. Psychol.* **89**, 827–844. Copyright 1975 by The American Psychological Association. Reprinted by permission.)

much less disruptive of responsiveness to food than the same procedure carried out when the bird is at ad lib weight. Three of the birds resumed eating within 1 to 3 days postoperatively, and the number of daily feedometer responses was close to or greater than its preoperative value. However, in succeeding weeks the retardation in the recovery of body weight typical of birds deafferented under ad lib conditions is also evident in the 80% group. Six weeks after the resumption of food intake, body weight in the deafferented pigeons ranges from 73% to 87% of preoperative values (for comparison with normal birds, see Fig. 9). Thus the facilitatory effect of weight loss seen in short-term tests with deafferented birds appears to be a relatively transient phenomenon and is not evident in a long-term test.

D. EFFECTS UPON FOOD-REINFORCED OPERANT RESPONSES

By providing an index of responsiveness to food independent of food intake, the feedometer data indicate that the effects of deafferentation, however they are mediated, are manifested behaviorally as a decreased probability of pecking at food. Since *pecking* is under the exteroceptive control of visual rather than somatosensory inputs, trigeminal deafferentation must produce its effects by altering the responsiveness of the sensorimotor mechanisms involved in pecking. This reduction in responsiveness may simply be indicative of a general loss of excitability in the sensorimotor systems underlying pecking per se, or it may reflect the disruption of processes specific to eating. In view of the convergence of primary trigeminal afferents upon neurons in the medulla and cervical spinal cord (Kerr, 1972; Dubbledam and Menken, 1973), the reduced responsiveness of deafferented birds may reflect a process analogous to *spinal shock,* which reduces the excitability of the interneurons and motoneurons that normally participate in pecking.

The extreme specificity of the deficit makes this an unlikely possibility, however. Trigeminal deafferentation does not disrupt either grooming or drinking, and both these behaviors involve patterns of neuromotor organization which must overlap extensively with those used in pecking at food. It therefore seems that deafferentation affects neural mechanisms specific to the control of responsiveness to food (i.e., hunger). However, since the morphology of the behavior patterns used in drinking and grooming differs somewhat from those used in pecking at grain, this interpretation would gain additional support from the demonstration that trigeminal deafferentation does not disrupt other behaviors which are even more similar to those involved in pecking at food.

Wolin (1968) and more recently Jenkins and Moore (1973) have shown that the form of the pecking responses used in the food- or water-reinforced key pecking of pigeons is very similar to that of the species-typical consummatory responses to food and water. Analysis of the effects of trigeminal deafferenta-

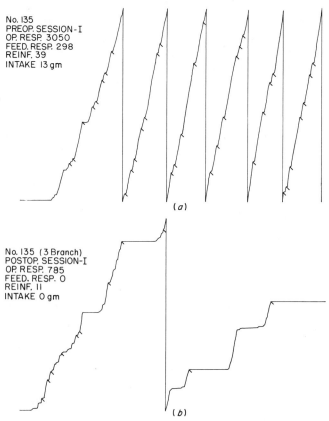

No. 135
PREOP. SESSION-I
OP. RESP. 3050
FEED. RESP. 298
REINF. 39
INTAKE 13 gm

(a)

No. 135 (3 Branch)
POSTOP. SESSION-I
OP. RESP. 785
FEED. RESP. 0
REINF. 11
INTAKE 0 gm

(b)

Fig. 36. Dissociation of operant and consummatory responses by trigeminal deafferenta-tion in the pigeon. Comparison of the cumulative records of key pecking for (a) the last preoperative and (b) the first postoperative test sessions in a pigeon subjected to bilateral, three-branch deafferentation. Despite the absence of feeding responses to the magazine, the deafferented bird emits bursts of key-pecking responses at the start of the session, but key pecking declines with times. (From Zeigler, 1975b.)

tion upon operant conditioning could therefore help clarify the problem of the specificity or generality of the deficit (Zeigler, 1975b).

In the light of our previous studies on the effects of central lesions we were surprised to find that trigeminal deafferentation appears to have no direct effect upon food-reinforced key pecking. Instead, its most obvious and immediate effect is to significantly reduce responses to food presented in the magazine during the reinforcement interval. This reduction in responsiveness ranged from 30 to 100%; indeed, during the first few postoperative sessions six of the eight birds made no feeding responses to magazine presentations produced either by

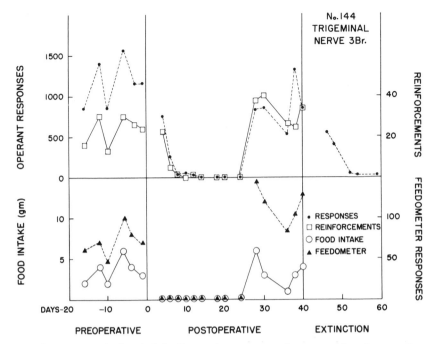

Fig. 37. Effects of trigeminal deafferentation upon several measures of performance in an operant conditioning situation. Although the bird makes 813 key pecks during the first postoperative session and delivers 28 reinforcements, it makes no feeding responses. Note the prolonged disruption of feeding responses (feedometer), the decline of key pecking, and its recovery simultaneously with the resumption of feeding. Initiation of an extinction procedure produces a decline in key pecking similar to that seen immediately after deafferentation. (From Zeigler, 1975b.)

their own key pecking or during "probe" trials during which the magazine was presented automatically.

Despite this absence of feeding responses in the Skinner box, key pecking was present in all birds during these sessions. Analysis of cumulative records such as those presented in Fig. 36 indicates that during their first postoperative sessions deafferented birds are capable of emitting bursts of operant responses at rates approximating their preoperative levels while simultaneously failing to respond to presentation of the food magazine.

In such cases there was a gradual decline in key pecking which resembles that seen during extinction. However, with continued testing there was a gradual increase in the number of feeding responses per reinforcement in some of the birds. With the resumption of measurable food intake, key pecking rapidly regained its preoperative levels. The time course of deafferentation effects for one such bird is illustrated in Fig. 37.

These findings are of interest in several respects. First, they demonstrate that trigeminal deafferentation can dissociate processes underlying the consummatory response to food and those controlling food-reinforced instrumental responses. Such a dissociation suggests that the mechanisms underlying operant key pecking involve different neural structures than those involved in responsiveness to food. Moreover, while trigeminal deafferentation disrupts feeding behavior without directly impairing operant conditioning, lesions of higher-order structures in the pigeon's feeding system appear to disrupt both types of behavior. Some of the implications of these findings will be discussed below (Section X).

E. EFFECTS UPON PATTERNS OF FEEDING BEHAVIOR

The evidence just summarized indicates that the reduced food intake of deafferented birds does not simply reflect an inability to perform the pecking response nor a reduction in the efficiency of eating. In order to clarify the nature of the deficit produced by trigeminal deafferentation we carried out a detailed analysis of long-term feeding behavior patterns in deafferented birds (Miller and Zeigler, 1974). Because such birds typically lose weight postoperatively, changes in feeding behavior patterns due to deafferentation could be confounded by the effects of body weight loss upon such patterns. Thus, in addition to a standard "surgical" control group, it was necessary to include a "deprivation" control group subjected to food deprivation sufficient to produce a weight loss equivalent to that produced by the postoperative aphagia of the deafferented birds.

In analyzing the feeding behavior patterns produced by either manipulation we focused on certain characteristic features which, although they may vary from bird to bird, tend to be stable for a given individual. These include ingestion rate, number of bouts, distribution of bout sizes, and temporal distribution of food intake within the daily feeding period (see Section V). Figure 38 illustrates the long-term feeding behavior patterns of a pigeon subjected to a bilateral, three-branch trigeminal deafferentation. Its feeding patterns should be compared with those of the subject illustrated in Fig. 16 that had been food deprived to produce a body weight loss (10%) equivalent to that which occurred in a deafferented bird as a consequence of several days of postoperative aphagia.

A comparison of the data of the "deprivation" and "deafferentation" groups reveals some striking similarities in their feeding behavior patterns. First, both groups eat exceptionally large meals during the initial portion of the daily feeding period. Second, both groups show a reduction in the number of feeding bouts made in the remainder of the feeding period. Third, there is in both groups an increase in the proportion of the total daily food intake that is consumed in medium- and large-size feeding bouts. Fourth, the rate of food ingestion in both groups is at or above normal levels for most of the period of observation.

It is clear that deafferented birds behave in many respects like food-deprived birds, which is not surprising since they too have undergone a period of food deprivation and body weight loss. Yet despite their similarities, the feeding patterns of the two groups lead to very different outcomes with respect to long-term food intake: compensatory overeating and body weight gain in the deprived birds; undereating and reduced body weight in the deafferented birds.

The difference in feeding behavior which mediate these differences in outcome become apparent when we examine the temporal distribution of food intake in the two groups. As we pointed out earlier (Section V) food intake in normal birds tends to be highest at the start of the daily feeding period, tapering off gradually thereafter. Following either deprivation or deafferentation, the initiation of eating is characterized by an exaggeration of this tendency, with both groups taking their largest meals during the initial portion of the feeding period. However, although both groups show a reduction in the frequency of subsequent feeding bouts, this reduction is not very marked in the deprived group and is compensated for by an increase in bout size. Thus the attenuation of feeding activity occurs at about its normal rate over the entire feeding period. In deafferented birds, on the other hand, the reduction of bout frequency after the initial burst of overeating is quite marked and is not accompanied by an increase in bout size. Thus the attenuation of feeding activity occurs much more rapidly in the deafferented group (Fig. 39).

In summary then, deprived birds respond to their body weight loss by increasing the size of the first few bouts while simultaneously sustaining the remainder of their daily feeding activity at its normal level. The result is a net increase in food intake and a rapid recovery of body weight. Deafferented birds also overeat in the first hour but fail to maintain normal levels of feeding activity during the rest of the day. The result is an insufficient increase or a net decrease in daily food intake and a retardation in the rate of body weight gain.

F. TRIGEMINAL DEAFFERENTATION AND THE CONCEPT OF TONIC SENSORY PROCESSES

The syndrome of deficits in feeding behavior seen after deafferentation is similar to that which follows lesions of central trigeminal structures. In both these preparations there is an immediate postoperative period of aphagia, varying in duration from several days to several months (Stage I) depending upon the bilateral extent of the lesions or the completeness of the deafferentation. This is followed by a period of hypophagia (Stage II) during which feeding efficiency is severely impaired and food intake is reduced below its preoperative level. Subsequently, there is a gradual improvement in feeding efficiency, and intake may approach or even exceed its preoperative level. Nevertheless, intake remains insufficient to compensate for the body weight lost during the period of aphagia, and during this period (Stage III) body weight, although it may be quite stable,

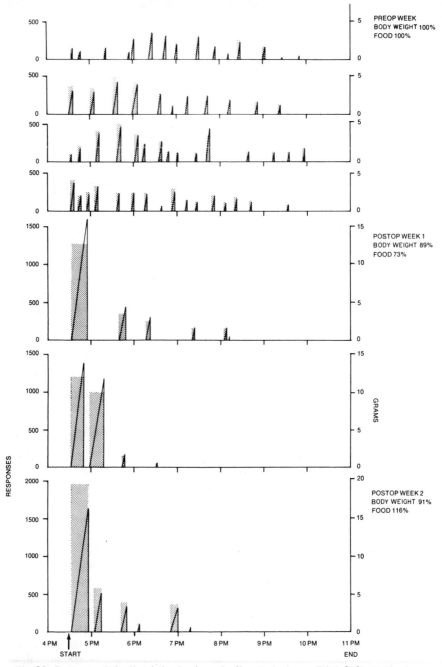

Fig. 38. Patterns of feeding behavior in a deafferented pigeon (Bird 373). Grids show intake (in grams), and lines within grids show responses. Note the increased size of the initial bout(s) and the marked reduction in the frequency of subsequent bouts. Compare with the case illustrated in Fig. 15, which has sustained an equivalent degree of body weight loss but without deafferentation.

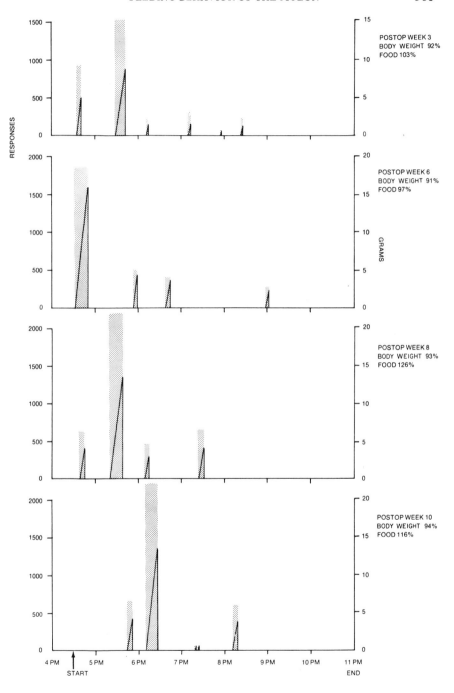

Fig. 38. See facing page for legend.

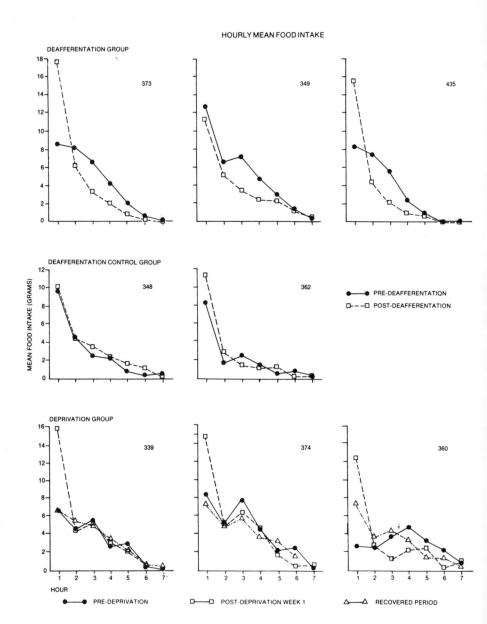

Fig. 39. Comparison of the rate of attenuation of food intake in deafferented, deprived, and surgical control birds.

is regulated at a level significantly below its preoperative value for prolonged periods.

The effects upon feeding efficiency have been shown to reflect a disruption of the phasic sensory inputs which mediate the trigeminal control of grasping and mandibulation. However, the reduction in responsiveness to food, that is, the decline in the initiation of pecking responses to food, is not readily explicable in these terms because the elicitation of pecking is under the control of visual rather than trigeminal inputs.

In order to account for these effects upon responsiveness we have hypothesized that, in addition to its *phasic* role in the neurosensory control of eating, trigeminal input has a *tonic* function in helping to maintain the excitability of central feeding behavior mechanisms. Given this "tonic" hypothesis, both the deafferentation effects and the effects of central trigeminal lesions may be accounted for by making the following corollary assumptions: (1) Neurons of the oropharyngeal components of the trigeminal system have both phasic and tonic outputs. (2) Trigeminal neurons have connections with other neuronal aggregates which function as components of a system controlling feeding behavior. (3) Inputs from these trigeminal neurons are primarily excitatory in their effects upon the activity of these feeding behavior mechanisms. (4) Other types of input (interoceptive and exteroceptive) may interact with that from trigeminal afferents to modulate the level of tonic activity in the pigeon's feeding system.

Accepting these assumptions, we may account for the two stages seen after trigeminal lesions or deafferentation as follows: The immediate postoperative reduction in responsiveness (Stage I—aphagia) is a consequence of the reduction in the level of tonic excitatory input from the trigeminal system to the sensorimotor mechanisms underlying responsiveness to food. The gradual decrease in body weight in the aphagic bird tends to increase responsiveness and leads to an increase in the probability of pecking at food (Stage II). The probability of eating in the deafferented bird will thus be a joint function of the extent of the deafferentation and the degree of body weight loss. However, even when eating is resumed in response to lost body weight, it will not be sustained in the normal manner because of the absence or reduction of the excitatory trigeminal inputs which are a normal accompaniment of eating in the intact animal. Consequently, feeding behavior, although initiated periodically, will be insufficient to compensate for the lost body weight (Stage III).

The assumptions upon which this analysis is based have a considerable amount of empirical support. (1) The trigeminal system of the pigeon contains neurons which are spontaneously active but which may also be driven by peripheral stimuli during feeding, as well as neurons active only in response to peripheral stimuli. (2) There are extensive connections between the trigeminal system and central neural structures implicated in both sensorimotor and responsiveness mechanisms. (3) Both peripheral deafferentation and lesions of central trigeminal structures produce a reduction in responsiveness to food, suggesting that the effects of trigeminal inputs upon these feeding mechanisms are primarily excitatory. (4) Body weight loss has a facilitory effect upon feeding behavior even in deafferented birds, which suggests that it can compensate to some extent for the reduction in trigeminal input after deafferentation. We have therefore concluded, tentatively, that trigeminal inputs have a tonic function in maintaining the excitability of central neural mechanisms involved in the initiation and persistence of feeding behavior.

The hypothesis that sensory systems, in addition to their informational (phasic) functions, may also have a (tonic) function in modulating the excitability of central neural mechanisms is not a novel proposition (cf. Buddenbrock, 1952; Pfaffman, 1961). However, as Bullock and Horridge (1965, p. 322) have pointed out, "...it has suffered from the ambiguity of the cases cited as evidence." Perhaps the least ambiguous source of support for the hypothesis comes from work on the neural mechanisms of invertebrate motor patterns (e.g., Wilson and Wyman, 1965). In recent years the "tonic hypothesis" gained a renewed impetus from a growing body of research on the functions of the mammalian olfactory system (Cain, 1974; Wenzel, 1975). These data suggest that olfactory inputs are involved in the expression of a wide variety of behaviors in a manner that is not readily explicable in terms of our current understanding of the role played by phasic olfactory inputs. However, so little is known about the phasic sensory determinants of many of the behaviors disrupted by olfactory lesions that it may be premature to invoke tonic processes.

On the other hand, analysis of the sensory determinants of eating in the pigeon show that pecking is visually elicited and that trigeminal deafferentation does not disrupt the spatiotemporal organization of the pecking response pattern. Rather it seems to decrease the probability of its elicitation by the appropriate visual stimuli. Such analyses make it highly unlikely that deafferentation exerts its effects by disrupting *phasic* inputs for pecking and therefore removes one source of ambiguity. Moreover, because of its "quantal" nature pecking may easily be recorded in digital fashion, providing an index of responsiveness that makes possible the experimental dissociation of the phasic and tonic effects of deafferentation upon feeding behavior. Finally, because the structures involved in the processing of trigeminal input have been identified and subjected to electrophysiological analysis, it is possible to study the effects of deafferentation upon the response properties of neurons at different levels of the trigeminal system. Ultimately, as the visual mechanisms underlying pecking behavior are elucidated it may be possible to clarify the relationship between trigeminal input and the excitability of the pecking mechanism. Against this background, the advantages of the pigeon as a preparation for the study of tonic sensory processes is readily apparent.

IX. IMPLICATIONS FOR THE STUDY OF
VERTEBRATE FEEDING BEHAVIOR

A. OROSENSORY MECHANISMS AND THE CONTROL OF FEEDING IN PIGEON AND RAT

It has long been evident that sensory factors, especially chemosensory inputs, play a critical role in both the initiation and maintenance of feeding behavior in invertebrates (Dethier, 1967, 1969). However, while there is considerable information on the role of oropharyngeal factors in the control of mammalian feeding behavior (Epstein, 1967), data on the effects of orosensory deafferentation have been sparse because of the difficulties involved in surgical denervation. Our current concepts of the role of orosensory factors are therefore based largely upon the classical experiments of Epstein and Teitelbaum involving a combination of intragastric feeding techniques and operant conditioning procedures (Epstein and Teitelbaum, 1962; Epstein, 1967). On the basis of such experiments it has been generally concluded that, in mammals, oropharyngeal sensations are not essential, either for the arousal of hunger and thirst or for the regulation of body weight (Epstein, 1967).

The technique of intragastric self-feeding has been criticized on methodological grounds by Holman (1969), and the problems raised in this paper have not been satisfactorily resolved. The procedure is also open to the logical criticism that it does not provide data on the role of oral sensations in feeding because it involves the decoupling rather than the elimination of oral sensations during feeding. As Oakley (1965, p. 209) puts it, "...the gastric tube preparation is logically unable to provide (an) answer ... for it eliminates the oral senses only by virtue of bypassing a normal step in feeding behavior, namely, the consummatory responses." Moreover, the techniques does not simply remove the species-typical consummatory response but also involves the performance of a learned operant response (bar pressing), reinforced by intragastric feeding. While it is undoubtedly true that there will be a close relation between the neural mechanisms controlling food intake and those controlling food-reinforced operant responses, these mechanisms may not be identical. Indeed, using the deafferented pigeon it is possible to dissociate performance of the operant key-pecking response from performance of the consummatory response of eating (Zeigler, 1975b). For all these reasons, generalizations about the role of oropharyngeal sensations based upon the intragastric/operant procedure must be advanced with caution.

It is therefore of particular interest that recent work from Epstein's laboratory suggests that earlier experiments using the intragastric/operant procedure had seriously underestimated the role of oropharyngeal sensations in "motivating and sustaining feeding behavior at optimal levels" in the rat (Snowdon, 1969, p.

98). In the absence of oropharyngeal sensations, bar pressing for intragastric feeding extinguishes rapidly. Although the rats could be retrained using an oral supplement, the subsequent intragastric feeding behavior of these animals differed in several respects from their response to oral feeding. Food intake was reduced to about 75% of oral feeding levels, bar pressing was brief and not sustained, and intragastric meals were smaller than oral ones. Body weight, although it remained stable, was regulated at a lower level and did not show normal increases over time. There are thus some obvious similarities between the deficits seen after trigeminal deafferentation in the pigeon (see Section VIII) and the effects of a partial "functional deafferentation" produced by the use of intragastric/operant procedures in the rat.

B. TRIGEMINAL DEAFFERENTATION AND FEEDING BEHAVIOR IN THE RAT

By contrast with the pigeon, the location and peripheral distribution of the trigeminal sensory nerves in the rat are such that extensive denervation of the face and oral region would involve unacceptable damage to the musculature of these regions. In collaboration with Marwine (Zeigler et al., 1974; Marwine and Zeigler, 1975) we have developed several surgical procedures which partially obviate this problem. The simplest procedure involves section of the infraorbital nerve which innervates the vibrissae. The consequent loss of somatosensory information results in postural adjustments involving the entire body. The posture of the normal rat (Fig. 40A) is characterized by relatively horizontal placement of the body with respect to the substrate and elevation of the head above the substrate, which is contacted only by the vibrissae. After denervation of the vibrissae, the rat assumes a hunched posture with an extension of the rear legs so that the snout is in *direct* contact with the substrate (Fig. 40B). Although the denervated rat is alert and active there are noticeable differences in its gait, and it will actually bump into objects placed in its path. As it moves about, its mandible generally remains in contact with the substrate, but its head may be elevated during olfactory scanning. Comparable deficits have been seen after lesions of the central nervous system (CNS) and are frequently characterized as "motor" deficits.

Because infraorbital section produces a relatively restricted focus of deafferentation, we have developed a procedure for more extensive denervation by electrolytic lesion of the trigeminal sensory roots. Employing stereotaxic procedures and an intracranial approach to the nerve, it is relatively easy to place lesions in the various roots (ophthalmic, mandibular, or maxillary) and in the Gasserian ganglion, under electrophysiological control, i.e., while recording the effects of tactile stimulation of the snout and jaw regions. Figure 41 presents a section through the rat brain at the level of the lateral hypothalamus indicating the location of the trigeminal nerve and ganglion at the base of the

Fig. 40. Effects of section of the infraorbital branch of the trigeminal nerve upon posture in the rat: (A) Normal rat. (B) Posture after intraorbital nerve section.

brain and illustrating the extent of the destruction of the ganglion produced by an electrolytic lesion of moderate size.

By varying the placement and extent of the lesions we can produce a continuum of effects upon ingestive behavior ranging from prolonged aphagia and adipsia to varying degrees of hypophagia and secondary hypodipsia (Fig. 42). All animals show a significant increase in food spillage. One incidental effect of deafferentation is an increase in the size of the incisors, which becomes noticeable within a few days after denervation. Incisor growth may become so extensive that it will interfere with eating unless the teeth are clipped at regular intervals. This phenomenon is, of course, not seen in normal rats, nor has it been reported after CNS lesions. Inspection of the dental literature indicates that there is probably no direct connection between the sensory innervation of the incisors and their rate of growth. Rather the incisors appear to be maintained at a functional length in normal rats by (1) the grinding action provided by eating hard foods, and (2) the use of gnawing behaviors—both of which are disrupted by trigeminal deafferentation (Marwine and Zeigler, 1975).

Observations on the feeding behavior of deafferented rats tested under depriva-

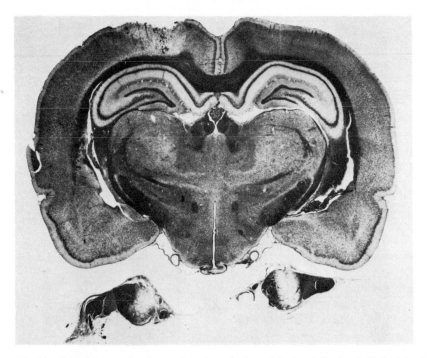

Fig. 41. Photomicrograph of a section through the rat brain at the level of the lateral hypothalamus, illustrating the extent of the damage produced in the trigeminal ganglion by an electrolytic lesion placed under electrophysiological control.

tion conditions with standard laboratory pellets show a significant increase in their latency to feed and a reduction in the amount eaten. Although the time spent in contact with food is also reduced, the deafferented rats do spend a significant amount of time manipulating the pellets. Their reduced food intake appears to reflect a disruption in the efficiency of their consummatory behavior toward the pellets. Some of the animals are able to pick up the pellets in their jaws but are unable to shave food off the pellet's surface in the normal fashion. (These observations are, of course, consistent with the disruptive effects of deafferentation upon gnawing behavior.) In order to clarify the extent to which such consummatory deficits mediate the disruption of food intake seen after denervation, we have examined the relationship between the sensory properties of the animal's diet and its food intake after trigeminal deafferentation.

The rats were offered a choice of four diets: two highly palatable soft diets (commercial dog food and a high fat diet), and two standard diets (pellets and powder) which differed in the ease with which they could be ingested. The amount of highly palatable food given each day was adjusted to a level which insured that the animal would consume some of the standard diets in order to

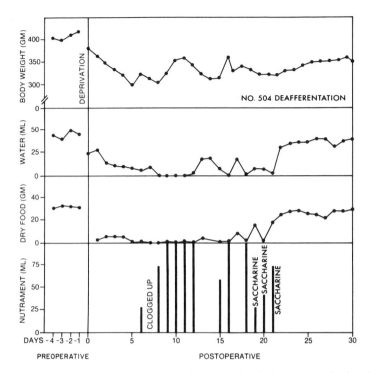

Fig. 42. Effects of trigeminal deafferentation (ganglion lesions) upon food and water intake and body weight in the rat.

maintain normal body weight. Following surgery, the amounts of palatable diets offered were further reduced at intervals to make it even more likely that pellets or powder would be ingested. The alignment of these four diets on the graphs presented in Fig. 43a,b reflect the relative preferences of rats in our laboratory, with dog food most preferred and powdered chow least preferred.

As might be expected, the response of control animals (Fig. 43a) to a 24-hour preoperative food deprivation and a reduction in the availability of palatable diets is a compensatory increase in the intake of pellets. (Reductions in high-fat consumption can be completely accounted for by the effects of increased spillage.) After deafferentation the most palatable diet continues to be consumed at nearly maximal levels, but there is a reduction in the high-fat diet which cannot be satisfactorily accounted for in terms of spillage. Moreover, the deafferented animals show no compensatory increase in pellet intake and are, in fact, aphagic with respect to the two standard diets, which parallels our original findings (Fig. 43b).

Further analyses of the behavioral capacities of the trigeminally deafferented rat are currently in progress. It is clear from even these preliminary data that abolition or reduction of sensory inputs provided by the peripheral trigeminal

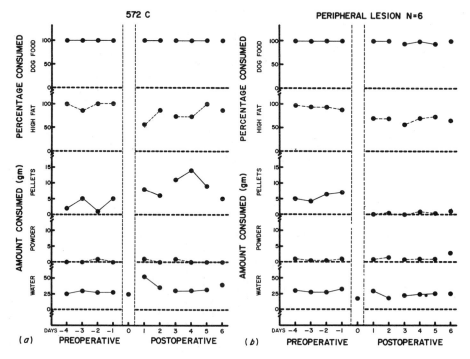

Fig. 43. Trigeminal deafferentation and feeding behavior in the rat, showing effects of varying texture and palatability of the diet: (a) Control subject. (b) Deafferented group.

system produces a profound disruption of ingestive behavior in the rat. The deficits appear to be obviously related to the sensory properties of the diet, i.e., texture and palatability, and are reflected in both "consummatory" and "motivational" measures of feeding behavior. We have already noted that there are striking similarities between the deficits seen after trigeminal deafferentation in the pigeon and the effects of reducing orosensory inputs in the rat by means of the intragastric/operant feeding procedure. In view of the even more striking disruptions produced by surgical deafferentation procedures in the rat, it would seem that our findings in the pigeon are not unique to an avian preparation but probably reflect the operation of neurosensory mechanisms which are widespread among vertebrates.

C. BRAIN MECHANISMS AND FEEDING BEHAVIOR IN PIGEON AND RAT

The study of brain mechanisms controlling feeding behavior in mammals has focused primarily on the role of one brain region—the lateral hypothalamic area.

It has long been known that lesions of this region disrupt both eating and drinking (Anand and Brobeck, 1951) and produce a complex syndrome of deficits in ingestive behavior which have been analyzed in considerable detail (Teitelbaum and Epstein, 1962; Epstein, 1971). Some of the deficits (e.g., aphagia, adipsia, finickiness, and food spillage) are relatively transient in the sense that animals may recover from them and still exhibit persistent deficits in other aspects of ingestive behavior. These "permanent" deficits include loss of the hydrational controls of drinking, loss of the glucoprivic control of eating, and the regulation of body weight at persistently lower levels than normal. Although earlier discussions of the lateral hypothalamic (LH) syndrome tended to minimize the prominence of sensorimotor deficits (Rodgers et al., 1965), the existence of such deficits is now acknowledged. Teitelbaum and his colleagues were the first to report that in rats made aphagic by LH lesions the transition from Stage I (complete aphagia) to Stage II (accepting only highly palatable foods) was preceded by or coincident with the recovery of head-orientation responses to olfactory and somatosensory stimuli (Marshall et al., 1971). The analysis of such sensorimotor deficits has become an additional focus of research on the LH syndrome (Turner, 1973).

In their interpretations of the deficits in feeding behavior which follow lateral hypothalamic lesions in the rat, different investigators have focused on different aspects of the syndrome. Teitelbaum and Epstein originally viewed the reduction in food intake as reflecting a "motivational" failure, i.e., a disruption of the major neural control systems "for the translation of internal states and afferent inputs into the energizing motives of hunger and thirst" (Epstein, 1971, p. 297). More recent studies from Teitelbaum's laboratory have emphasised sensorimotor dysfunctions, particularly a "sensory neglect" involving somatosensory, olfactory, and visual stimuli (Marshall et al., 1971; Turner, 1973). Keesey (1973), on the other hand, has suggested that the LH syndrome, rather than involving the disruption of a neural system crucial to free feeding, reflects an adaptive response to a reduced "set-point" for body weight. None of these alternatives is entirely satisfactory, however, since each of them accounts for only certain types of deficit and none can account for the mixture of sensorimotor dysfunctions, responsiveness changes, and weight regulation effects seen after LH lesions.

It is therefore of interest that precisely such a combination of deficits is seen to follow trigeminal deafferentation or lesions of central trigeminal structures in the pigeon. Both the trigeminal syndrome in the pigeon and the LH syndrome in the rat include periods of aphagia and hypophagia, somatosensory deficits, food spillage, and regulation of body weight at reduced levels. However, the trigeminal syndrome in the pigeon does not involve the hypothalamus but is produced by peripheral deafferentation or extrahypothalamic lesions of central trigeminal structures. Indeed, lesions of the lateral hypothalamic area of the pigeon that do

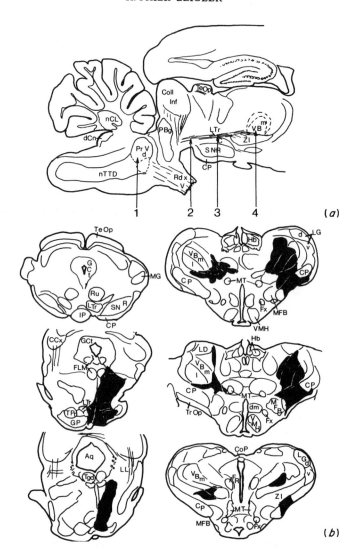

Fig. 44. (a) Sagittal section through the rat brain, illustrating the trajectory of the trigeminal lemniscus (LTr) from its origin in PrV (level 1) to its termination in the medial portion of the ventrobasal complex of the thalamus (level 4). (b) Sections through the maximal extent of the lesions in two cases with damage to trigeminal structures at extrahypothalamic loci. (From Zeigler and Karten, 1974. Copyright 1974 by The American Association for the Advancement of Science.) Abbreviations:

Aq, aqueductus
CCx, n. centralis colliculus inferioris
Coll. Inf., colliculus inferioris

CP, pendunculus cerebri
nCL, n. cerebellaris lateralis
dCn, n. cochlearis dorsalis

not impinge upon trigeminal structures have no effect upon eating (see Section VII; also Zeigler and Karten, 1973a, Fig. 10A).

Despite their functional similarities, therefore, the two syndromes seemed originally to have completely different structural bases. However, recent experiments carried out in collaboration with Karten have implicated *central* trigeminal structures in the neural control of feeding in the rat and in so doing have clarified the relation between the trigeminal syndrome and the LH syndrome.

D. CENTRAL TRIGEMINAL STRUCTURES AND THE LATERAL HYPOTHALAMIC SYNDROME IN THE RAT

Our experiments were greatly facilitated by the publication of an anatomical study delineating the ascending projections of the trigeminal lemniscus (LTr) in the rat (Smith, 1973). The lemniscus originates in the Principal Sensory Trigeminal Nucleus, decussates at the level of the interpeduncular nucleus, and continues through the mesencephalon, lying immediately dorsal to the medial portion of the substantia nigra at the level of the ventral tegmentum. At the diencephalic level, the lemniscus gives off collaterals to the posterior thalamic region and to zona incerta before terminating in the medial portion of the ventrobasal complex of the thalamus. Figure 44 (*a*) illustrates the longitudinal trajectory of the trigeminal lemniscus at several levels of the rat brain.

A review of the histological materials accompanying published studies of the LH syndrome suggested to us that the "characteristic" lateral hypothalamic lesion always impinges either upon LTr fibers of passage of upon their areas of termination within the diencephalon. Indeed, it may be difficult to place a typical lesion in the LH area without doing some damage to central trigeminal structures. On the other hand, it is possible to place lesions in trigeminal structures outside the hypothalamus, as we had previously done in the pigeon. Reconstructions of such extrahypothalamic lesions are presented in Fig. 44 (*b*), and their effects on ingestive behavior are shown in Fig. 45. While lesions of

---

FLM, fasciculus medialis longitudinalis
FX, fornix
GP, peontine gray
Hb, habenula
LG, lateral geniculate nucleus
LL, lemniscus lateralis
LTr, lemniscus trigeminalis
MFB, medial forebrain bundle
MT, tractus mammillothalamicus
PBg, n. parabigeminalis
PrVd, n. sensibilis trigemini, pars dorsalis
RdxV, radix nervi trigemini

Sn-R;C, substantia nigra, pars reticulata; pars compacta
TeOp, tectum opticum
Tgd, n. tegmentalis Guddeni, pars dorsalis
Tpr, tractus pyramidalis
nTTD, nucleus et tractus trigeminalis descendens
VBm, n. ventrobasalis, pars medialis, thalami
VMH, n. ventromedialis hypothalami
ZI, zona incerta

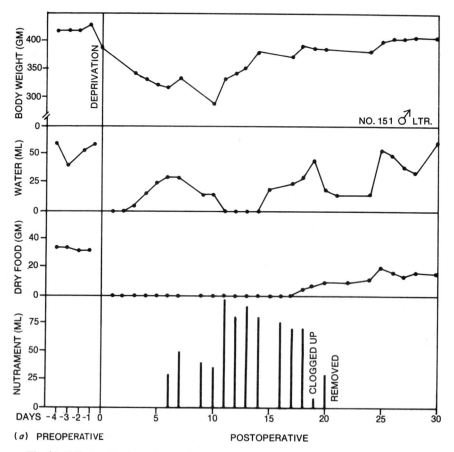

Fig. 45. Effects of lesions of central trigeminal structures upon food and water intake and body weight in the rat: (a) Effects of a lesion of LTr at the level of the interpeduncular nucleus. Case 151 did not respond to the food pellets until the fourth day postoperatively. From days 5 to 14 there was considerable gnawing at the food but no measurable intake until day 18. From days 18 to 30 daily spillage ranged from 55 to 65% of the ration given. (b) Effects of a lesion of VBm at level 4. Case 156 made no responses to either food or water until the thirteenth postoperative day. Spillage over the next two weeks ranged between 55 and 75%. In both cases the rats were "finicky" in the sense that they ingested large quantities of Choc-Nutrament during periods when intake of dry food or water was absent or reduced below preoperative levels. The lesions of these rats are shown in Fig. 44b. (From Zeigler and Karten, 1974. Copyright 1974 by The American Association for the Advancement of Science.)

central trigeminal structures in the rat do not produce the prolonged periods of debilitation reported after LH lesions, nor any signs of aversion to contact with food and water, they are followed by a syndome of deficits in ingestive behavior including aphagia, adipsia, anorexia, finickiness, food spillage, and somatosensory neglect (Zeigler and Karten, 1974). On the basis of these studies we may

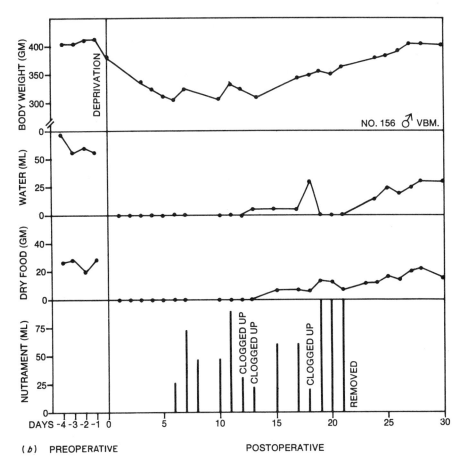

Fig. 45(b). See facing page for legend.

tentatively conclude that to the extent that lesions of the lateral hypothalamic region impinge on central trigeminal structures, such lesions will produce in the rat all three types of deficit (sensorimotor, responsiveness, and weight regulation) seen after comparable lesions in the pigeon.

Our findings suggest that some of the most important deficits formerly attributed to LH lesions in the rat are not due to hypothalamic damage but—as in the pigeon—are the result of incidental damage to trigeminal fibers of passage coursing through adjacent portions of the diencephalon. Thus in both species the trigeminal system appears to play a critical role in the neural control of feeding. This is not surprising since the trigeminal system is very highly developed in both the rat (Welker, 1973) and the pigeon (Zeigler and Karten, 1973a) and may be expected to play a major role in the oral monitoring of intake and in the neurosensory control of eating and drinking. Moreover, in both species inputs from the oral region have been characterized as having "motivational" as well as sensory properties (Snowdon, 1969; Zeigler, 1973a).

There is yet another sense in which our findings are not unexpected. It has long been evident that the deficits in eating and drinking seen after LH lesions are due, in part, to lesion effects upon fibers of passage rather than to the disruption of synaptic networks within the hypothalamus itself (Albert *et al.*, 1970; Ellison *et al.*, 1970; Gold, 1967; Grossman and Grossman, 1971; Morgane, 1969). Indeed, as Epstein (1971, p. 306) has cogently noted:

> The(se) neurological systems for the initiation of ingestive behavior are not centered in the lateral hypothalamus except in the sense that an unusually large number of their partial components are focused there. An obvious task now is the identification and analysis of these partial components. . . .

The studies reviewed above suggest that the trigeminal system is an important "partial component" of the neural systems controlling feeding. Studies currently in progress in our laboratory will enable us to specify more precisely the differences between the LH syndrome and the trigeminal syndrome in the rat and to identify the anatomical substrates related to these differences. However, to the extent that the deficits seen after LH lesions do indeed reflect trigeminal damage, several hitherto puzzling aspects of the LH syndrome (spillage, somato-sensory neglect, and perhaps, finickiness) would become more readily explicable. On the other hand, the significance of our findings is obviously *not* that they "account" in any sense for the LH syndrome—a task requiring the identification and analysis of neural circuits involved in a variety of disparate behaviors (drinking, response to glucoprivation, etc.). Indeed, it is precisely the differences between the trigeminal syndrome and the LH syndome that promise to be most informative. An analysis of these differences should enable us to partial out the unique contributions of central trigeminal structures to the control of feeding behavior in vertebrates.

Finally, our studies may shed some light on the well-established relationship between oropharyngeal inputs and central neural mechanisms underlying feeding (e.g., Teitelbaum and Epstein, 1963). It will be recalled that the effects of trigeminal deafferentation in the pigeon resemble to a remarkable degree the "motivational" and weight-regulation deficits seen after the reversible, func-tional "deafferentation" produced by use of intragastric/operant procedures in the rat. That is, in both rat and pigeon, massive deprivation of the inputs which normally accompany the consummatory response appears to profoundly reduce responsiveness to food as well as the level at which body weight is regulated. (The fact that such disruptions are produced by *peripheral* manipulations tenta-tively suggests that the effect upon intake is *primary* and the reduction in body weight a *secondary* effect.) Against this background it might be suggested that at least some of the deficits in ingestive behavior seen after LH lesions reflect a massive *central deafferentation* produced by interruption of trigeminal taste, and possibly olfactory pathways ascending in the basolateral diencephalon (Smith, 1973; Norgren and Leonard, 1973; Heimer, 1972). The implications of such an interpretation remain to be explored.

X. CONCLUSIONS: "SENSORY" VERSUS "MOTIVATIONAL" MECHANISMS AND THE NEURAL CONTROL OF FEEDING

In a paper entitled "The Relations of Comparative Anatomy to Comparative Psychology," Edinger (1908) made the observation that in many species of birds and reptiles there is a large fiber tract leading from the nucleus of the trigeminal nerve and terminating at the level of the forebrain in a field located close behind the olfactory apparatus. On the basis of other anatomical data and his own "naturalistic" observations of their feeding behavior, Edinger suggested that these forebrain regions might be the locus of an "oral sense." In principle, at least, Edinger's approach to the problem of feeding behavior mechanisms was correct. Like other great comparative anatomists of his time—Herrick, Coghill, Ariëns Kappers, etc.—Edinger assumed that the study of sensory systems could be a source of productive insights for the analysis of brain function. Similarly, the early behaviorists—Watson, Lashley, Von Frisch, etc.—also assumed that the study of sensory mechanisms was an appropriate starting point for the analysis of behavior. For a variety of reasons, some of them having to do with the dramatic "effectiveness" of hypothalamic lesions, many physiological psychologists have abandoned the comparative neurosensory approach to the study of feeding. Indeed, much research on the neural control of mammalian feeding behavior has actually been predicated on the existence of a dichotomy between sensory and motivational mechanisms.

The most explicit statement of such a dichotomy, with respect to feeding behavior mechanisms, was advanced by Teitelbaum (1967, p. 58) in an attempt to distinguish between "reflexes" and "voluntary motivated behavior":

> Clearly, when an act is a completely automatic consequence of a stimulus we need not speak of motivation. As long as a fixed, built-in relation exists between a stimulus and a response we have no justification for inferring the existence of a motivational state underlying that response to the stimulus. . . . To infer motivation, we must break the fixed connection between stimulus and response. The learning process enables us to do so. . . . The(se) characteristics of the learned act—the arbitrary, essentially interchangeable nature of the act and of the stimulus that elicits it, as well as the measure of control the animal exerts over the response—distinguish it as a voluntary act. Once learned such a voluntary act can be used for any reinforcement. Thus, unlike many instinctive responses, the bar-press response can be separated from the animal's internal state. In effect, in

any operant situation, the stimulus, the response and the reinforcement are completely arbitrary. No one of them bears any biologically built-in, fixed connection to the others. . . . If an operant occurs motivation exists.

Unfortunately such a formulation begs more questions than it answers. First, it assumes that something called the "operant" (i.e., the rate of key pecking or bar pressing) reflects a unitary process. In fact, the rate measure actually reflects the output of a response system whose operation must itself be characterized in terms of at least three parameters (duration, force, and interresponse time), and the mechanisms controlling variations in these three parameters may be experimentally dissociable (Zeigler and Hunter, 1976). Moreover recent work by Schwartz and Williams suggests that the operant key peck subsumes two different classes of peck, varying both in their duration and in their sensitivity to contingent reinforcement. Such findings "belie the notion that members of an operant class are homogeneous with respect to their sensitivity to environmental consequences" (Schwartz and Williams, 1972, p. 214). Finally, the relation between deprivation conditions and the rate of responding will be a function of the schedule of reinforcement under which the operant is measured. Such schedules may not be equally sensitive throughout the entire range of food deprivation, and their sensitivity may vary with the parameters of the schedule and the extent of the organism's experience with the schedule.

Second, the proposition that any operant response is "biologically" *arbitrary* with respect either to the stimulus or the reinforcer is no longer self-evident. The phenomenon of autoshaping, for example, suggests that at least some proportion of the key pecks made by the pigeon in an "operant" conditioning situation are under the control of the same types of variables which control its consummatory responses (Schwartz and Williams, 1972; Jenkins and Moore, 1973). Collier and associates (1975) have suggested that we may, perhaps, regard the typical Skinner box session as a meal: ". . . one in which the experimenter initiates and terminates the meal and controls the rate of ingestion. The manipulandum (bar, lever or key) can be viewed as a feeding utensil, a fancy fork." While we need not go quite so far, we must certainly entertain the proposition that the rat's operant bar pressing has a more direct relationship to its consummatory response than we have hitherto assumed. Indeed, a growing body of research testifies to the subtle ways in which species-typical processes interact with learning paradigms to effect an organism's performance (Shettleworth, 1972).

The most cogent criticism of such a dichotomy relates not to its empirical validity, but to its heuristic or conceptual utility. If our aim is merely to categorize various behaviors as reflecting processes of different orders of complexity, then a variety of such distinctions, perhaps ordered along a continuum of complexity, would be defensible. However, if our aim is not categorization but explanation, it is not easy to demonstrate the utility of such distinctions or to defend the dichotomy implicit in the statement that "if an operant occurs motivation exists." Such dichotomous formulations provide no useful insights into causal mechanisms and may even subtly retard the analysis of such mechanisms.

Over the years the dichotomy between "reflexes" and "motivated behavior" was generalized almost imperceptibly from the categorization of behavioral processes to the categorization of behavioral deficits and, by implication, of causal mechanisms (e.g., consummatory versus regulatory; sensorimotor versus motivational). Now at an initial level of analysis such categories or distinctions may be helpful. It is obviously important to distinguish between deficits which are relatively specific to ingestive behavior and those resulting from gross disruptions of posture, locomotion, orientation, or metabolism, which are likely to have rather generalized effects upon a variety of behaviors. [The akinesia and catalepsy which follow LH lesions or 6-hydroxydopamine (6-HDA) injections are good examples of the latter.] At the same time we must remember that the deficits in behavior seen after brain lesions can only be the result of a disruption in the normal mechanisms controlling that behavior. Exactly how "higher-level" *motivational* deficits are presumed to be causally mediated—other than by disruption of the normal spatiotemporal organization of eating behavior—was never very satisfactorily explained.

Having adopted such dichotomies, many investigators implicitly assumed that *motivational* deficits were somehow more significant than "mere" *sensorimotor* or consummatory deficits. This assumption has had several deleterious consequences for the study of the neural control of feeding:

1. It has led investigators to deny, ignore, or minimize the role played by "sensorimotor" deficits in the LH syndrome, although there has long been abundant evidence for the existence of such deficits (e.g., Teitelbaum and Epstein, 1962). Moreover, we have seen that the identification of behavioral deficits as "sensory" or "motor" is not a simple matter. For example, deficits in mandibulation may be produced by impairments of either afferent or efferent systems in the pigeon, but their effects upon the efficiency of the pigeon's eating will be the same, regardless of their origin. Similarly, the dramatic changes in posture seen after CNS lesions or 6-HDA injections in rats are often characterized as "motor" deficits, but similar effects upon posture can be produced by peripheral damage to an afferent system (i.e., by infraorbital nerve section). Because investigators have devoted little attention to the study of sensory and motor control mechanisms in feeding, they are likely to be insensitive to the complex manner in which afferent and efferent systems may interact to control behavior.

2. It has discouraged studies on the relation between central sensory systems and ingestive behavior, although such reports as are available (Castro, 1972; Oakley, 1965; Wolf and DiCara, 1974; Zeigler and Karten, 1974), suggest

that the problem is of considerable importance. Moreover, the design of such investigations has been facilitated by the publication of experimental anatomical studies of the ascending pathways of the major afferent systems involved in the rat's feeding behavior (Heimer, 1972; Norgren and Leonard, 1973; Smith, 1973).

3. It has contributed to a state of affairs in which, after 50 years of studying feeding behavior in the rat, we still do not have either a qualitative or a quantitative analysis of the spatiotemporal organization of feeding in this species. Such analyses have become commonplace in neurobiology, and our studies have shown them to be immensely useful tools for microbehavioral analysis (see also Pfaff et al., 1974). Moreover, had such analyses been carried out earlier it is most unlikely that the critical role of trigeminal structures in the control of the rat's feeding behavior would have gone unnoticed. Even granting the subtle anthropocentrism that has led psychologists to focus their investigations on the rat, the restriction of those investigations to chemosensory (olfactory, gustatory) systems surely reflects the absence of detailed information about the sensory control of eating.

In neglecting or minimizing the study of neurosensory mechanisms, physiological psychologists lost one important source of insights into brain-behavior relationships in feeding. The decline of comparative studies has removed still another source. In our concern with developing "general" laws of behavior we have lost sight of the fact that the feeding behavior of any species reflects both its structure and the ecological constraints imposed by its environment (Collier et al., 1972; Zeigler, 1973c). The evolutionary process has provided us with a wide variety of vertebrate "preparations" for the comparative study of feeding. The diversity of structure and ecology available are such that we could undoubtedly select, from within any vertebrate class, species differing with respect to the relative significance of somatosensory, visual, or chemosensory feeding mechanisms.

Our past neglect of comparative studies was due, in part, to some widely held assumptions about the functional significance of certain morphological differences between the forebrain of mammals and that of other vertebrates. It is now clear that the mammalian forebrain does not represent a different direction of evolution from that of other vertebrates and that, in fact, there have been many important continuities in the evolution of the vertebrate forebrain (Karten, 1969; Cogen and Karten, 1974; Ebbesson, 1970; Ebbesson, 1972; Ebbesson et al., 1972; Halpern, 1972, etc.). Moreover, recent technical advances in histology and histochemistry have stimulated renewed interest in comparative neuroanatomy, and there is now available a large and growing body of comparative data on the neurosensory organization of the brain in many nonmammalian vertebrates (see, e.g., Masterton et al., 1976).

These data could provide the anatomical foundations for comparative studies of the relationship between neurosensory mechanisms and ingestive behaviors across a broad spectrum of vertebrate classes. Our studies of the rat and pigeon testify to the utility of such an approach to the analysis of vertebrate feeding behavior mechanisms.

Acknowledgments

The work described in this review was supported by Research Grant MH-08366 and Research Career Development Award K-2-6391, both from the National Institute of Mental Health, U.S. Public Health Service. Preparation of the review was supported by a Fellowship from the John Simon Guggenheim Foundation, 1974–1975.

References

Åkerman, B., Anderson, B., Fabricius, E., and Svenson, L. 1960. Observations on central regulation of body temperature and of food and water intake in the pigeon (*Columba livia*). *Acta Physiol. Scand.*, **50**, 323–336.

Åkerman, B., Fabricius, E., Larsson, B., and Steen, L. 1962. Observations on pigeons with prethalamic radiolesions in the nervous pathways from the telencephalon. *Acta Physiol. Scand.* **56**, 286–298.

Albert, D. J., Storlien, L. H., Wood, D. J., and Ehman, G. K. 1970. Further evidence for a complex system controlling feeding behavior. *Physiol. Behav.* **5**, 1075–1082.

Anand, B. K., and Brobeck, J. R. 1951. Hypothalamic control of food intake in rats and cats. *Yale J. Biol. Med.* **24**, 123–140.

Andersen, A. E., and Nafstad, P. H. T. 1968. An electron microscopic investigation of the sensory organs in the hard palate region of the hen (*Gallus domesticus*). *Z. Zellforsch.* **91**, 391–401.

Barlow, G. 1968. Ethological units of behavior. *In* "The Central Nervous System and Fish Behavior" (D. H. Ingle, ed.), Univ. of Chicago Press, Chicago, Illinois.

Barnikol, A. 1953. Zür Morphologie des Nervus trigeminus der Vögel unter besonderer Berucksichtingung der Acciptres, Cathartidae, Striges und Anseriformes. *Z. Wiss. Zool.* **157**, 285–332.

Bolles, R. C. 1961. The interaction of hunger and thirst in the rat. *J. Comp. Physiol. Psych.* **54**, 580–584.

Bolles, R. C. 1965. Readiness to eat: effects of age, sex and weight loss. *J. Comp. Physiol. Psycho.l.* **60**, 88–92.

Bolles, R. C. 1967. "Theory of Motivation." Harper & Row, New York.

Bolton, W. 1965. Digestion in the crop of the fowl. *Brit. Poultry Sci.* **6**, 97–102.

Buddenbrock, W. von. 1952. "Vergleichende Physiologie," Vol. 1: Sinnesphysiologie. Birkenhauser, Basel.

Bullock, T. H. 1961. The origin of patterned nervous discharge. *Behavior* **17**, 48–59.

Bullock, T. H., and Horridge, G. A. 1965. "Structure and Function in the Nervous System of Invertebrates." Freeman, San Francisco.

Cain, D. P. 1974. The role of the olfactory bulb in limbic mechanisms. *Psychol. Bull.* **81**, 654–671.

Campbell, B. A., and Misanin, J. R. 1969. Basic drives. *Annu. Rev. Psychol.* **20**, 57–83.

Cardini, F. P. 1971. Eating after intracrop preloading in the pigeon. *Physiol. Behav.* **7**, 443–446.

Castro, A. J. 1972. The effects of cortical ablations on tongue usage in the rat. *Brain Res.* 45, 251–253.

Cizek, L. J. 1959. Long-term observations on relationship between food and water ingestion in the dog. *Amer. J. Physiol.* 197, 242–246.

Code, C. E., ed. 1967. "Handbook of Physiology," Sect. 6: Alimentary Canal, Vol. 1: Control of Food and Water Intake. Amer. Physiol. Soc., Washington, D.C.

Cohen, D. H. 1975. The neural pathways and informational flow mediating a conditioned autonomic response. *In* "The Limbic and Autonomic Nervous Systems" (L. DiCara, ed.), Plenum, New York.

Cohen, D. H., and Karten, H. J. 1974. The structural organization of avian brain: An overview. *In* "Birds: Brain and Behavior" (I. J. Goodman and M. Schein, ed.), Academic Press, New York.

Collier, G. 1969. Body weight loss as a measure of motivation in hunger and thirst. *Ann. N. Y. Acad. Sci.* 157, 594–609.

Collier, G., Hirsch, E., and Hamlin, P. H. 1972. The ecological determinants of reinforcement in the rat. *Physiol. Behav.* 9, 705–716.

Collier, G., Kanarek, R., Hirsch, E., and Marwine, A. 1975. Environmental determinants of feeding behavior: or How to turn a rat into a tiger. *In* "Psychological Research: The Inside Story" (M. Siegel and H. P. Zeigler, eds.), Harper and Row, New York.

Cords, E. 1904. Beitrage zur Lehre vom Kopfnervensystm der Vogel. *Anat. Hefte* 26, 49–100.

Davis, A. H., Davison, M. C., and Webster, D. M. 1972. Intracranial reinforcement in pigeons: An analysis using concurrent schedules. *Physiol. Behav.* 9, 385–390.

Davis, J. D., and Campbell, C. S. 1973. Peripheral control of meal size in the rat. *J. Comp. Physiol. Psychol.* 83, 379–387.

Dawkins, R. 1968. The ontogeny of a pecking preference in domestic chicks. *Z. Tierpsychol.* 25, 170–186.

Dawkins, R. and M. 1973. Decisions and the uncertainty of behavior. *Behavior* 45, 83–103.

Delius, J. D. 1971. Foraging behavior patterns of Herring Gulls elicited by electrical forebrain stimulation. *Experientia (Basel)* 27, 1287–1289.

Delius, J. D., and Bennetto, K. 1972. Cutaneous sensory projections in the avian forebrain. *Brain Res.* 37, 205–221.

Dethier, V. G. 1967. Feeding and drinking behavior of invertebrates. *In* "Handbook of Physiology" (C. E. Code, ed.), Sect. 6: Alimentary Canal, Vol. 1: Control of Food and Water Intake. Amer. Physiol. Soc., Washington, D.C.

Dethier, V. G. 1969. Feeding behavior in the blowfly. This series. 2.

Dethier, V. G., and Gelperin, A. 1967. Hyperphagia in the blowfly. *J. Exp. Biol.* 47, 191–200.

Doty, R. W., and Bosma, J. F. 1956. An electromyographic analysis of reflex deglutition. *J. Neurophysiol.* 19, 44–60.

Dubbeldam, J., and Menken, S. 1973. Central projections of the trigeminal, facial and vagal nerves in the Mallard Duck. *Proc. 3rd Eur. Anat. Congr., 3rd.*

Duncan, I. J. H., Horne, A. R., Hughes, B. O., and Wood-Gush, D. G. M. 1970. The pattern of food intake in female Brown Leghorn fowls as recorded in a Skinner box. *Anim. Behav.* 18, 245–255.

Ebbesson, S. O. E. 1970. On the organization of central visual pathways in vertebrates. *Brain, Behav. Evol.* 3, 178–194.

Ebbesson, S. O. E. 1972. A proposal for a common nomenclature for some optic nuclei in vertebrates and evidence for a common origin of two such cell groups. *Brain, Behav. Evol.* 6, 75–91.

Ebbesson, S. O. E., Jane, J. A., and Schroeder, D. M. 1972. A general overview of major interspecific variations in thalamic organization. *Brain, Behav. Evol.* **6**, 92–131.

Edinger, L. 1908. The relations of comparative anatomy to comparative psychology. *J. Comp. Neurol.* **18**, 437–457.

Ellison, G. D., Sorenson, C. A., and Jacobs, B. L. 1970. Two feeding syndromes following surgical isolation of the hypothalamus in rats. *J. Comp. Physiol. Psychol.* **70**, 173–188.

Epstein, A. N. 1967. Oropharyngeal factors in feeding and drinking. *In* "Handbook of Psychiology" (C. E. Code, ed.), Sect. 6: Alimentary Canal, Vol. 1: Control of Food and Water Intake. Amer. Physiol. Soc., Washington, D.C.

Epstein, A. N. 1971. The lateral hypothalamic syndrome: its implications for the physiological psychology of hunger and thirst. *Progr. Physiol. Psychol.* **4**.

Epstein, A. N., and Teitelbaum, P. 1962. Regulation of food intake in the absence of taste, smell and other oropharyngeal sensations. *J. Comp. Physiol. Psychol.* **55**, 753–759.

Ewert, J. P. 1974. The neural basis of visually guided behavior. *Sci. Amer.* **230**, 34–42.

Fantz, R. L. 1957. Form preferences in newly hatched chicks. *J. Comp. Physiol. Psychol.* **50**, 422–430.

Feldman, S. E., Larsson, S., Dimick, M. K., and Lepkovsky, S. 1957. Aphagia in chickens. *Amer. J. Physiol.* **191**, 259–261.

Ferster, C. B., and Skinner, B. F. 1957. "Schedules of Reinforcement." Appleton-Century-Crofts, New York.

Fisher, H., and Weiss, H. S. 1956. Food consumption in relation to dietary bulk and energy level: the effect of surgical removal of the crop. *Poultry Sci.* **35**, 418–431.

Fitzsimmons, J. T. 1971. The physiology of thirst: A review of the extraneural aspects of the mechanisms of drinking. *Progr. Physiol. Psychol.* **4**.

Flourens, P. 1824. "Recherches expéreimentales sur les propriétés les fonctions du système nerveux dan les animaux vertébrés." Baillière, Paris.

Friedman, M. 1975. How birds use their eyes. *In* "Neural and Endocrine Aspects of Behavior in Birds" (P. Wright, P. G. Caryl, and D. M. Vowles, eds.), Elsevier, Amsterdam.

Gentle, M. J. 1971. Taste and its importance to the domestic chicken. *Brit. Poultry Sci.* **12**, 77–86.

Gentle, M. J. 1975. Gustatory behavior of the chicken and other birds. *In* "Neural and Endocrine Aspects of Behavior in Birds" (P. Wright, P. G. Caryl, and D. M. Vowles, eds.), Elsevier, Amsterdam.

Gold, R. M. 1967. Aphagia and adipsia following unilateral and bilaterally asymmetrical lesions in rats. *Physiol. Behav.* **2**, 211–220.

Goodman, I. J., and Brown, J. L. 1966. Stimulation of positively and negatively reinforcing sites in the avian brain. *Life Sci.* **5**, 693–704.

Goodman, I. J., and Schein, M. 1974. "Birds: Brain and Behavior." Academic Press, New York.

Gottschaldt, K. M., and Lausmann, S. 1974. Mechanoreceptors and their properties in the beak skin of geese (*Anser anser*). *Brain Res.* **65**, 510–515.

Gregory, J. E. 1973. An electrophysiological investigation of the receptor apparatus of the duck's bill. *J. Physiol.* **229**, 151–164.

Grossman, S. P., and Grossman, L. 1971. Food and water intake in rats with parasaggital knife cuts medial or lateral to the lateral hypothalamus. *J. Comp. Physiol. Psychol.* **74**, 148–156.

Haartsen, A. B., and Verhaart, W. J. C. 1967. Cortical projections to brainstem and spinal cord in the goat by way of pyramidal tract and bundle of Bagley. *J. Comp. Neurol.* **129**, 189–202.

Halpren, M. 1972. Some connections of the telenecphalon of the frong, *Rana pipiens*. An experimental study. *Brain, Behav. Evol.* **6**, 42–68.

Harwood, D., and Vowles, D. M. 1966. Forebrain stimulation and feeding behavior in the Ring Dove (*Streptopelia risoria*). *J. Comp. Physiol. Psychol.* **62**, 388–396.

Heimer, L. 1972. The olfactory connections of the diencephalon of the rat: An experimental light- and electron-microscopic study with special emphasis on the problem of terminal degeneration. *Brain, Behav. Evol.* **6**, 484–523.

Henry, K. M., MacDonald, A. J., and Magee, H. E. 1933. Observations on the function of the alimentary canal in fowls. *J. Exp. Biol.* **10**, 153–171.

Hinde, R. A. 1970. "Animal Behaviour." McGraw-Hill, New York.

Holman, G. L. 1969. Intragastric reinforcement effect. *J. Comp. Physiol. Psychol.* **69**, 432–441.

Hutchinson, J. C. D., and Taylor, W. W. 1962. Mechanics of pecking grain. *Proc. World's Poultry Congr., 12th* pp. 112–116.

Janowitz, H. D. 1967. Role of the gastrointestinal tract in regulation of food intake. *In* "Handbook of Physiology" (C. E. Code, ed.), Sect. 6: Alimentary Canal, Vol. 1: Control of Food and Water Intake. Amer. Physiol. Soc., Washington, D.C.

Jenkins, H. M., and Moore, B. R. 1973. The form of the auto-shaped response with food or water reinforcers. *J. Exp. Anal. Behav.* **20**, 163–181.

Jerge, C. R. 1963. The organization and function of the trigeminal mesencephalic nucleus. *J. Neurophysiol.* **26**, 379–392.

Kandel, E. 1974. An invertebrate system for the cellular analysis of simple behaviors and their modification. *In* "The Neurosciences: Third Study Program" (F. O. Schmitt and F. G. Worden, eds.), pp. 347–370. MIT Press, Cambridge, Massachusetts.

Karten, H. J. 1969. The organization of the avian telencephalon and some speculations on the phylogeney of the amniote telencephalon. *Ann. N. Y. Acad. Sci.* **167**, 164–179.

Karten, H. J. 1975. Unpublished observations.

Karten, H. J., and Hodos, W. 1967. "A Stereotaxic Atlas of the Brain of the Pigeon (*Columba livia*)." Johns Hopkins Univ. Press, Baltimore, Maryland.

Keesey, R. E. 1973. Weight regulation and the lateral hypothalamic feeding syndrome. *Bull. Neurosci. Res. Progr.* **11**, 342–353.

Kerr, F. W. 1972. Central relationships of trigeminal and cervical primary afferents in the spinal cord and medulla. *Brain Res.* **43**, 561–572.

Kitchell, R. L., Strom, L., and Zotterman, Y. 1959. Electrophysiological studies of thermal and taste reception in chickens and pigeons. *Acta Physiol. Scand.* **46**, 133–151.

Kutscher, C. L. 1969. Species differences in the interaction of feeding and drinking. *Ann. N. Y. Acad. Sci.* **157**, 539–551.

Lack, D. 1947. "Darwin's Finches." Cambridge Univ. Press, London and New York.

Lashley, K. S. 1938. Experimental analysis of instinctive behavior. *Psychol. Rev.* **45**, 445–471.

Lepkovsky, S., Chari-Bitron, A., Lyman, R. L., and Dimick, M. K. 1960. Food intake, water intake and body water regulation. *Poul. Sci.* **30**, 390–394.

Lettvin, J. Y., Maturana, H. R., McCulloch, W., and Pitts, W. H. 1959. What the frog's eye tells the frog's brain. *Proc. IRE* **47**, 1940–1951.

Levine, R. R. 1976. Efferent pathways and feeding behavior in pigeon. Unpublished doctoral dissertation. City University of New York.

McFarland, D. 1964. Interaction of hunger and thirst in the Barbary Dove. *J. Comp. Physiol. Psychol.* **58**, 174–179.

McFarland, D. 1967. Phase relationships between feeding and drinking in the Barbary Dove. *J. Comp. Physiol. Psychol.* **63**, 208–213.

McFarland, D. 1969. Separation of satiating and rewarding consequences of drinking. *Physiol. Behav.* **4**, 987–989.

McFarland, D. J., and Lloyd, I. H. 1973. Time-shared feeding and drinking. *Quart. J. Exp. Psychol.* **25**, 48–61.

MacPhail, E. M. 1966. Self-stimulation in pigeons: The problem of "priming." *Psychonom. Sci.* **5**, 7–8.

MacPhail, E. M. 1967. Positive and negative reinforcement from intracranial stimulation in pigeons. *Nature (London)* **213**, 947–948.

Maley, M. J. 1969. Electrical stimulation of agonistic behavior in the Mallard. *Behavior* **34**, 138–160.

Manni, G. R., Bortolami, R., and Azzena, G. B. 1965. Jaw muscle proprioception and mesencephalic trigeminal cells in birds. *Exp. Neurol.* **12**, 320–328.

Marshall, J. F., Turner, B. H., and Teitelbaum, P. 1971. Sensory neglect produced by lateral hypothalamic damage. *Science* **174**, 523–525.

Marwine, A., and Zeigler, H. P. 1975. Trigeminal deafferentation and ingestive behavior in the rat. Paper presented at the meeting of the Eastern Psychological Association, New York.

Masterton, R. B., Bitterman, M. E., Campbell, B., and Hotton, N. (eds.), 1976. "Evolution of Brain and Behavior in Vertebrates." Erlbaum Assoc., Potomac, Maryland.

Megibow, M., and Zeigler, H. P. 1968. Readiness to eat in the pigeon. *Psychonom. Sci.* **12**, 17–18.

Miller, M. 1974. Trigeminal deafferentation and feeding behavior patterns in the pigeon. Unpublished doctoral dissertation, City University of New York.

Miller, M., and Zeigler, H. P. 1974. Trigeminal deafferentation and feeding patterns in pigeons. Paper presented at the meeting of the Eastern Psychological Association, Philadelphia, Pennsylvania, April.

Miller, N. E. 1967. Behavioral and physiological techniques. *In* "The Handbook of Physiology" (C. E. Code, ed.), Sect. 6: The Alimentary Canal, Vol. 1: Control of Food and Water Intake. Amer. Physiol. Soc., Washington, D.C.

Mittelstaedt, H. 1962. Control systems of orientation in insects. *Annu. Rev. Entomol.* **7**, 177–198.

Mook, D. G. 1963. Oral and postingestional determinants of the intake of various solutions in rats with esophageal fistulas. *J. Comp. Physiol. Psychol.* **56**, 645–659.

Moon, R. M. 1975. Food preferences in the pigeon. Unpublished doctoral dissertation, City University of New York.

Morgane, P. J. 1969. The function of the limbic and rhinic forebrain-limbic midbrain systems and reticular formation in the regulation of food and water intake. *Ann. N. Y. Acad. Sci.* **157**, 806–848.

Murton, R. K. 1965. "The Wood-Pigeon." Collins, London.

Nauta, W. J. H., and Karten, H. J. 1970. A general profile of the vertebrate brain with sidelights on the ancestry of the cerebral cortex. *In* "The Neurosciences, Second Study Program" (F. O. Schmitt, ed.), Rockefeller Univ. Press, New York.

Necker, R. 1972. Response of trigeminal ganglion neurons to thermal stimulation of the beak in pigeons. *J. Comp. Physiol.* **78**, 307–314.

Necker, R. 1973. Temperature sensitivity of thermoreceptors and mechanoreceptors on the beak of pigeons. *J. Comp. Physiol.* **87**, 379–391.

Norgren, R., and Leonard, C. 1973. Ascending central gustatory pathways. *J. Comp. Neurol.* **150**, 217–238.

Oakley, B. 1965. Impaired operant behavior following lesions of the thalamic taste nucleus. *J. Comp. Physiol. Psychol.* **59**, 202–210.

Orians, G. 1971. Ecological aspects of behavior. *In* "Avian Biology" (D. S. Farner and J. R. King, eds.), Vol. 1, pp. 513–546. Academic Press, New York.

Panksepp, J. 1973. Reanalysis of feeding patterns in the rat. *J. Comp. Physiol. Psychol.* 82, 78–94.

Pearson, R. 1972. "The Avian Brain." Academic Press, New York.

Pfaff, D., Diakow, C., Zigmond, R., and Kow, L. M. 1974. Neural and hormonal determinants of female mating behavior in rats. *In* "The Neurosciences: Third Study Program" (F. O. Schmitt and F. Worden, eds.), pp. 621–650. MIT Press, Cambridge, Massachusetts.

Pfaffman, C. 1961. The sensory and motivating properties of the sense of taste. *In* "Nebraska Symposium on Motivation" (M. R. Jones, ed.), pp. 71–108. Univ. of Nebraska, Press, Lincoln, Nebraska.

Phillips, R. E. 1964. Wildness in the Mallard duck: Effects of brain lesions and stimulation on "escape behavior" and reproduction. *J. Comp. Neurol.* 116, 139–155.

Phillips, R. E., and Youngren, O. M. 1971. Brain stimulation and species-typical behavior: activities evoked by electrical stimulation of the brains of chickens (*Gallus gallus*). *Anim. Behav.* 19, 757–779.

Putkonen, P. T. S. 1967. Electrical stimulation of the avian brain. *Ann. Acad. Sci. Fenn. Ser. A5* 130, 9–95.

Reese, T. W., and Hogenson, M. J. 1962. Food satiation in the pigeon. *J. Exp. Anal. Behav.* 5, 239–245.

Richardson, A. J. 1970. The role of the crop in the feeding behavior of the domestic chicken. *Anim. Behav.* 18, 633–639.

Richardson, A. J. 1972. The effect of duodenal constriction on food and water intake of the Brown Leghorn cockerel. *Brit. J. Poult. Sci.* 13, 175–177.

Roeder, K. 1959. A physiological approach to the relation between prey and predator. *Smithson. Misc. Collect.* 137, 287–306.

Rodgers, W. L., Epstein, A. N., and Teitelbaum, P. 1965. Lateral hypothalamic aphagia: motor failure or motivational deficit? *Amer. J. Physiol.* 208, 334–342.

Rogers, F. T. 1922. Studies on the brain stem. VI. An experimental study of the corpus striatum of the pigeon as related to various instinctive types of behavior. *J. Comp. Neurol.* 35, 21–60.

Rozin, P., and Mayer, J. 1964. Some factors influencing short-term food intake of the goldfish. *Amer. J. Physiol.* 206, 1430–1436.

Schiff, W. A. 1965. Perception of impending collision. *Psychol. Monogr.* 79, (11).

Schleidt, W. M. 1974a. The comparative study of behavior. *In* "Birds: Brain and Behavior" (I. J. Goodman and M. Schien, eds.), pp. 3–12. Academic Press, New York.

Schleidt, W. M. 1974b. How "fixed" is the Fixed Action Pattern. *Z. Tierpsychol.* 34, 181–211.

Schmid, W. D. 1965. Energy intake of the Mourning Dove *Zenaidoura macroura marginella*. *Science* 150, 1171–1172.

Schwartz, B., and Williams, D. R. 1972. Two different kinds of key-peck in the pigeon: Some properties of responses maintained by negative and positive response-reinforcer contingencies. *J. Exp. Anal. Behav.* 18, 201–216.

Shettleworth, S. 1972. Constraints on learning. This series. 4.

Silver, R., and Witkovsky, P. 1973. Functional characteristics of single units in the spinal trigeminal nucleus of the pigeon. *Brain Behav. Evol.*, 8, 287–303.

Smith, R. J. 1967. Behavioral responses other than key striking which are counted as responses during pigeon pecking. Unpublished doctoral dissertation, Indiana University.

Smith, R. L. 1973. The ascending fiber projections from the principal sensory trigeminal nucleus in the rat. *J. Comp. Neurol.* 148, 423–446.

Snowdon, C. T. 1969. Motivation, regulation and the control of meal parameters with oral and intragastric feeding. *J. Comp. Physiol. Psychol.* **69**, 91–100.

Snowdon, C. T. 1970. Gastrointestinal sensory and motor control of food intake. *J. Comp. Physiol. Psychol.* **71**, 68–76.

Stellar, E., and Hill, H. H. 1952. The rat's rate of drinking as a function of water deprivation. *J. Comp. Physiol. Psychol.* **45**, 96–102.

Sterritt, G. M., and Smith, M. P. 1965. Reinforcement effects of specific components of feeding in young Leghorn chicks. *J. Comp. Physiol. Psychol.* **59**, 171–175.

Stevenson, J. F. 1969. Mechanisms in the control of food and water intake. *Ann. N. Y. Acad. Sci.* **157**, 1069–1083.

Stingelin, W. 1961. Grossenunterschiede des sensiblen Trigeminuskern bein verschiedenen Vogeln. *Rev. Suisse Zool.* **68**, 247–251.

Storer, R. W. 1971. Adaptive radiation of birds. *In* "Avian Biology" (D. S. Farner and J. R. King, eds.), Vol. 1, pp. 150–188. Academic Press, New York.

Strominger, J. L. 1947. The relation between water intake and food intake in normal rats and in rats with hypothalamic hyperphagia. *Yale J. Biol. Med.* **19**, 279–288.

Szentagothai, J. 1948. Anatomical considerations of monosynaptic reflex arcs. *J. Neurophysiol.* **11**, 445–454.

Teitelbaum, P. 1967. "Physiological Psychology" Prentice-Hall, Englewood Cliffs, New Jersey.

Teitelbaum, P., and Epstein, A. N. 1962. The lateral hypothalamic syndrome: Recovery of feeding and drinking after lateral hypothalamic lesions. *Psychol. Rev.* **69**, 94–90.

Teitelbaum, P., and Epstein, A. N. 1963. The role of taste and smell in the regulation of food and water intake. *In* "Olfaction and Taste" (Y. Zotterman, ed.), pp. 347–360. Pergamon, London.

Towe, A. L. 1973. Motor cortex and the pyramidal system. *In* "Efferent Organization and the Integration of Behavior" (J. D. Maser, ed.), Academic Press, New York.

Tucker, D. 1971. Nonolfactory responses from the nasal cavity: Jacobson's organ and the trigeminal system. *In* "Handbook of Sensory Physiology" (L. M. Beidler, ed.), Vol. IV: Chemical Senses, Part 1, pp. 151–181. Olfaction. Springer-Verlag, Berlin and New York.

Turner, B. H. 1973. Sensorimotor syndrome produced by lesions of the amygdala and lateral hypothalamus. *J. Comp. Physiol. Psychol.* **82**, 37–47.

Tweeton, J. R., Phillips, R. E., and Peek, F. W. 1973. Feeding behavior elicited by electrical stimulation of the brain in chickens (*Gallus Gallus*). *Poult. Sci.* **52**, 165–172.

Valenstein, E. 1968. The anatomical locus of reinforcement. *Progr. Physiol. Psychol.* **1**,

Van Hemel, S. B., and Meyer, J. S. 1969. Feeding patterns and response to caloric dilutions in the Japanese Quail. *Physiol. Behav.* **4**, 339–344.

von Ihnen, K. 1928. Beitrage zur Physiologie des Kropfes bei Huhn und Taube. *Pfluger's Arch. Physiol.* **218**, 767–769.

Vonk, H. J., and Postma, N. 1949. X-ray studies on the movements of the hen's intestines. *Physiol. Comp. Oecol.* **1**, 15–23.

Wallenberg, A. 1903. Der Urspring des Tractus isthmo-striatus (oder bulbostriatus) der Taube. *Neurol. Zbl.* **22**, 98–101.

Watanabe, T., and Yasuda, M. 1970. Comparative and topographical anatomy of the fowl. XXVI. Peripheral course of the trigeminal nerve. *Japan. J. Anat.* **32**, 43–57.

Webster, D. M., and Beale, I. L. 1970. Intracranial self-stimulation in the pigeon: The effects of current intensity. *Psychonom. Sci.* **20**, 15–17.

Welker, W. I. 1973. Principles of organization of the ventrobasal complex in mammals. *Brain, Behav. Evol.* **7**, 253–336.

Welker, W. I. 1976. Brain evolution in mammals. A review of concepts, problems and methods. *In* "Evolution of Brain and Behavior in Vertebrates" (Masterton, R. B.,

Bitterman, M. E., Campbell, B. and Hotton, N. (Eds.). Erlbaum Assoc., Potomac, Maryland.

Wenzel, B. M. 1971. Olfaction in birds. *In* "Handbook of Sensory Physiology" (L. M. Beidler, ed.), Vol. IV: Chemical Senses, Part 1: Olfaction, pp. 432–448. Springer-Verlag, Berlin and New York.

Wenzel, B. M. 1975. The olfactory system and behavior. *In* "Advances in Limbic and Autonomic Research" (L. V. DiCara, ed.), Plenum, New York.

White, S. S. 1969. Mechanisms involved in deglutition in *Gallus domesticus. J. Anat. (London)* **104,** 177 (abstr.).

Wilson, D. M., and Wyman, R. 1965. Motor output patterns during random and rhythmic stimulation of locust thoracic ganglia. *Biophys. J.* **5,** 121–143.

Witkovsky, P., Zeigler, H. P., and Silver, R. 1973. The nucleus basalis of the pigeon: A single-unit analysis. *J. Comp. Neurol.* **147,** 119–128.

Wolf, G., and DiCara, L. 1974. Impairments in sodium appetite after lesions of gustatory thalamus: Replication and extension. *Behav. Biol.* **10,** 105–112.

Wolin, B. R. 1968. Difference in manner of pecking a key between pigeons reinforced with food and with water. *In* "Contemporary Research in Operant Behavior" (A. C. Cantania, ed.), p. 286. Scott, Foresman, Glenview, Illinois.

Woodburne, R. T. 1936. A phylogenetic consideration of primary and secondary centers and connections of the trigeminal complex in a series of vertebrates. *J. Comp. Neurol.* **65,** 403–501.

Wright, P. 1968. Hypothalamic lesions and food and water intake in the Barbary dove. *Psychonom. Sci.* **13,** 133–134.

Wright, P. 1975. The neural substrates of feeding behavior in birds. *In* "Neural and Endocrine Aspects of Behavior in Birds" (P. Wright, P. G. Caryl, and D. M. Vowles, eds.) Elsevier, Amsterdam.

Wright, P., Caryl, P. G., and Vowles, D. M., eds. 1975. "Neural and Endocrine Aspects of Behavior in Birds." Elsevier, Amsterdam.

Zeier, H. 1971. Archistriatal lesions and response inhibition in the pigeon. *Brain Res.* **31,** 327–339.

Zeier, H. 1974. Behavioral adaptations on operant schedules after forebrain lesions in the pigeon. *In* "Birds: Brain and Behavior" (I. J. Goodman and M. Schein, eds.), pp. 153–163. Academic Press, New York.

Zeier, H., and Karten, H. J. 1971. The archistriatum of the pigeon: Organization of afferent and efferent connections. *Brain Res.* **31,** 313–326.

Zeigler, H. P. 1963. Effects of forebrain lesions upon activity in pigeons. *J. Comp. Neurol.* **120,** 183–194.

Zeigler, H. P. 1973a. Trigeminal deafferentation and feeding behavior in the pigeon: Sensorimotor and motivational effects. *Science* **182,** 1155–1158.

Zeigler, H. P. 1973b. The "consummatory act" of eating in the pigeon: Spatiotemporal organization and neurosensory control. Paper presented at the XIII International Congress of Ethology, Washington, D.C.

Zeigler, H. P. 1973c. The problem of comparison in comparative psychology. *Ann. N. Y. Acad. Sci.* **223,** 126–134.

Zeigler, H. P. 1974. Feeding behavior in the pigeon: A neurobehavioral analysis. *In* "Birds: Brain and Behavior" (I. Goodman and M. Schein, eds.), pp. 101–132. Academic Press, New York.

Zeigler, H. P. 1975a. Trigeminal deafferentation and hunger in the pigeon (*Columba livia*). *J. Comp. Physiol. Psychol.* **89,** 827–844.

Zeigler, H. P. 1975b. Dissociation of operant and consummatory responses by trigeminal deafferentation in the pigeon. *Physiol. Behav.* **14,** 871–874.

Zeigler, H. P., and Feldstein, S. 1971. A feedometer for the pigeon. *J. Exp. Anal. Behav.* **16,** 181–187.

Zeigler, H. P., and Hunter, I. 1977. In preparation.

Zeigler, H. P., and Karten, H. J. 1973a. Brain mechanisms and feeding behavior in the pigeon (*Columba livia*): I. Quinto-frontal structures. *J. Comp. Neurol.* **152,** 59–82.

Zeigler, H. P., and Karten, H. J. 1973b. Brain mechanisms and feeding behavior in the pigeon (*Columba livia*): II. Analysis of feeding behavior deficits following lesions of quinto-frontal structures. *J. Comp. Neurol.* **152,** 83–102.

Zeigler, H. P., and Karten, H. J. 1974. Central trigeminal structures and the lateral hypothalamic syndrome in the rat. *Science* **186,** 636–638.

Zeigler, H. P., and Witkovsky, P. 1968. The main sensory trigeminal nucleus in the pigeon: A single-unit analysis. *J. Comp. Neurol.* **134,** 255–264.

Zeigler, H. P., Karten, H. J., and Green, H. L. 1969a. Neural control of feeding in the pigeon. *Psychonom. Sci.* **15,** 156–157.

Zeigler, H. P., Silver, R., and Karten, H. J. 1969b. Archistriate lesions and feeding behavior in the pigeon. Paper presented at Eastern Psychological Association.

Zeigler, H. P., Green, H. L., and Lehrer, R. 1971. Patterns of feeding behavior in the pigeon. *J. Comp. Physiol. Psychol.* **76,** 468–477.

Zeigler, H. P., Green, H. L., and Siegel, J. 1972. Food and water intake and weight regulation in the pigeon. *Physiol. Behav.* **8,** 127–134.

Zeigler, H. P., Marwine, A., and Karten, H. J. 1974. Central trigeminal structures and the lateral hypothalamic syndrome in the rat. Paper presented at the meeting of the Eastern Psychological Association, Philadelphia, Pennsylvania.

Zeigler, H. P., Miller, M., and Levine, R. R. 1975. Trigeminal nerve and eating in the pigeon (*Columba livia*): Neurosensory control of the consummatory response. *J. Comp. Physiol. Psychol.* **89,** 845–858.

Zeigler, H. P., Hollard, V., Webster, D. M., and Wild, M. 1977. Reinforcement elicited by intracranial self-stimulation of visual and trigeminal relay nuclei in the pigeon. In preparation.

Zisweiler, V., and Farner, D. S. 1972. Digestion and the digestive system. *In* "Avian Biology" (D. S. Farner and J. King, eds.), Vol. 2, pp. 343–430. Academic Press, New York.

Zweers, G., and Wouterlood, F. 1973. Functional anatomy of the feeding apparatus of the Mallard (*Anas platyrhynchos* L.). Proceedings of the Third European Anatomical Congress, Manchester, England.

Zweers, G. A. 1974. Structure, movement, and myography of the feeding apparatus of the Mallard. A functional study of anatomy. *Neth. J. Zool.* **24,** 323–467.

Subject Index